Shojo Beat

Tail of the Moon™

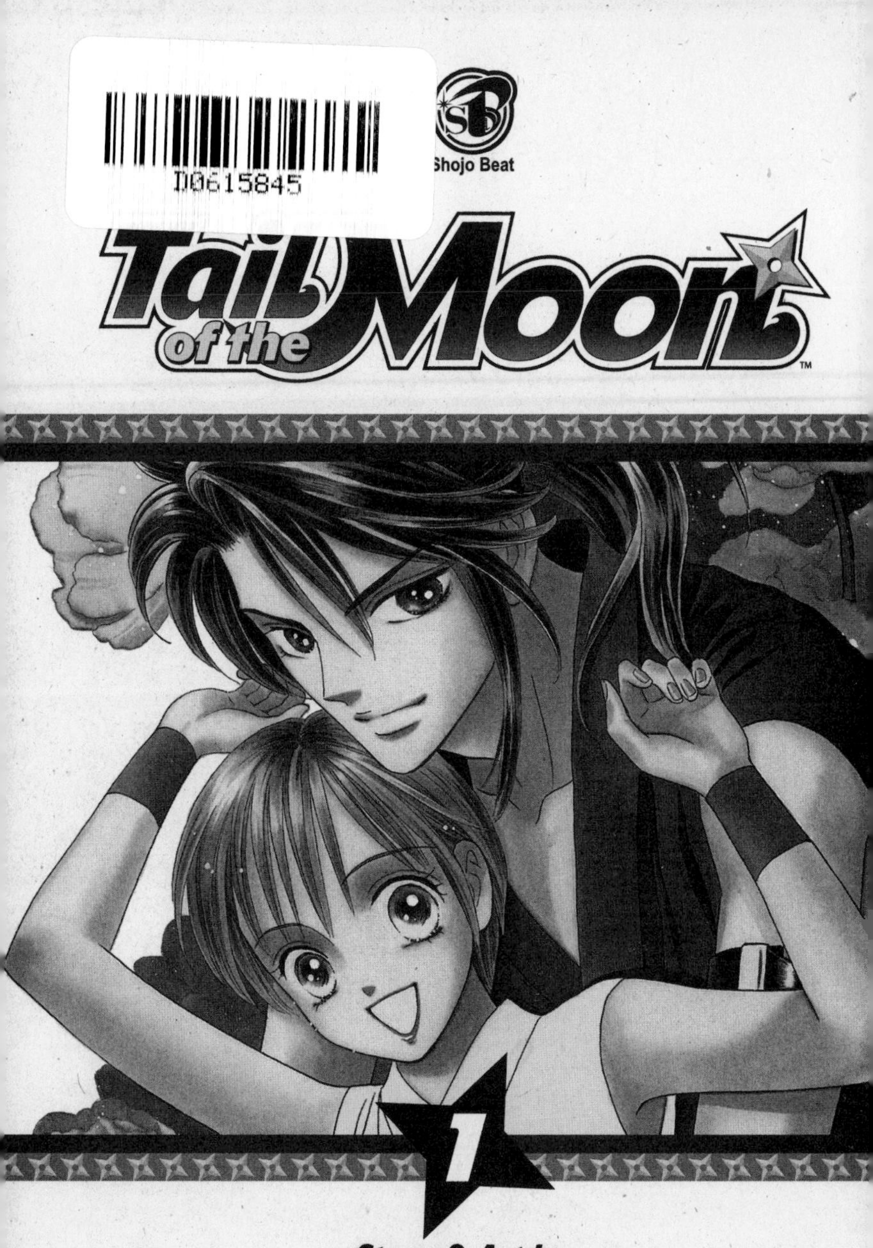

1

Story & Art by

Rinko Ueda

Tail of the Moon
of the

Volume 1

CONTENTS

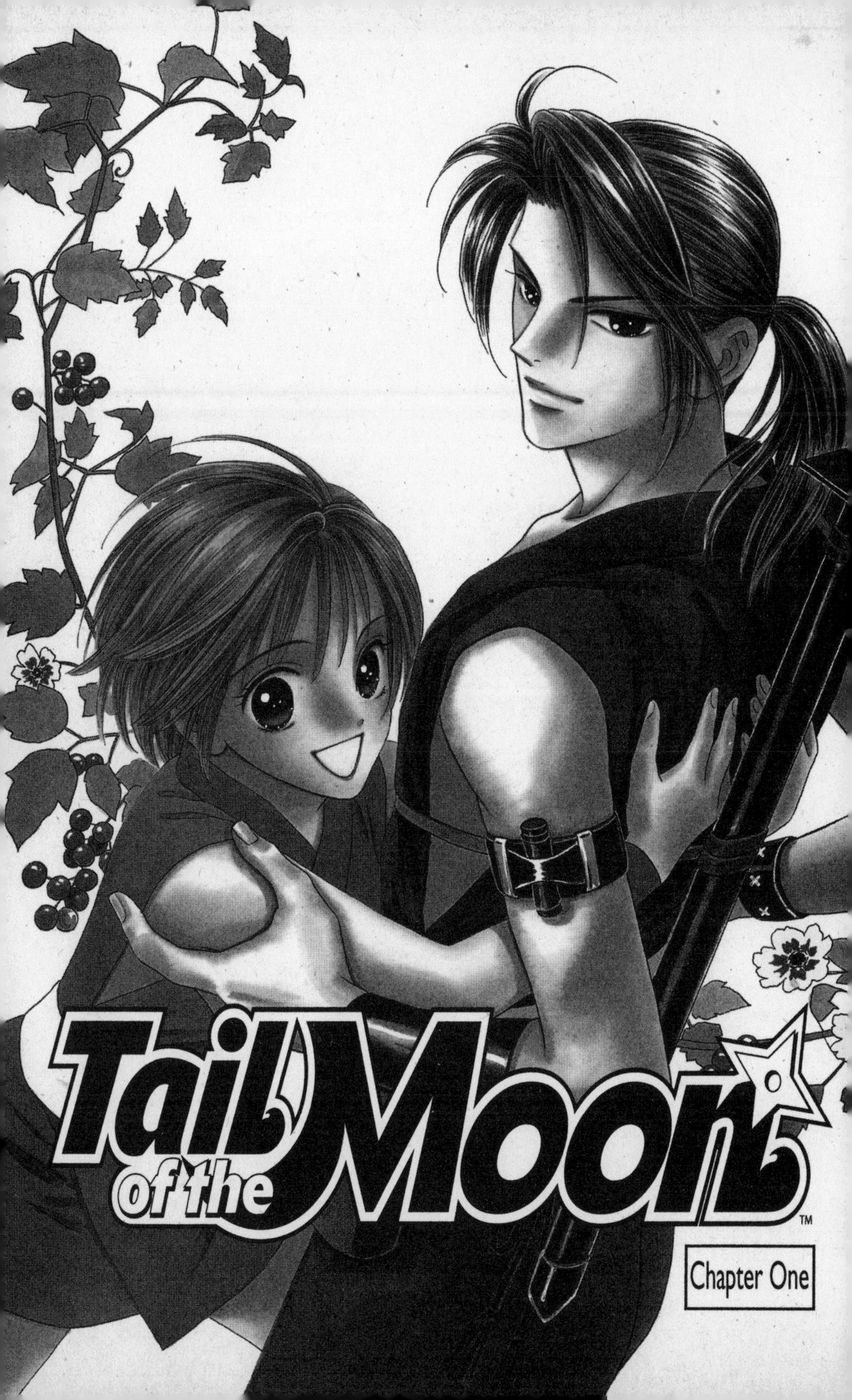
Tail of the Moon™
Chapter One

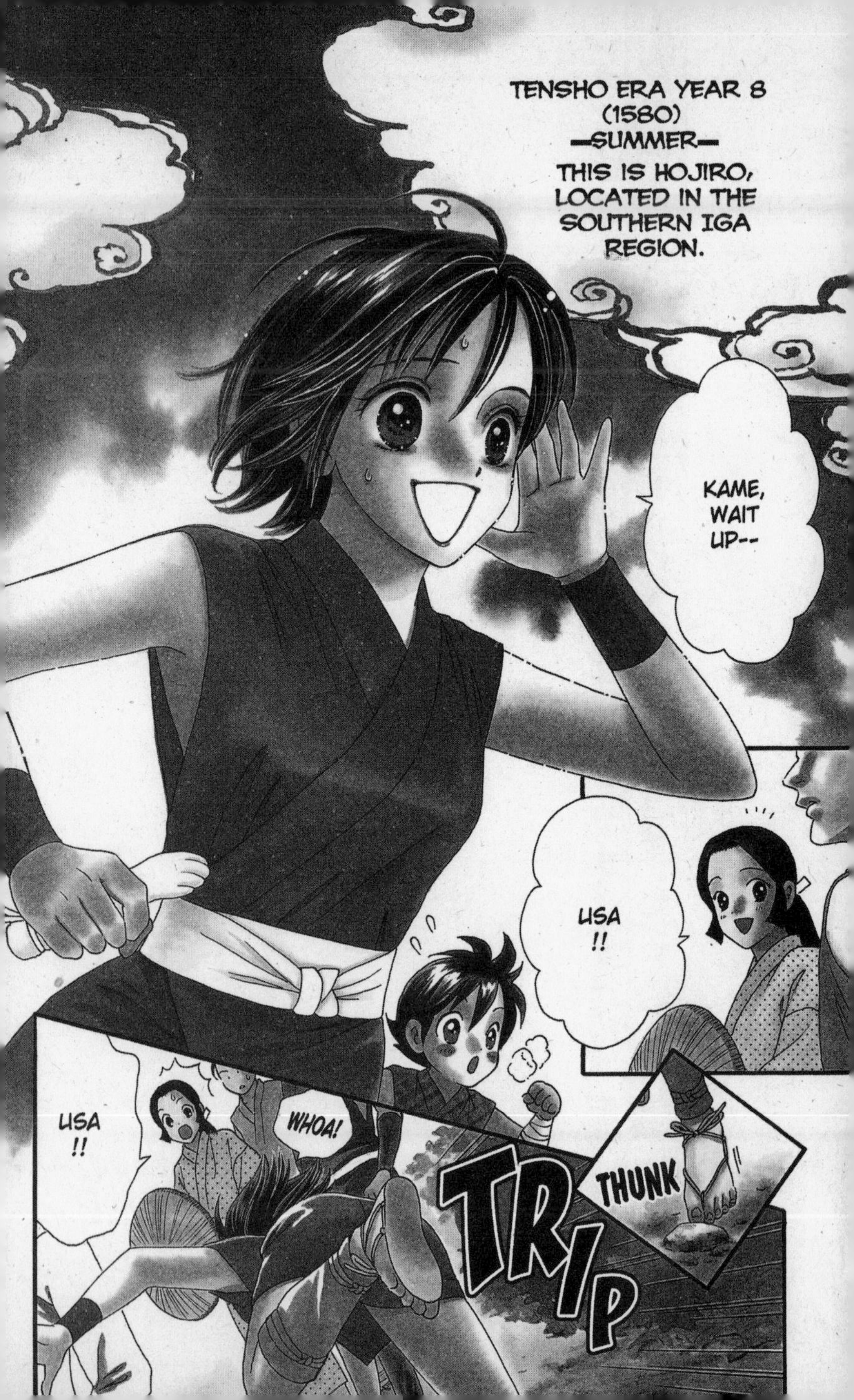
TENSHO ERA YEAR 8 (1580) —SUMMER—
THIS IS HOJIRO, LOCATED IN THE SOUTHERN IGA REGION.
KAME, WAIT UP--
USA !!
THUNK
TRIP
WHOA!
USA !!

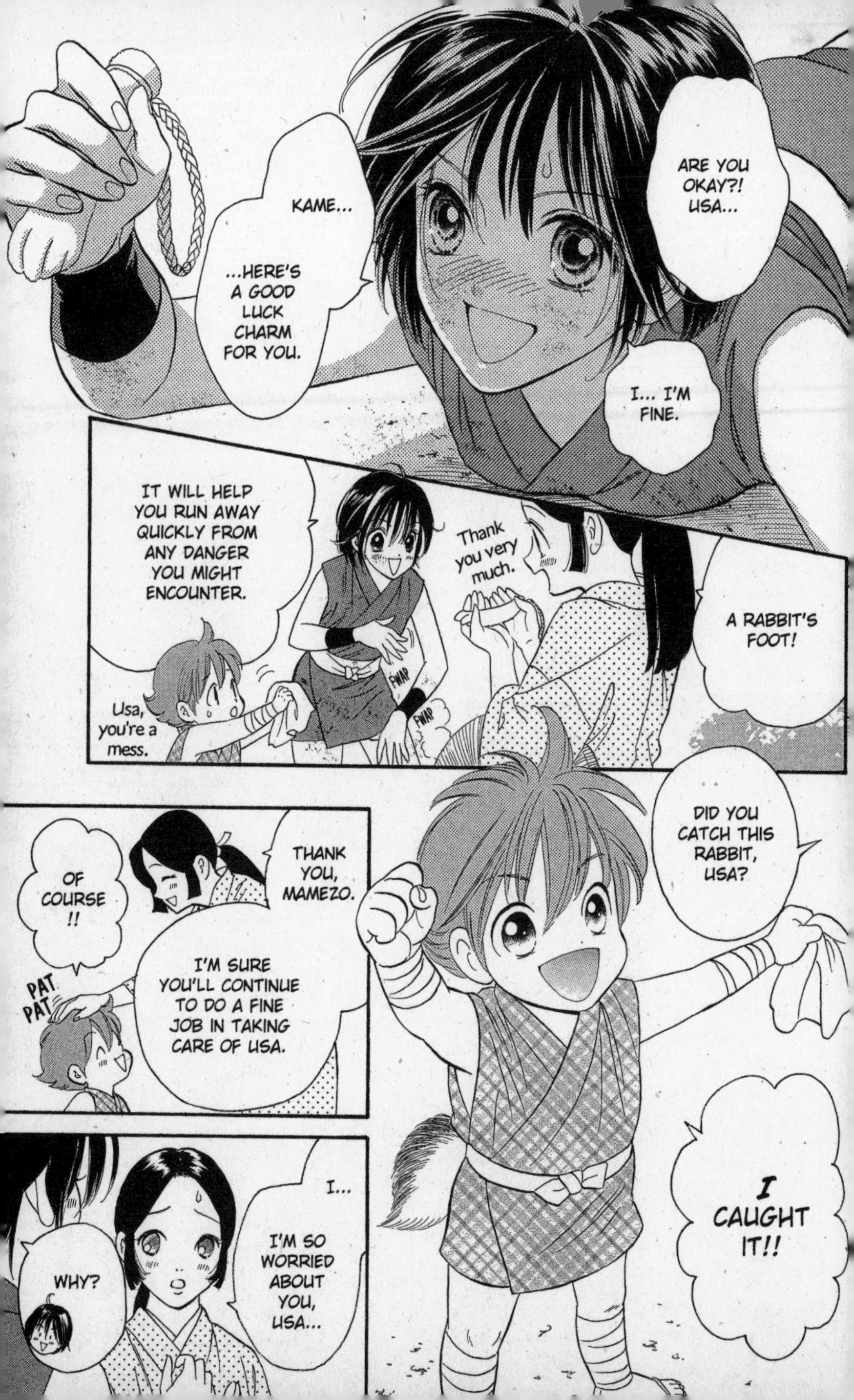
ARE YOU OKAY?! USA...
I... I'M FINE.
KAME...
...HERE'S A GOOD LUCK CHARM FOR YOU.
A RABBIT'S FOOT!
Thank you very much.
IT WILL HELP YOU RUN AWAY QUICKLY FROM ANY DANGER YOU MIGHT ENCOUNTER.
FWAP
FWAP
Usa, you're a mess.
DID YOU CATCH THIS RABBIT, USA?
I CAUGHT IT!!
THANK YOU, MAMEZO.
OF COURSE!!
I'M SURE YOU'LL CONTINUE TO DO A FINE JOB IN TAKING CARE OF USA.
PAT PAT
I...
I'M SO WORRIED ABOUT YOU, USA...
WHY?

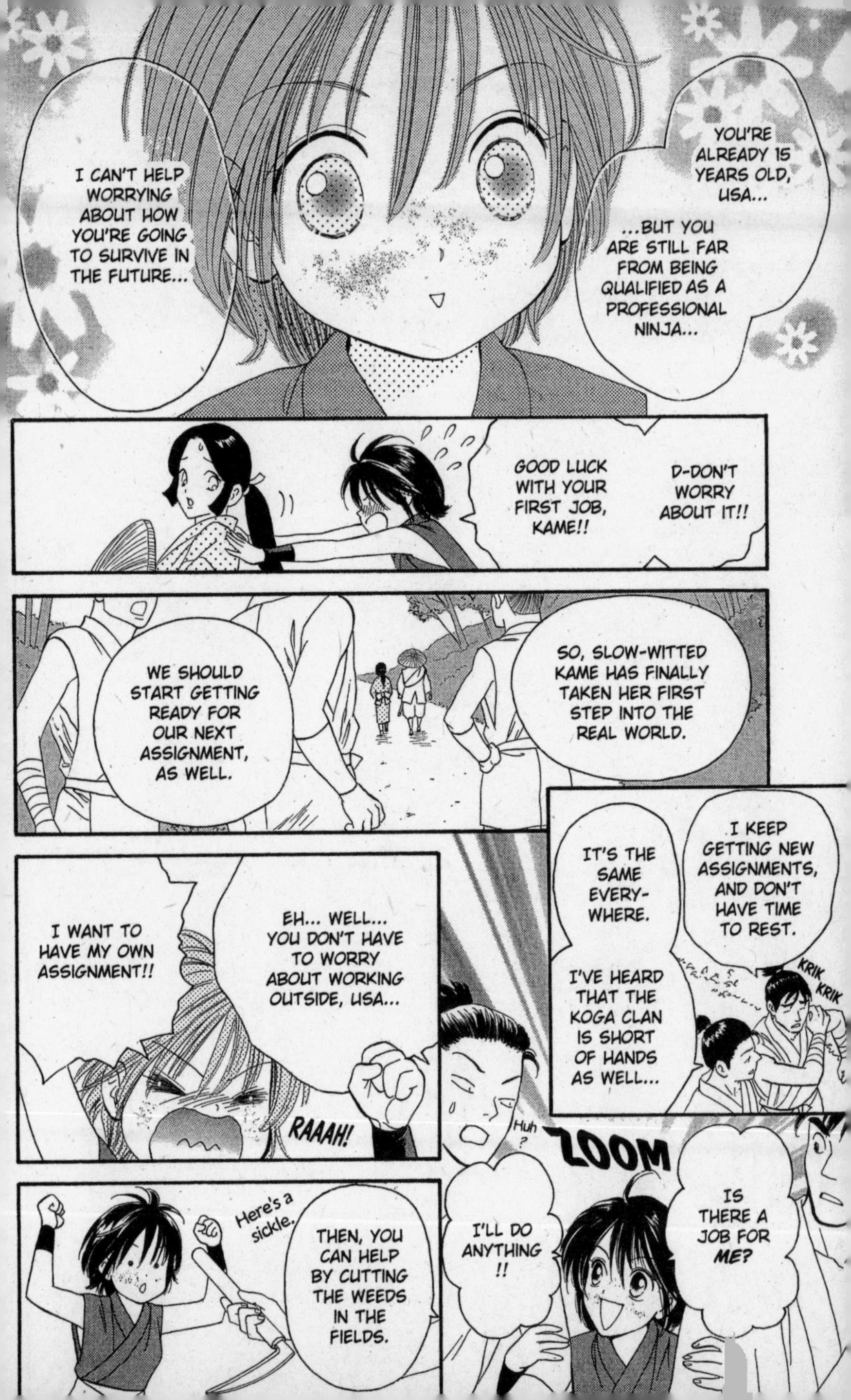
YOU'RE ALREADY 15 YEARS OLD, USA...
...BUT YOU ARE STILL FAR FROM BEING QUALIFIED AS A PROFESSIONAL NINJA...
I CAN'T HELP WORRYING ABOUT HOW YOU'RE GOING TO SURVIVE IN THE FUTURE...
D-DON'T WORRY ABOUT IT!!
GOOD LUCK WITH YOUR FIRST JOB, KAME!!
SO, SLOW-WITTED KAME HAS FINALLY TAKEN HER FIRST STEP INTO THE REAL WORLD.
WE SHOULD START GETTING READY FOR OUR NEXT ASSIGNMENT, AS WELL.
I KEEP GETTING NEW ASSIGNMENTS, AND DON'T HAVE TIME TO REST.
IT'S THE SAME EVERY-WHERE.
KRIK KRIK
I'VE HEARD THAT THE KOGA CLAN IS SHORT OF HANDS AS WELL...
EH... WELL... YOU DON'T HAVE TO WORRY ABOUT WORKING OUTSIDE, USA...
I WANT TO HAVE MY OWN ASSIGNMENT!!
RAAAH!
ZOOM
IS THERE A JOB FOR ME?
Huh?
I'LL DO ANYTHING!!
THEN, YOU CAN HELP BY CUTTING THE WEEDS IN THE FIELDS.
Here's a sickle.

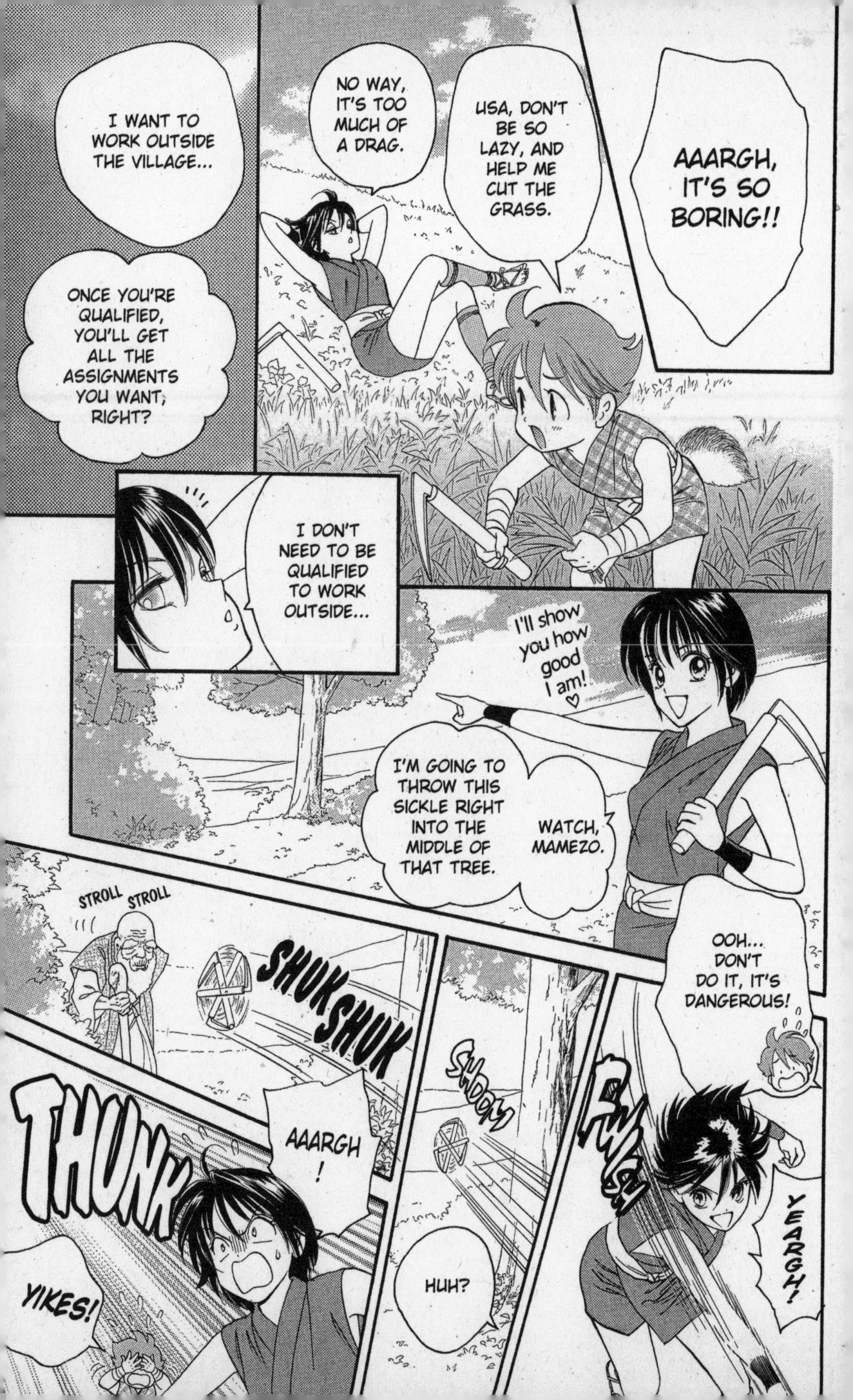
AAARGH, IT'S SO BORING!!
USA, DON'T BE SO LAZY, AND HELP ME CUT THE GRASS.
NO WAY, IT'S TOO MUCH OF A DRAG.
I WANT TO WORK OUTSIDE THE VILLAGE...
ONCE YOU'RE QUALIFIED, YOU'LL GET ALL THE ASSIGNMENTS YOU WANT, RIGHT?
I DON'T NEED TO BE QUALIFIED TO WORK OUTSIDE...
I'll show you how good I am! ♡
WATCH, MAMEZO.
I'M GOING TO THROW THIS SICKLE RIGHT INTO THE MIDDLE OF THAT TREE.
OOH... DON'T DO IT, IT'S DANGEROUS!
FWISH
YEARGH!
SHOOM
HUH?
STROLL STROLL
SHUK SHUK
THUNK
AAARGH!
YIKES!

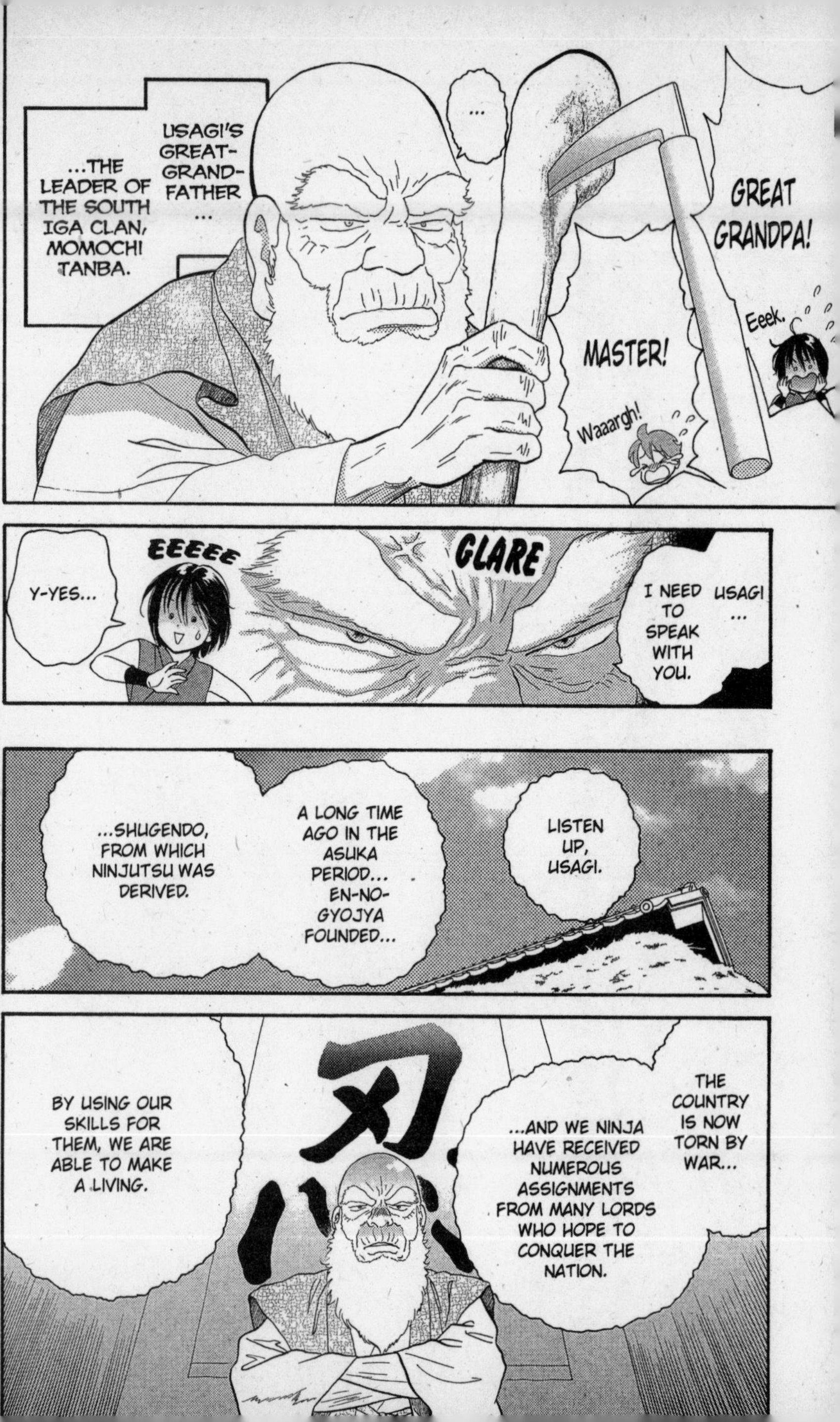
GREAT GRANDPA!
Eeek.
MASTER!
Waaargh!
...
USAGI'S GREAT-GRANDFATHER...
...THE LEADER OF THE SOUTH IGA CLAN, MOMOCHI TANBA.
USAGI...
I NEED TO SPEAK WITH YOU.
GLARE
EEEEE
Y-YES...
LISTEN UP, USAGI.
A LONG TIME AGO IN THE ASUKA PERIOD... EN-NO-GYOJYA FOUNDED...
...SHUGENDO, FROM WHICH NINJUTSU WAS DERIVED.
THE COUNTRY IS NOW TORN BY WAR...
...AND WE NINJA HAVE RECEIVED NUMEROUS ASSIGNMENTS FROM MANY LORDS WHO HOPE TO CONQUER THE NATION.
BY USING OUR SKILLS FOR THEM, WE ARE ABLE TO MAKE A LIVING.

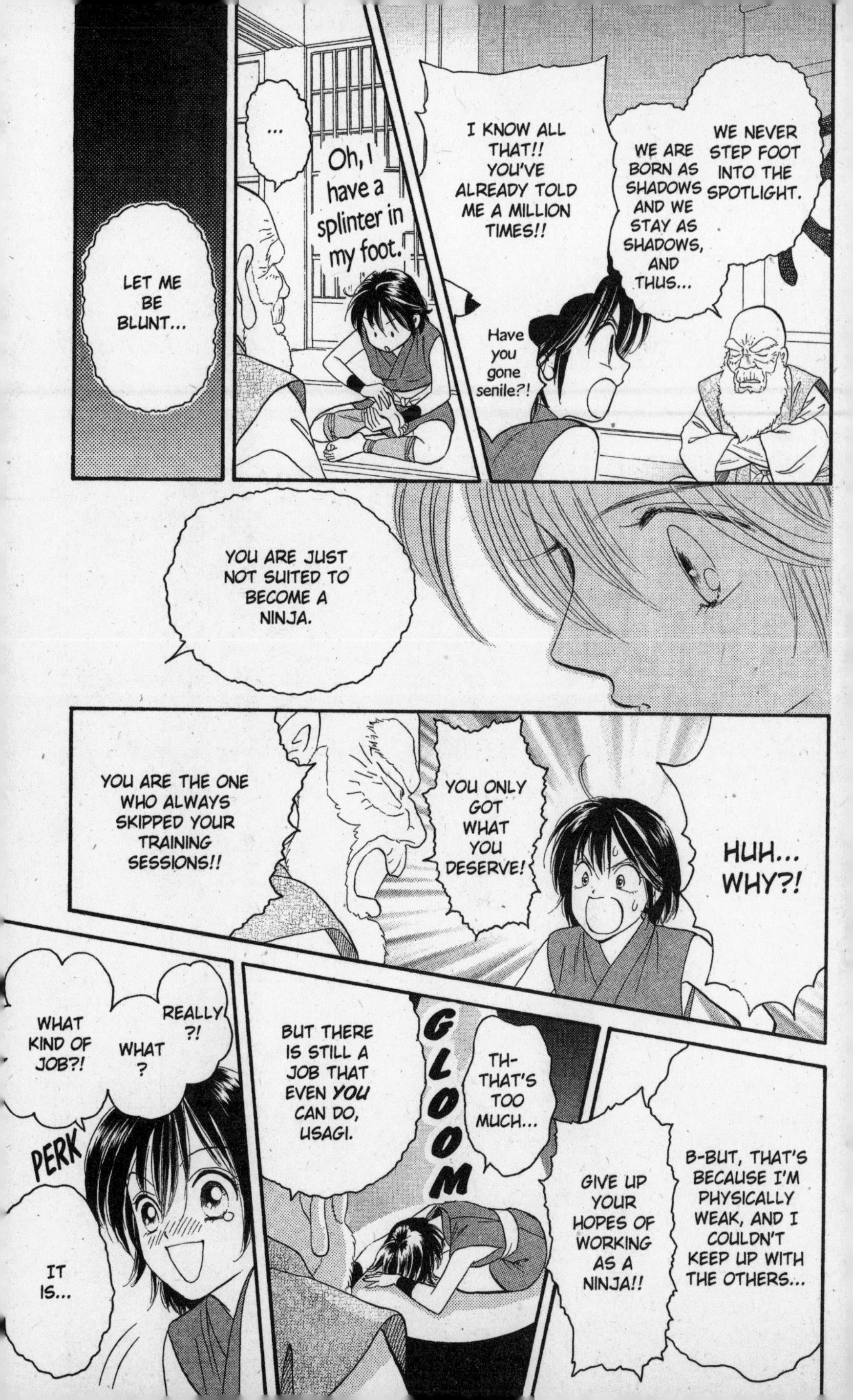
WE NEVER STEP FOOT INTO THE SPOTLIGHT.
WE ARE BORN AS SHADOWS AND WE STAY AS SHADOWS, AND THUS...
I KNOW ALL THAT!! YOU'VE ALREADY TOLD ME A MILLION TIMES!!
Have you gone senile?!
...
Oh, I have a splinter in my foot.
LET ME BE BLUNT...
YOU ARE JUST NOT SUITED TO BECOME A NINJA.
HUH... WHY?!
YOU ONLY GOT WHAT YOU DESERVE!
YOU ARE THE ONE WHO ALWAYS SKIPPED YOUR TRAINING SESSIONS!!
B-BUT, THAT'S BECAUSE I'M PHYSICALLY WEAK, AND I COULDN'T KEEP UP WITH THE OTHERS...
GIVE UP YOUR HOPES OF WORKING AS A NINJA!!
TH-THAT'S TOO MUCH...
GLOOM
BUT THERE IS STILL A JOB THAT EVEN *YOU* CAN DO, USAGI.
REALLY?!
WHAT?
WHAT KIND OF JOB?!
PERK
IT IS...

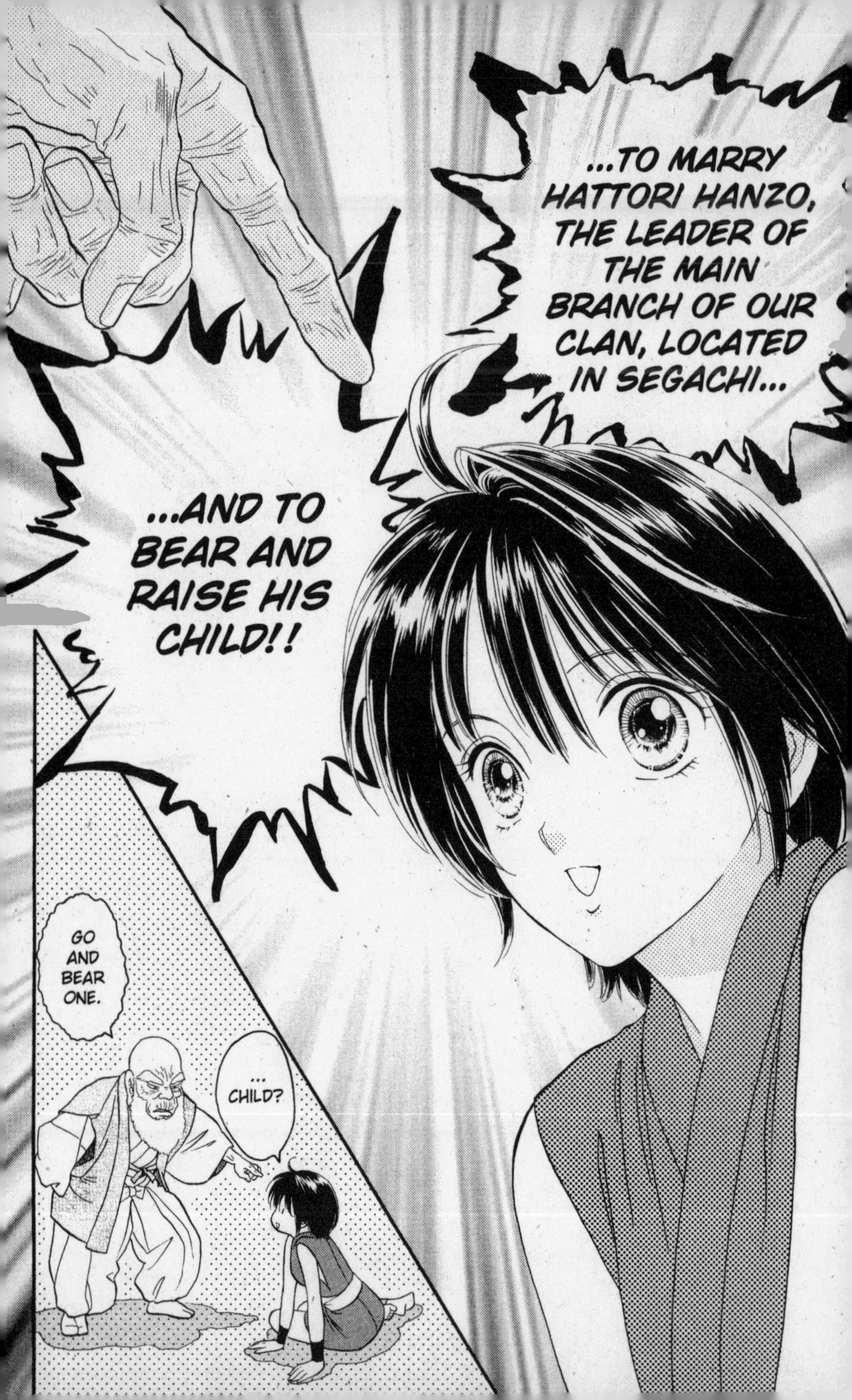
...TO MARRY HATTORI HANZO, THE LEADER OF THE MAIN BRANCH OF OUR CLAN, LOCATED IN SEGACHI...
...AND TO BEAR AND RAISE HIS CHILD!!
... CHILD?
GO AND BEAR ONE.

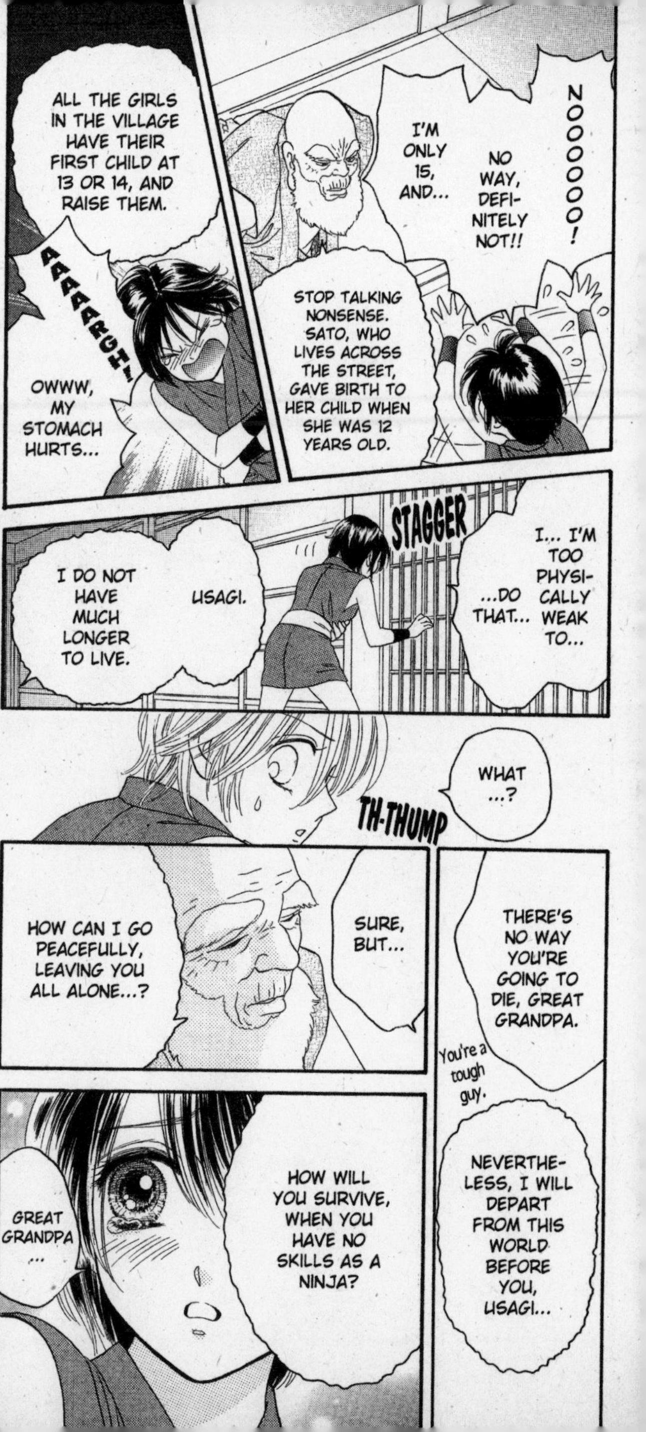
NOOOOOOO!
NO WAY, DEFI-NITELY NOT!!
I'M ONLY 15, AND...
STOP TALKING NONSENSE. SATO, WHO LIVES ACROSS THE STREET, GAVE BIRTH TO HER CHILD WHEN SHE WAS 12 YEARS OLD.
ALL THE GIRLS IN THE VILLAGE HAVE THEIR FIRST CHILD AT 13 OR 14, AND RAISE THEM.
AAAAARGH!
OWWW, MY STOMACH HURTS...
I... I'M TOO PHYSI-CALLY WEAK TO...
...DO THAT...
STAGGER
USAGI.
I DO NOT HAVE MUCH LONGER TO LIVE.
WHAT ...?
TH-THUMP
THERE'S NO WAY YOU'RE GOING TO DIE, GREAT GRANDPA.
You're a tough guy.
NEVERTHE-LESS, I WILL DEPART FROM THIS WORLD BEFORE YOU, USAGI...
SURE, BUT...
HOW CAN I GO PEACEFULLY, LEAVING YOU ALL ALONE...?
HOW WILL YOU SURVIVE, WHEN YOU HAVE NO SKILLS AS A NINJA?
GREAT GRANDPA ...

This and that from the author #1

Hello, and welcome!! I'm Rinko Ueda aka Ue-Rin!! I intend to write bits and pieces about the creation of *Tail of the Moon* here. I know my handwriting is bad, so you may have some trouble reading it...

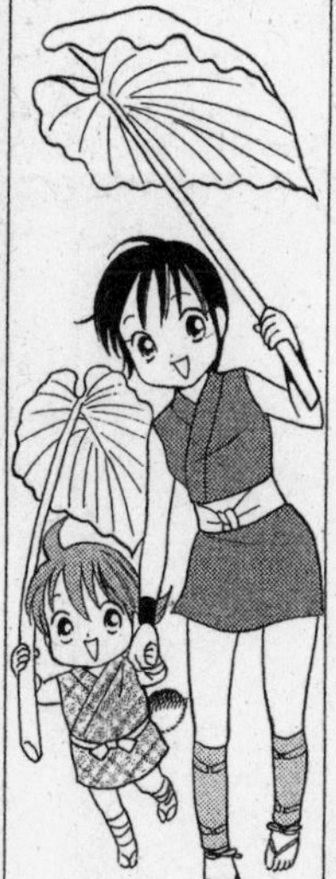

...but I hope you will all hang on with me to the very end.

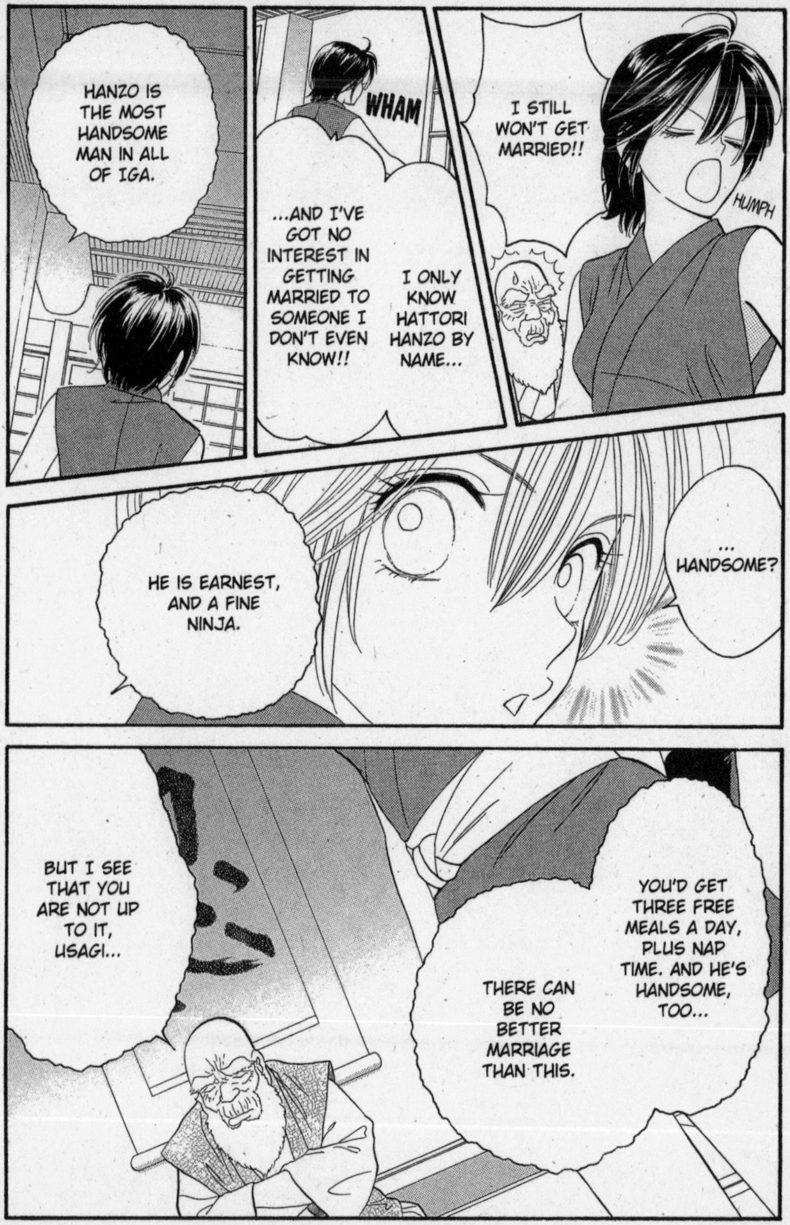
I STILL WON'T GET MARRIED!!
HUMPH
WHAM
I ONLY KNOW HATTORI HANZO BY NAME...
...AND I'VE GOT NO INTEREST IN GETTING MARRIED TO SOMEONE I DON'T EVEN KNOW!!
HANZO IS THE MOST HANDSOME MAN IN ALL OF IGA.
... HANDSOME?
HE IS EARNEST, AND A FINE NINJA.
YOU'D GET THREE FREE MEALS A DAY, PLUS NAP TIME. AND HE'S HANDSOME, TOO...
THERE CAN BE NO BETTER MARRIAGE THAN THIS.
BUT I SEE THAT YOU ARE NOT UP TO IT, USAGI...

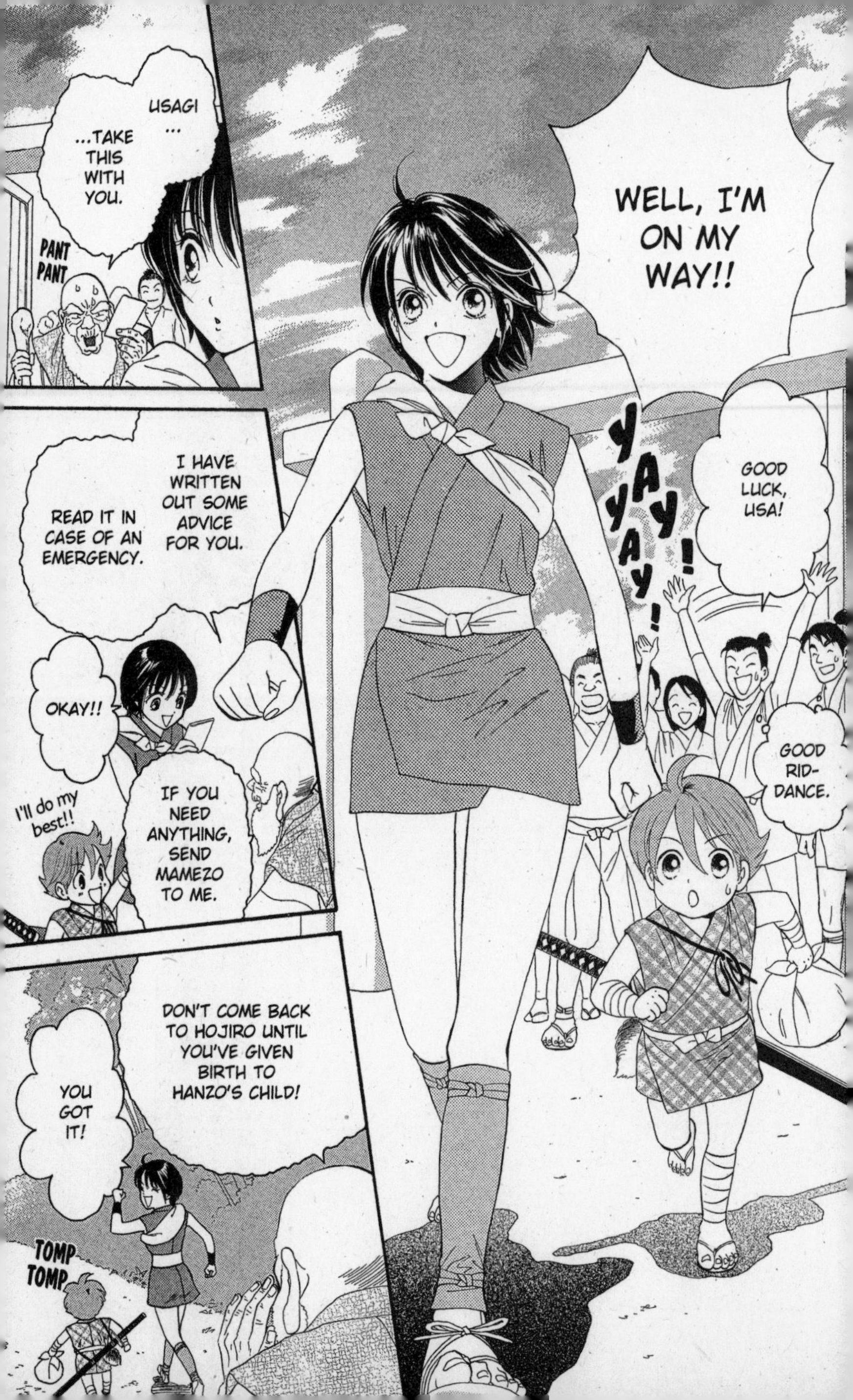

WELL, I'M ON MY WAY!!
GOOD LUCK, USA!
YAY YAY!!
GOOD RID-DANCE.
USAGI ...
...TAKE THIS WITH YOU.
PANT PANT
I HAVE WRITTEN OUT SOME ADVICE FOR YOU.
READ IT IN CASE OF AN EMERGENCY.
OKAY!!
IF YOU NEED ANYTHING, SEND MAMEZO TO ME.
I'll do my best!!
DON'T COME BACK TO HOJIRO UNTIL YOU'VE GIVEN BIRTH TO HANZO'S CHILD!
YOU GOT IT!
TOMP TOMP

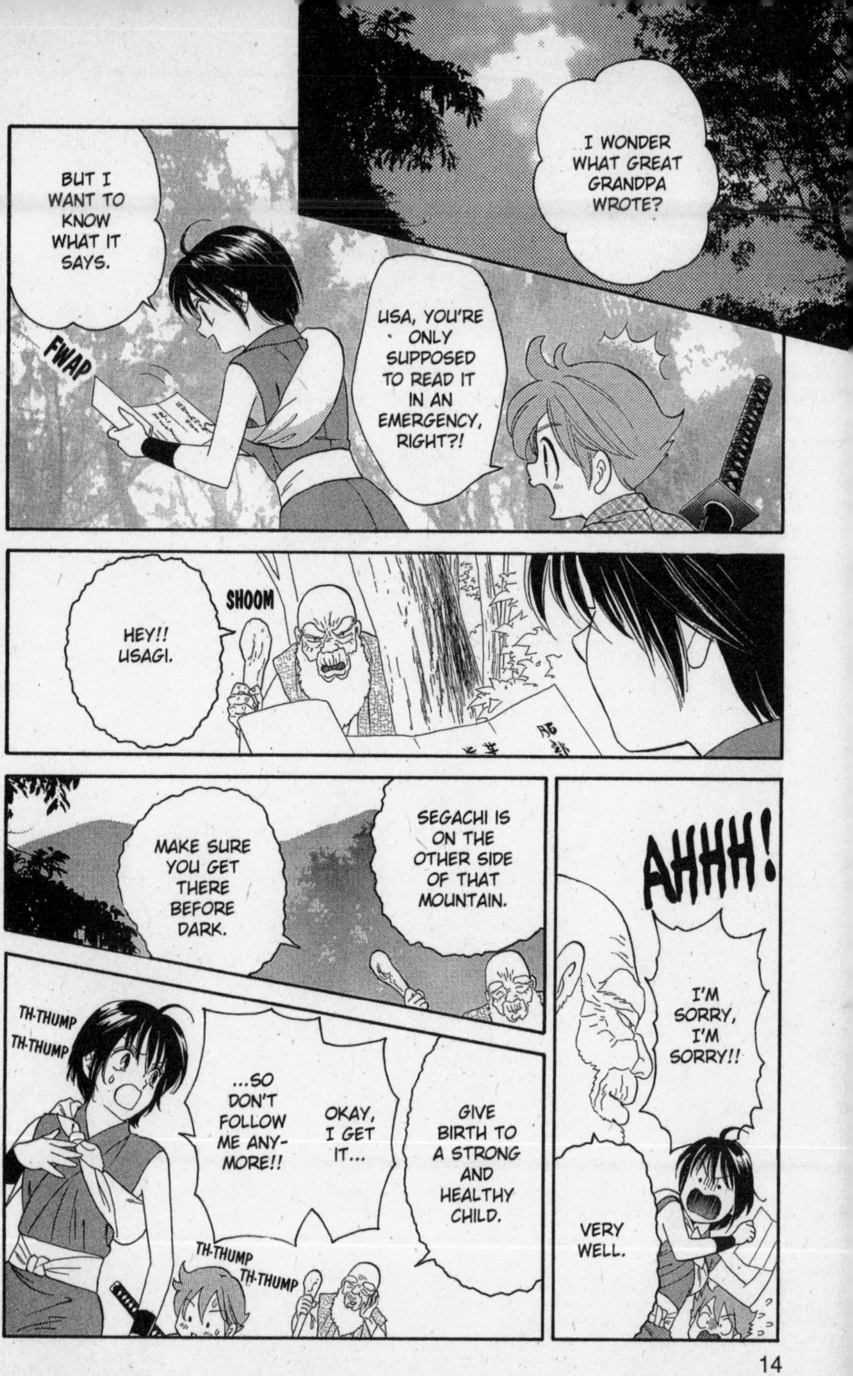
I WONDER WHAT GREAT GRANDPA WROTE?
USA, YOU'RE ONLY SUPPOSED TO READ IT IN AN EMERGENCY, RIGHT?!
BUT I WANT TO KNOW WHAT IT SAYS.
FWAP
SHOOM
HEY!! USAGI.
AHHH!
I'M SORRY, I'M SORRY!!
VERY WELL.
SEGACHI IS ON THE OTHER SIDE OF THAT MOUNTAIN.
MAKE SURE YOU GET THERE BEFORE DARK.
GIVE BIRTH TO A STRONG AND HEALTHY CHILD.
OKAY, I GET IT...
...SO DON'T FOLLOW ME ANY-MORE!!
TH-THUMP TH-THUMP
TH-THUMP TH-THUMP

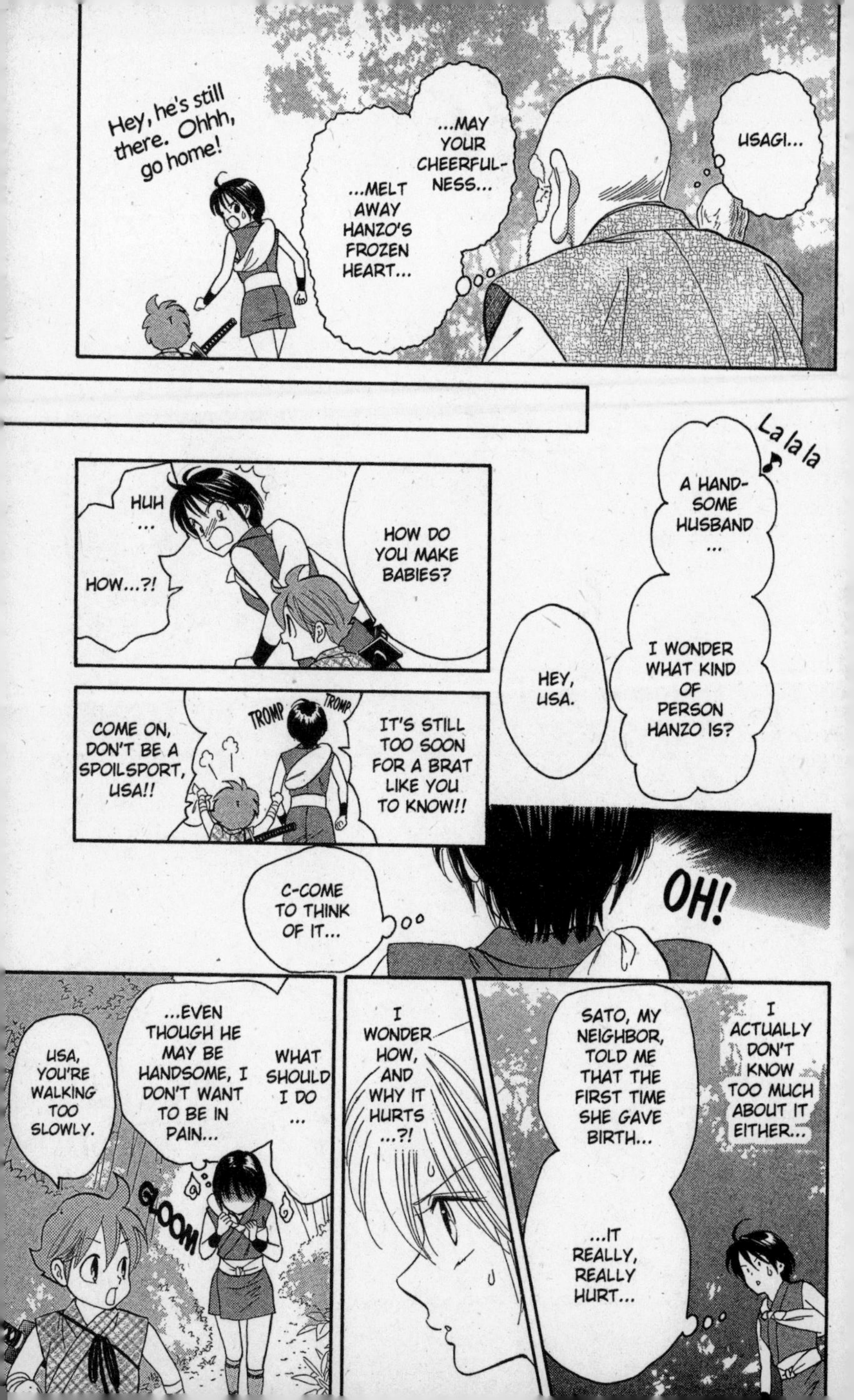
USAGI...
...MAY YOUR CHEERFULNESS...
...MELT AWAY HANZO'S FROZEN HEART...
Hey, he's still there. Ohhh, go home!
La la la
A HANDSOME HUSBAND...
I WONDER WHAT KIND OF PERSON HANZO IS?
HEY, USA.
OH!
C-COME TO THINK OF IT...
HOW DO YOU MAKE BABIES?
HUH... HOW...?!
IT'S STILL TOO SOON FOR A BRAT LIKE YOU TO KNOW!!
TROMP TROMP
COME ON, DON'T BE A SPOILSPORT, USA!!
I ACTUALLY DON'T KNOW TOO MUCH ABOUT IT EITHER...
SATO, MY NEIGHBOR, TOLD ME THAT THE FIRST TIME SHE GAVE BIRTH...
...IT REALLY, REALLY HURT...
I WONDER HOW, AND WHY IT HURTS...?!
WHAT SHOULD I DO...
...EVEN THOUGH HE MAY BE HANDSOME, I DON'T WANT TO BE IN PAIN...
GLOOM
USA, YOU'RE WALKING TOO SLOWLY.

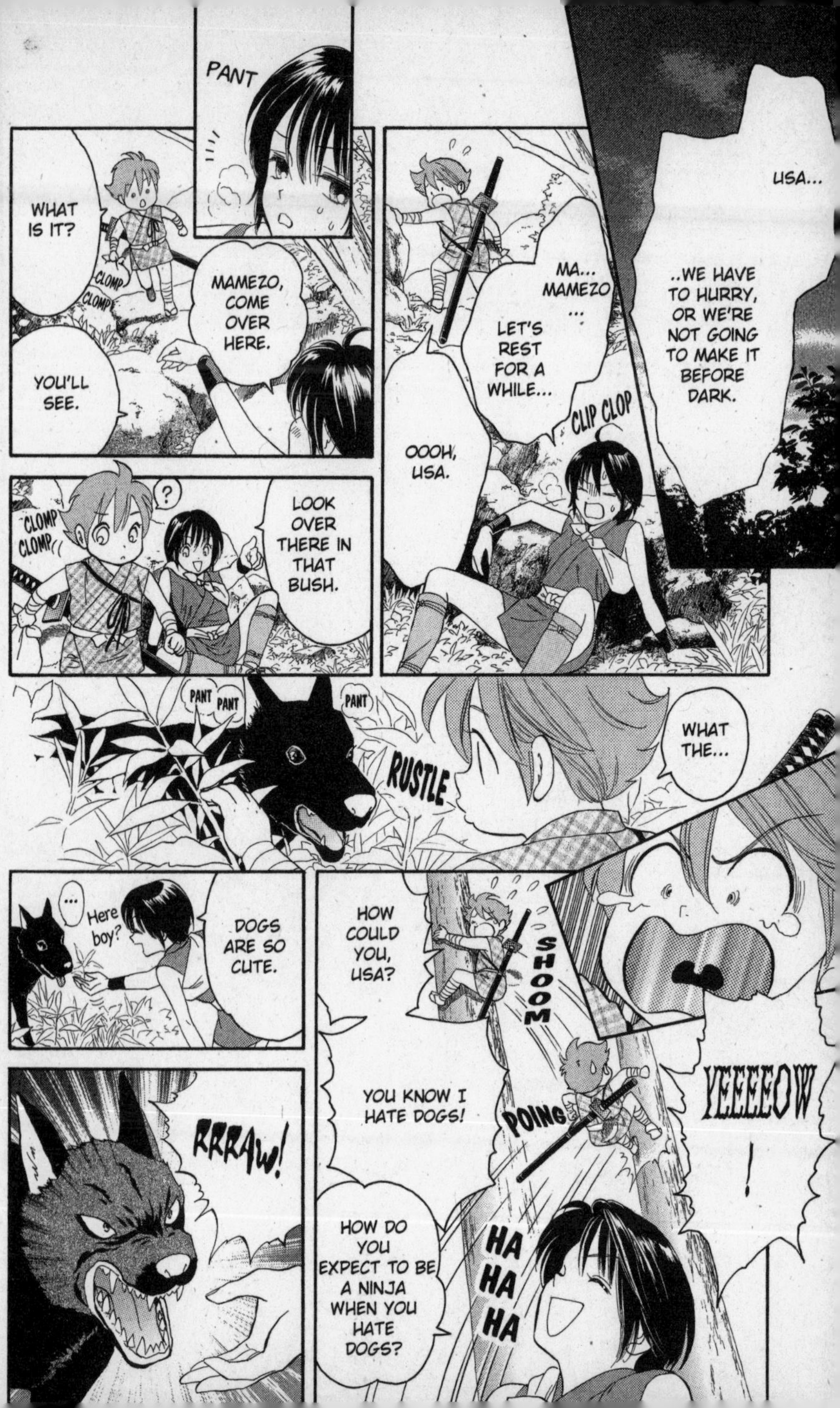
USA...
..WE HAVE TO HURRY, OR WE'RE NOT GOING TO MAKE IT BEFORE DARK.
PANT
MA... MAMEZO...
LET'S REST FOR A WHILE...
CLIP CLOP
OOOH, USA.
MAMEZO, COME OVER HERE.
WHAT IS IT?
CLOMP
CLOMP
YOU'LL SEE.
?
LOOK OVER THERE IN THAT BUSH.
CLOMP CLOMP
WHAT THE...
PANT
PANT PANT
RUSTLE
YEEEEOW !
SHOOM
HOW COULD YOU, USA?
POING
YOU KNOW I HATE DOGS!
HA HA HA
HOW DO YOU EXPECT TO BE A NINJA WHEN YOU HATE DOGS?
DOGS ARE SO CUTE.
...
Here boy?
RRRAW!

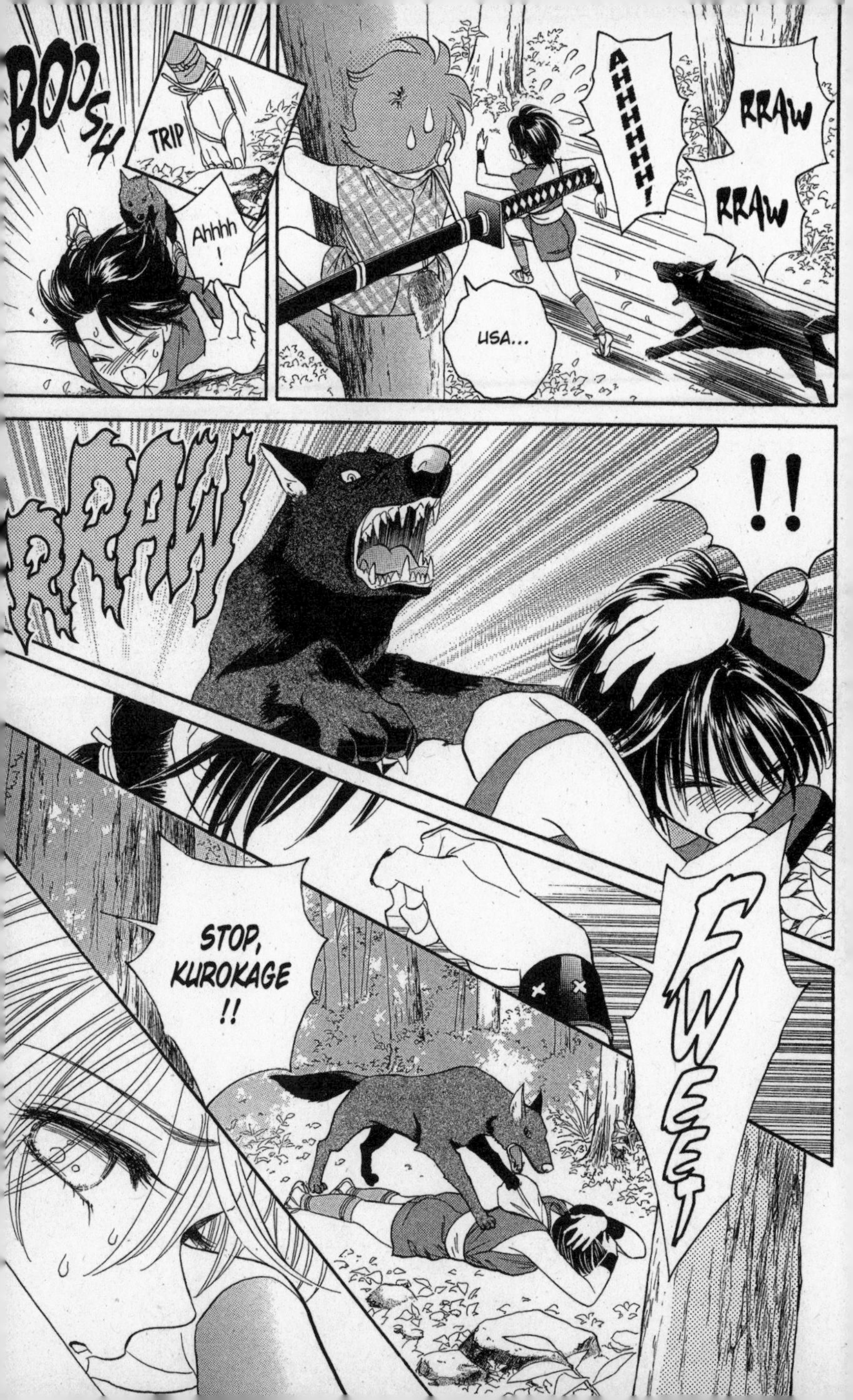
RRAW
RRAW
AHHHHHH!
USA...
TRIP
BOOSH
Ahhhh!
!!
RRAW
FWEEET
STOP, KUROKAGE!!

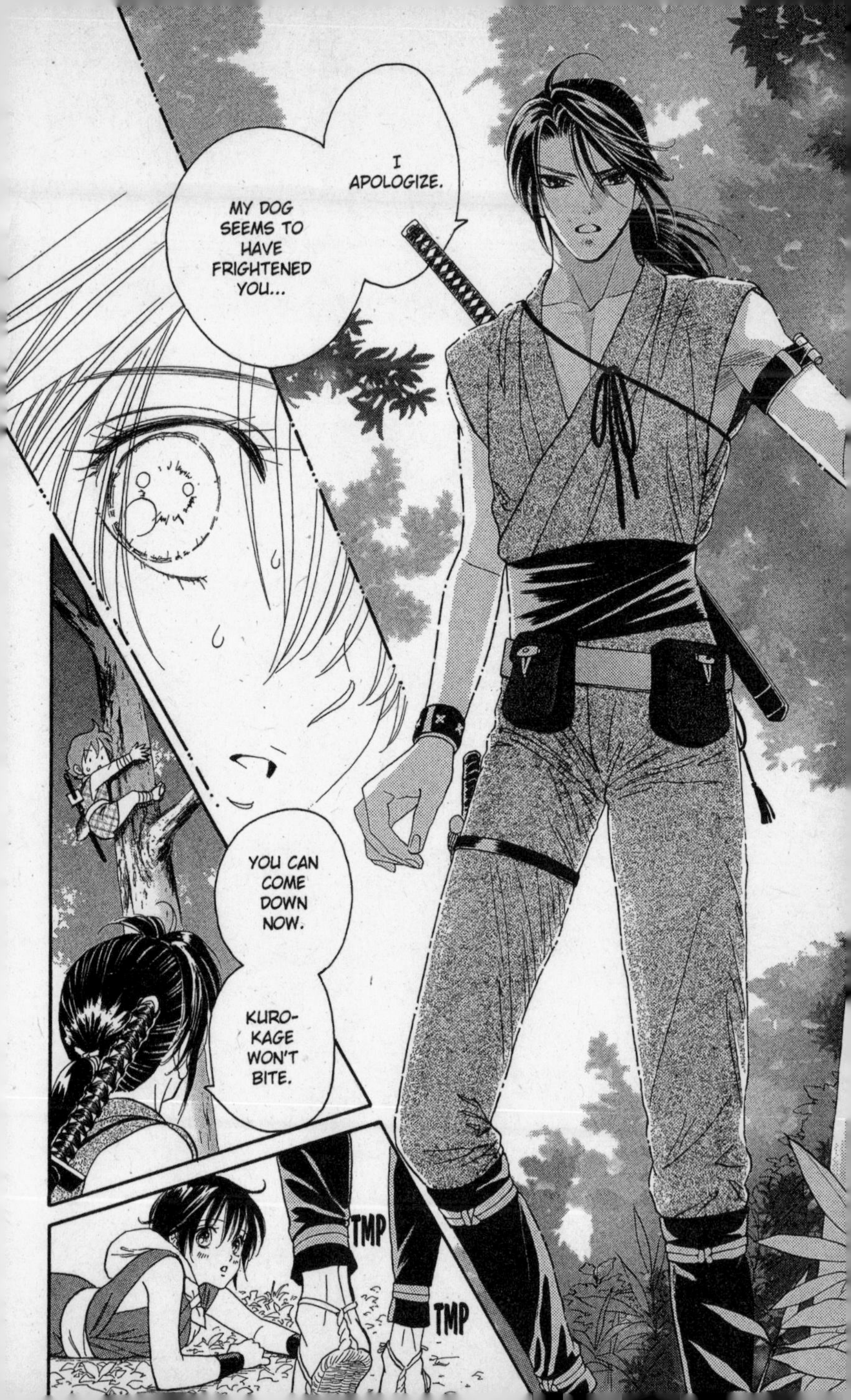
I APOLOGIZE.
MY DOG SEEMS TO HAVE FRIGHTENED YOU...
YOU CAN COME DOWN NOW.
KURO-KAGE WON'T BITE.
TMP
TMP

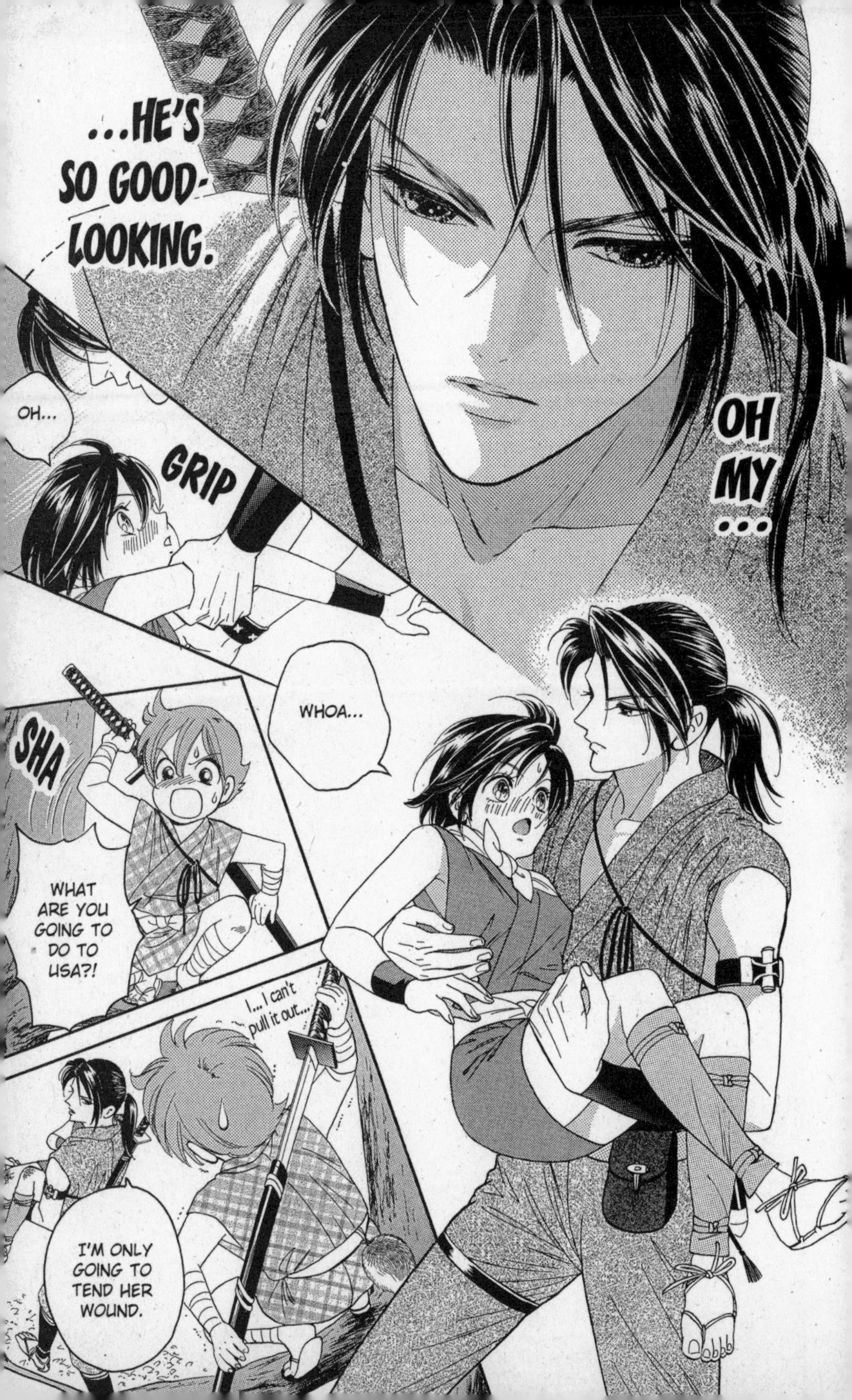
...HE'S SO GOOD-LOOKING.
OH MY...
OH...
GRIP
WHOA...
SHA
WHAT ARE YOU GOING TO DO TO USA?!
I... I can't pull it out...
I'M ONLY GOING TO TEND HER WOUND.

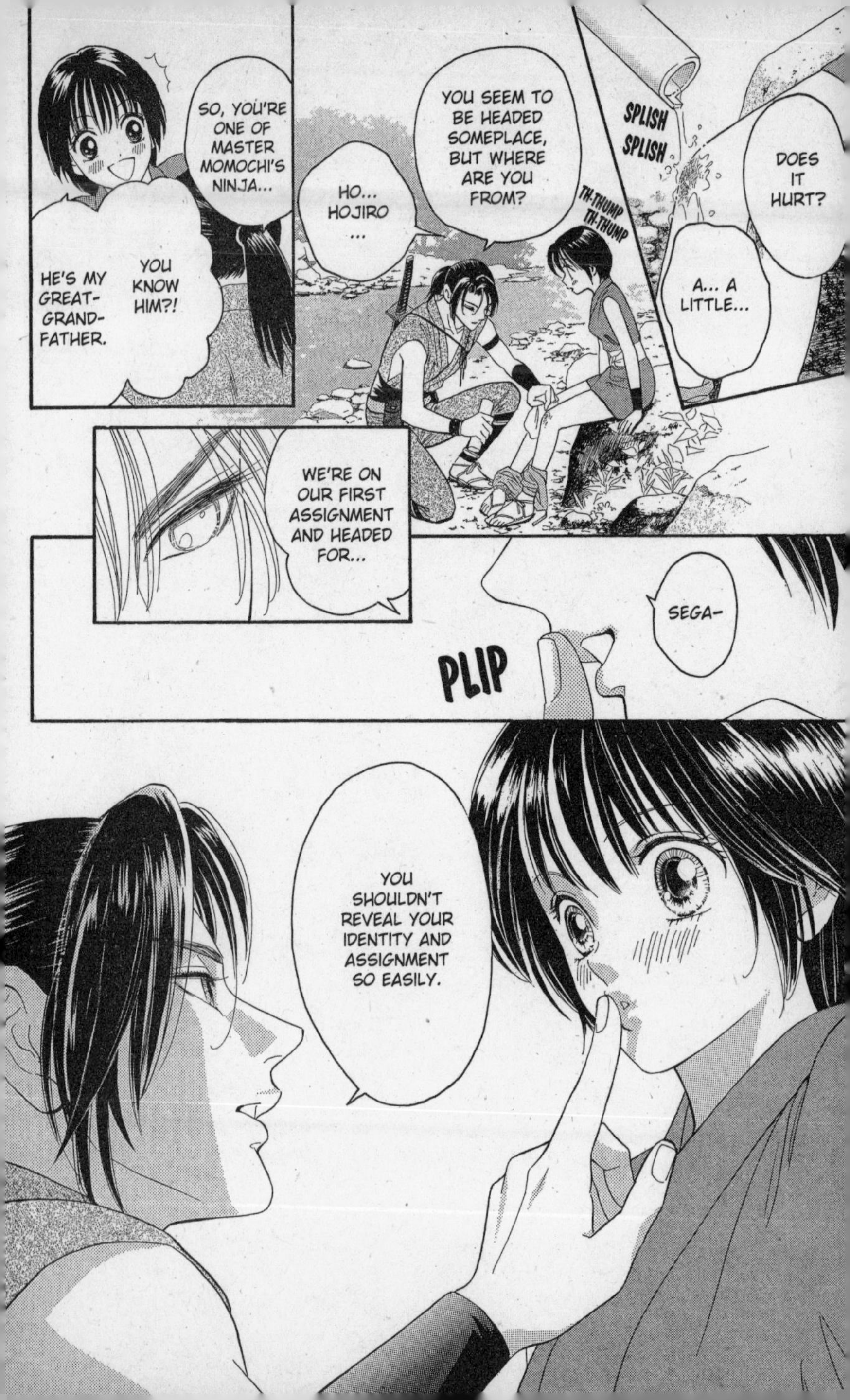
SPLISH SPLISH
DOES IT HURT?
A... A LITTLE...
TH-THUMP TH-THUMP
YOU SEEM TO BE HEADED SOMEPLACE, BUT WHERE ARE YOU FROM?
HO... HOJIRO ...
SO, YOU'RE ONE OF MASTER MOMOCHI'S NINJA...
YOU KNOW HIM?!
HE'S MY GREAT-GRANDFATHER.
WE'RE ON OUR FIRST ASSIGNMENT AND HEADED FOR...
SEGA-
PLIP
YOU SHOULDN'T REVEAL YOUR IDENTITY AND ASSIGNMENT SO EASILY.

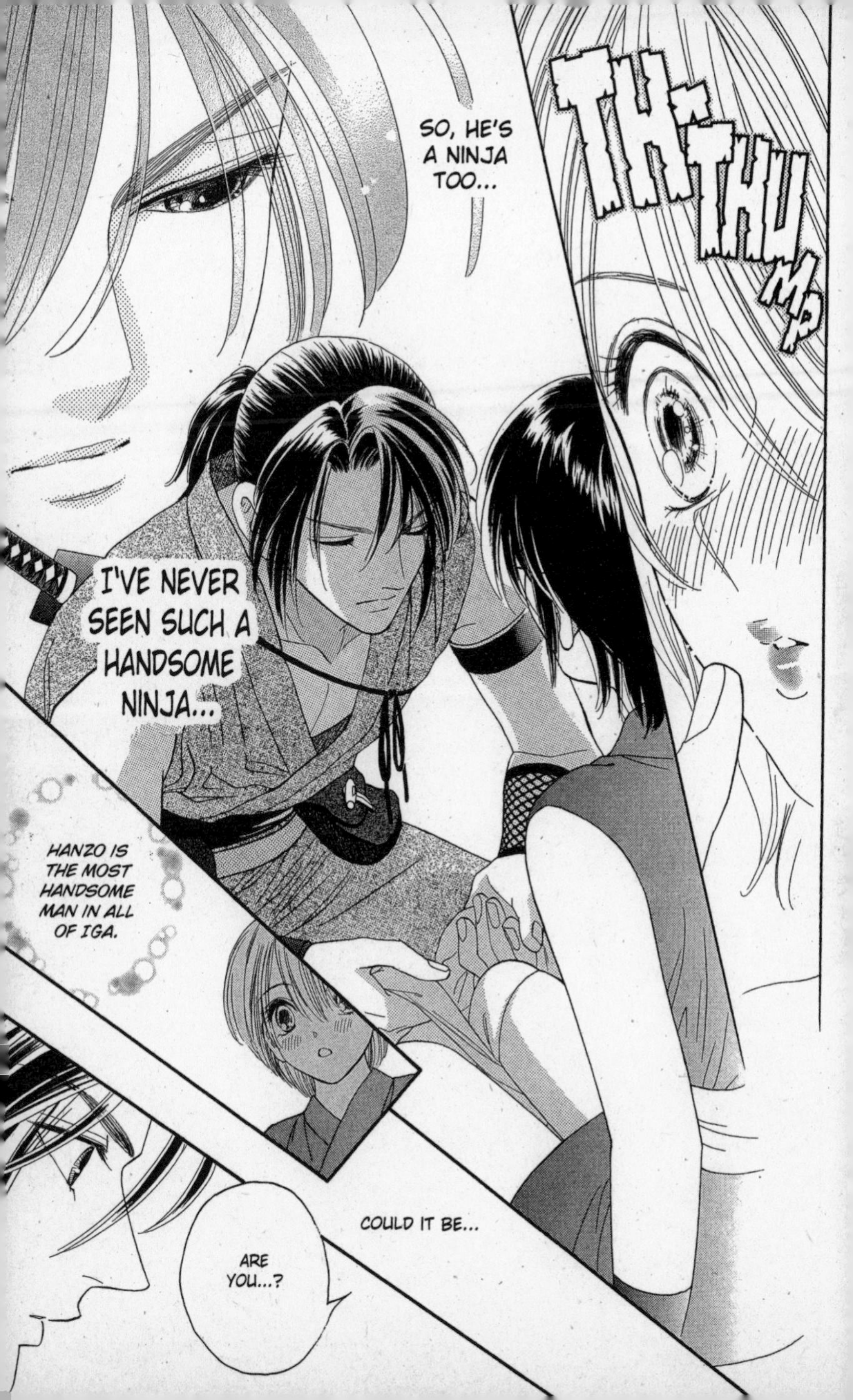
TH-THUMP
SO, HE'S A NINJA TOO...
I'VE NEVER SEEN SUCH A HANDSOME NINJA...
HANZO IS THE MOST HANDSOME MAN IN ALL OF IGA.
COULD IT BE...
ARE YOU...?

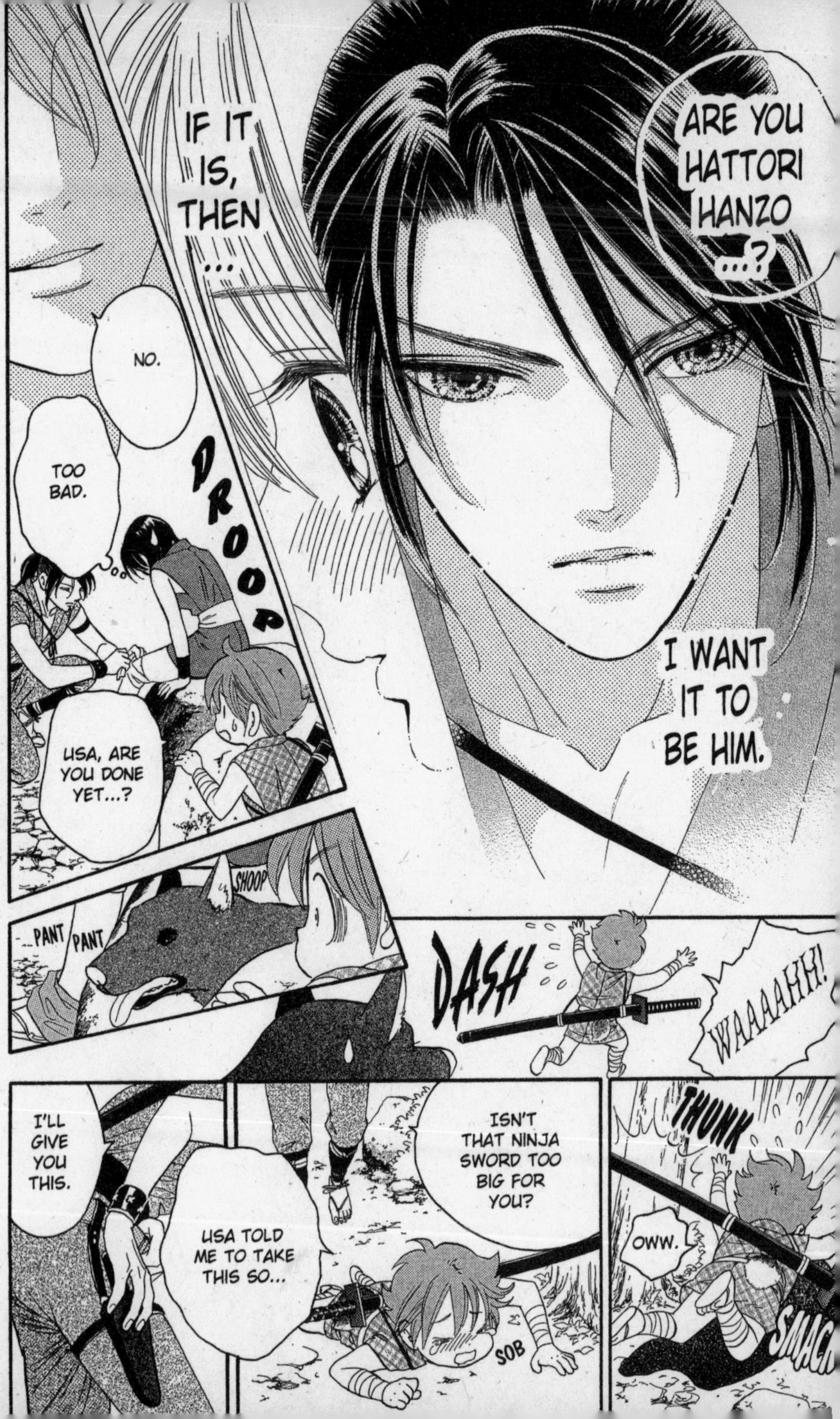
ARE YOU HATTORI HANZO ...?
IF IT IS, THEN ...
I WANT IT TO BE HIM.
NO.
DROOP
TOO BAD.
USA, ARE YOU DONE YET...?
WAAAAHH!
DASH
SHOOP
PANT PANT
THUNK
OWW.
SMACK
ISN'T THAT NINJA SWORD TOO BIG FOR YOU?
USA TOLD ME TO TAKE THIS SO...
SOB
I'LL GIVE YOU THIS.

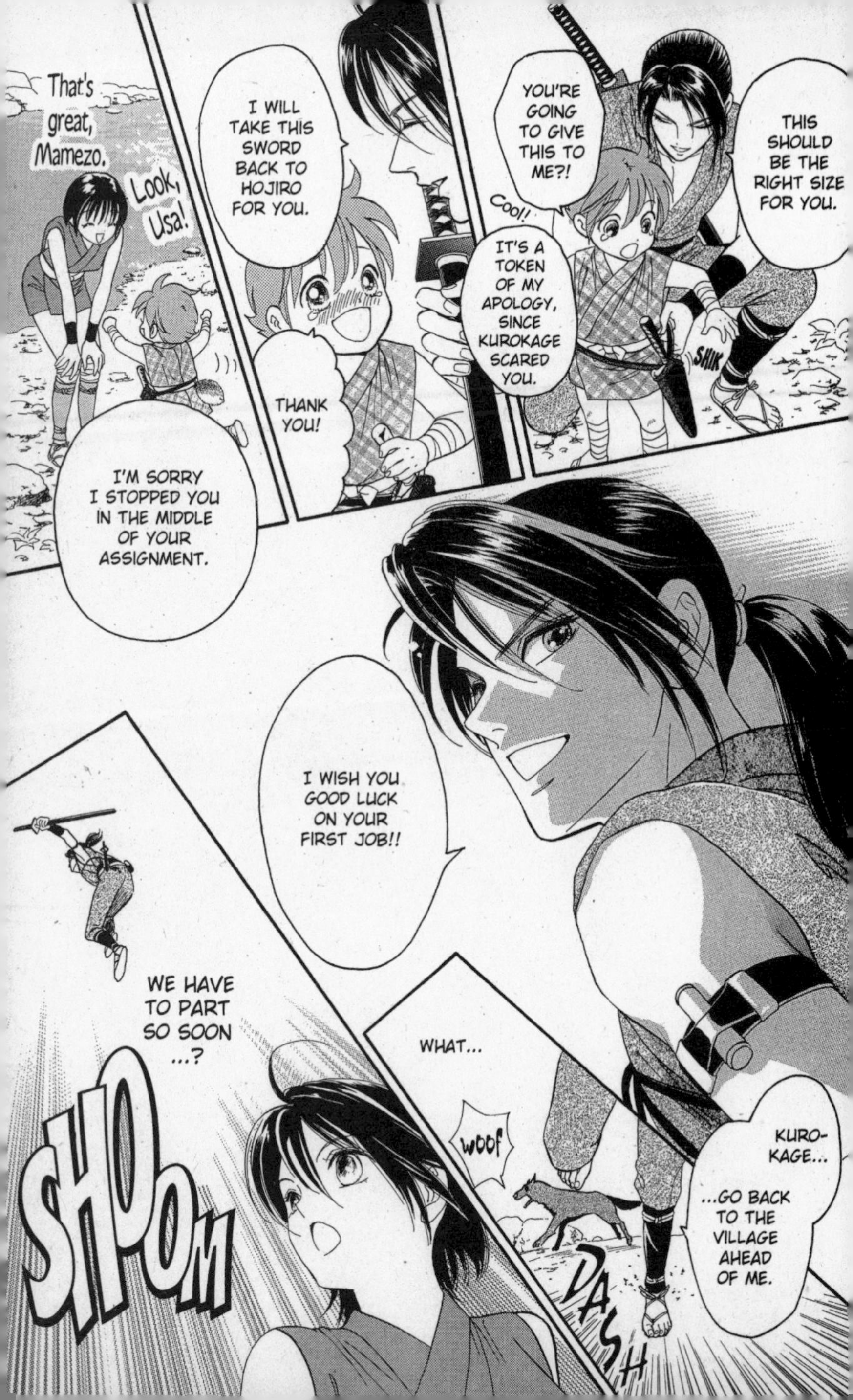
THIS SHOULD BE THE RIGHT SIZE FOR YOU.
SHIK
YOU'RE GOING TO GIVE THIS TO ME?!
Cool!!
IT'S A TOKEN OF MY APOLOGY, SINCE KUROKAGE SCARED YOU.
I WILL TAKE THIS SWORD BACK TO HOJIRO FOR YOU.
THANK YOU!
That's great, Mamezo.
Look, Usa!
I'M SORRY I STOPPED YOU IN THE MIDDLE OF YOUR ASSIGNMENT.
I WISH YOU GOOD LUCK ON YOUR FIRST JOB!!
KURO-KAGE...
...GO BACK TO THE VILLAGE AHEAD OF ME.
DASH
woof
WHAT...
WE HAVE TO PART SO SOON ...?
SHOOM

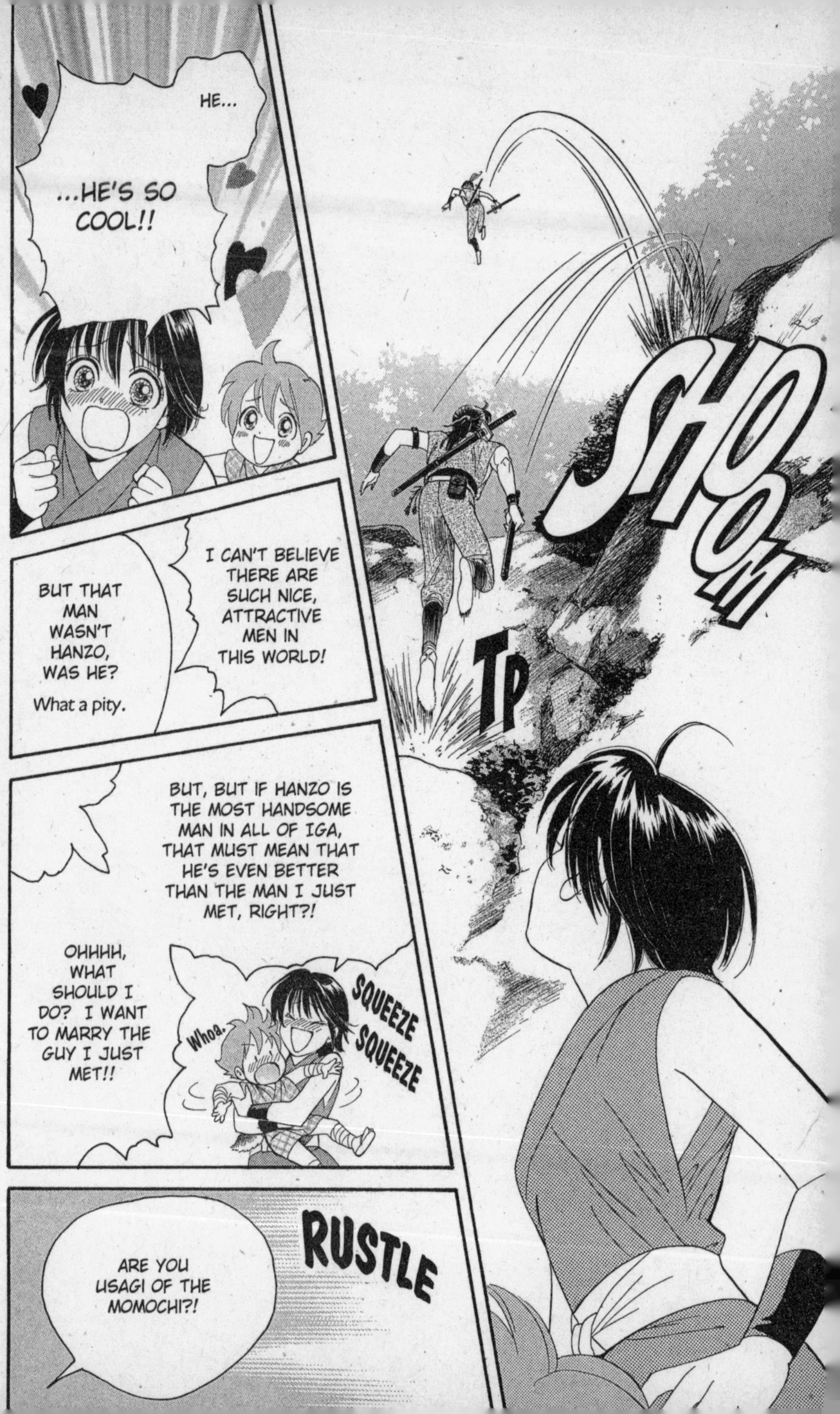
SHOOM
TP
HE...
...HE'S SO COOL!!
I CAN'T BELIEVE THERE ARE SUCH NICE, ATTRACTIVE MEN IN THIS WORLD!
BUT THAT MAN WASN'T HANZO, WAS HE?
What a pity.
BUT, BUT IF HANZO IS THE MOST HANDSOME MAN IN ALL OF IGA, THAT MUST MEAN THAT HE'S EVEN BETTER THAN THE MAN I JUST MET, RIGHT?!
SQUEEZE SQUEEZE
OHHHH, WHAT SHOULD I DO? I WANT TO MARRY THE GUY I JUST MET!!
Whoa.
RUSTLE
ARE YOU USAGI OF THE MOMOCHI?!

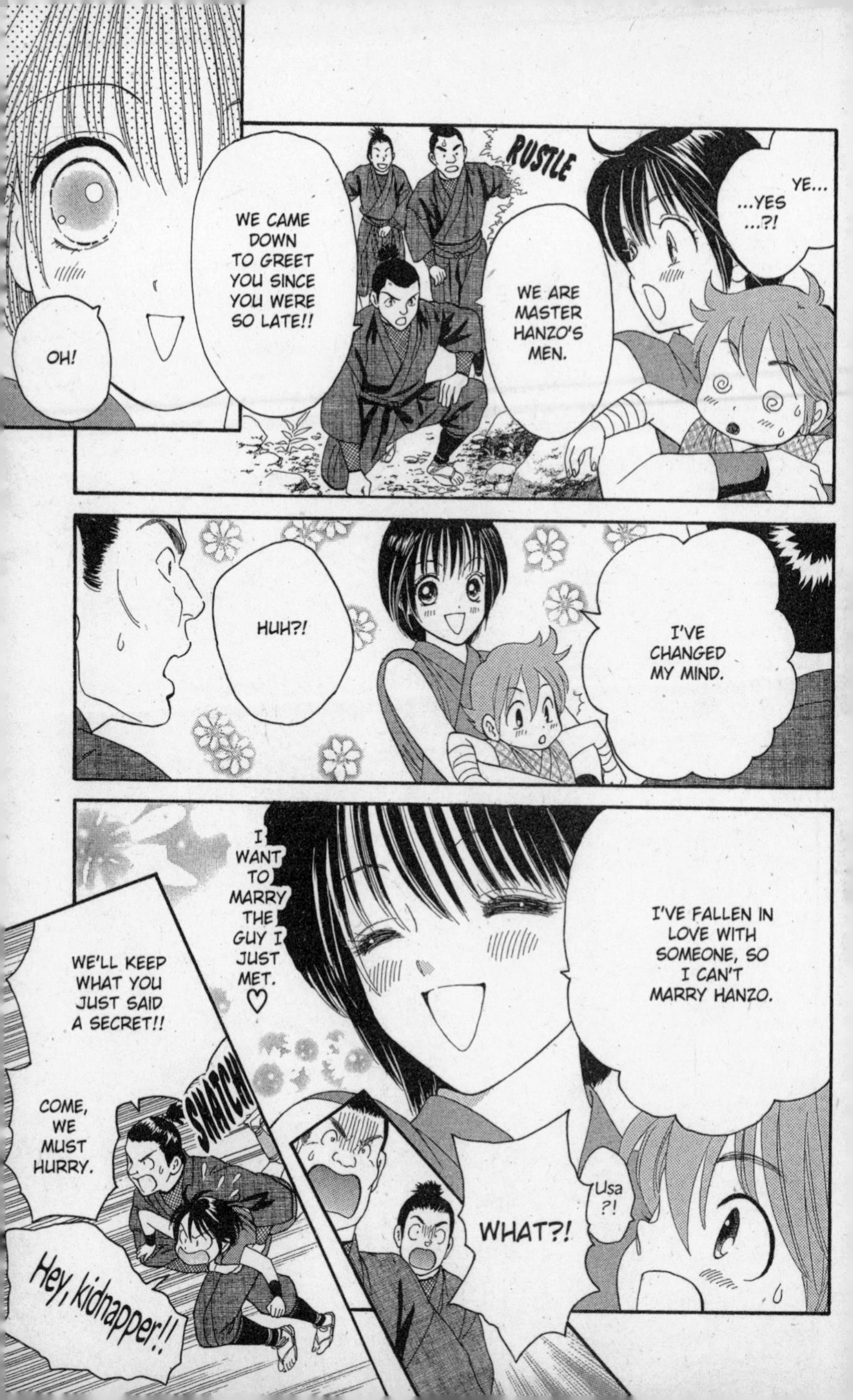
RUSTLE
YE... ...YES ...?!
WE ARE MASTER HANZO'S MEN.
WE CAME DOWN TO GREET YOU SINCE YOU WERE SO LATE!!
OH!
I'VE CHANGED MY MIND.
HUH?!
I'VE FALLEN IN LOVE WITH SOMEONE, SO I CAN'T MARRY HANZO.
I WANT TO MARRY THE GUY I JUST MET. ♡
Usa?!
WHAT?!
WE'LL KEEP WHAT YOU JUST SAID A SECRET!!
SNATCH
COME, WE MUST HURRY.
Hey, kidnapper!!

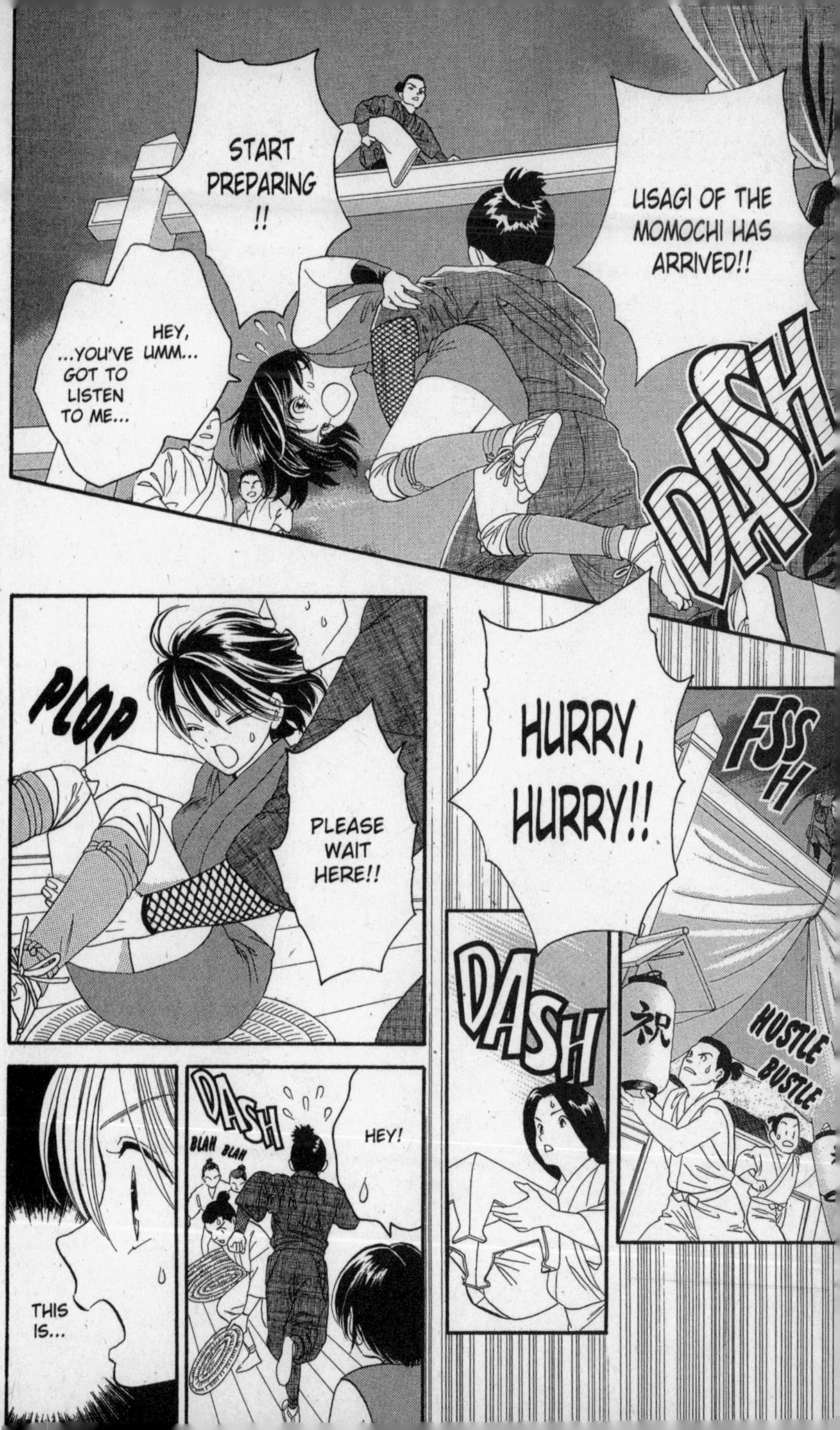

USAGI OF THE MOMOCHI HAS ARRIVED!!
START PREPARING!!
HEY, UMM...
...YOU'VE GOT TO LISTEN TO ME...
DASH
HURRY, HURRY!!
FSSH
HUSTLE BUSTLE
DASH
PLOP
PLEASE WAIT HERE!!
HEY!
DASH
BLAH BLAH
THIS IS...

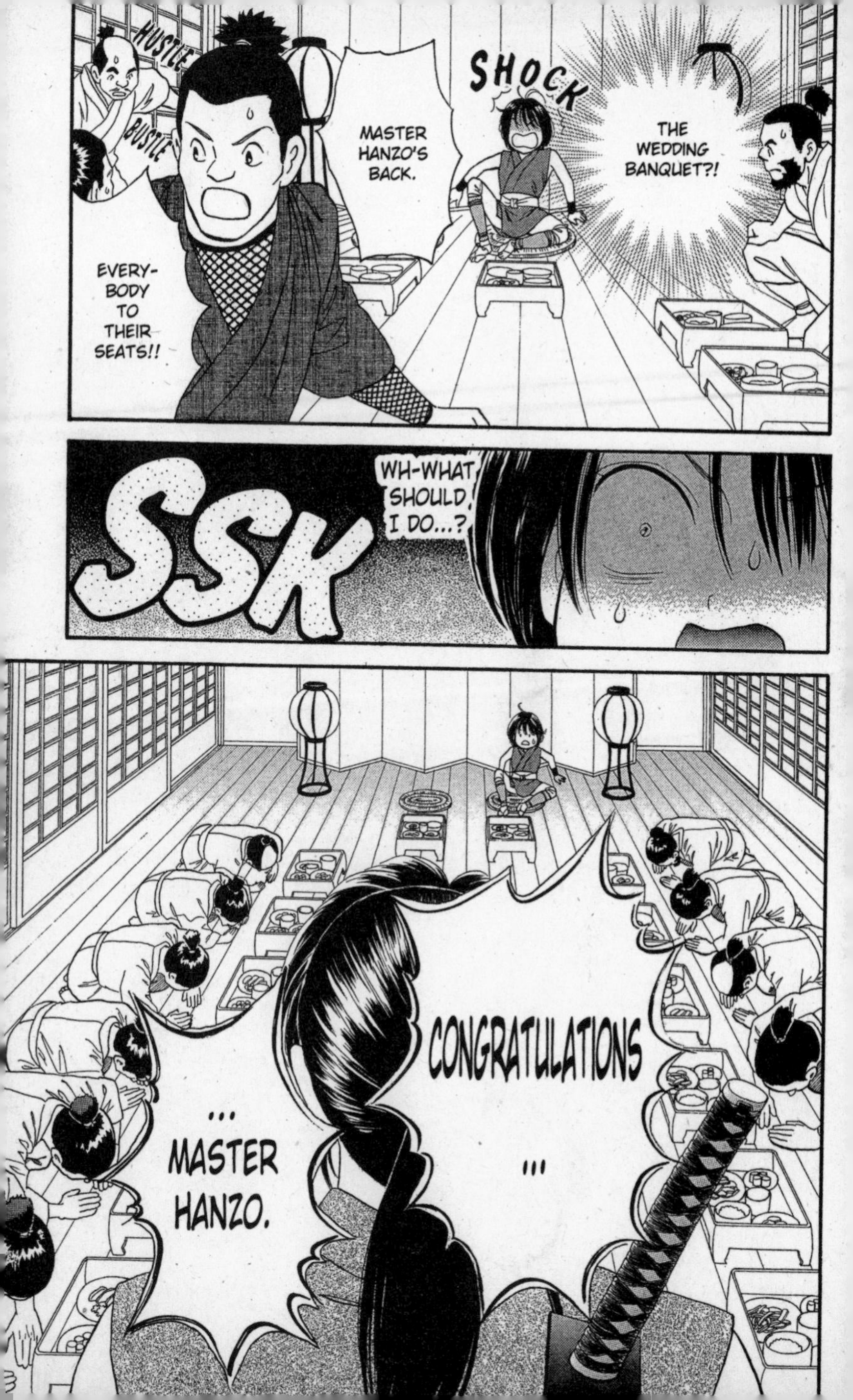

THE WEDDING BANQUET?!
SHOCK
MASTER HANZO'S BACK.
HUSTLE
BUSTLE
EVERYBODY TO THEIR SEATS!!
WH-WHAT SHOULD I DO...?
SSK
CONGRATULATIONS
...
... MASTER HANZO.

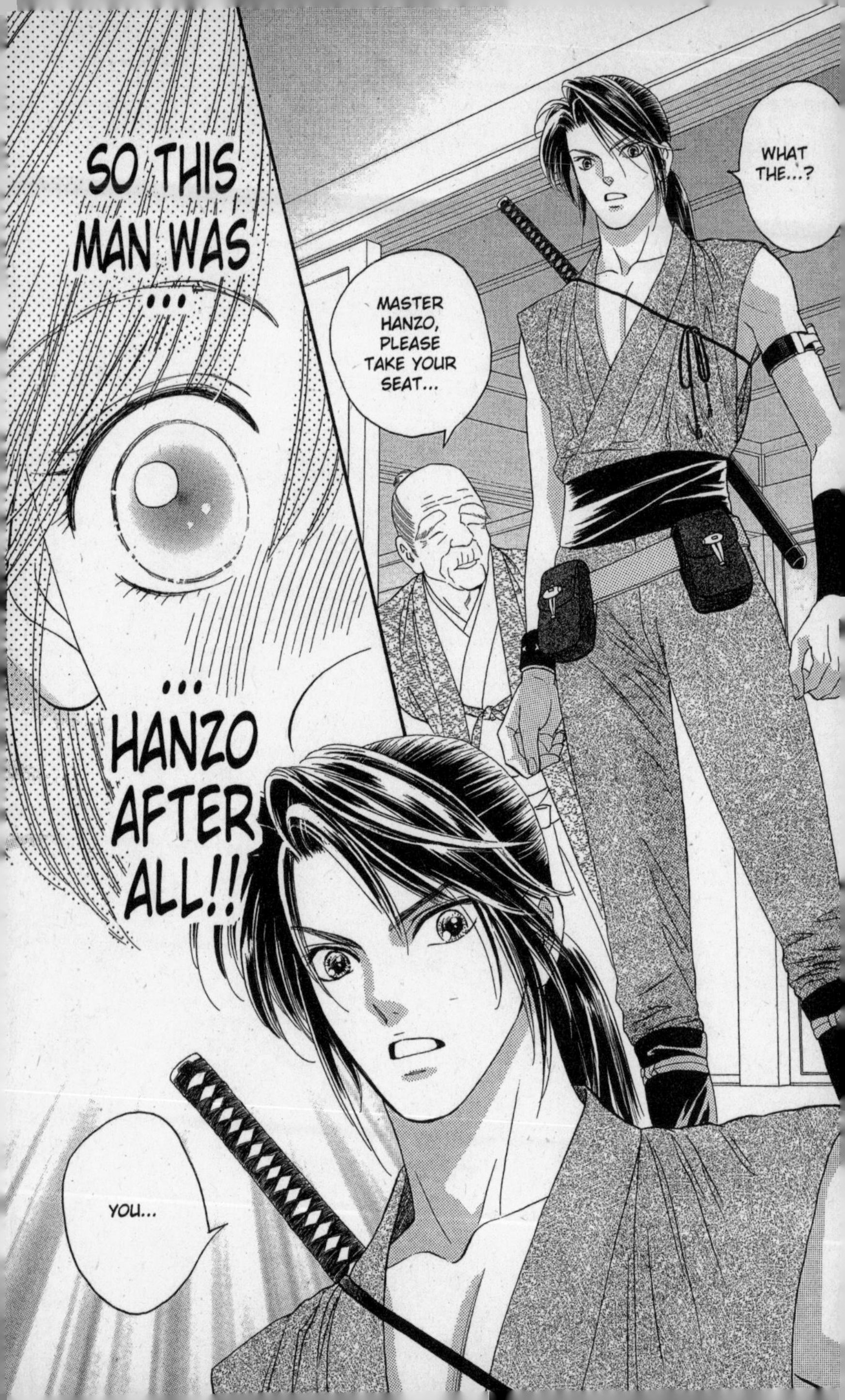
WHAT THE...?
MASTER HANZO, PLEASE TAKE YOUR SEAT...
SO THIS MAN WAS ...
... HANZO AFTER ALL!!
YOU...

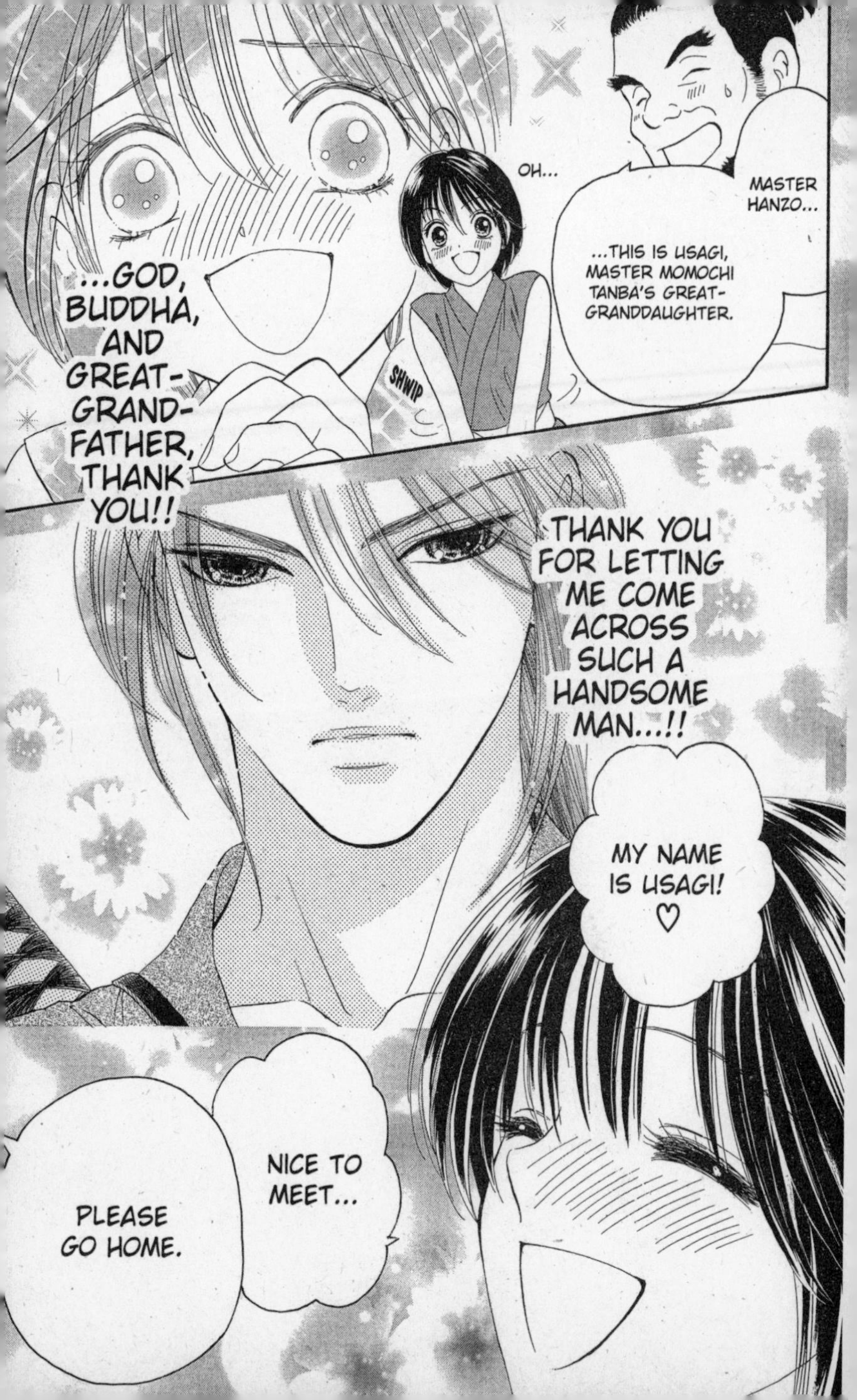
MASTER HANZO...
...THIS IS USAGI, MASTER MOMOCHI TANBA'S GREAT-GRANDDAUGHTER.
OH...
SHWIP
...GOD, BUDDHA, AND GREAT-GRAND-FATHER, THANK YOU!!
THANK YOU FOR LETTING ME COME ACROSS SUCH A HANDSOME MAN...!!
MY NAME IS USAGI! ♡
NICE TO MEET...
PLEASE GO HOME.

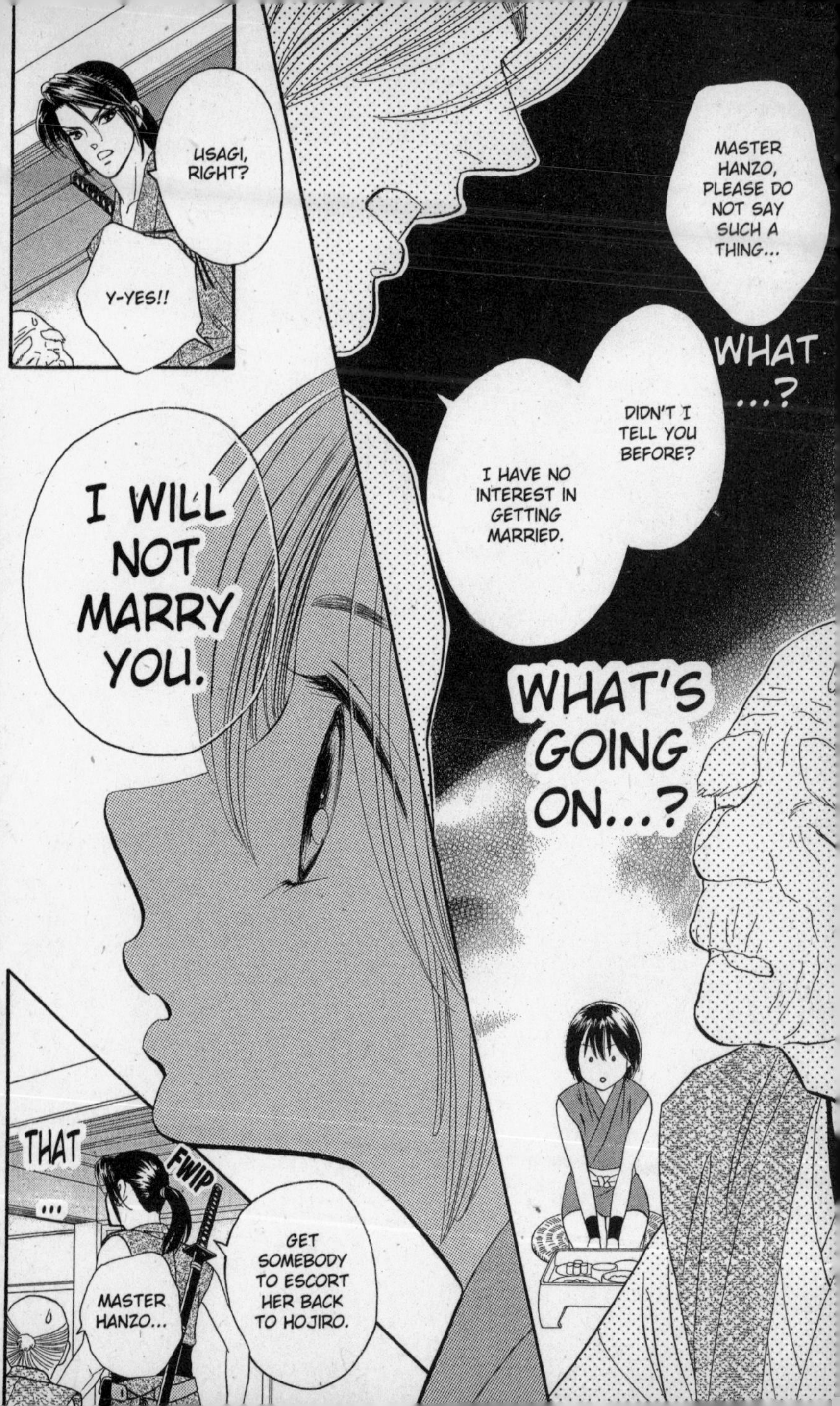
USAGI, RIGHT?
Y-YES!!
I WILL NOT MARRY YOU.
MASTER HANZO, PLEASE DO NOT SAY SUCH A THING...
DIDN'T I TELL YOU BEFORE?
I HAVE NO INTEREST IN GETTING MARRIED.
WHAT ...?
WHAT'S GOING ON...?
THAT ...
FWIP
GET SOMEBODY TO ESCORT HER BACK TO HOJIRO.
MASTER HANZO...

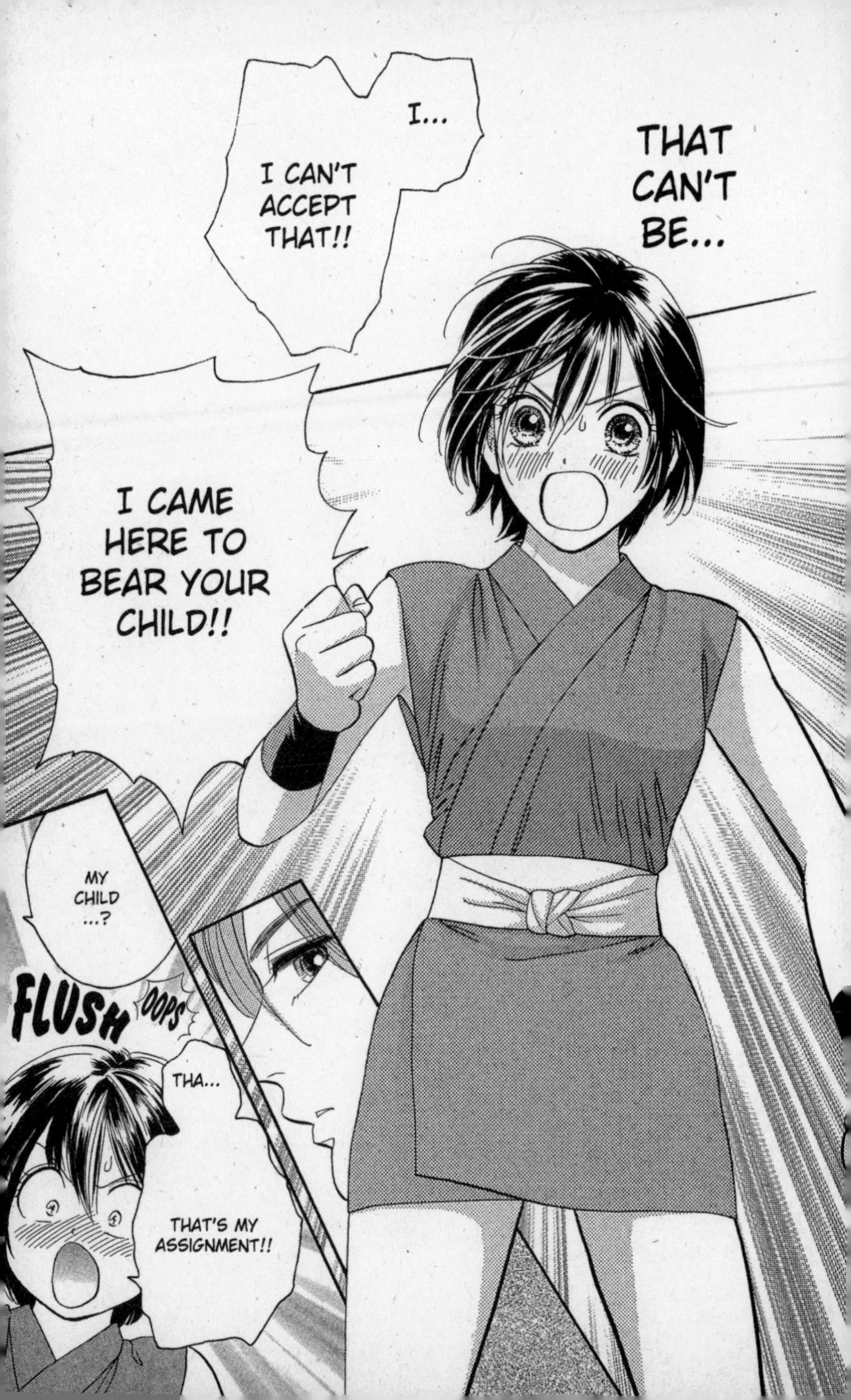
THAT CAN'T BE...
I...
I CAN'T ACCEPT THAT!!
I CAME HERE TO BEAR YOUR CHILD!!
MY CHILD ...?
OOPS
FLUSH
THA...
THAT'S MY ASSIGNMENT!!

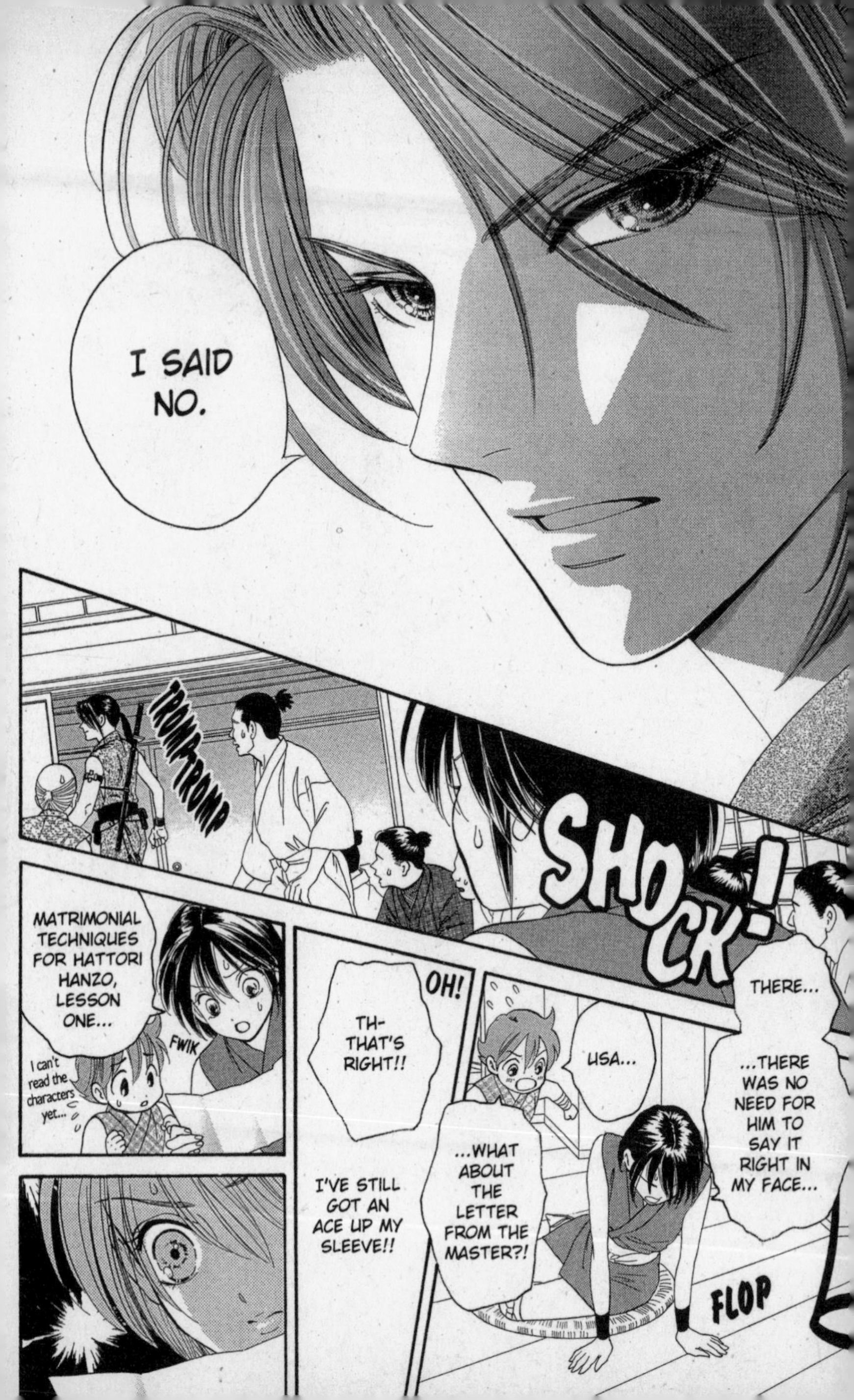
I SAID NO.
TROMP TROMP
SHOCK!
THERE...
...THERE WAS NO NEED FOR HIM TO SAY IT RIGHT IN MY FACE...
FLOP
USA...
...WHAT ABOUT THE LETTER FROM THE MASTER?!
OH!
TH-THAT'S RIGHT!!
I'VE STILL GOT AN ACE UP MY SLEEVE!!
MATRIMONIAL TECHNIQUES FOR HATTORI HANZO, LESSON ONE...
FWIK
I can't read the characters yet...

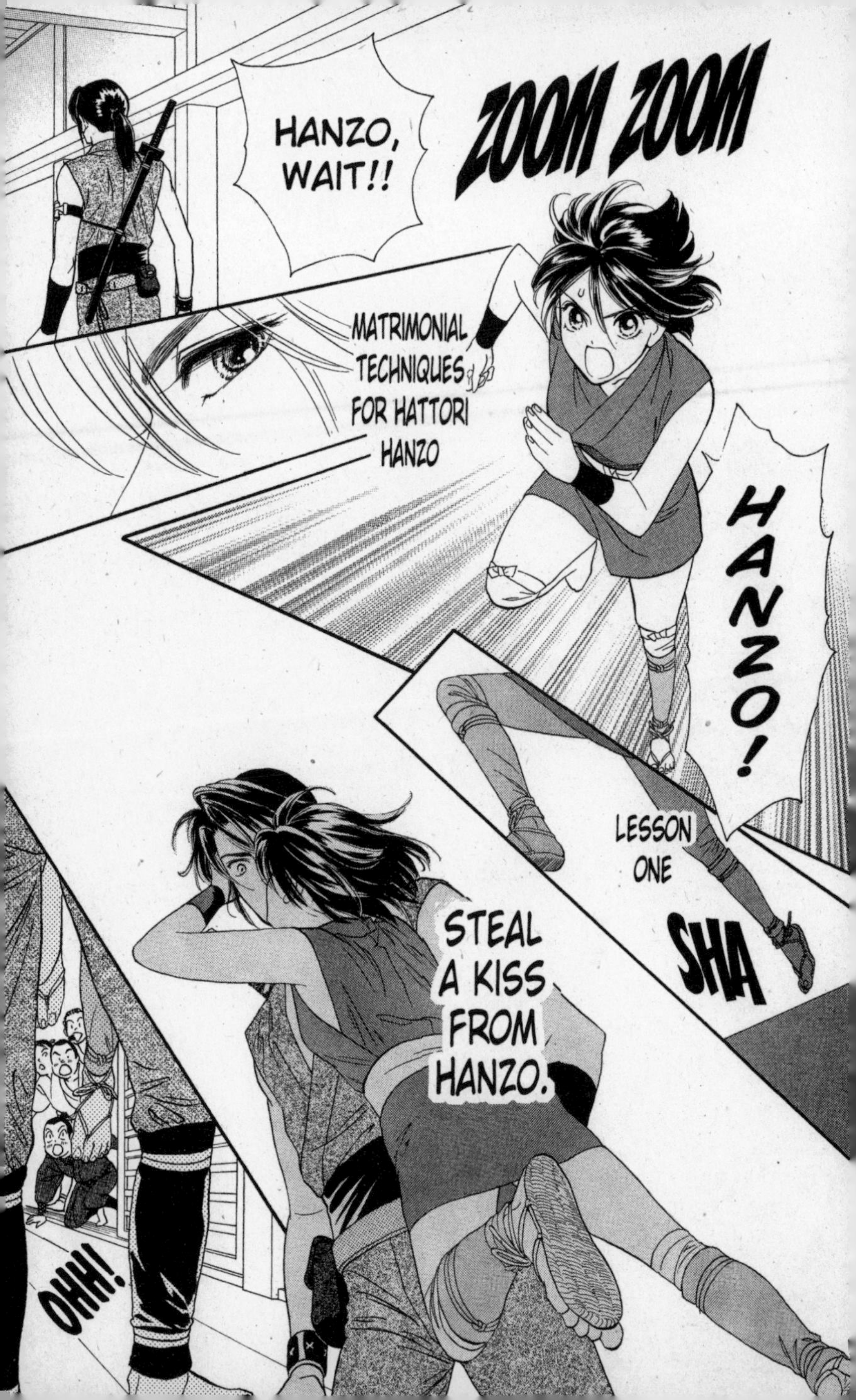
ZOOM ZOOM
HANZO, WAIT!!
HANZO!
MATRIMONIAL TECHNIQUES FOR HATTORI HANZO
LESSON ONE
SHA
STEAL A KISS FROM HANZO.
OHH!

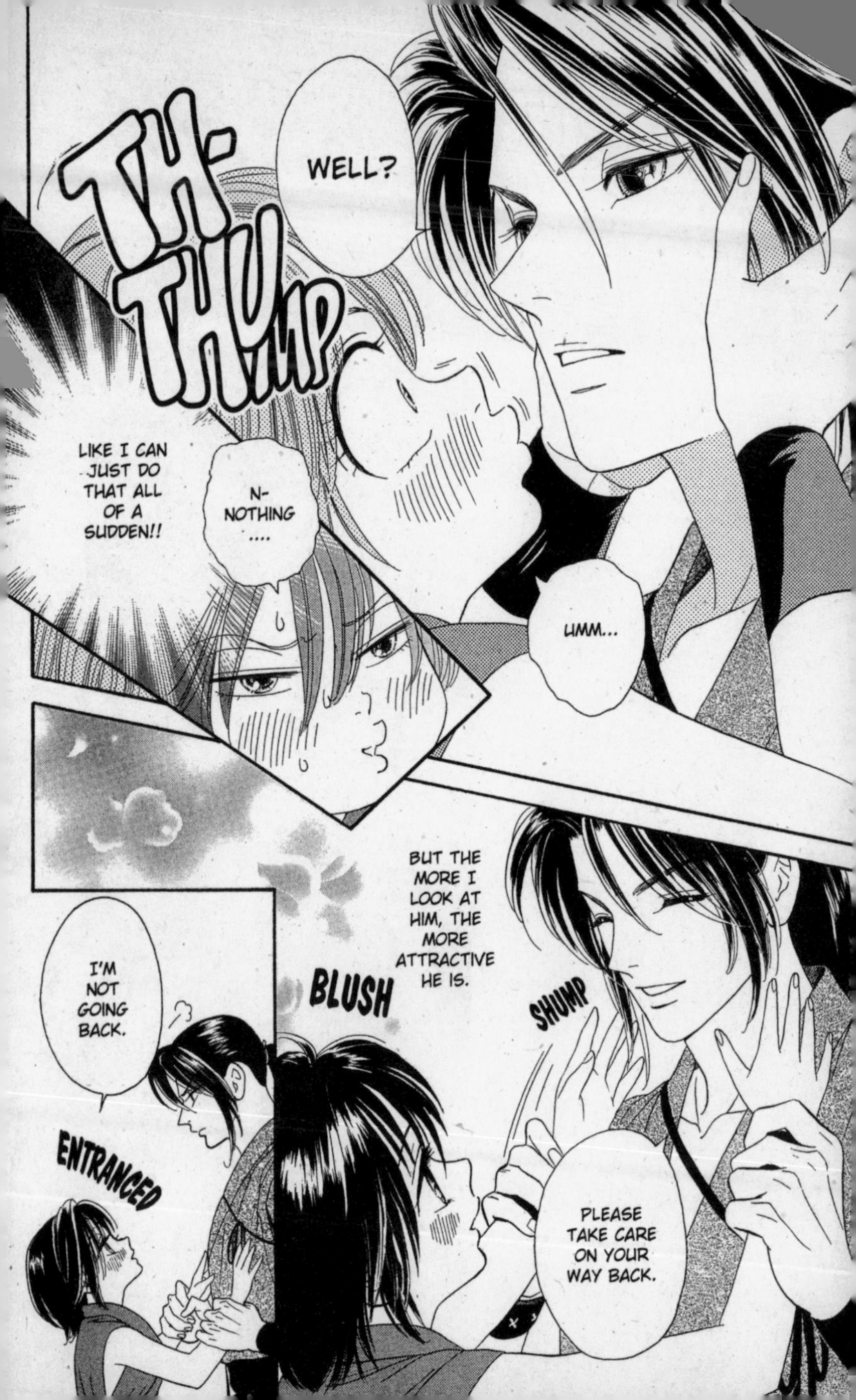
WELL?
TH-THUMP
UMM...
N-NOTHING ....
LIKE I CAN JUST DO THAT ALL OF A SUDDEN!!
BUT THE MORE I LOOK AT HIM, THE MORE ATTRACTIVE HE IS.
SHUMP
BLUSH
PLEASE TAKE CARE ON YOUR WAY BACK.
I'M NOT GOING BACK.
ENTRANCED

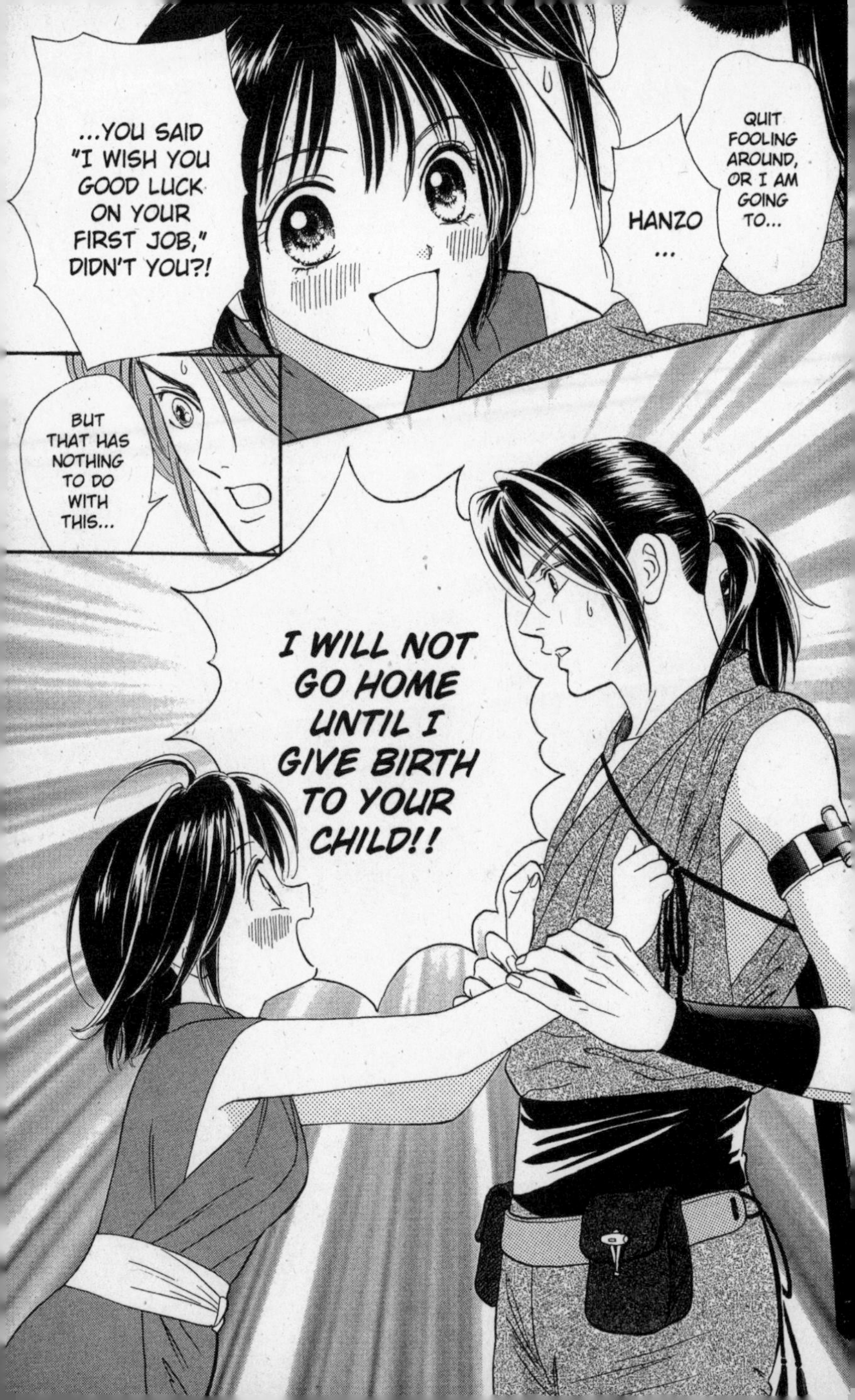
QUIT FOOLING AROUND, OR I AM GOING TO...
HANZO ...
...YOU SAID "I WISH YOU GOOD LUCK ON YOUR FIRST JOB," DIDN'T YOU?!
BUT THAT HAS NOTHING TO DO WITH THIS...
I WILL NOT GO HOME UNTIL I GIVE BIRTH TO YOUR CHILD!!

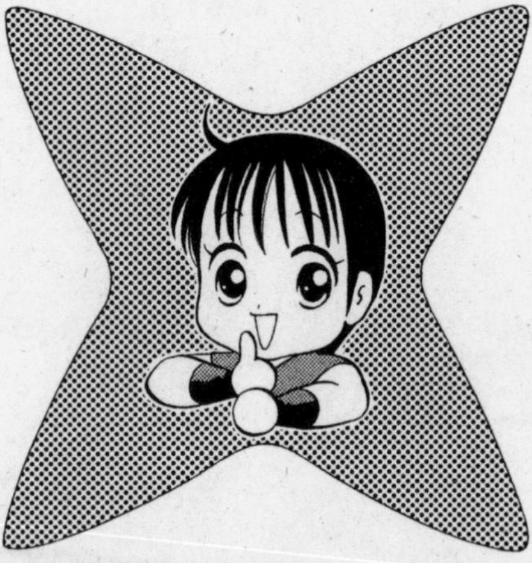

Tail of the Moon™

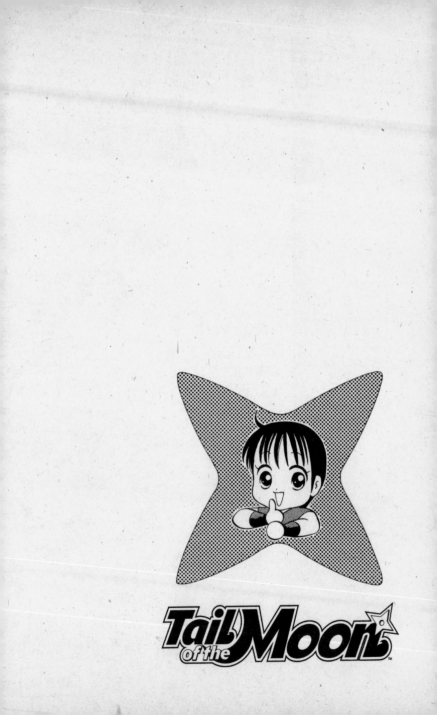

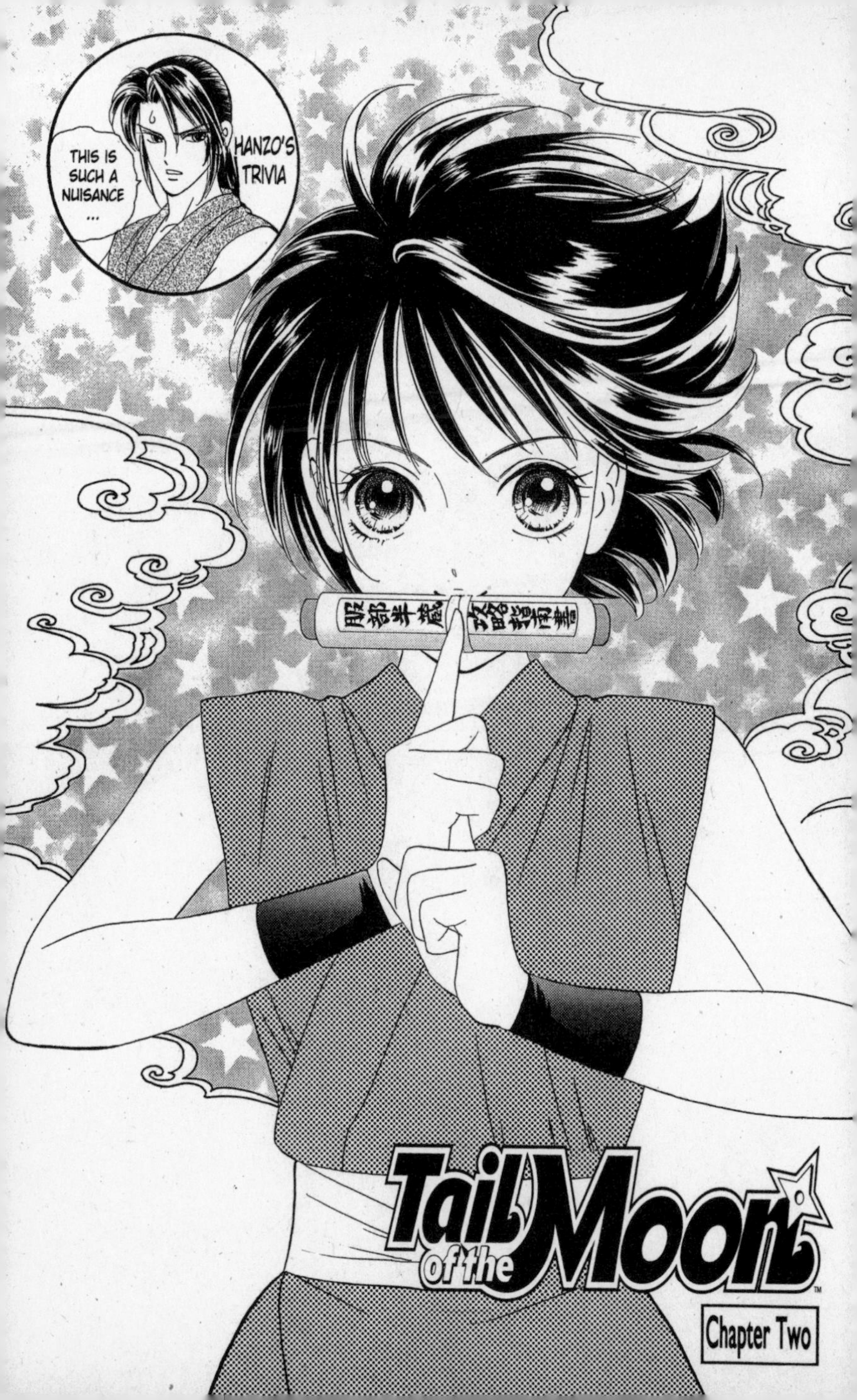
HANZO'S TRIVIA
THIS IS SUCH A NUISANCE ...
服部半蔵 攻略指南書
Tail of the Moon™
Chapter Two

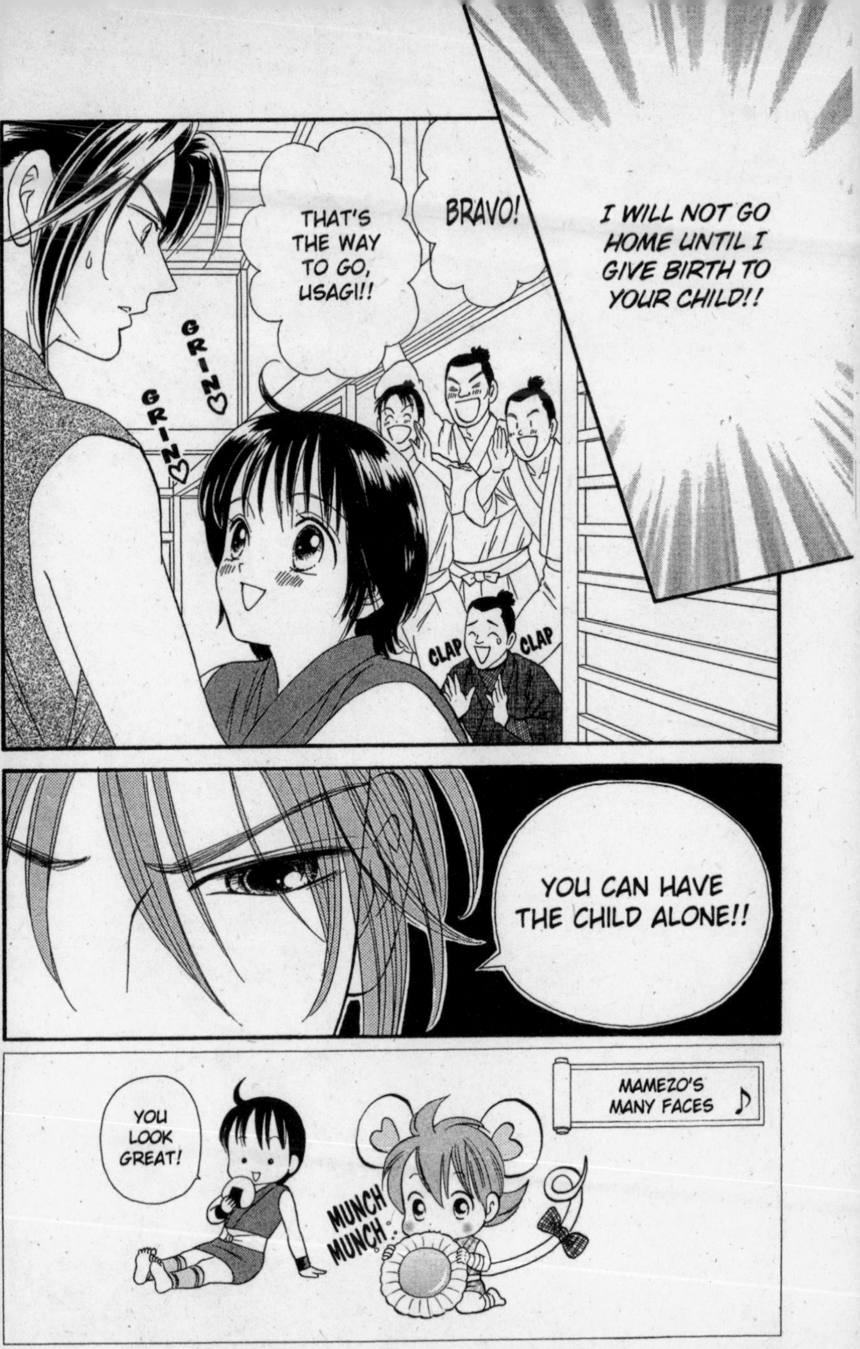
I WILL NOT GO HOME UNTIL I GIVE BIRTH TO YOUR CHILD!!
BRAVO!
THAT'S THE WAY TO GO, USAGI!!
GRIN♡
GRIN♡
CLAP
CLAP
YOU CAN HAVE THE CHILD ALONE!!
MAMEZO'S MANY FACES ♪
MUNCH MUNCH
YOU LOOK GREAT!

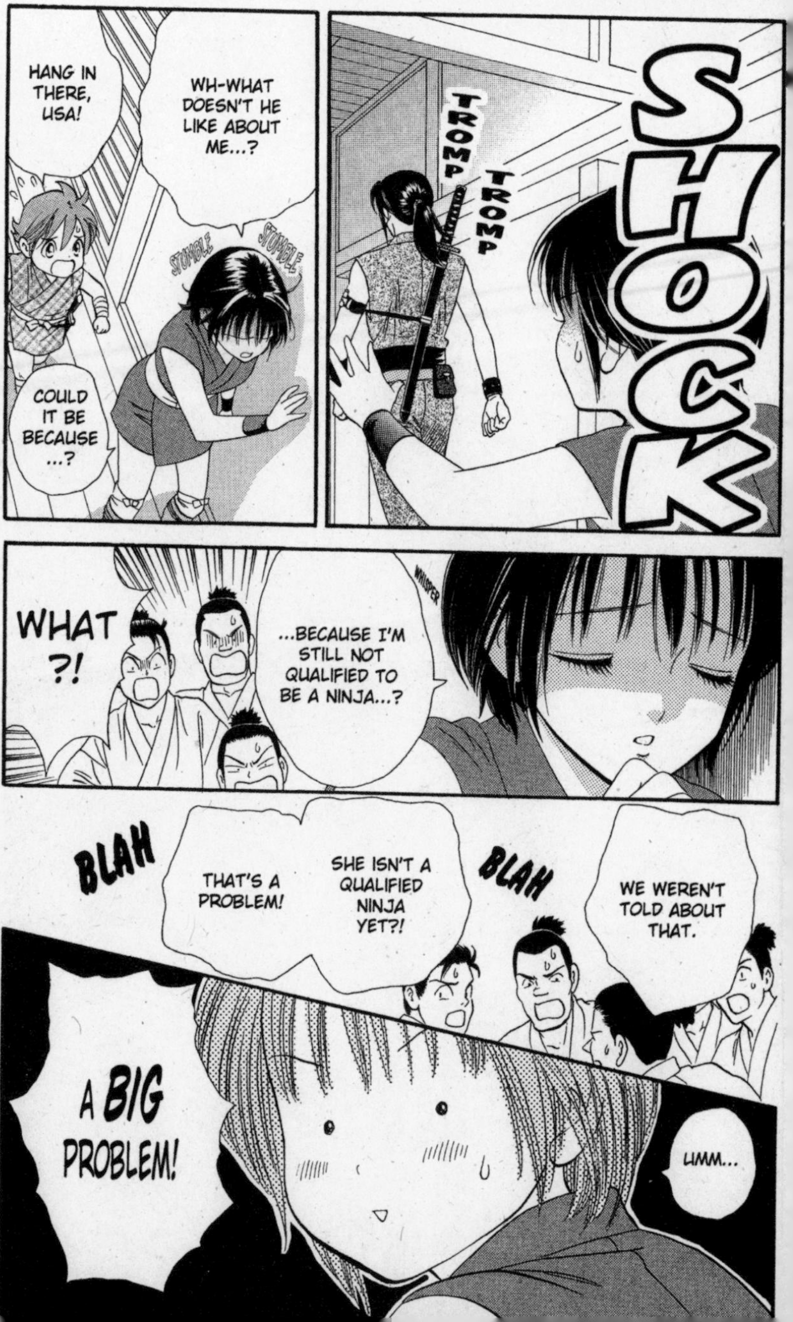
SHOCK
TROMP
TROMP
WH-WHAT DOESN'T HE LIKE ABOUT ME...?
HANG IN THERE, USA!
STUMBLE
STUMBLE
COULD IT BE BECAUSE ...?
WHISPER
...BECAUSE I'M STILL NOT QUALIFIED TO BE A NINJA...?
WHAT ?!
WE WEREN'T TOLD ABOUT THAT.
BLAH
SHE ISN'T A QUALIFIED NINJA YET?!
THAT'S A PROBLEM!
BLAH
UMM...
A BIG PROBLEM!

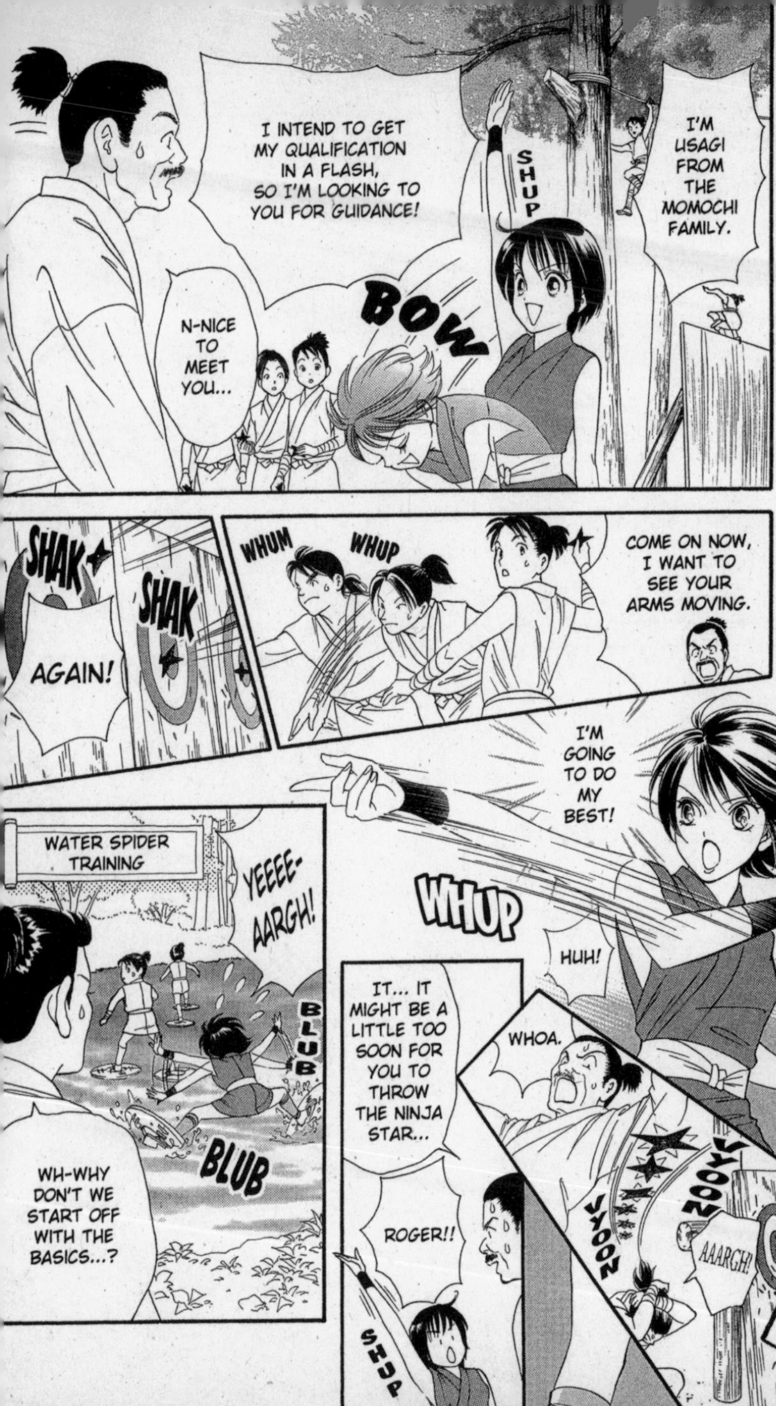
I'M USAGI FROM THE MOMOCHI FAMILY.
SHUP
I INTEND TO GET MY QUALIFICATION IN A FLASH, SO I'M LOOKING TO YOU FOR GUIDANCE!
BOW
N-NICE TO MEET YOU...
COME ON NOW, I WANT TO SEE YOUR ARMS MOVING.
WHUP
WHUM
SHAK
SHAK
AGAIN!
I'M GOING TO DO MY BEST!
WHUP
HUH!
WHOA.
VYOON
VYOON
AAARGH!
TARGET
IT... IT MIGHT BE A LITTLE TOO SOON FOR YOU TO THROW THE NINJA STAR...
ROGER!!
SHUP
WATER SPIDER TRAINING
YEEEE-AARGH!
BLUB
BLUB
WH-WHY DON'T WE START OFF WITH THE BASICS...?

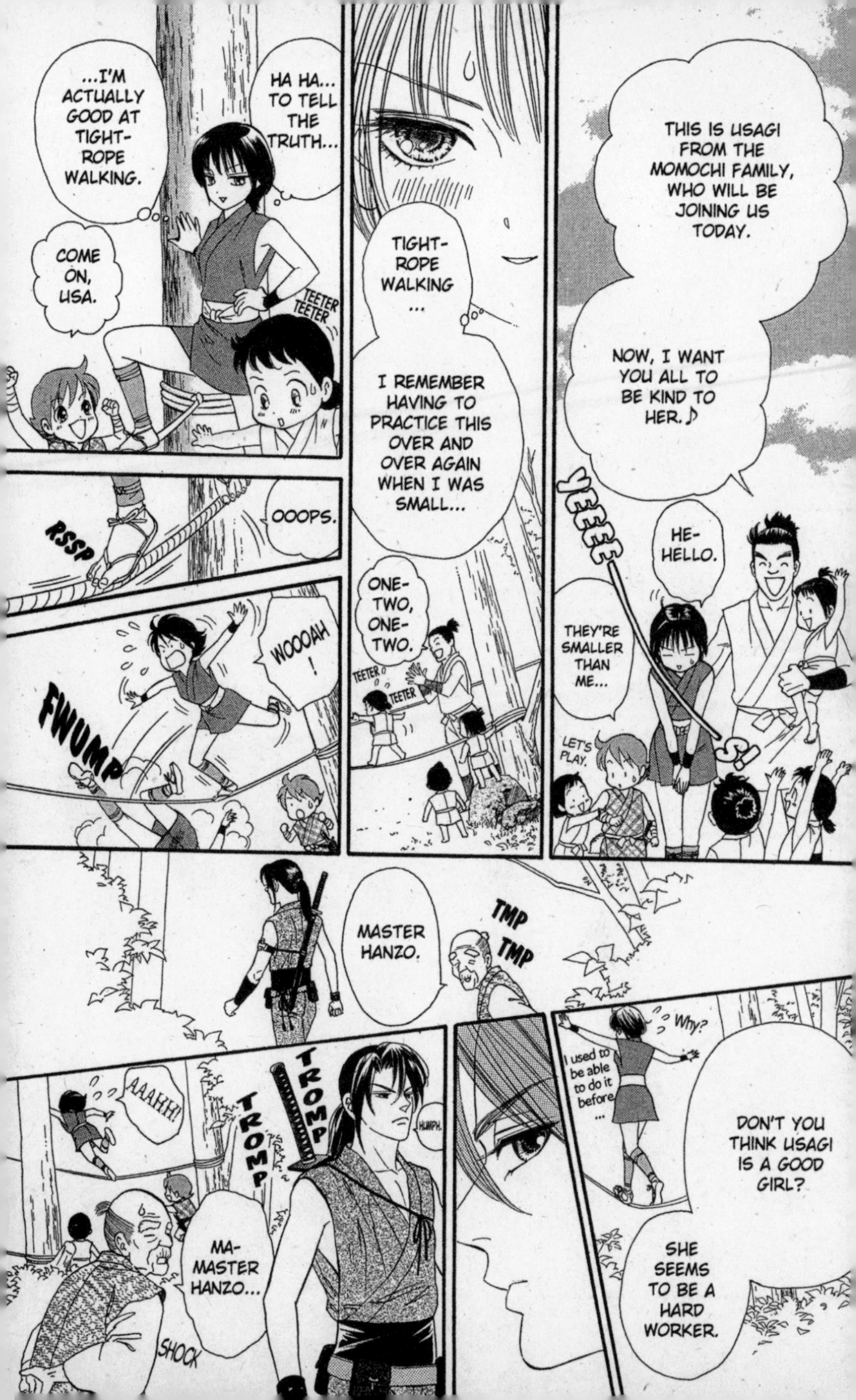
THIS IS USAGI FROM THE MOMOCHI FAMILY, WHO WILL BE JOINING US TODAY.
NOW, I WANT YOU ALL TO BE KIND TO HER.♪
YEEEEES!
HE-HELLO.
THEY'RE SMALLER THAN ME...
LET'S PLAY.
TIGHT-ROPE WALKING...
I REMEMBER HAVING TO PRACTICE THIS OVER AND OVER AGAIN WHEN I WAS SMALL...
ONE-TWO, ONE-TWO.
TEETER
TEETER
HA HA... TO TELL THE TRUTH...
...I'M ACTUALLY GOOD AT TIGHT-ROPE WALKING.
TEETER TEETER
COME ON, USA.
OOOPS.
RSSP
WOOOAH!
FWUMP
TMP TMP
MASTER HANZO.
DON'T YOU THINK USAGI IS A GOOD GIRL?
SHE SEEMS TO BE A HARD WORKER.
Why?
I used to be able to do it before...
TROMP
TROMP
HUMPH.
AAAHH!
MA-MASTER HANZO...
SHOCK

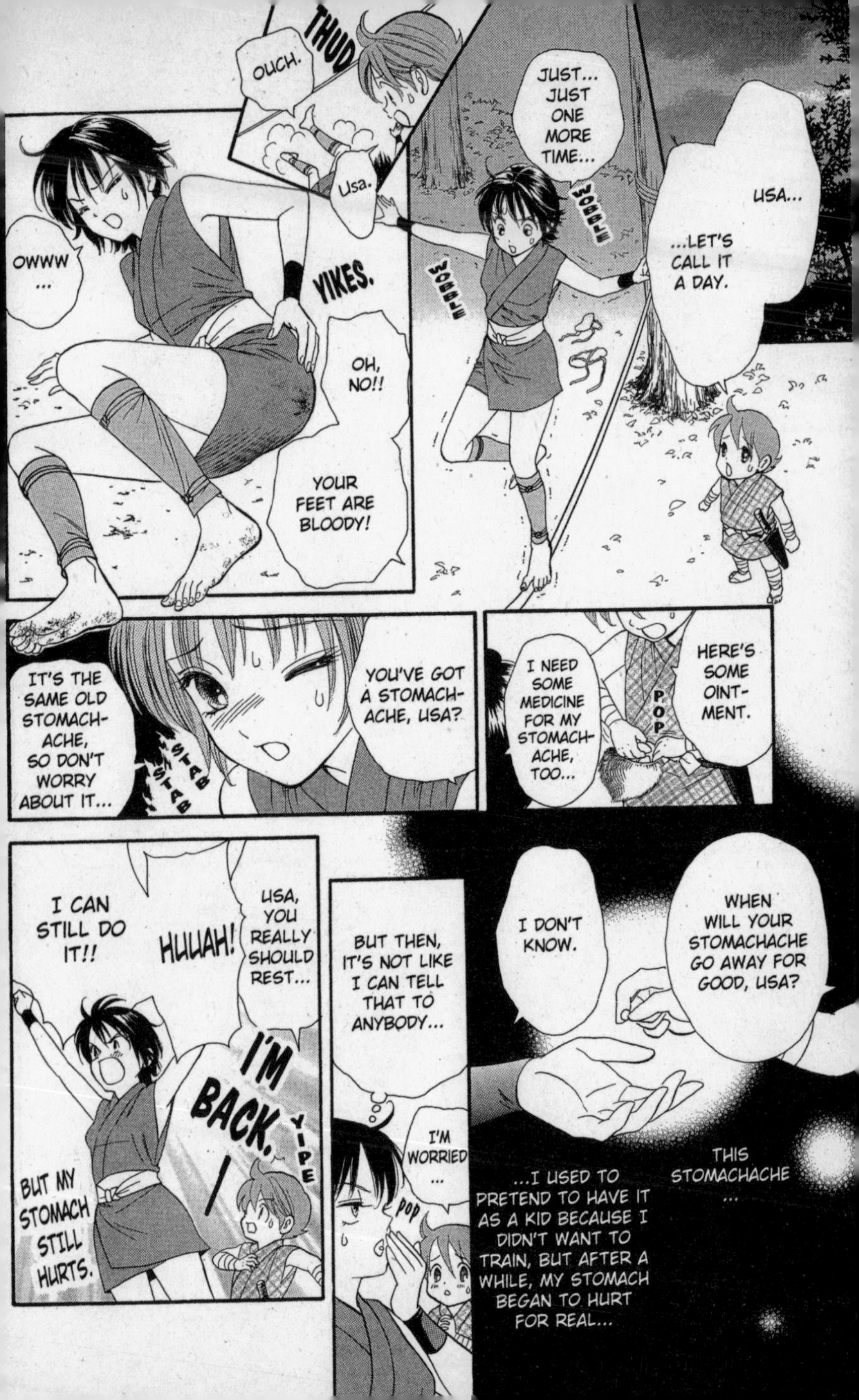
USA...
...LET'S CALL IT A DAY.
JUST... JUST ONE MORE TIME...
WOBBLE
WOBBLE
THUD
OUCH.
Usa.
OH, NO!!
YOUR FEET ARE BLOODY!
YIKES.
OWWW ...
HERE'S SOME OINT-MENT.
POP
I NEED SOME MEDICINE FOR MY STOMACH-ACHE, TOO...
YOU'VE GOT A STOMACH-ACHE, USA?
IT'S THE SAME OLD STOMACH-ACHE, SO DON'T WORRY ABOUT IT...
STAB STAB
WHEN WILL YOUR STOMACHACHE GO AWAY FOR GOOD, USA?
I DON'T KNOW.
THIS STOMACHACHE ...
...I USED TO PRETEND TO HAVE IT AS A KID BECAUSE I DIDN'T WANT TO TRAIN, BUT AFTER A WHILE, MY STOMACH BEGAN TO HURT FOR REAL...
BUT THEN, IT'S NOT LIKE I CAN TELL THAT TO ANYBODY...
I'M WORRIED ...
POP
USA, YOU REALLY SHOULD REST...
HUUAH!
I CAN STILL DO IT!!
I'M BACK.
YIPE
BUT MY STOMACH STILL HURTS.

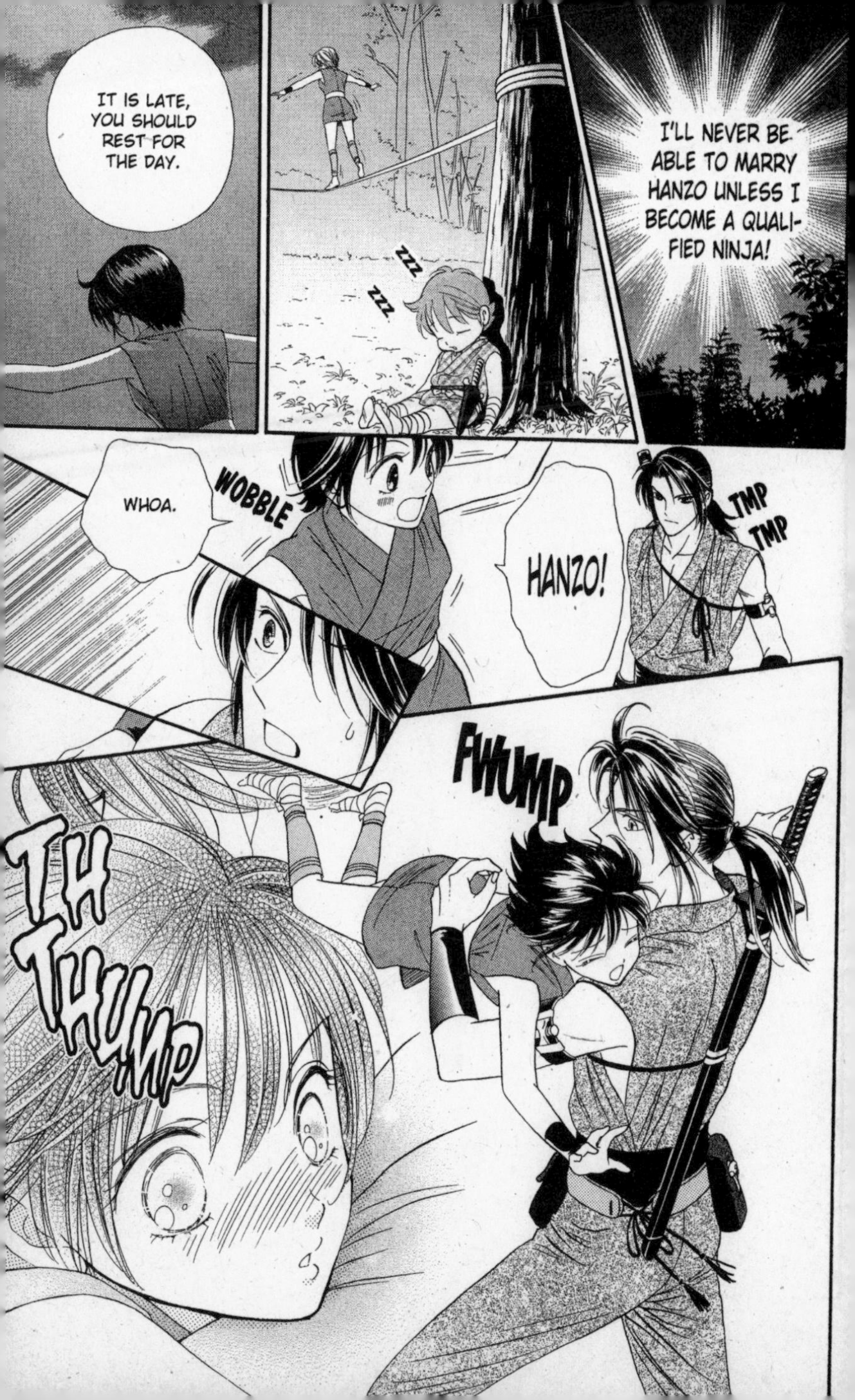
I'LL NEVER BE ABLE TO MARRY HANZO UNLESS I BECOME A QUALI-FIED NINJA!
ZZZ
ZZZ
IT IS LATE, YOU SHOULD REST FOR THE DAY.
TMP TMP
HANZO!
WOBBLE
WHOA.
FWUMP
TH THUMP

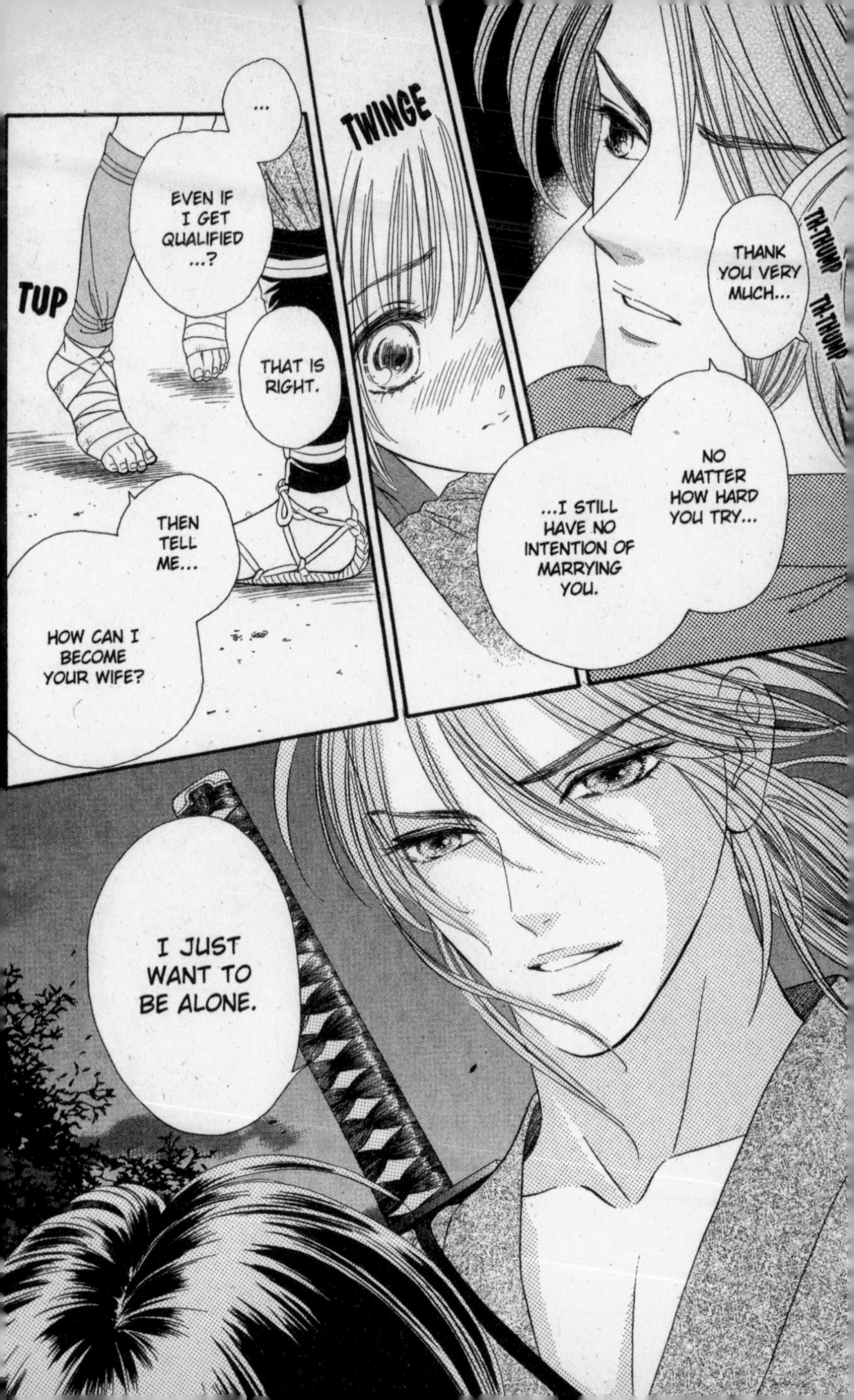

THANK YOU VERY MUCH...
TH-THUMP
TH-THUMP
NO MATTER HOW HARD YOU TRY...
...I STILL HAVE NO INTENTION OF MARRYING YOU.
TWINGE
...
EVEN IF I GET QUALIFIED ...?
THAT IS RIGHT.
TUP
THEN TELL ME...
HOW CAN I BECOME YOUR WIFE?
I JUST WANT TO BE ALONE.

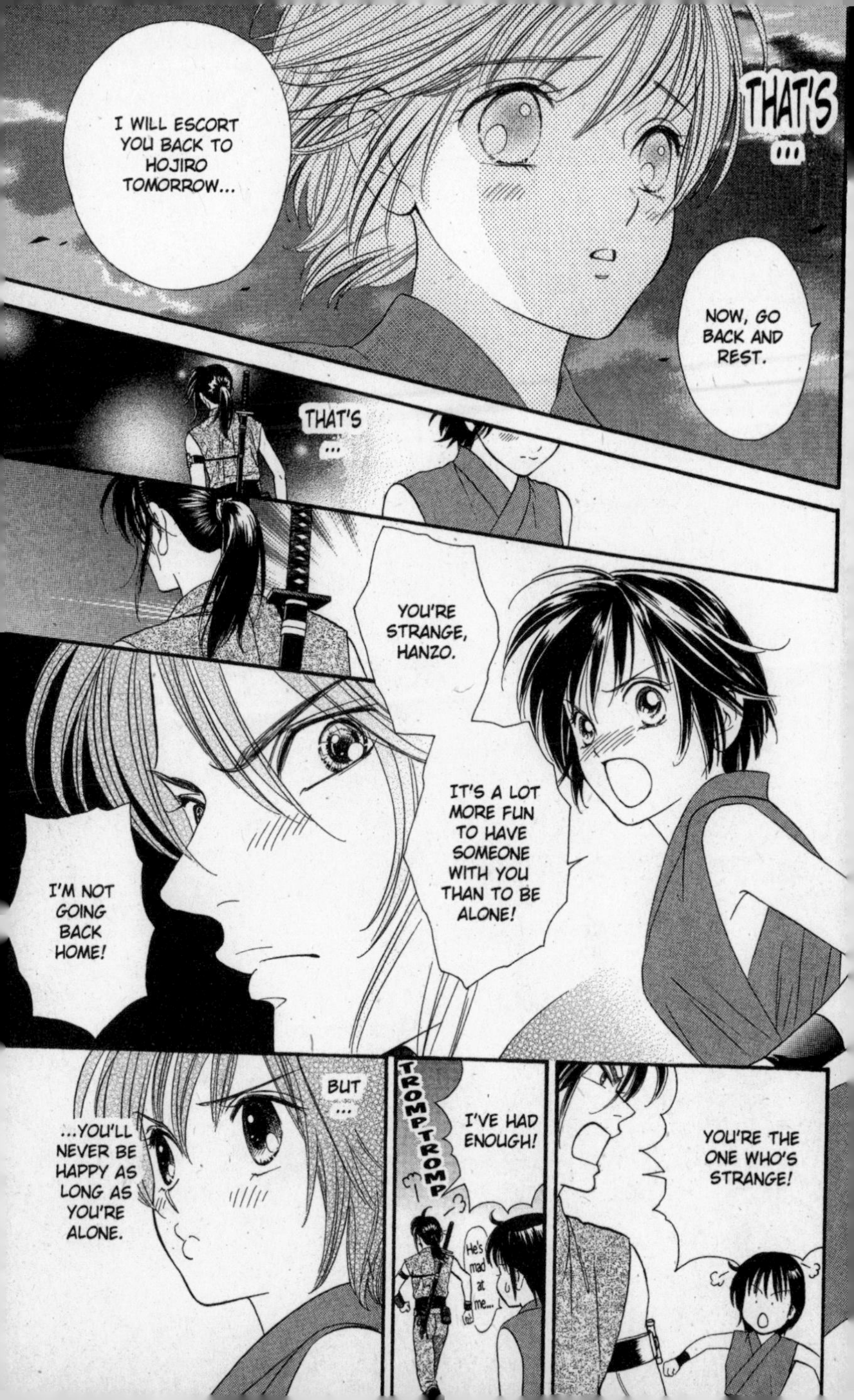
THAT'S ...
I WILL ESCORT YOU BACK TO HOJIRO TOMORROW...
NOW, GO BACK AND REST.
THAT'S ...
YOU'RE STRANGE, HANZO.
IT'S A LOT MORE FUN TO HAVE SOMEONE WITH YOU THAN TO BE ALONE!
I'M NOT GOING BACK HOME!
YOU'RE THE ONE WHO'S STRANGE!
I'VE HAD ENOUGH!
TROMP TROMP
He's mad at me...
BUT ...
...YOU'LL NEVER BE HAPPY AS LONG AS YOU'RE ALONE.

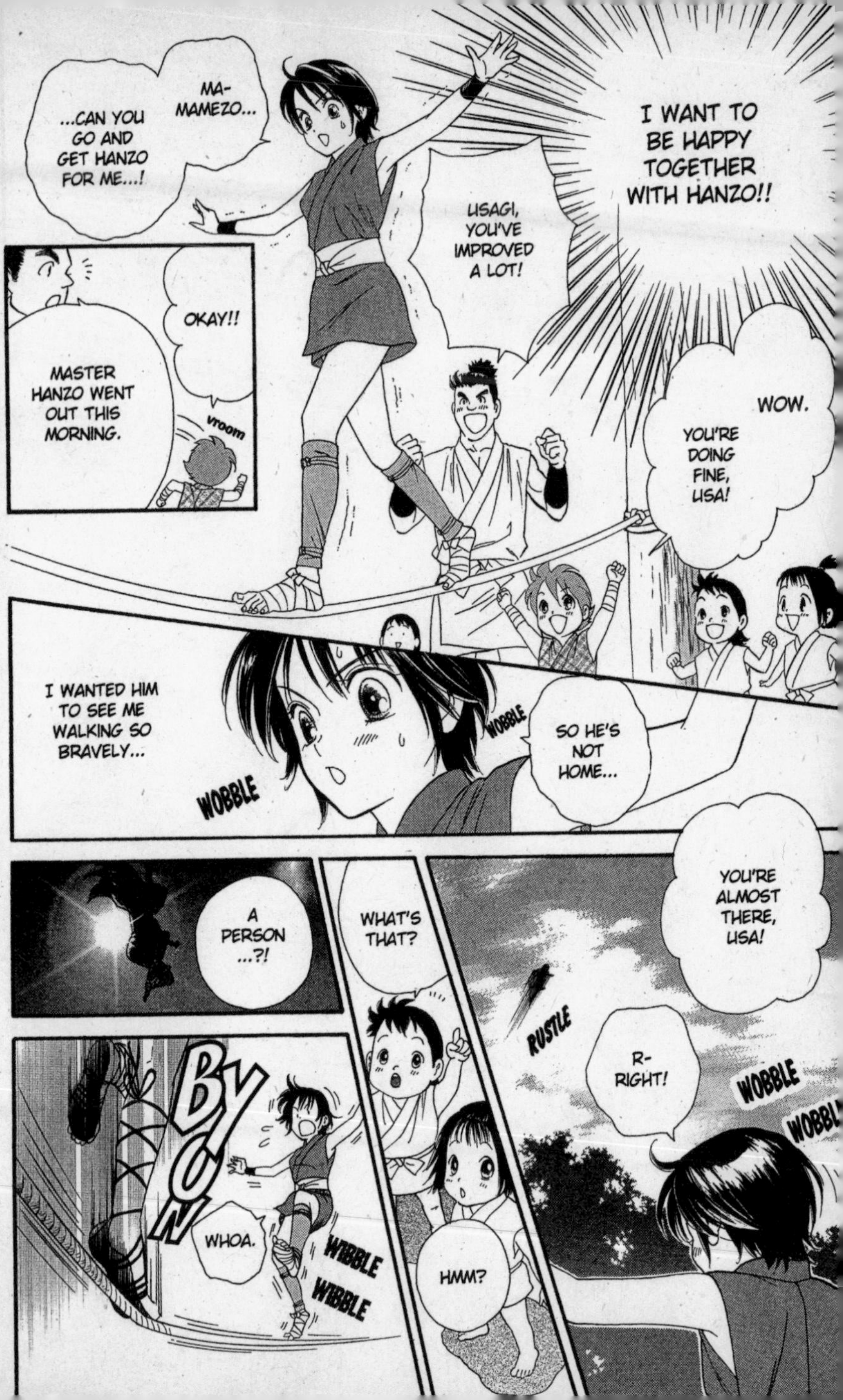

I WANT TO BE HAPPY TOGETHER WITH HANZO!!
USAGI, YOU'VE IMPROVED A LOT!
WOW.
YOU'RE DOING FINE, USA!
MA-MAMEZO...
...CAN YOU GO AND GET HANZO FOR ME...!
OKAY!!
vroom
MASTER HANZO WENT OUT THIS MORNING.
SO HE'S NOT HOME...
WOBBLE
I WANTED HIM TO SEE ME WALKING SO BRAVELY...
WOBBLE
YOU'RE ALMOST THERE, USA!
R-RIGHT!
WOBBLE
WOBBLE
RUSTLE
WHAT'S THAT?
HMM?
A PERSON ...?!
BYOON
WHOA.
WIBBLE
WIBBLE

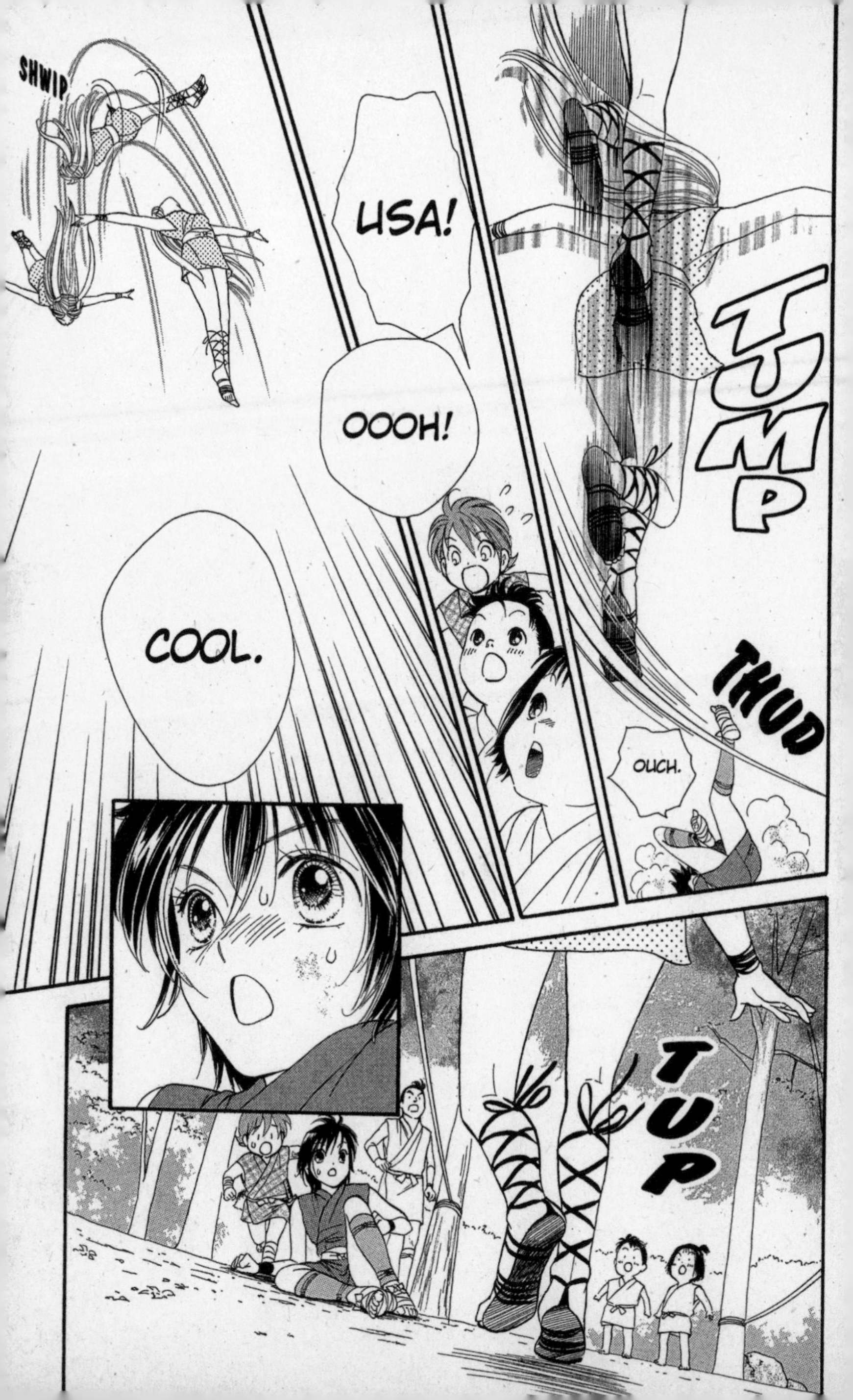
TUMP
THUD
OUCH.
OOOH!
USA!
SHWIP
COOL.
TUP

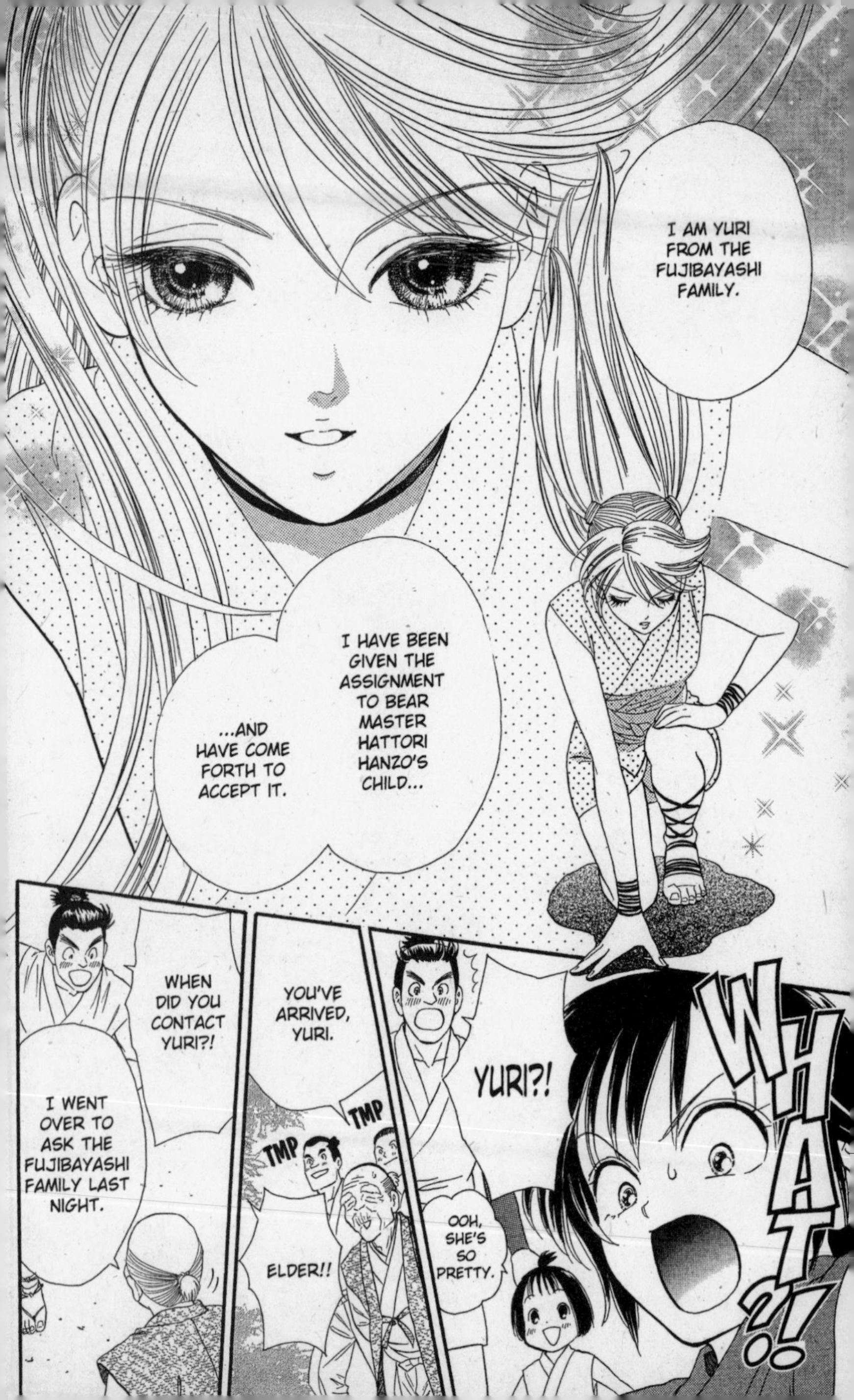

I AM YURI FROM THE FUJIBAYASHI FAMILY.
I HAVE BEEN GIVEN THE ASSIGNMENT TO BEAR MASTER HATTORI HANZO'S CHILD...
...AND HAVE COME FORTH TO ACCEPT IT.
WHAT?!
YURI?!
OOH, SHE'S SO PRETTY.
YOU'VE ARRIVED, YURI.
TMP
TMP
ELDER!!
WHEN DID YOU CONTACT YURI?!
I WENT OVER TO ASK THE FUJIBAYASHI FAMILY LAST NIGHT.

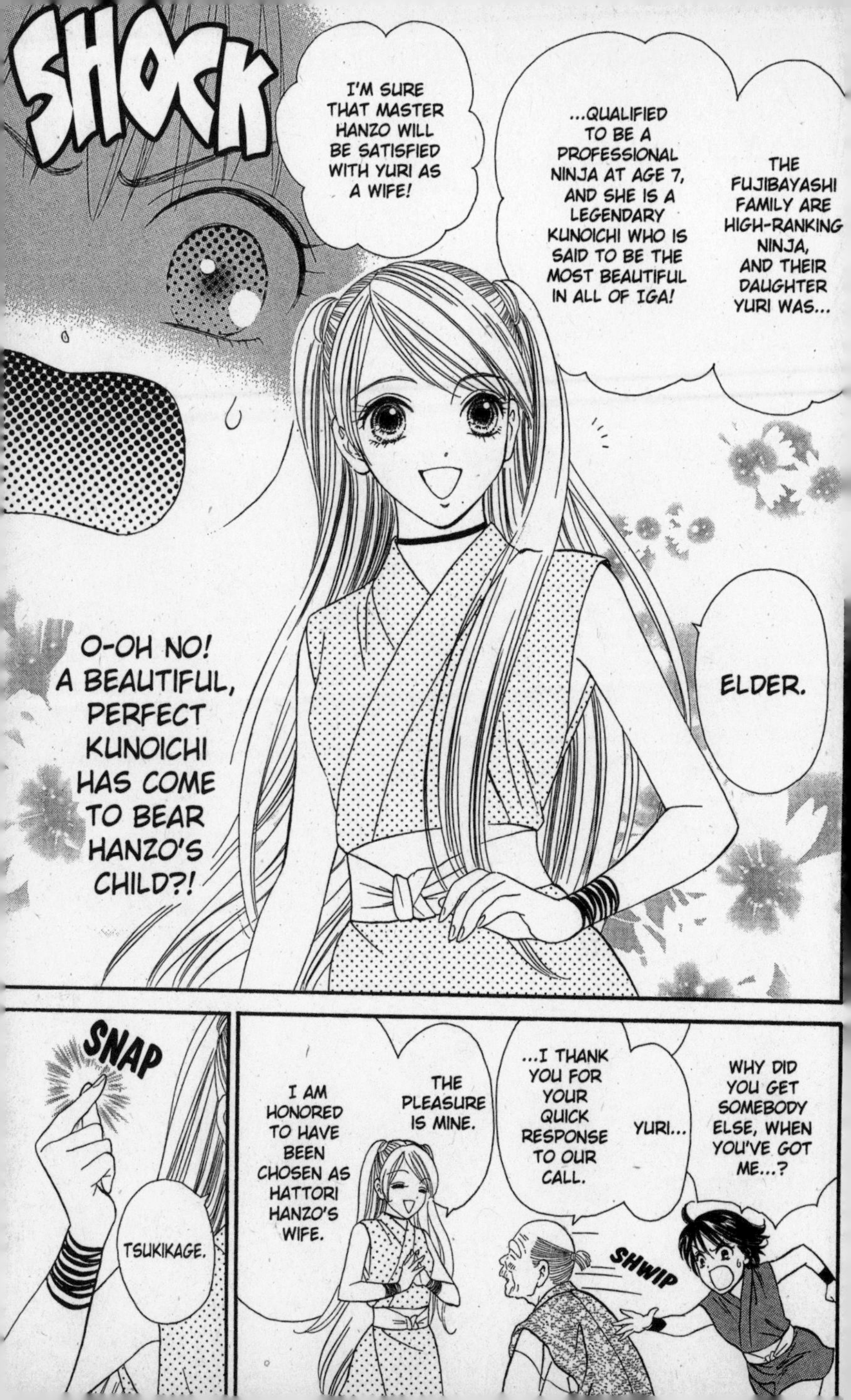
THE FUJIBAYASHI FAMILY ARE HIGH-RANKING NINJA, AND THEIR DAUGHTER YURI WAS...
...QUALIFIED TO BE A PROFESSIONAL NINJA AT AGE 7, AND SHE IS A LEGENDARY KUNOICHI WHO IS SAID TO BE THE MOST BEAUTIFUL IN ALL OF IGA!
I'M SURE THAT MASTER HANZO WILL BE SATISFIED WITH YURI AS A WIFE!
SHOCK
ELDER.
O-OH NO! A BEAUTIFUL, PERFECT KUNOICHI HAS COME TO BEAR HANZO'S CHILD?!
WHY DID YOU GET SOMEBODY ELSE, WHEN YOU'VE GOT ME...?
YURI...
...I THANK YOU FOR YOUR QUICK RESPONSE TO OUR CALL.
THE PLEASURE IS MINE.
I AM HONORED TO HAVE BEEN CHOSEN AS HATTORI HANZO'S WIFE.
SHWIP
SNAP
TSUKIKAGE.

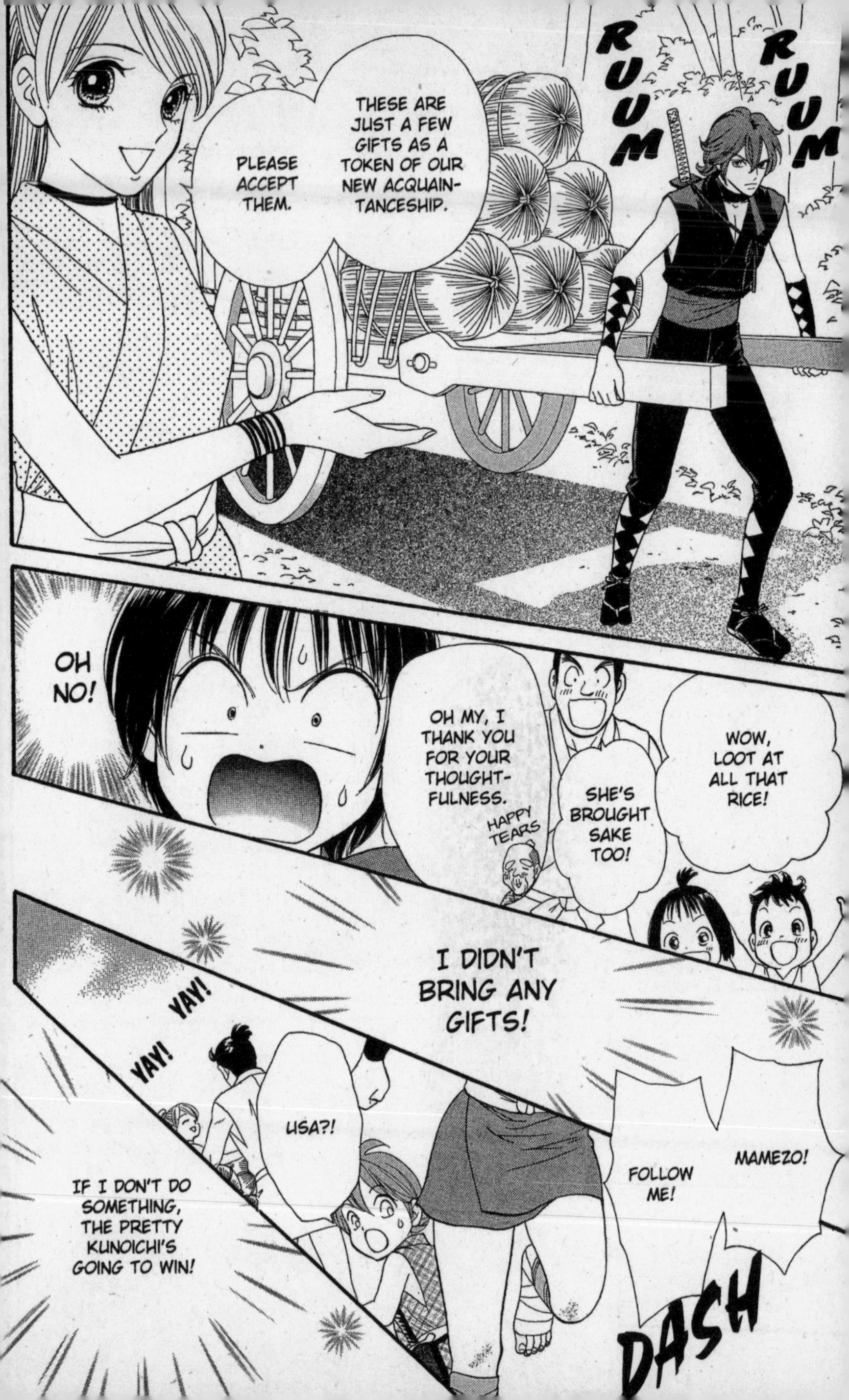
RUUM RUUM
THESE ARE JUST A FEW GIFTS AS A TOKEN OF OUR NEW ACQUAINTANCESHIP.
PLEASE ACCEPT THEM.
WOW, LOOT AT ALL THAT RICE!
SHE'S BROUGHT SAKE TOO!
HAPPY TEARS
OH MY, I THANK YOU FOR YOUR THOUGHTFULNESS.
OH NO!
I DIDN'T BRING ANY GIFTS!
MAMEZO!
FOLLOW ME!
DASH
USA?!
YAY! YAY!
IF I DON'T DO SOMETHING, THE PRETTY KUNOICHI'S GOING TO WIN!

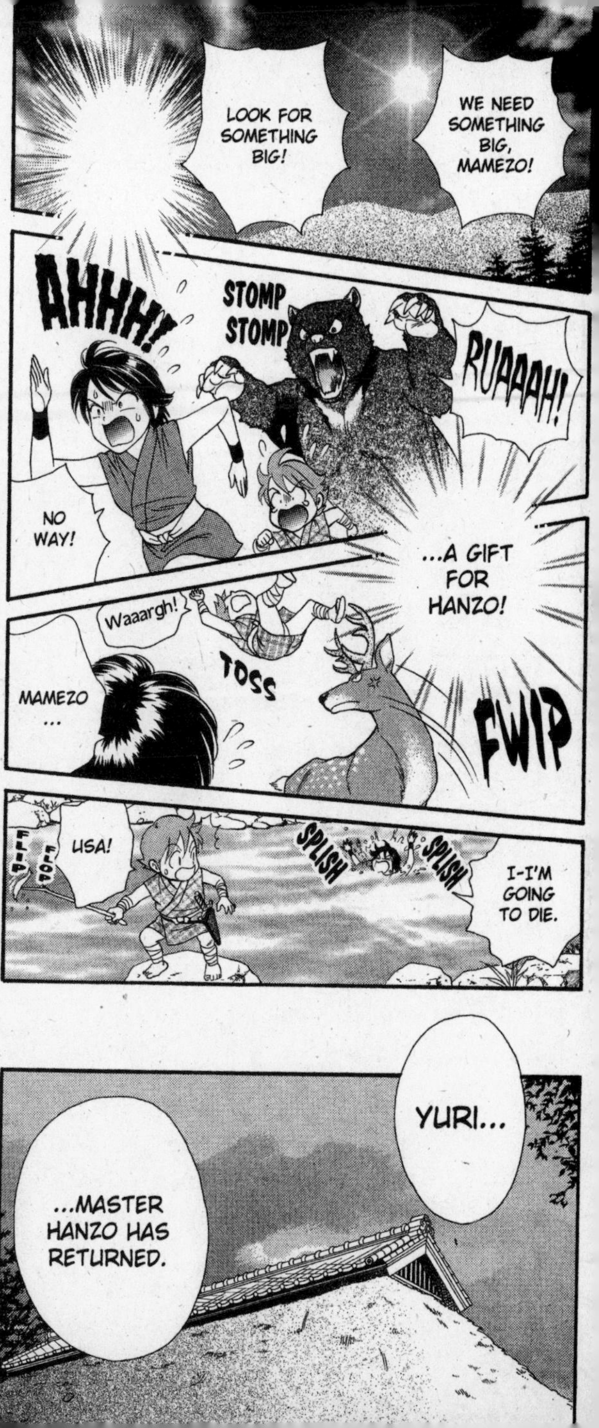
WE NEED SOMETHING BIG, MAMEZO!
LOOK FOR SOMETHING BIG!
RUAAAH!
STOMP STOMP
AHHH!
NO WAY!
...A GIFT FOR HANZO!
FWIP
TOSS
Waaargh!
MAMEZO ...
I-I'M GOING TO DIE.
SPLISH
SPLISH
FLIP FLOP
USA!
YURI...
...MASTER HANZO HAS RETURNED.

This and that from the author 2

Tail of the Moon is the sequel to a long, one-volume manga I wrote called "Tsuki no Toiki, Ai no Kizu" (Sigh of the Moon--The Wound of Love) and "Tsuki no Toiki, Natsu no Yume" (Sigh of the Moon--A Summer's Dream). I had a lot of fun writing "Tsuki no Toiki, Ai no Kizu," since it was a love/suspense story about a person with amnesia, which happens to be one of my very very very favorite topics.

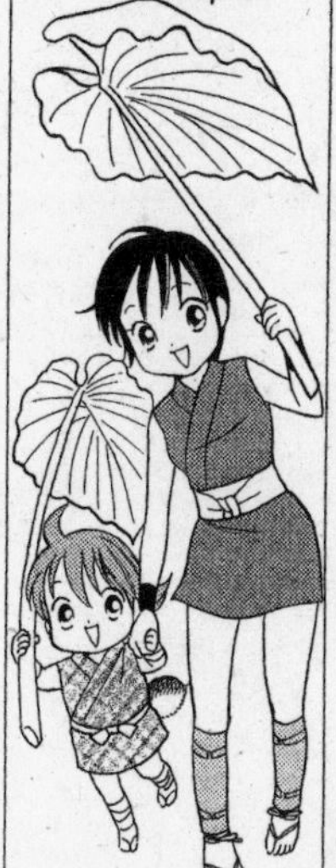

And in the second story, "Tsuki no Toiki, Natsu no Yume," Hanzo appears as a bit player, but I always had regrets about how poorly he was treated in it...

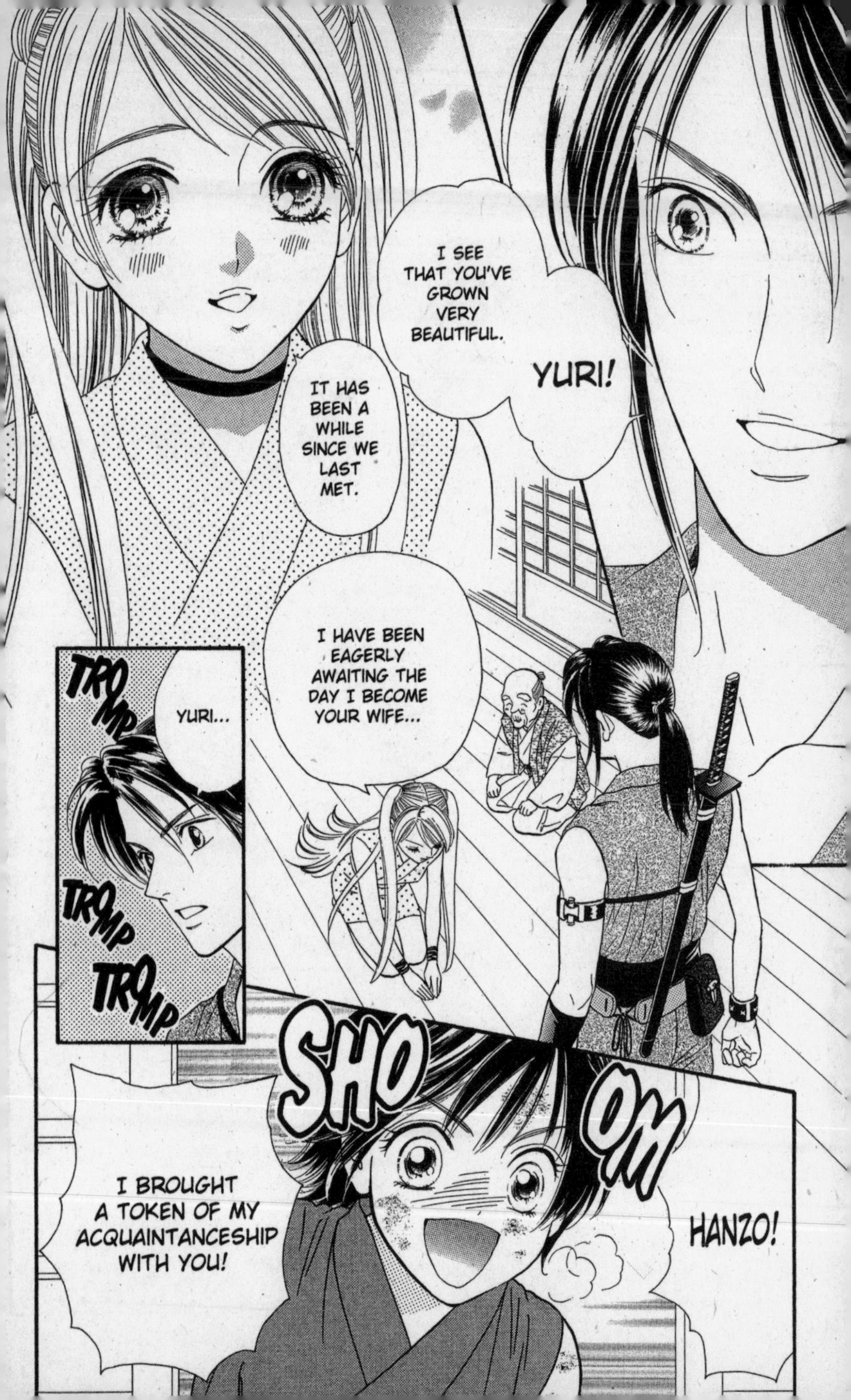
YURI!
I SEE THAT YOU'VE GROWN VERY BEAUTIFUL.
IT HAS BEEN A WHILE SINCE WE LAST MET.
I HAVE BEEN EAGERLY AWAITING THE DAY I BECOME YOUR WIFE...
YURI...
TROMP
TROMP
TROMP
SHOOM
HANZO!
I BROUGHT A TOKEN OF MY ACQUAINTANCESHIP WITH YOU!

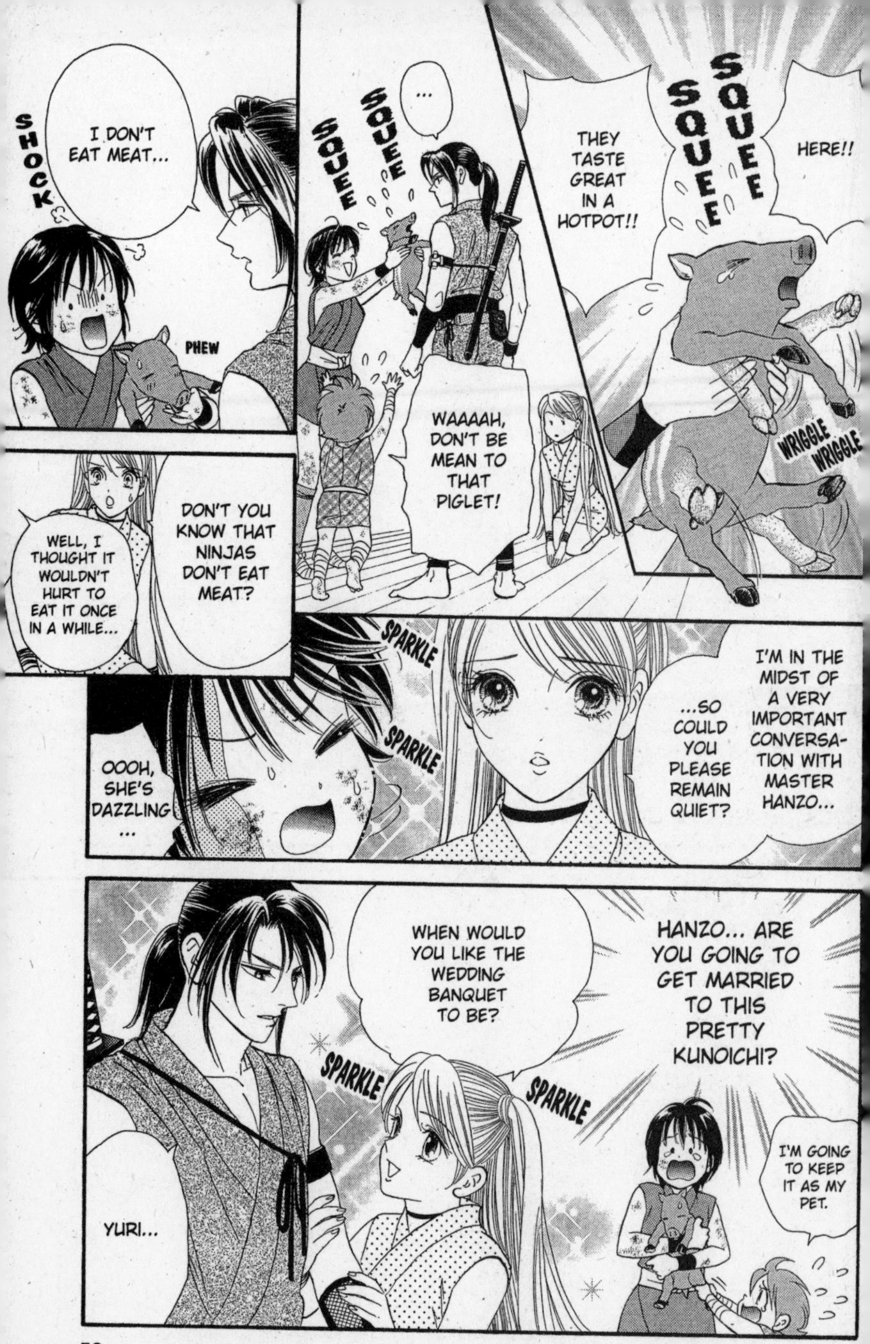
HERE!!
SQUEE SQUEE
THEY TASTE GREAT IN A HOTPOT!!
WRIGGLE WRIGGLE
...
SQUEE SQUEE
WAAAAH, DON'T BE MEAN TO THAT PIGLET!
I DON'T EAT MEAT...
SHOCK
PHEW
DON'T YOU KNOW THAT NINJAS DON'T EAT MEAT?
WELL, I THOUGHT IT WOULDN'T HURT TO EAT IT ONCE IN A WHILE...
I'M IN THE MIDST OF A VERY IMPORTANT CONVERSATION WITH MASTER HANZO...
...SO COULD YOU PLEASE REMAIN QUIET?
SPARKLE
SPARKLE
OOOH, SHE'S DAZZLING...
HANZO... ARE YOU GOING TO GET MARRIED TO THIS PRETTY KUNOICHI?
I'M GOING TO KEEP IT AS MY PET.
WHEN WOULD YOU LIKE THE WEDDING BANQUET TO BE?
SPARKLE
SPARKLE
YURI...

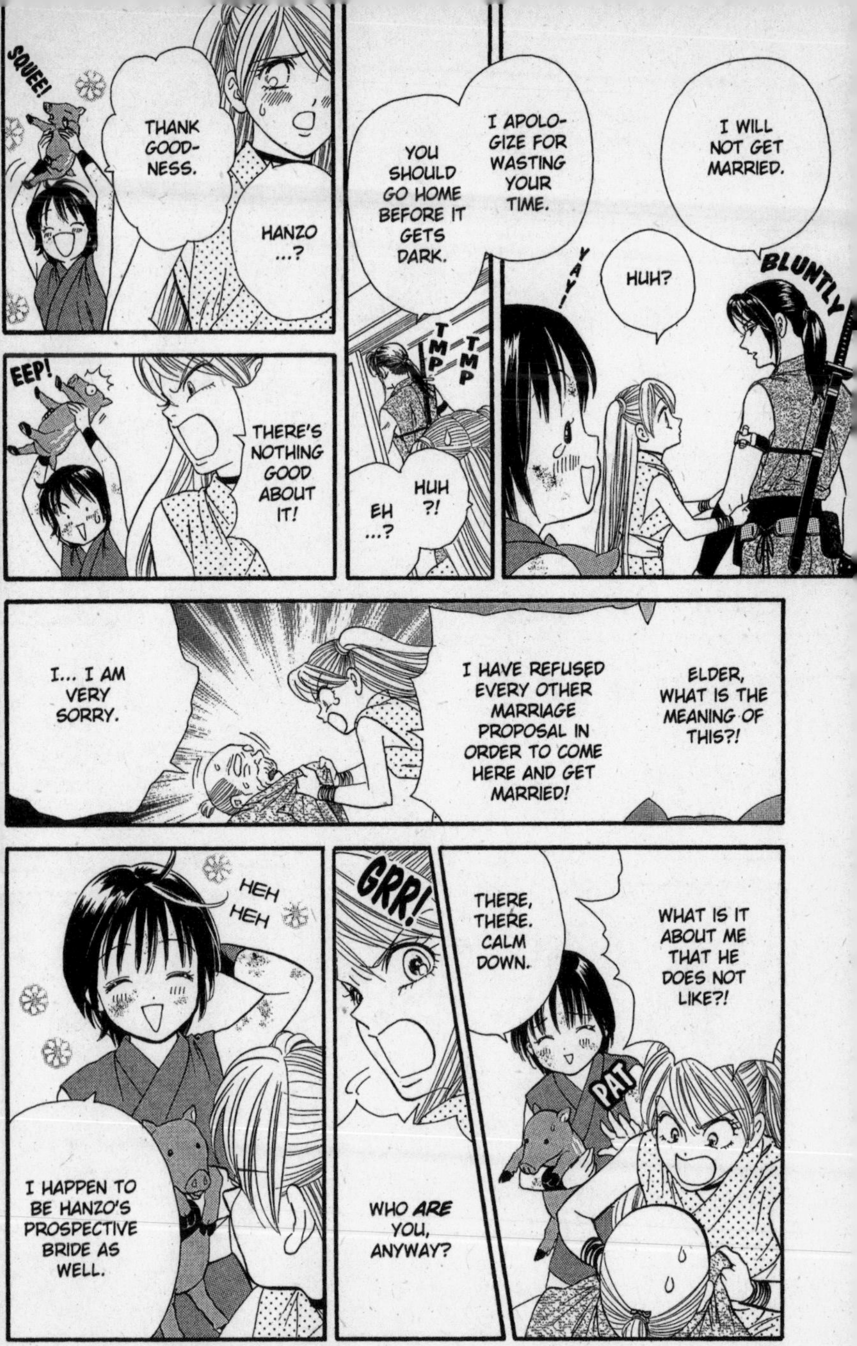
I WILL NOT GET MARRIED.
BLUNTLY
HUH?
YAY!
I APOLOGIZE FOR WASTING YOUR TIME.
YOU SHOULD GO HOME BEFORE IT GETS DARK.
TMP TMP
HUH?!
EH ...?
SQUEE!
THANK GOODNESS.
HANZO ...?
EEP!
THERE'S NOTHING GOOD ABOUT IT!
ELDER, WHAT IS THE MEANING OF THIS?!
I HAVE REFUSED EVERY OTHER MARRIAGE PROPOSAL IN ORDER TO COME HERE AND GET MARRIED!
I... I AM VERY SORRY.
WHAT IS IT ABOUT ME THAT HE DOES NOT LIKE?!
THERE, THERE. CALM DOWN.
PAT
GRR!
WHO *ARE* YOU, ANYWAY?
HEH HEH
I HAPPEN TO BE HANZO'S PROSPECTIVE BRIDE AS WELL.

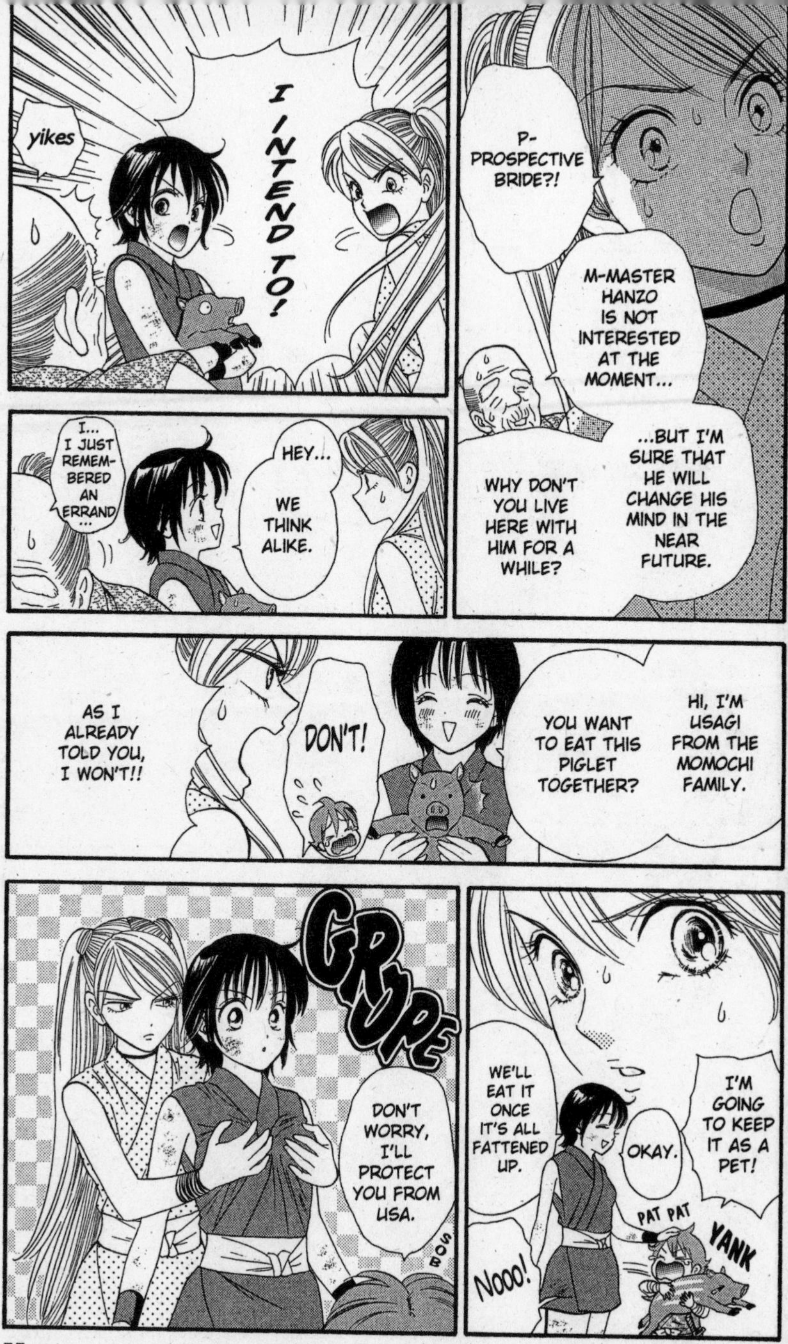
P-PROSPECTIVE BRIDE?!
M-MASTER HANZO IS NOT INTERESTED AT THE MOMENT...
...BUT I'M SURE THAT HE WILL CHANGE HIS MIND IN THE NEAR FUTURE.
WHY DON'T YOU LIVE HERE WITH HIM FOR A WHILE?
I INTEND TO!
yikes
HEY...
WE THINK ALIKE.
I... I JUST REMEMBERED AN ERRAND...
HI, I'M USAGI FROM THE MOMOCHI FAMILY.
YOU WANT TO EAT THIS PIGLET TOGETHER?
DON'T!
AS I ALREADY TOLD YOU, I WON'T!!
I'M GOING TO KEEP IT AS A PET!
OKAY.
WE'LL EAT IT ONCE IT'S ALL FATTENED UP.
PAT PAT
YANK
Nooo!
DON'T WORRY, I'LL PROTECT YOU FROM USA.

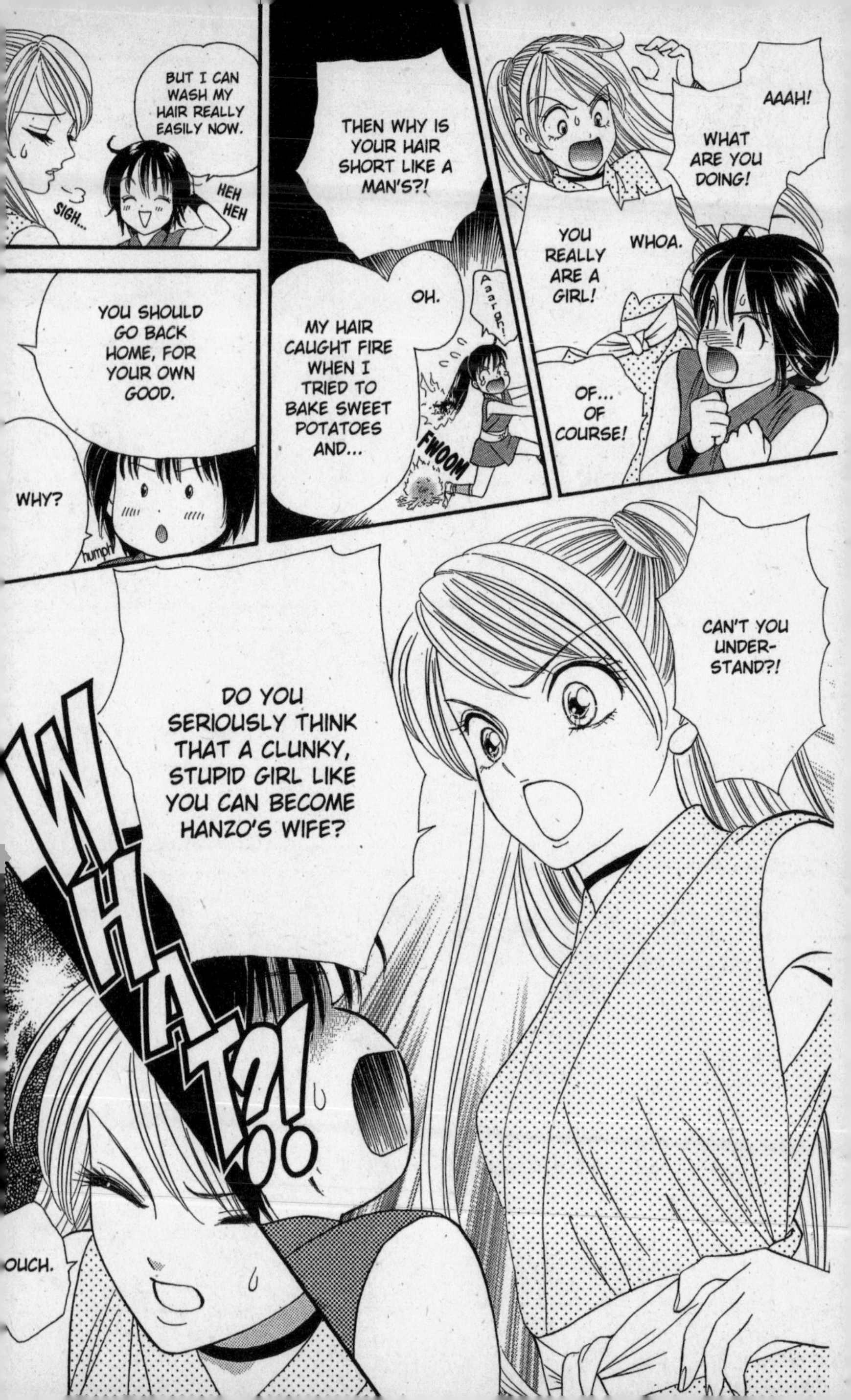
AAAH!
WHAT ARE YOU DOING!
WHOA.
YOU REALLY ARE A GIRL!
OF... OF COURSE!
THEN WHY IS YOUR HAIR SHORT LIKE A MAN'S?!
OH.
MY HAIR CAUGHT FIRE WHEN I TRIED TO BAKE SWEET POTATOES AND...
Aaargh!
FWOOM
BUT I CAN WASH MY HAIR REALLY EASILY NOW.
HEH HEH
SIGH...
YOU SHOULD GO BACK HOME, FOR YOUR OWN GOOD.
WHY?
humph
CAN'T YOU UNDER-STAND?!
DO YOU SERIOUSLY THINK THAT A CLUNKY, STUPID GIRL LIKE YOU CAN BECOME HANZO'S WIFE?
WHAT?!
OUCH.

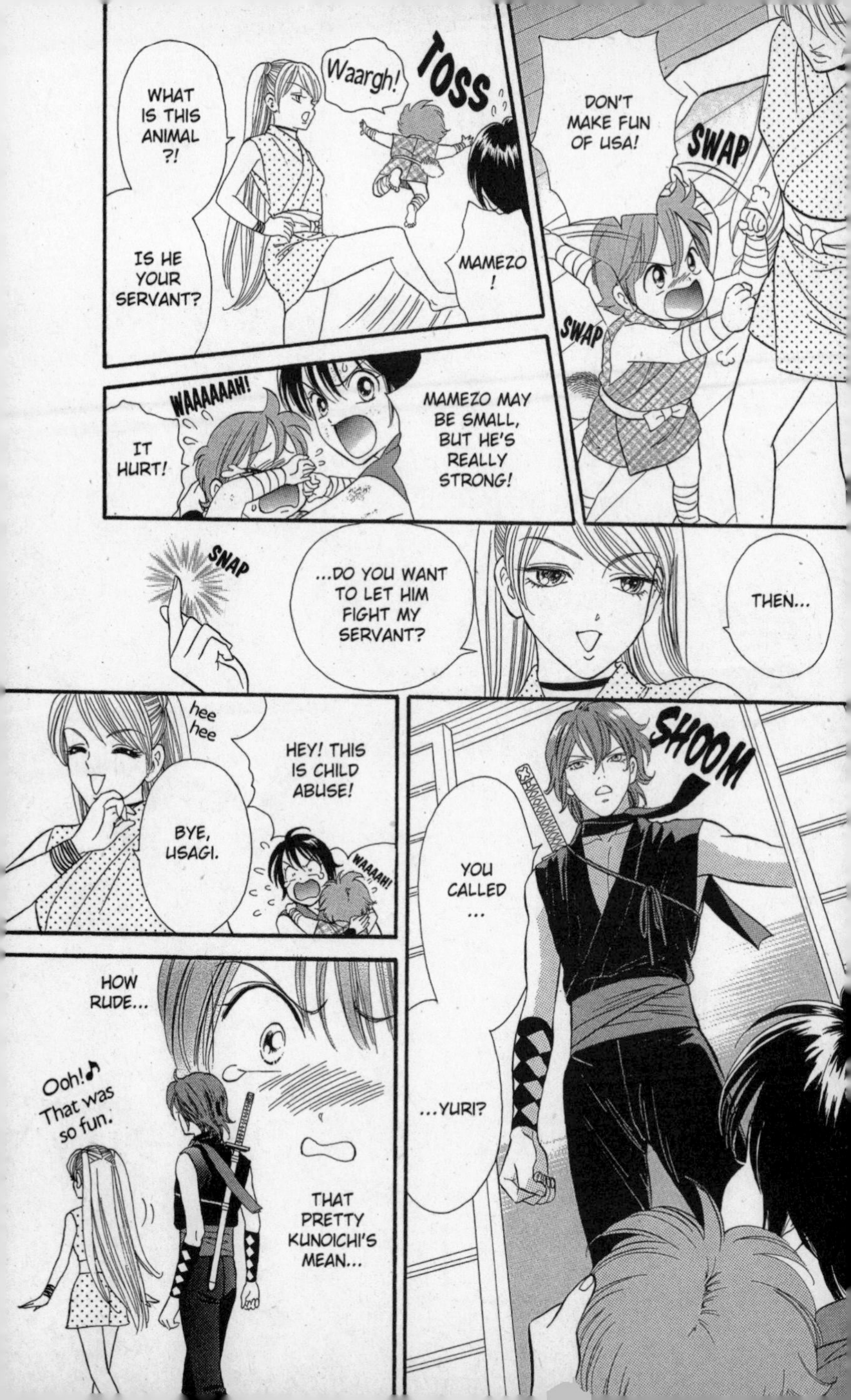
DON'T MAKE FUN OF USA!
SWAP
SWAP
TOSS
Waargh!
WHAT IS THIS ANIMAL ?!
MAMEZO !
IS HE YOUR SERVANT?
MAMEZO MAY BE SMALL, BUT HE'S REALLY STRONG!
WAAAAAAH!
IT HURT!
THEN...
...DO YOU WANT TO LET HIM FIGHT MY SERVANT?
SNAP
SHOOM
YOU CALLED ...
...YURI?
HEY! THIS IS CHILD ABUSE!
WAAAAH!
hee hee
BYE, USAGI.
HOW RUDE...
THAT PRETTY KUNOICHI'S MEAN...
Ooh!♪ That was so fun.

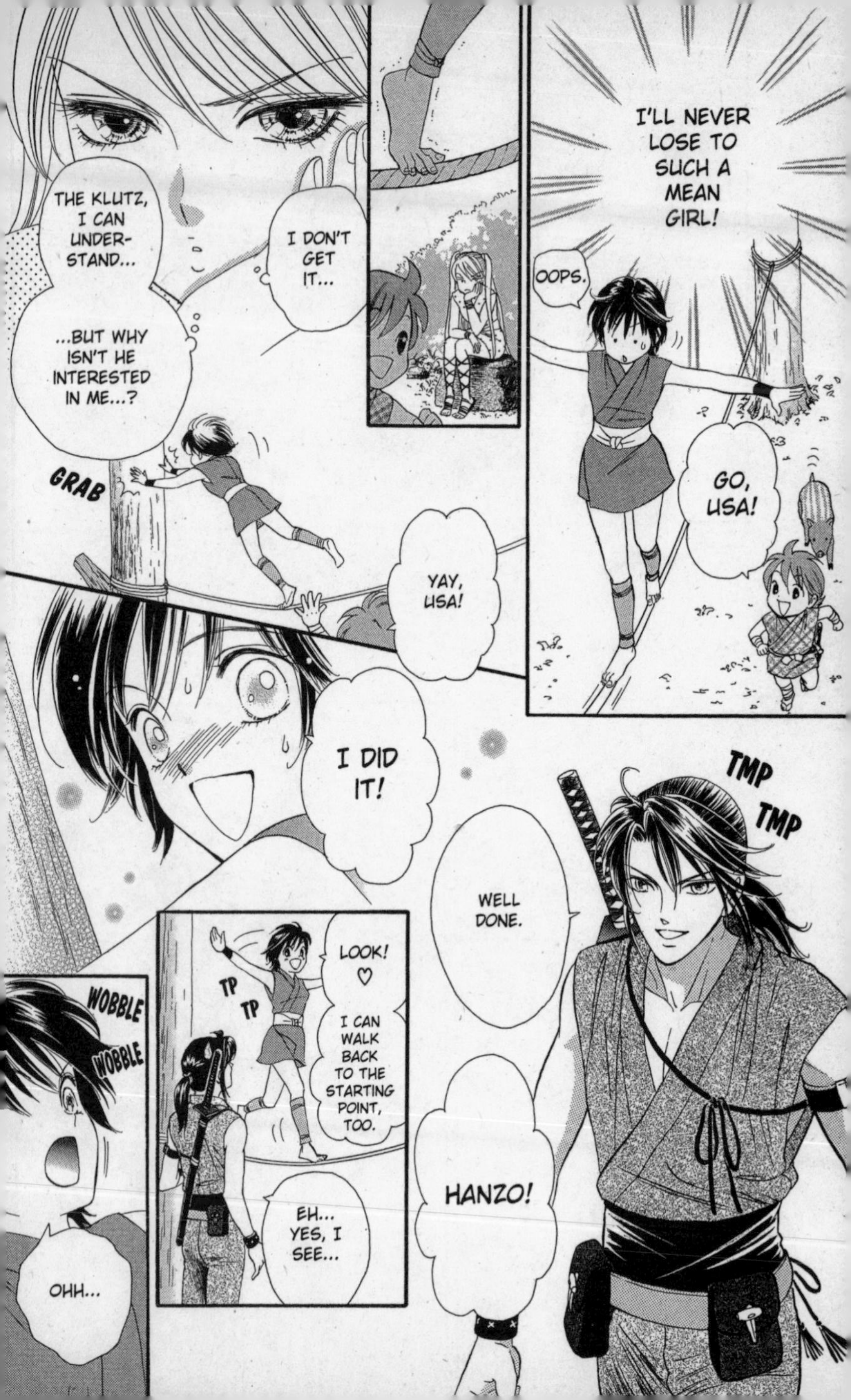
I'LL NEVER LOSE TO SUCH A MEAN GIRL!
OOPS.
GO, USA!
I DON'T GET IT...
THE KLUTZ, I CAN UNDERSTAND...
...BUT WHY ISN'T HE INTERESTED IN ME...?
GRAB
YAY, USA!
I DID IT!
TMP TMP
WELL DONE.
HANZO!
LOOK! ♡
I CAN WALK BACK TO THE STARTING POINT, TOO.
TP TP
EH... YES, I SEE...
WOBBLE WOBBLE
OHH...

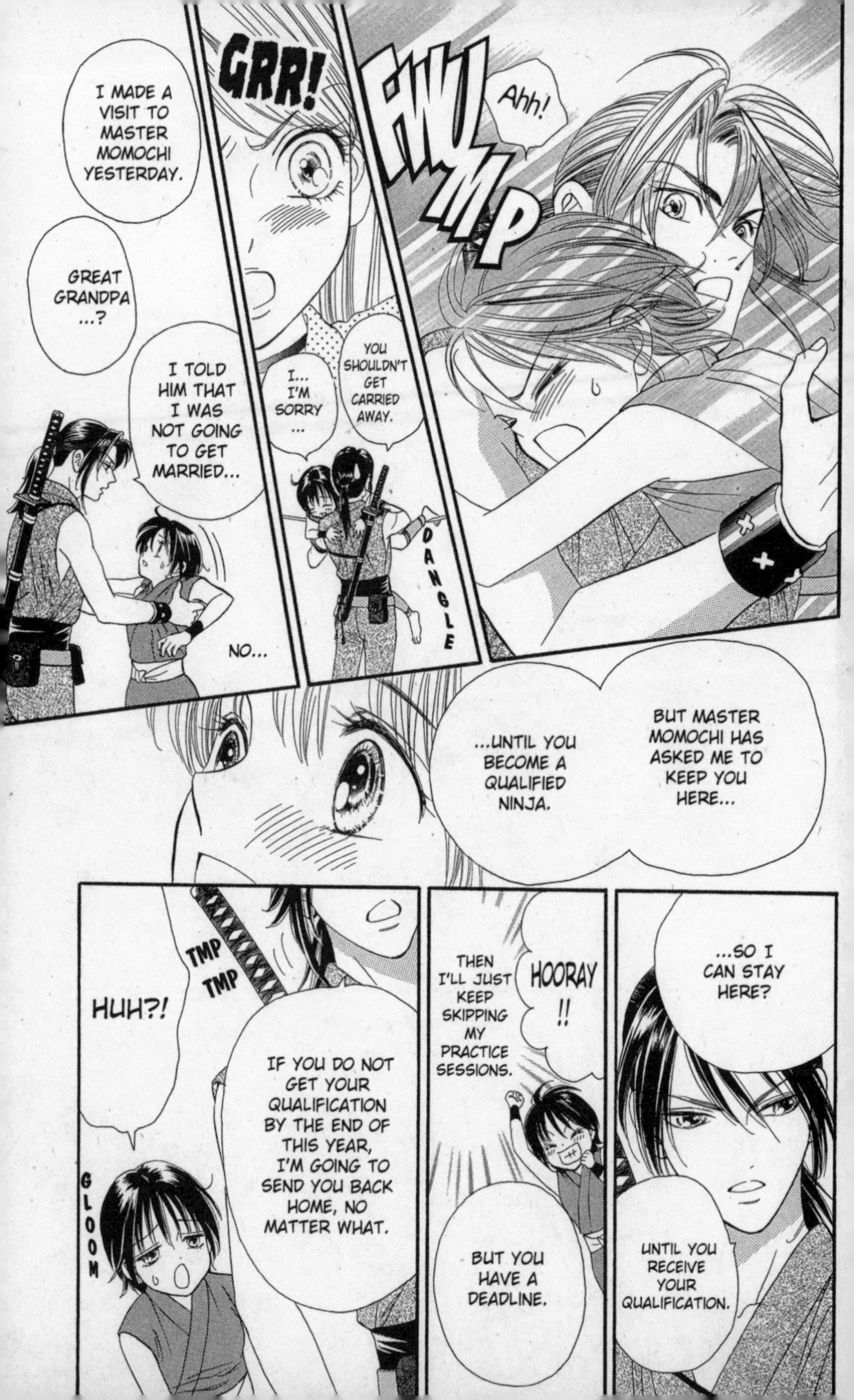
FWUMP
Ahh!
GRR!
YOU SHOULDN'T GET CARRIED AWAY.
I... I'M SORRY ...
DANGLE
I MADE A VISIT TO MASTER MOMOCHI YESTERDAY.
GREAT GRANDPA ...?
I TOLD HIM THAT I WAS NOT GOING TO GET MARRIED...
NO...
BUT MASTER MOMOCHI HAS ASKED ME TO KEEP YOU HERE...
...UNTIL YOU BECOME A QUALIFIED NINJA.
...SO I CAN STAY HERE?
UNTIL YOU RECEIVE YOUR QUALIFICATION.
HOORAY !!
THEN I'LL JUST KEEP SKIPPING MY PRACTICE SESSIONS.
BUT YOU HAVE A DEADLINE.
TMP TMP
IF YOU DO NOT GET YOUR QUALIFICATION BY THE END OF THIS YEAR, I'M GOING TO SEND YOU BACK HOME, NO MATTER WHAT.
HUH?!
GLOOM

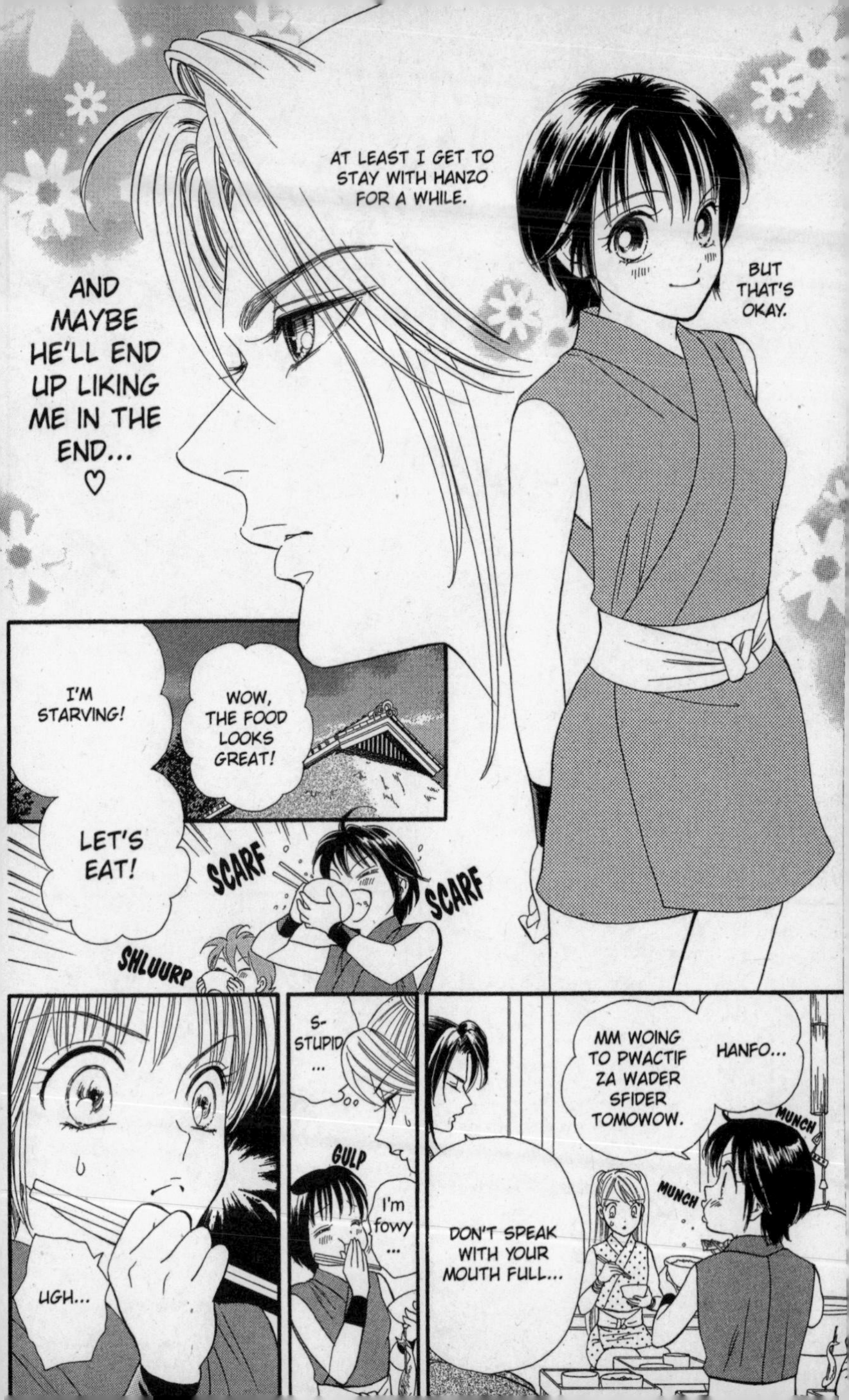
BUT THAT'S OKAY.
AT LEAST I GET TO STAY WITH HANZO FOR A WHILE.
AND MAYBE HE'LL END UP LIKING ME IN THE END... ♡
WOW, THE FOOD LOOKS GREAT!
I'M STARVING!
SCARF
SCARF
LET'S EAT!
SHLUURP
HANFO...
MM WOING TO PWACTIF ZA WADER SFIDER TOMOWOW.
MUNCH
MUNCH
DON'T SPEAK WITH YOUR MOUTH FULL...
S- STUPID ...
GULP
I'm fowy ...
UGH...

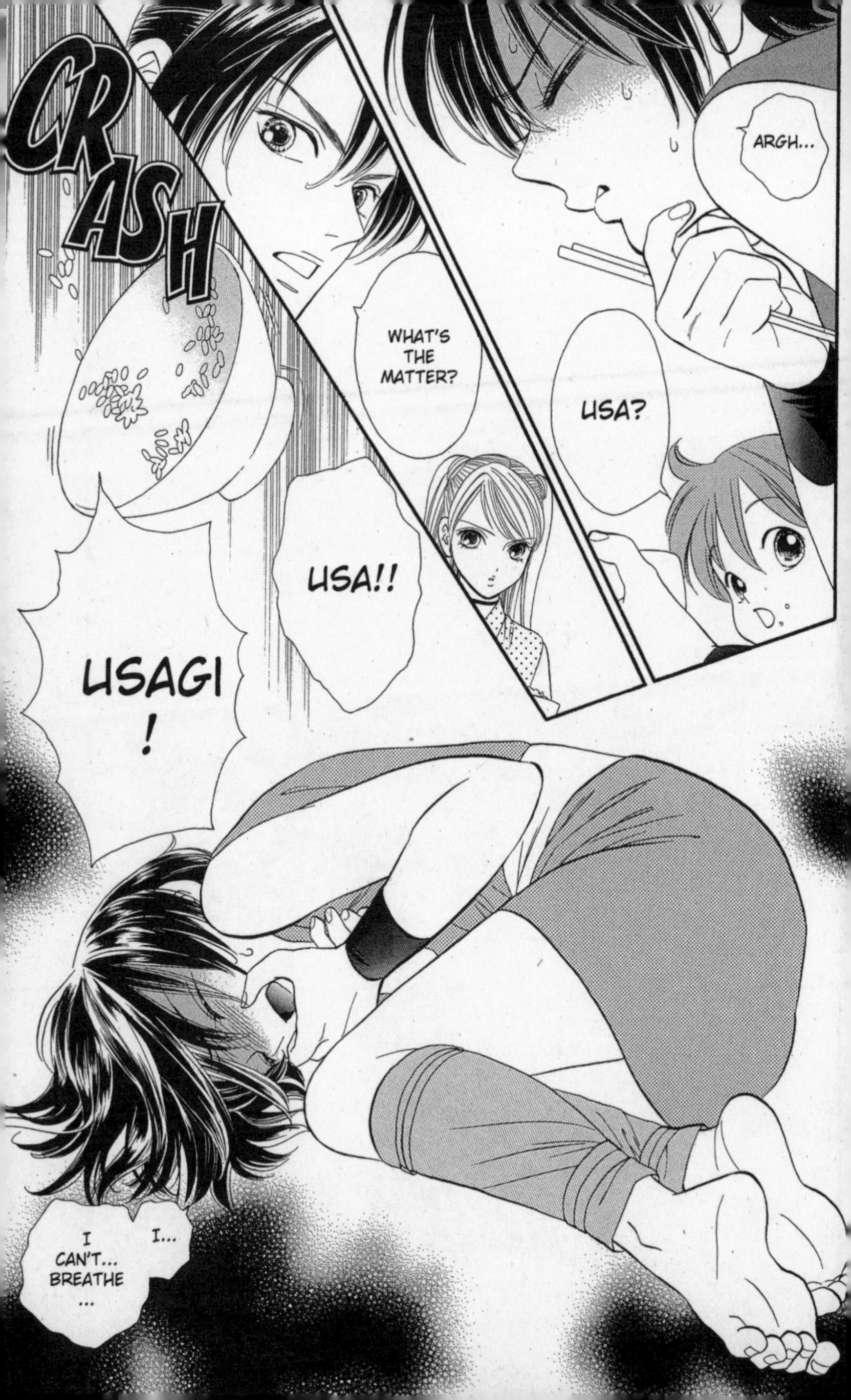
ARGH...
USA?
WHAT'S THE MATTER?
USA!!
CRASH
USAGI!
I...
I CAN'T... BREATHE ...

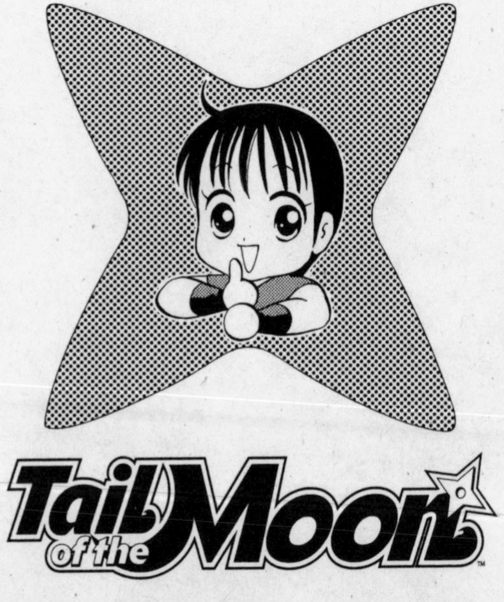

Tail of the Moon™

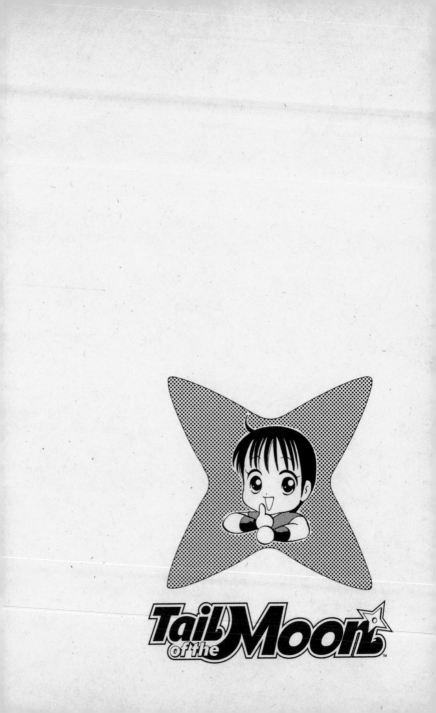

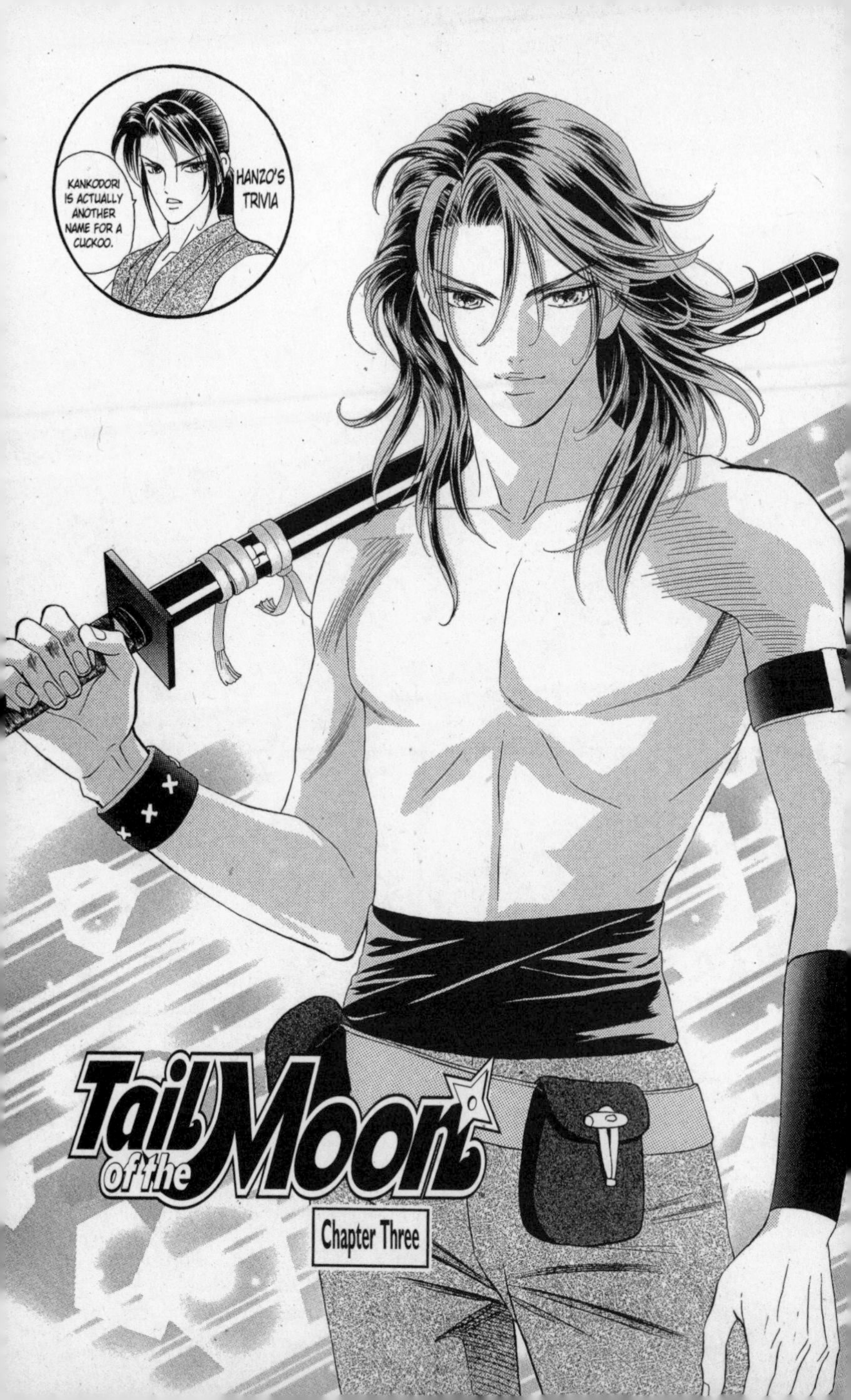
HANZO'S TRIVIA
KANKODORI IS ACTUALLY ANOTHER NAME FOR A CUCKOO.
Tail of the Moon
Chapter Three

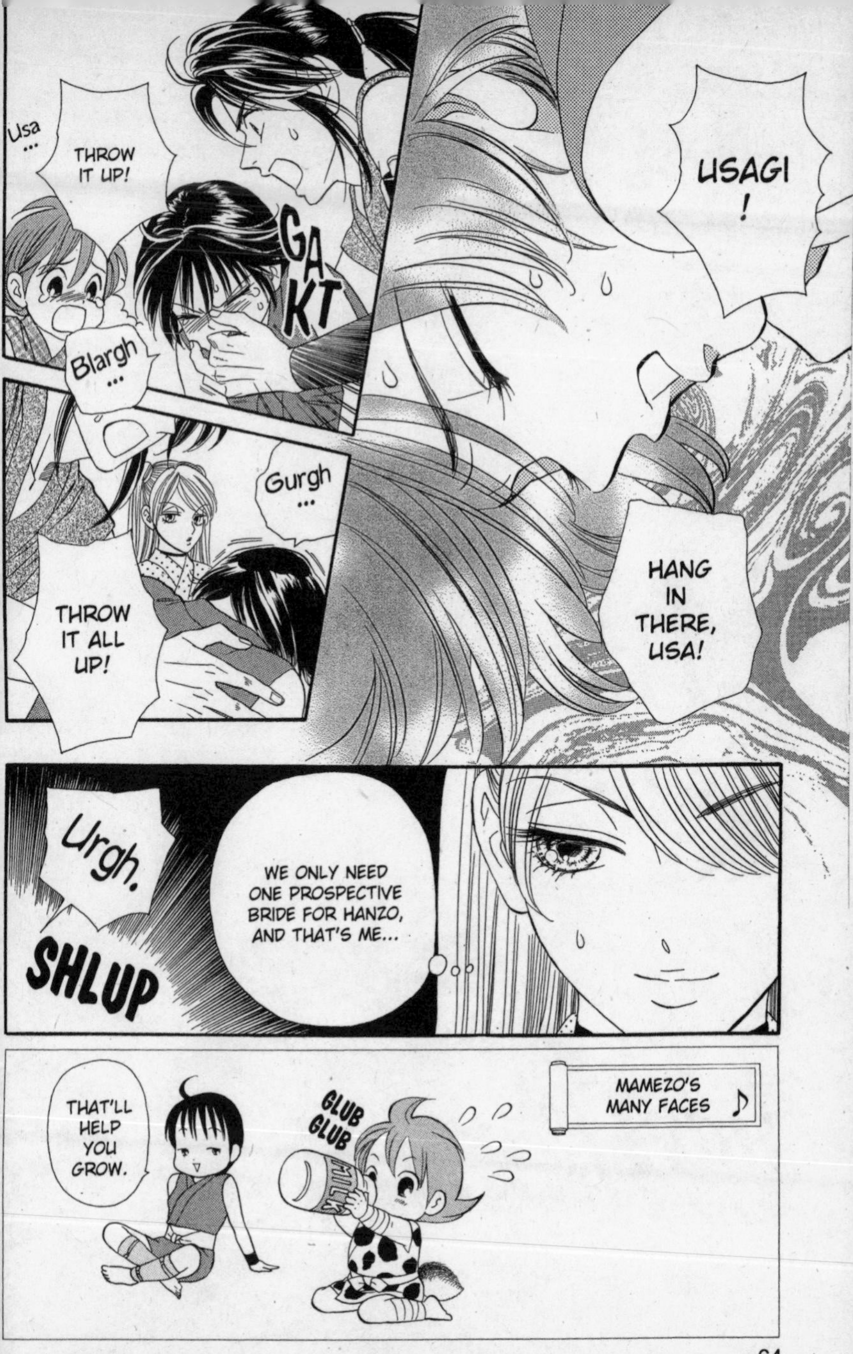
USAGI!
HANG IN THERE, USA!
Usa...
THROW IT UP!
GAKT
Blargh...
Gurgh...
THROW IT ALL UP!
WE ONLY NEED ONE PROSPECTIVE BRIDE FOR HANZO, AND THAT'S ME...
Urgh.
SHLUP
MAMEZO'S MANY FACES ♪
GLUB GLUB
MILK
THAT'LL HELP YOU GROW.

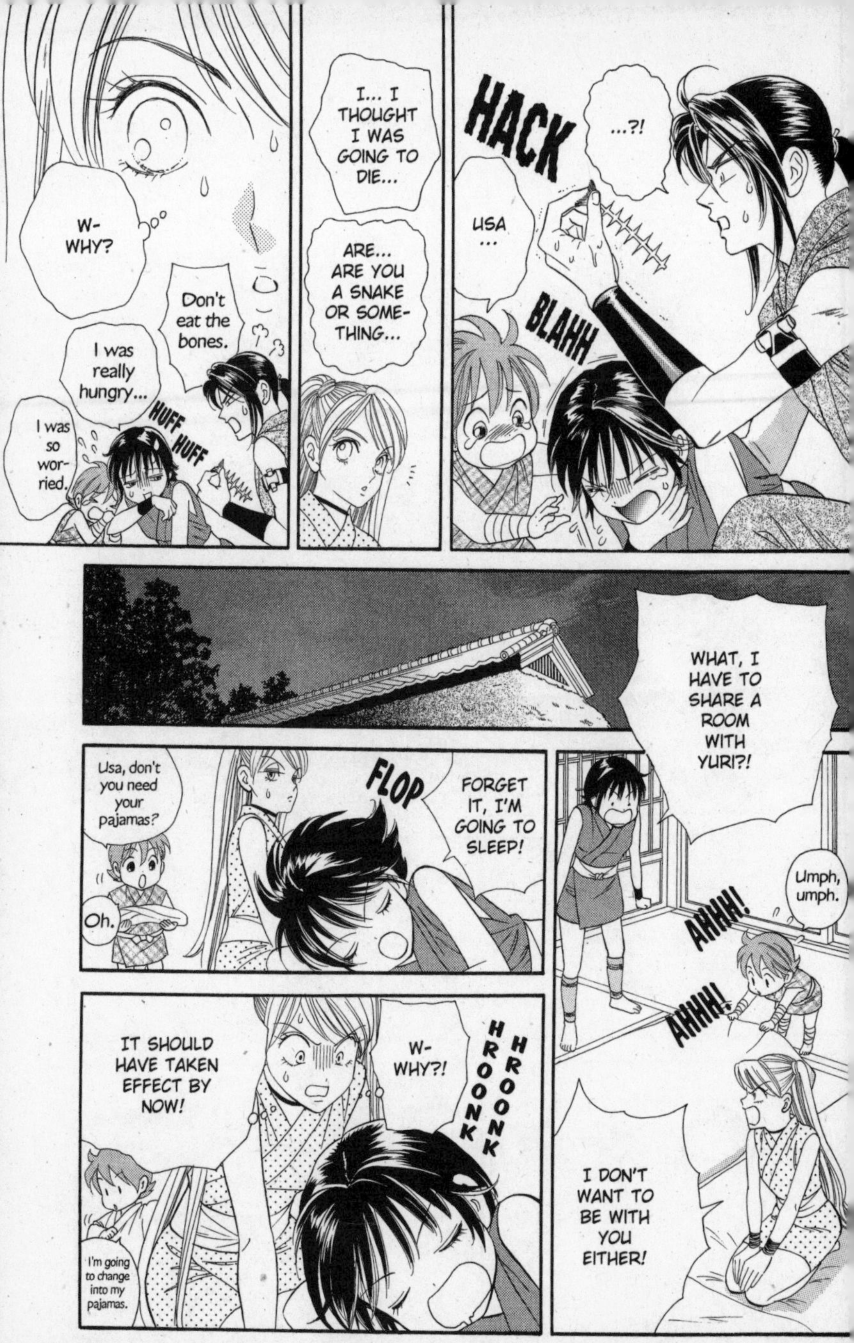
HACK
...?!
USA ...
BLAHH
I... I THOUGHT I WAS GOING TO DIE...
ARE... ARE YOU A SNAKE OR SOMETHING...
W- WHY?
Don't eat the bones.
I was really hungry...
HUFF HUFF
I was so worried.
WHAT, I HAVE TO SHARE A ROOM WITH YURI?!
Umph, umph.
AHHH!
AHHH!
I DON'T WANT TO BE WITH YOU EITHER!
FLOP
FORGET IT, I'M GOING TO SLEEP!
Usa, don't you need your pajamas?
Oh.
HROONK HROONK
W- WHY?!
IT SHOULD HAVE TAKEN EFFECT BY NOW!
I'm going to change into my pajamas.

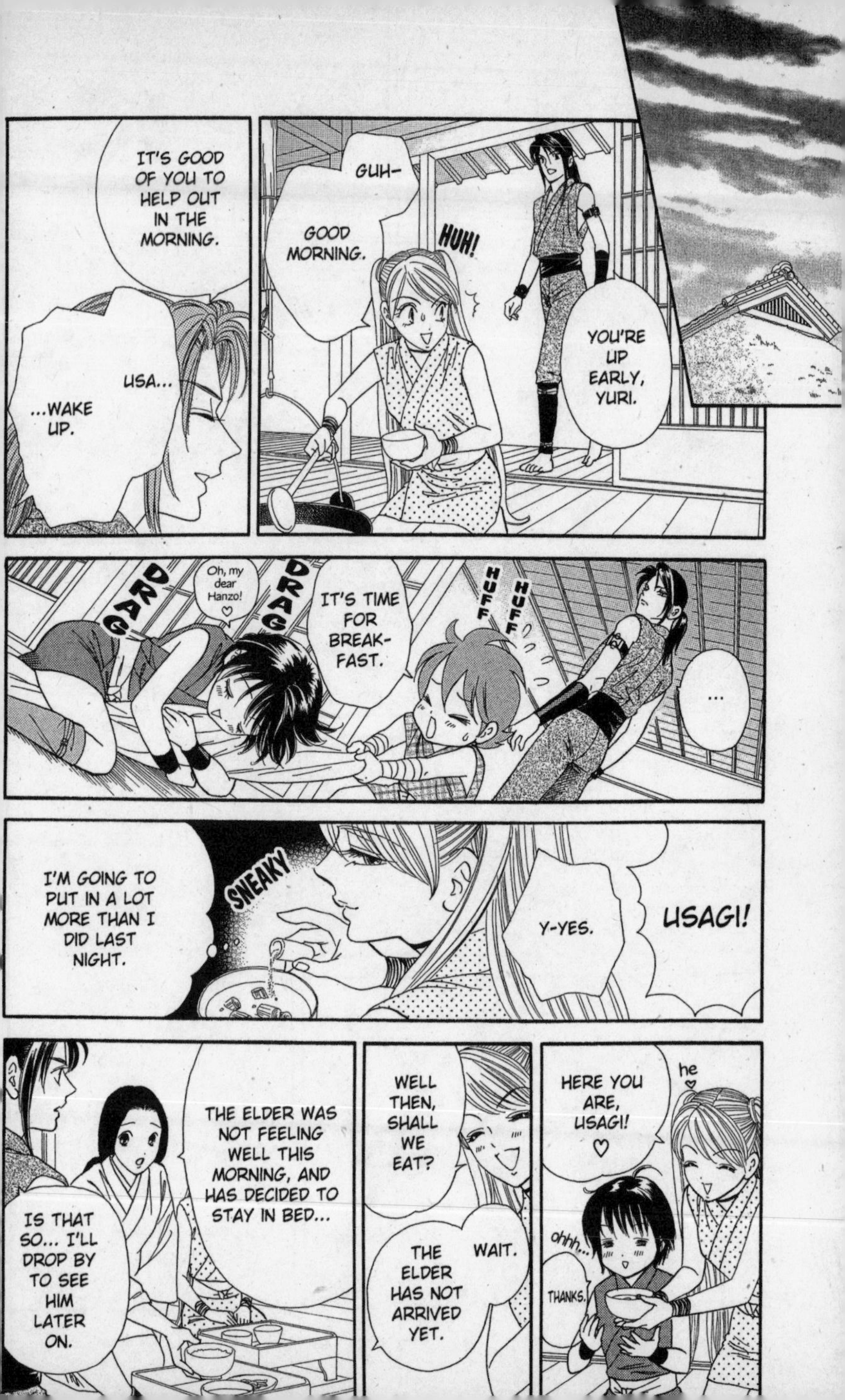
YOU'RE UP EARLY, YURI.
HUH!
GUH-
GOOD MORNING.
IT'S GOOD OF YOU TO HELP OUT IN THE MORNING.
USA...
...WAKE UP.
...
HUFF HUFF
IT'S TIME FOR BREAK-FAST.
DRAG
Oh, my dear Hanzo! ♡
DRAG
USAGI!
Y-YES.
SNEAKY
I'M GOING TO PUT IN A LOT MORE THAN I DID LAST NIGHT.
he ♡
HERE YOU ARE, USAGI! ♡
ohhh...
THANKS.
WELL THEN, SHALL WE EAT?
WAIT.
THE ELDER HAS NOT ARRIVED YET.
THE ELDER WAS NOT FEELING WELL THIS MORNING, AND HAS DECIDED TO STAY IN BED...
IS THAT SO... I'LL DROP BY TO SEE HIM LATER ON.

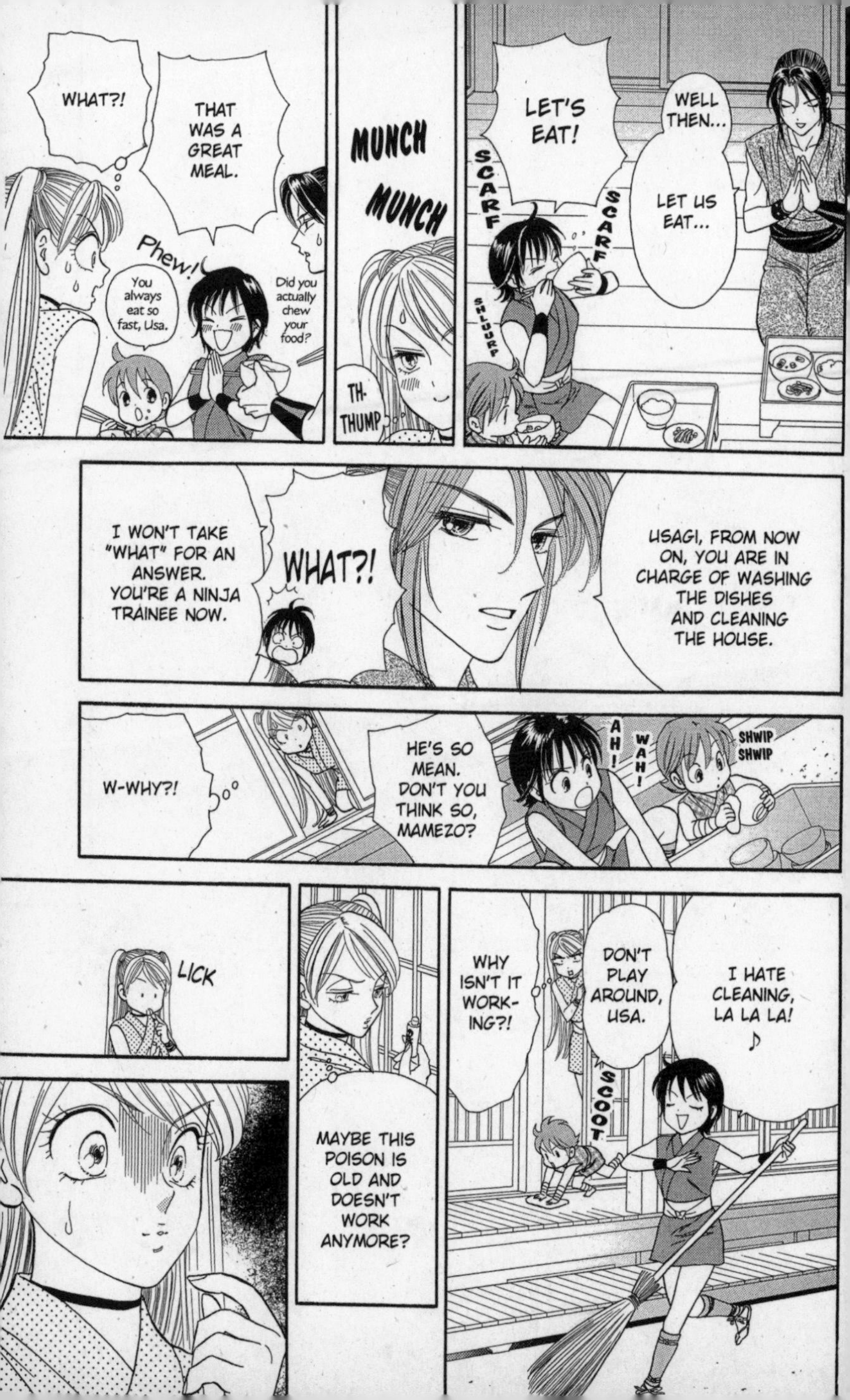
WELL THEN...
LET US EAT...
LET'S EAT!
SCARF
SCARF
SHLUURP
MUNCH
MUNCH
TH-THUMP
THAT WAS A GREAT MEAL.
WHAT?!
Did you actually chew your food?
Phew!
You always eat so fast, Usa.
USAGI, FROM NOW ON, YOU ARE IN CHARGE OF WASHING THE DISHES AND CLEANING THE HOUSE.
WHAT?!
I WON'T TAKE "WHAT" FOR AN ANSWER. YOU'RE A NINJA TRAINEE NOW.
SHWIP SHWIP
WAH!
AH!
HE'S SO MEAN. DON'T YOU THINK SO, MAMEZO?
W-WHY?!
I HATE CLEANING, LA LA LA! ♪
DON'T PLAY AROUND, USA.
SCOOT
WHY ISN'T IT WORKING?!
MAYBE THIS POISON IS OLD AND DOESN'T WORK ANYMORE?
LICK

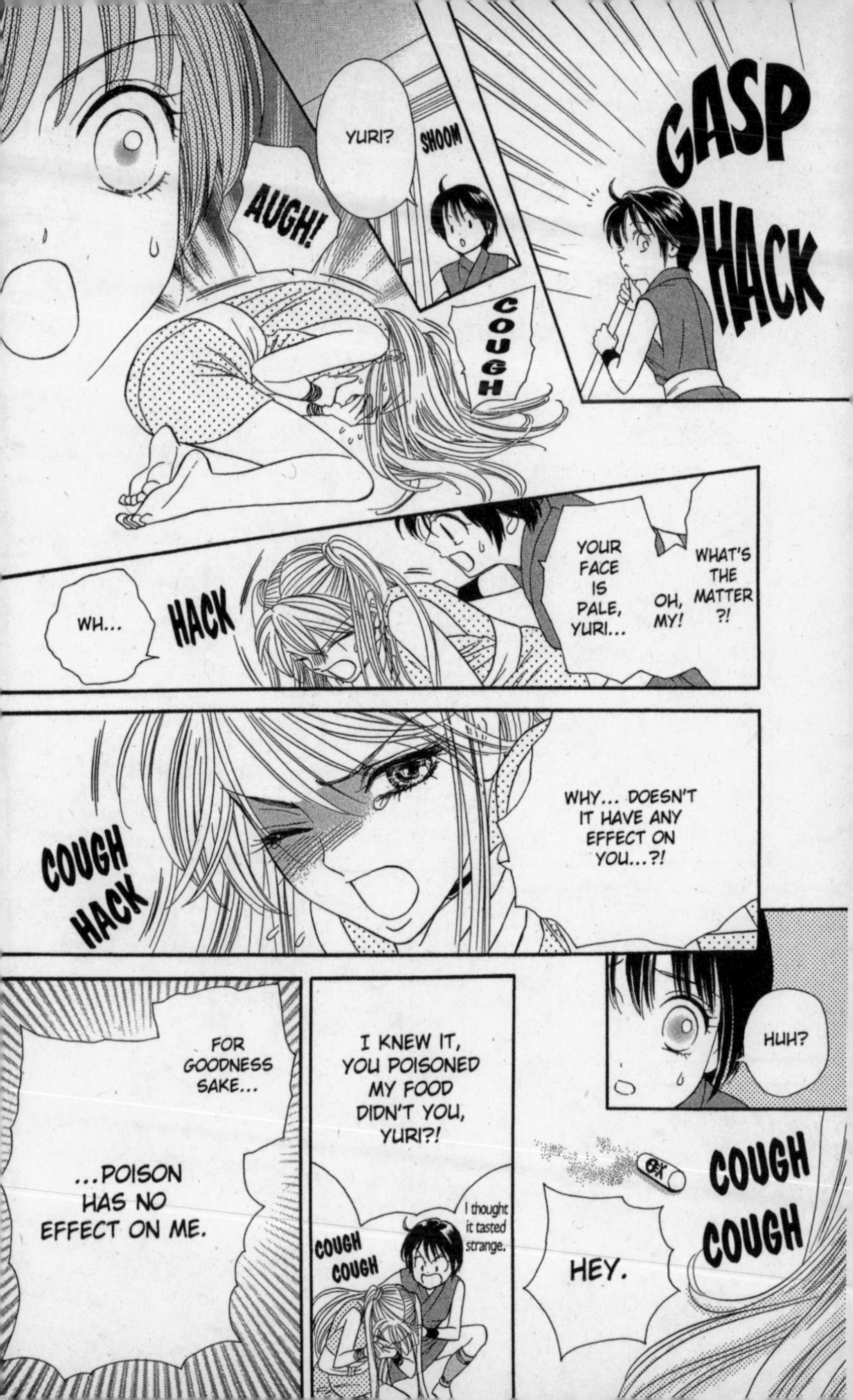
GASP
HACK
YURI?
SHOOM
AUGH!
COUGH
WHAT'S THE MATTER?!
OH, MY!
YOUR FACE IS PALE, YURI...
HACK
WH...
WHY... DOESN'T IT HAVE ANY EFFECT ON YOU...?!
COUGH HACK
HUH?
COUGH COUGH
HEY.
I KNEW IT, YOU POISONED MY FOOD DIDN'T YOU, YURI?!
I thought it tasted strange.
COUGH COUGH
FOR GOODNESS SAKE...
...POISON HAS NO EFFECT ON ME.

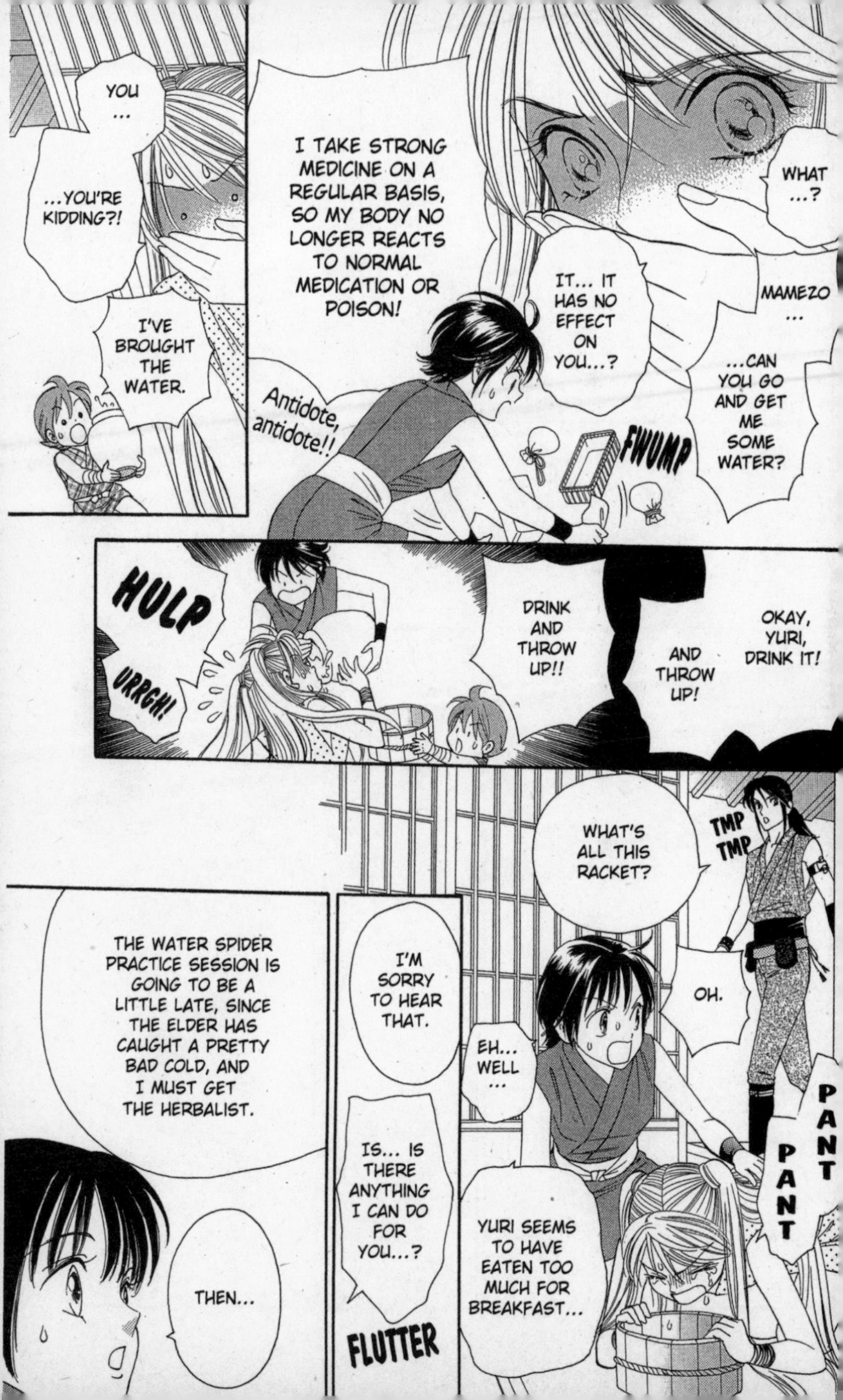
WHAT ...?
MAMEZO ...
...CAN YOU GO AND GET ME SOME WATER?
IT... IT HAS NO EFFECT ON YOU...?
I TAKE STRONG MEDICINE ON A REGULAR BASIS, SO MY BODY NO LONGER REACTS TO NORMAL MEDICATION OR POISON!
FWUMP
Antidote, antidote!!
YOU ...
...YOU'RE KIDDING?!
I'VE BROUGHT THE WATER.
OKAY, YURI, DRINK IT!
AND THROW UP!
DRINK AND THROW UP!!
HULP
URRGH!
TMP TMP
WHAT'S ALL THIS RACKET?
OH.
PANT PANT
EH... WELL ...
YURI SEEMS TO HAVE EATEN TOO MUCH FOR BREAKFAST...
I'M SORRY TO HEAR THAT.
IS... IS THERE ANYTHING I CAN DO FOR YOU...?
FLUTTER
THE WATER SPIDER PRACTICE SESSION IS GOING TO BE A LITTLE LATE, SINCE THE ELDER HAS CAUGHT A PRETTY BAD COLD, AND I MUST GET THE HERBALIST.
THEN...

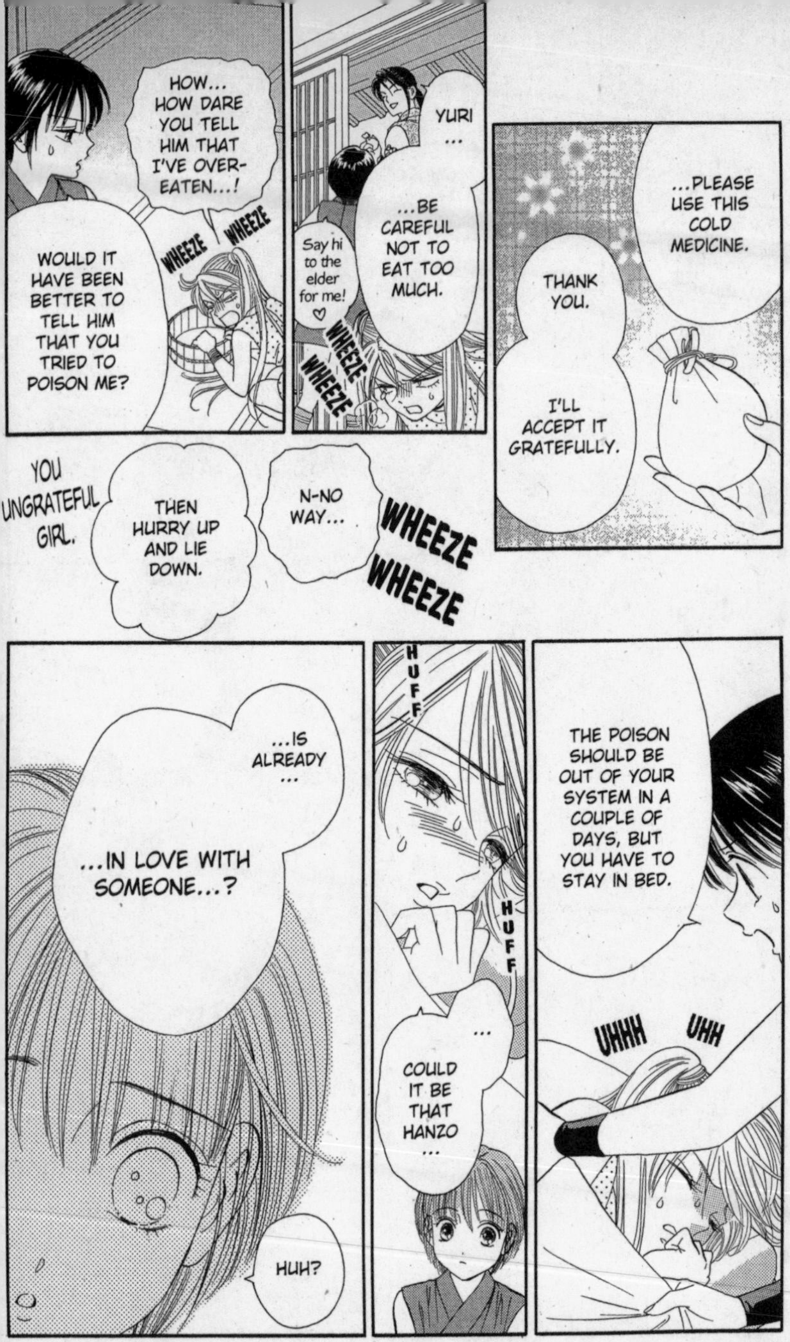
...PLEASE USE THIS COLD MEDICINE.
THANK YOU.
I'LL ACCEPT IT GRATEFULLY.
YURI ...
...BE CAREFUL NOT TO EAT TOO MUCH.
Say hi to the elder for me! ♡
WHEEZE WHEEZE
HOW... HOW DARE YOU TELL HIM THAT I'VE OVER-EATEN...!
WHEEZE WHEEZE
WOULD IT HAVE BEEN BETTER TO TELL HIM THAT YOU TRIED TO POISON ME?
WHEEZE WHEEZE
N-NO WAY...
THEN HURRY UP AND LIE DOWN.
YOU UNGRATEFUL GIRL.
THE POISON SHOULD BE OUT OF YOUR SYSTEM IN A COUPLE OF DAYS, BUT YOU HAVE TO STAY IN BED.
UHHH UHH
HUFF
HUFF
...
COULD IT BE THAT HANZO ...
...IS ALREADY ...
...IN LOVE WITH SOMEONE...?
HUH?

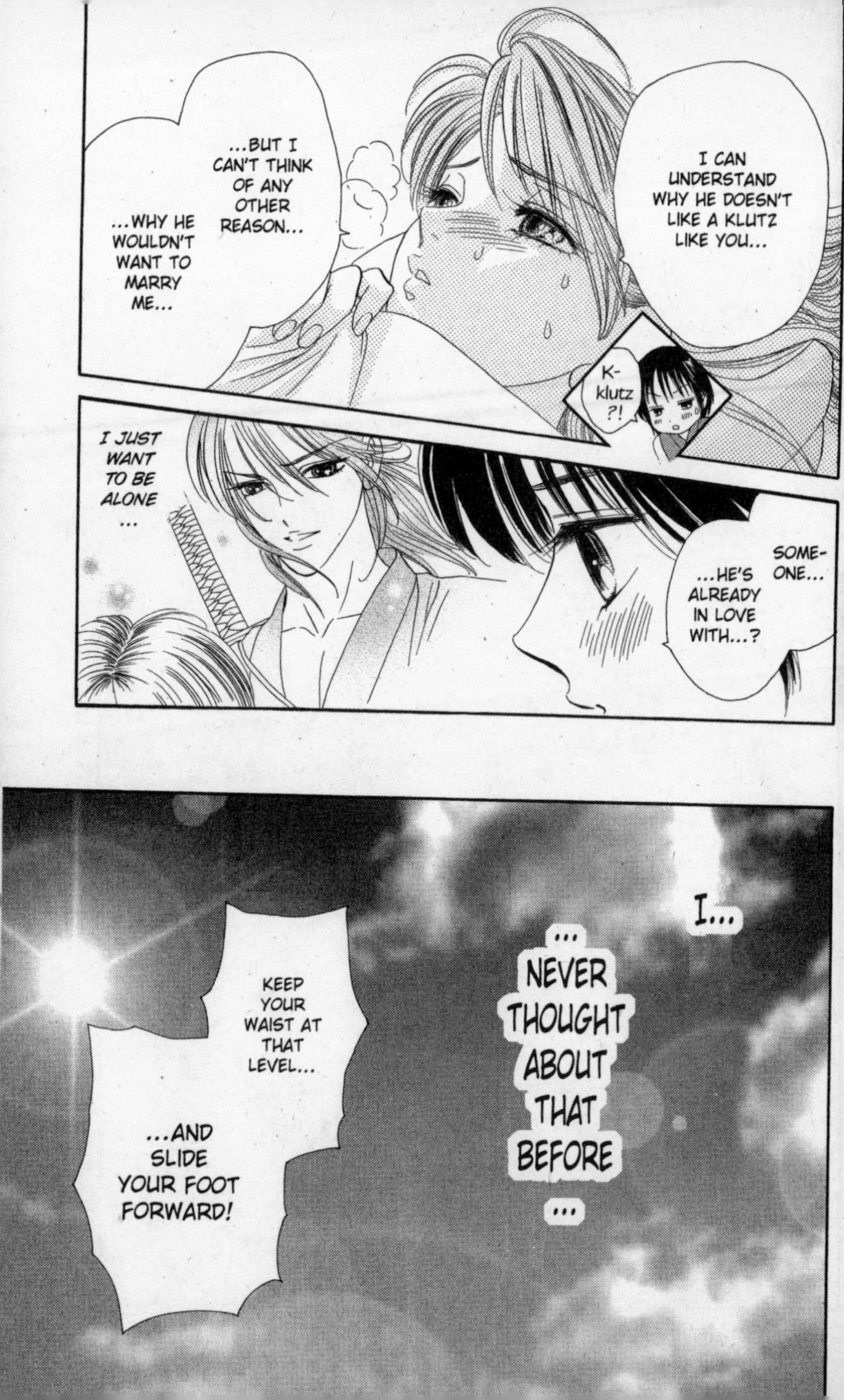
I CAN UNDERSTAND WHY HE DOESN'T LIKE A KLUTZ LIKE YOU...
K-klutz?!
...BUT I CAN'T THINK OF ANY OTHER REASON...
...WHY HE WOULDN'T WANT TO MARRY ME...
SOME-ONE...
...HE'S ALREADY IN LOVE WITH...?
I JUST WANT TO BE ALONE...
I...
...NEVER THOUGHT ABOUT THAT BEFORE...
KEEP YOUR WAIST AT THAT LEVEL...
...AND SLIDE YOUR FOOT FORWARD!

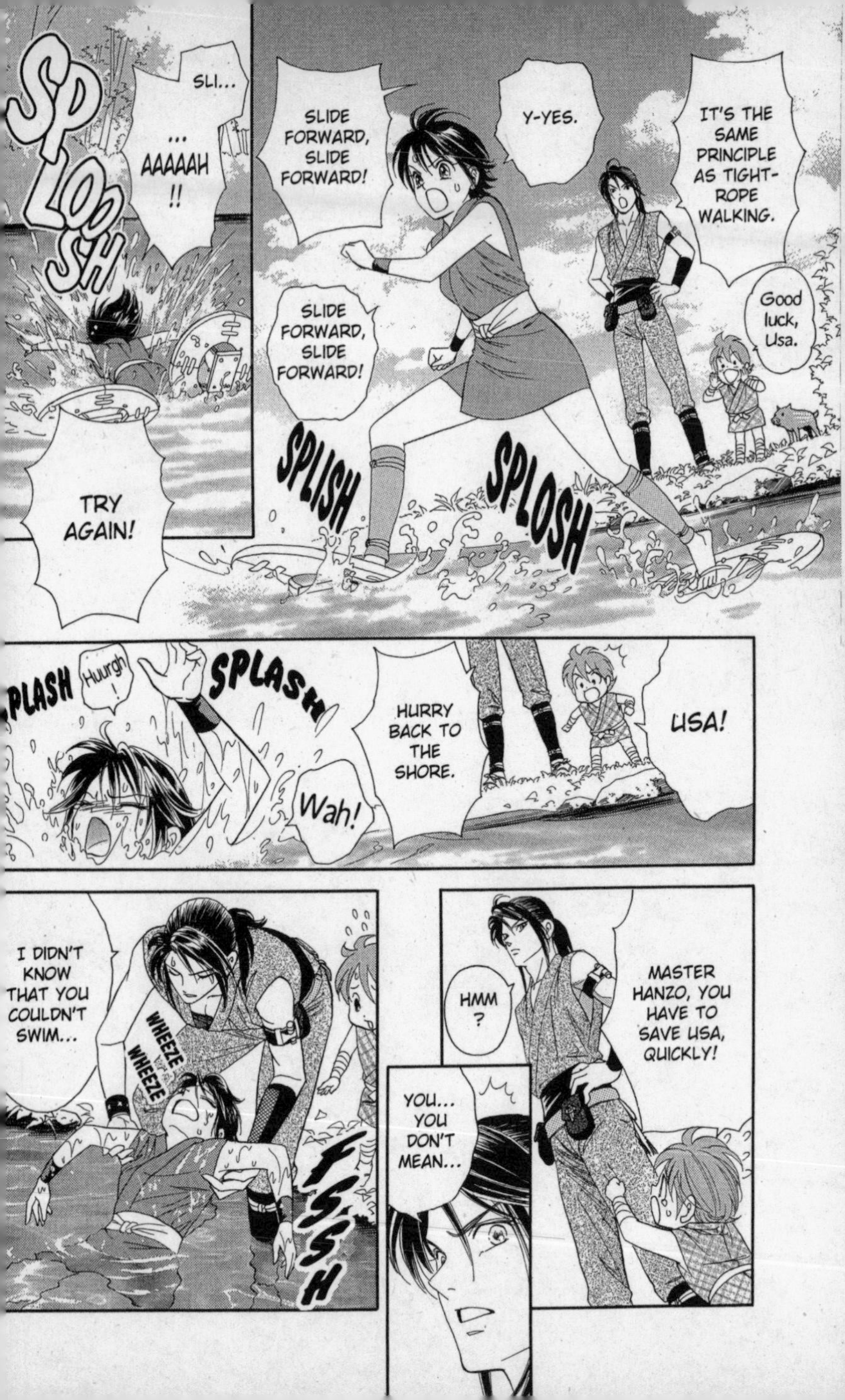
IT'S THE SAME PRINCIPLE AS TIGHT-ROPE WALKING.
Y-YES.
SLIDE FORWARD, SLIDE FORWARD!
Good luck, Usa.
SLIDE FORWARD, SLIDE FORWARD!
SPLOSH
SPLISH
SLI...
... AAAAAH!!
SPLOOSH
TRY AGAIN!
USA!
HURRY BACK TO THE SHORE.
Wah!
SPLASH
Huurgh!
SPLASH
MASTER HANZO, YOU HAVE TO SAVE USA, QUICKLY!
HMM?
YOU... YOU DON'T MEAN...
I DIDN'T KNOW THAT YOU COULDN'T SWIM...
WHEEZE
WHEEZE
FSSSH

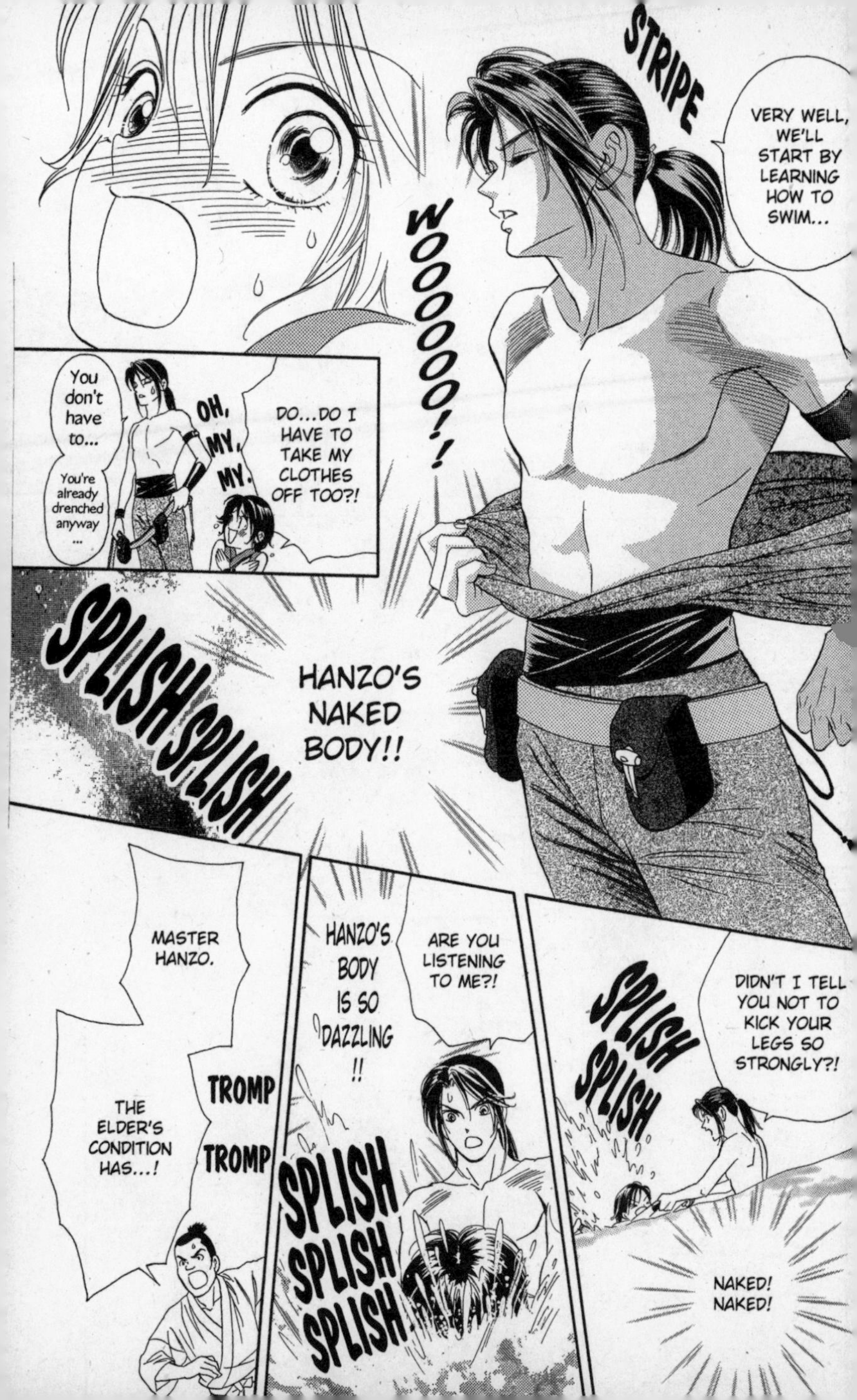
STRIPE
VERY WELL, WE'LL START BY LEARNING HOW TO SWIM...
WOOOOOOO!!
HANZO'S NAKED BODY!!
SPLISH SPLISH SPLISH
DO...DO I HAVE TO TAKE MY CLOTHES OFF TOO?!
OH, MY, MY.
You don't have to...
You're already drenched anyway ...
DIDN'T I TELL YOU NOT TO KICK YOUR LEGS SO STRONGLY?!
SPLISH SPLISH.
NAKED! NAKED!
ARE YOU LISTENING TO ME?!
HANZO'S BODY IS SO DAZZLING !!
SPLISH SPLISH SPLISH
TROMP TROMP
MASTER HANZO.
THE ELDER'S CONDITION HAS...!

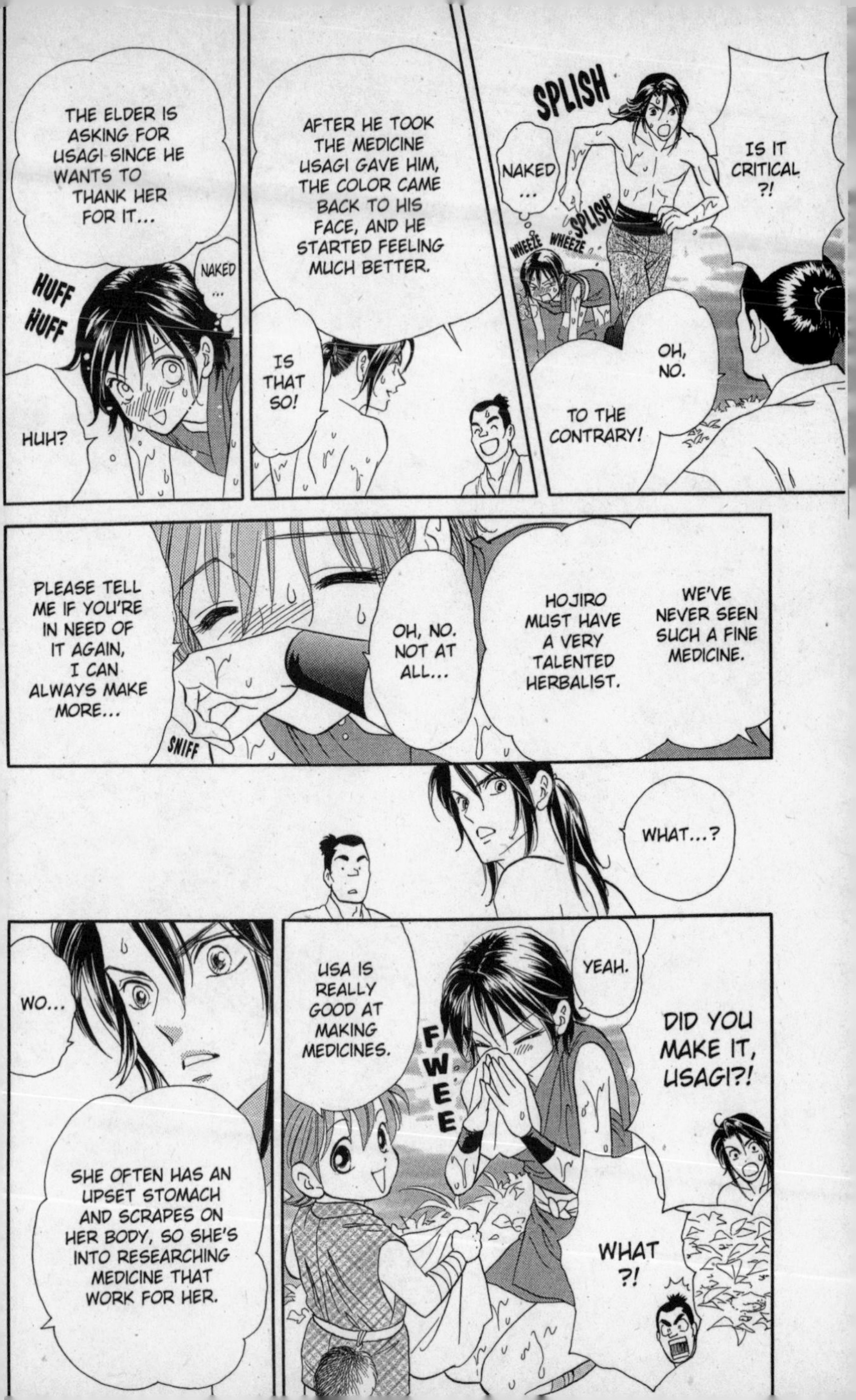
IS IT CRITICAL ?!
SPLISH
NAKED ...
SPLISH
WHEEZE WHEEZE
OH, NO.
TO THE CONTRARY!
AFTER HE TOOK THE MEDICINE USAGI GAVE HIM, THE COLOR CAME BACK TO HIS FACE, AND HE STARTED FEELING MUCH BETTER.
IS THAT SO!
THE ELDER IS ASKING FOR USAGI SINCE HE WANTS TO THANK HER FOR IT...
NAKED ...
HUFF HUFF
HUH?
WE'VE NEVER SEEN SUCH A FINE MEDICINE.
HOJIRO MUST HAVE A VERY TALENTED HERBALIST.
OH, NO. NOT AT ALL...
PLEASE TELL ME IF YOU'RE IN NEED OF IT AGAIN, I CAN ALWAYS MAKE MORE...
SNIFF
WHAT...?
DID YOU MAKE IT, USAGI?!
YEAH.
USA IS REALLY GOOD AT MAKING MEDICINES.
FWEE
WHAT ?!
WO...
SHE OFTEN HAS AN UPSET STOMACH AND SCRAPES ON HER BODY, SO SHE'S INTO RESEARCHING MEDICINE THAT WORK FOR HER.

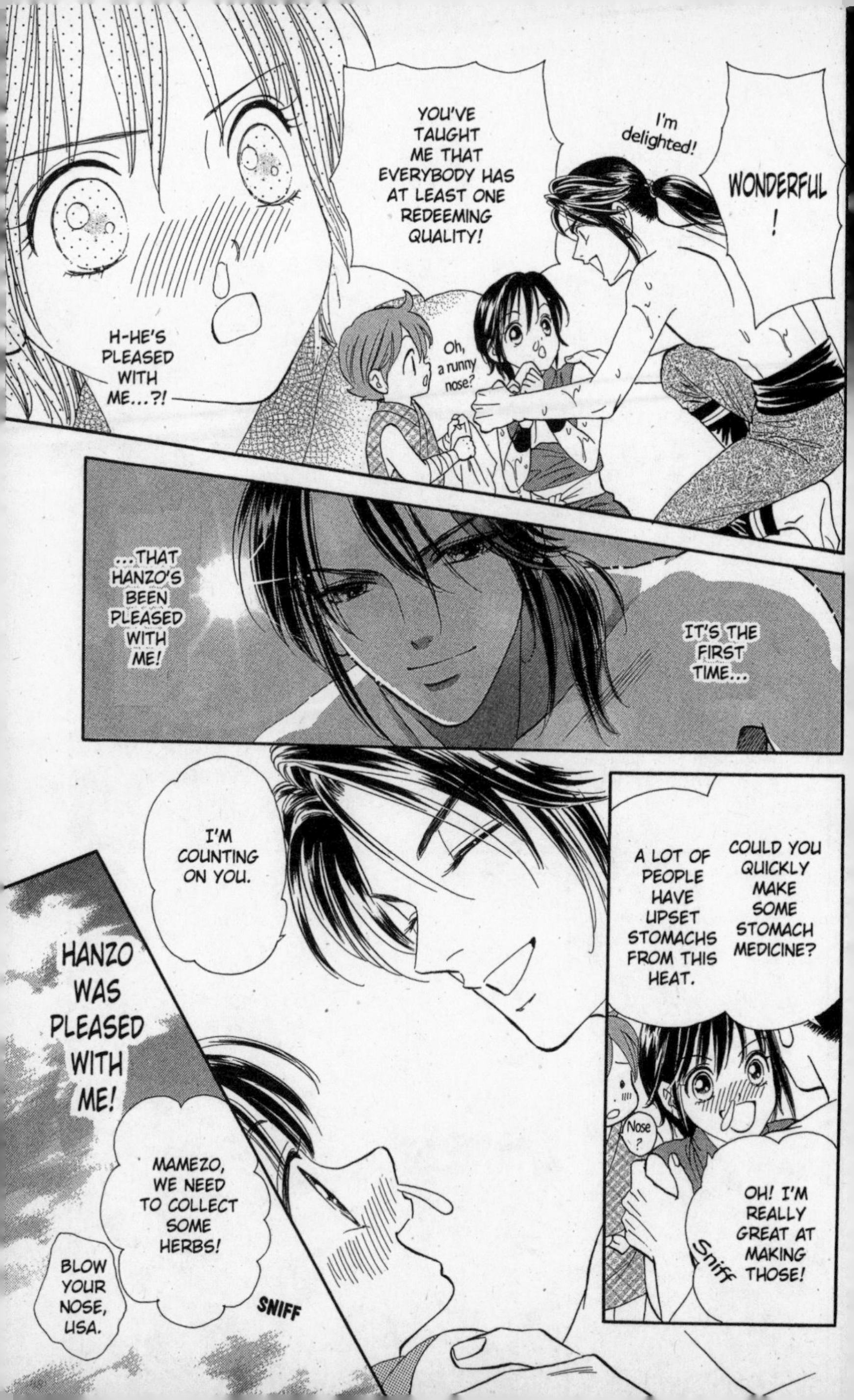
WONDERFUL!
I'm delighted!
YOU'VE TAUGHT ME THAT EVERYBODY HAS AT LEAST ONE REDEEMING QUALITY!
Oh, a runny nose?
H-HE'S PLEASED WITH ME...?!
IT'S THE FIRST TIME...
...THAT HANZO'S BEEN PLEASED WITH ME!
COULD YOU QUICKLY MAKE SOME STOMACH MEDICINE?
A LOT OF PEOPLE HAVE UPSET STOMACHS FROM THIS HEAT.
Nose?
OH! I'M REALLY GREAT AT MAKING THOSE!
Sniff
I'M COUNTING ON YOU.
HANZO WAS PLEASED WITH ME!
MAMEZO, WE NEED TO COLLECT SOME HERBS!
SNIFF
BLOW YOUR NOSE, USA.

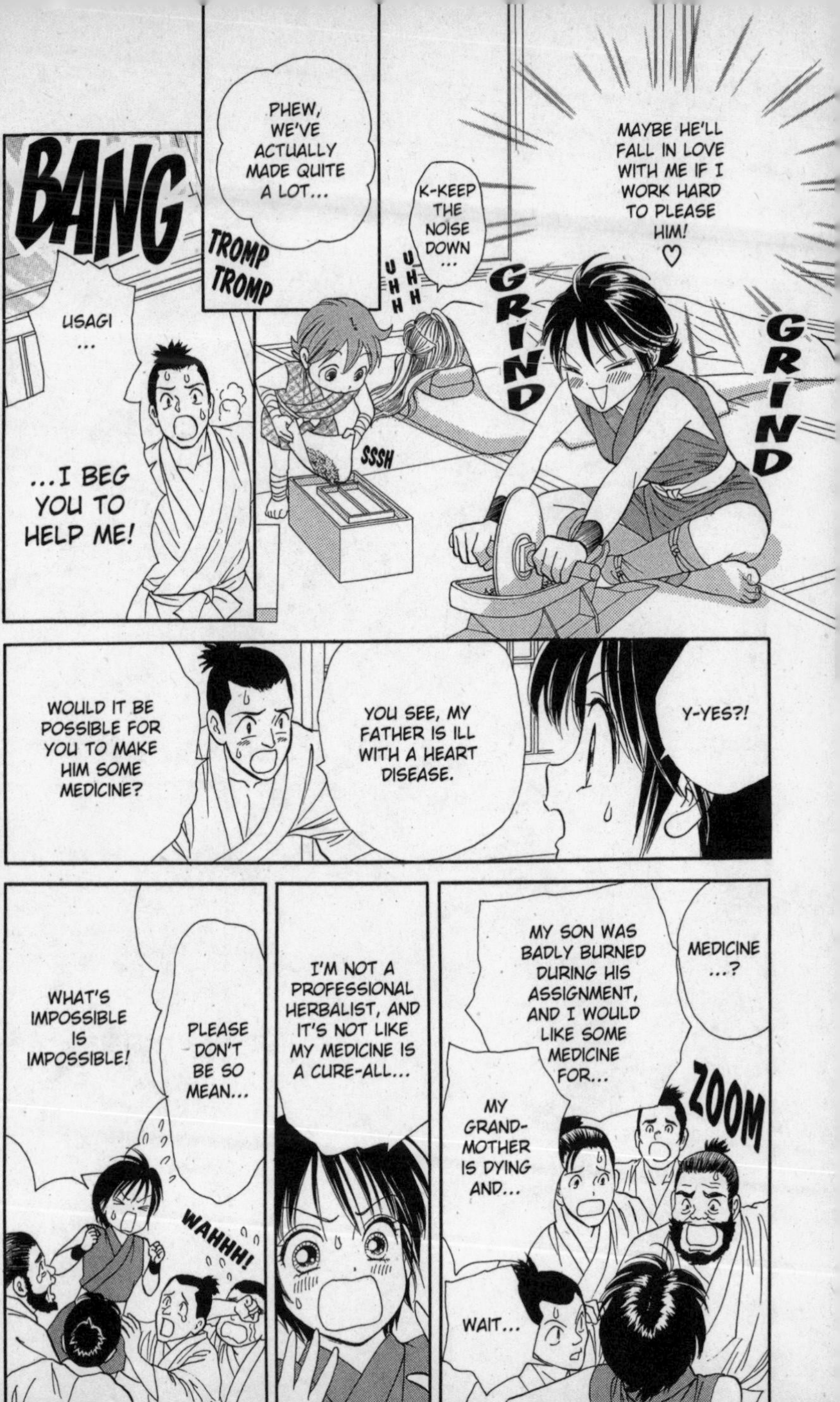
MAYBE HE'LL FALL IN LOVE WITH ME IF I WORK HARD TO PLEASE HIM! ♡
GRIND GRIND
GRIND
K-KEEP THE NOISE DOWN...
UHH UHH
PHEW, WE'VE ACTUALLY MADE QUITE A LOT...
SSSH
TROMP TROMP
BANG
USAGI...
...I BEG YOU TO HELP ME!
Y-YES?!
YOU SEE, MY FATHER IS ILL WITH A HEART DISEASE.
WOULD IT BE POSSIBLE FOR YOU TO MAKE HIM SOME MEDICINE?
MEDICINE...?
MY SON WAS BADLY BURNED DURING HIS ASSIGNMENT, AND I WOULD LIKE SOME MEDICINE FOR...
ZOOM
MY GRAND-MOTHER IS DYING AND...
WAIT...
I'M NOT A PROFESSIONAL HERBALIST, AND IT'S NOT LIKE MY MEDICINE IS A CURE-ALL...
PLEASE DON'T BE SO MEAN...
WHAT'S IMPOSSIBLE IS IMPOSSIBLE!
WAHHH!

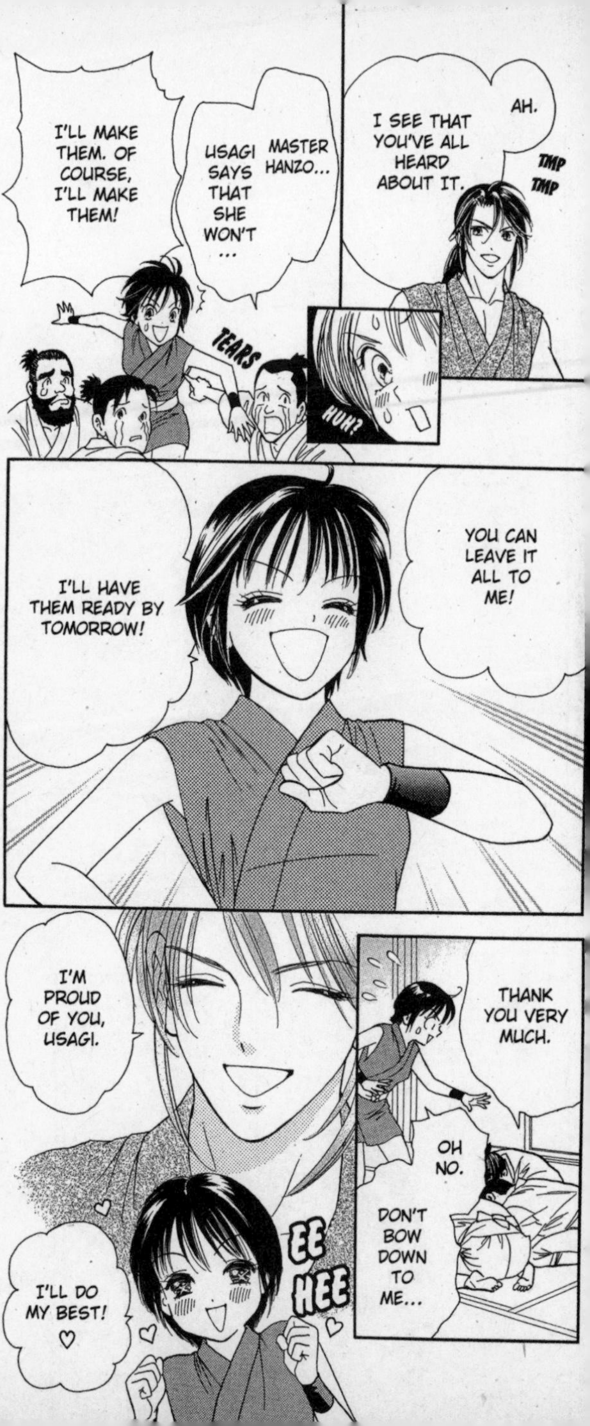
AH.
I SEE THAT YOU'VE ALL HEARD ABOUT IT.
TMP TMP
HUH?
MASTER HANZO...
USAGI SAYS THAT SHE WON'T ...
I'LL MAKE THEM. OF COURSE, I'LL MAKE THEM!
TEARS
YOU CAN LEAVE IT ALL TO ME!
I'LL HAVE THEM READY BY TOMORROW!
THANK YOU VERY MUCH.
OH NO.
DON'T BOW DOWN TO ME...
I'M PROUD OF YOU, USAGI.
EE HEE
I'LL DO MY BEST! ♡

This and that from the author 3

I had a small regret... And I wanted Hanzo to be happy as well, and that is why I created this manga, *Tail of the Moon*.

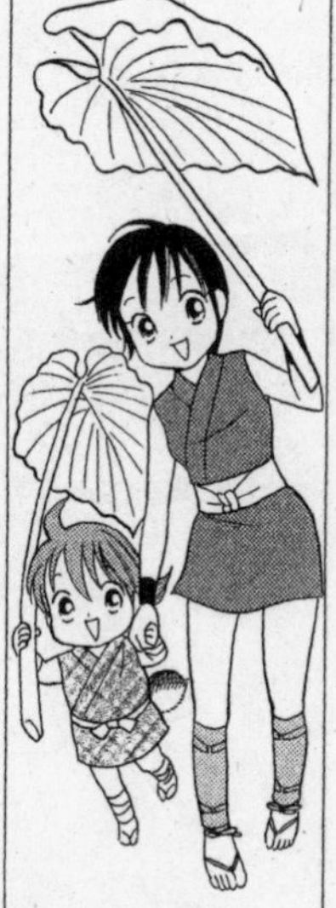

And the girl I created to be Hanzo's partner is Usagi.

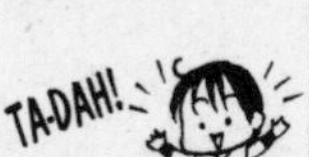
TA-DAH!

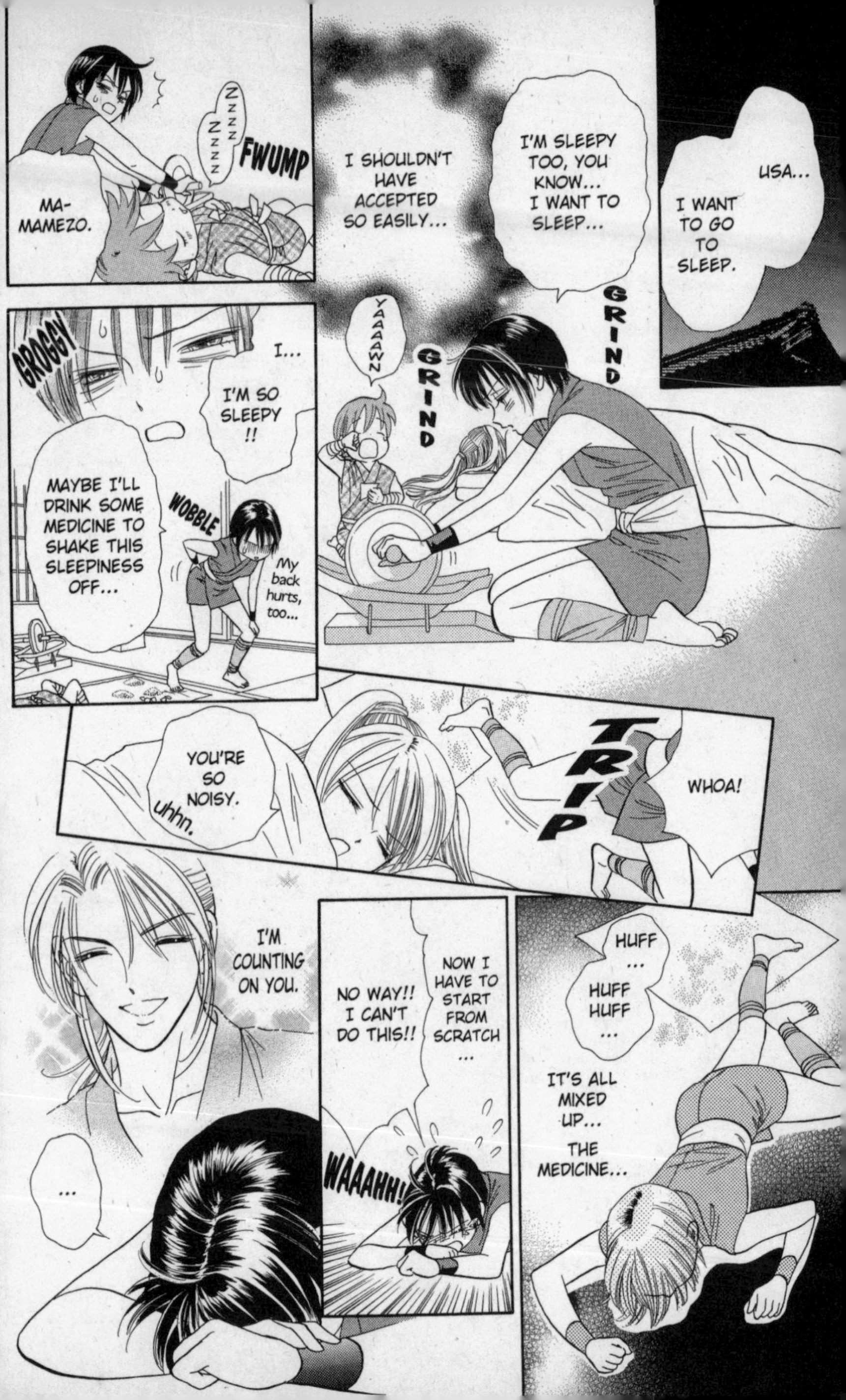
USA...
I WANT TO GO TO SLEEP.
I'M SLEEPY TOO, YOU KNOW... I WANT TO SLEEP...
GRIND
I SHOULDN'T HAVE ACCEPTED SO EASILY...
GRIND
YAAAAWN
FWUMP
ZZZZ ZZZ
MA-MAMEZO.
GROGGY
I...
I'M SO SLEEPY !!
MAYBE I'LL DRINK SOME MEDICINE TO SHAKE THIS SLEEPINESS OFF...
WOBBLE
My back hurts, too...
WHOA!
TRIP
YOU'RE SO NOISY.
uhhn.
HUFF... HUFF HUFF...
IT'S ALL MIXED UP... THE MEDICINE...
NOW I HAVE TO START FROM SCRATCH...
NO WAY!! I CAN'T DO THIS!!
WAAAHH!!
I'M COUNTING ON YOU.
...

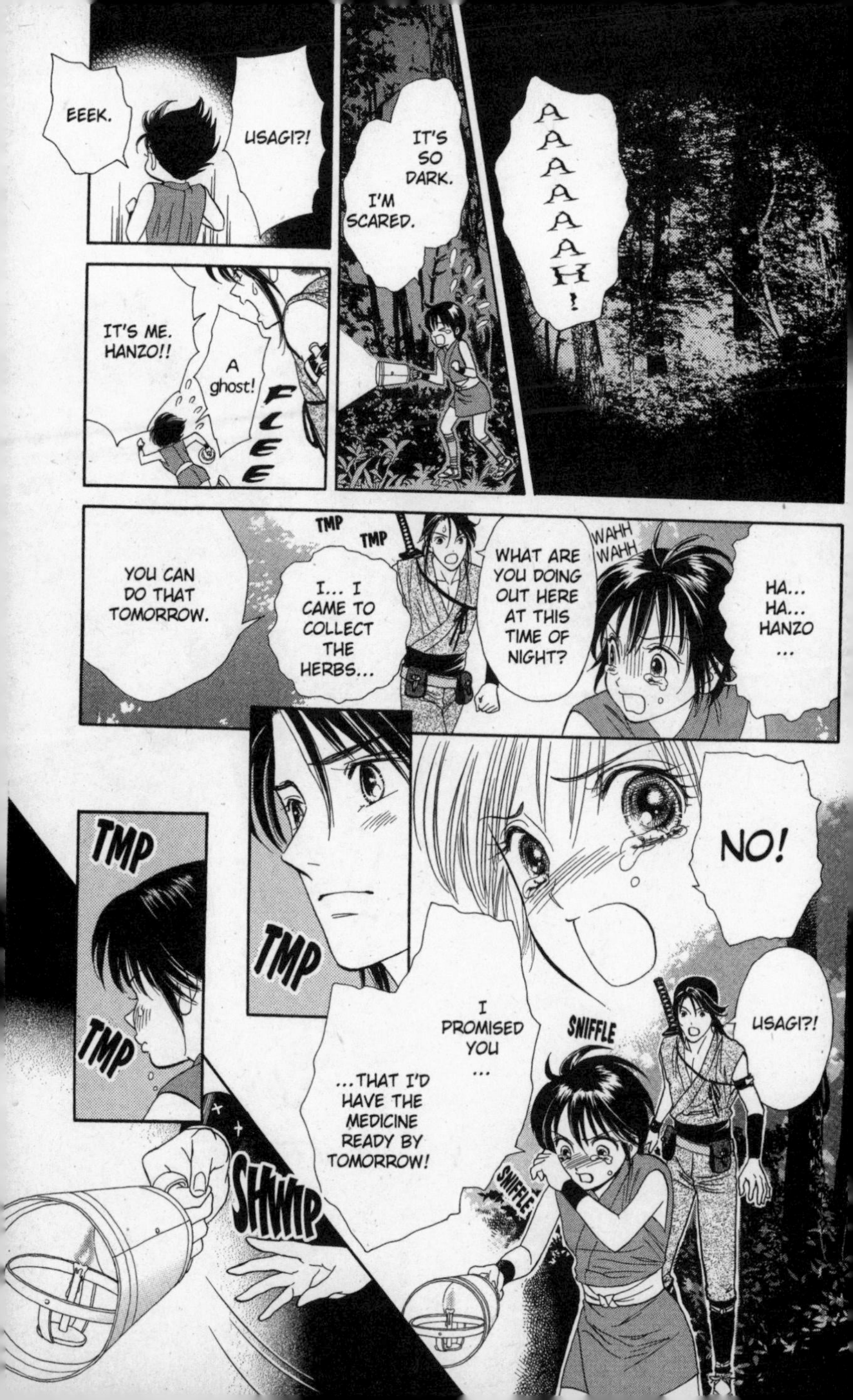
AAAAAAH!
IT'S SO DARK.
I'M SCARED.
USAGI?!
EEEK.
A ghost!
IT'S ME. HANZO!!
FLEEE
HA... HA... HANZO...
WAHH WAHH
WHAT ARE YOU DOING OUT HERE AT THIS TIME OF NIGHT?
TMP
TMP
I... I CAME TO COLLECT THE HERBS...
YOU CAN DO THAT TOMORROW.
NO!
USAGI?!
SNIFFLE
I PROMISED YOU...
...THAT I'D HAVE THE MEDICINE READY BY TOMORROW!
SNIFFLE
SHWIP
TMP
TMP
TMP

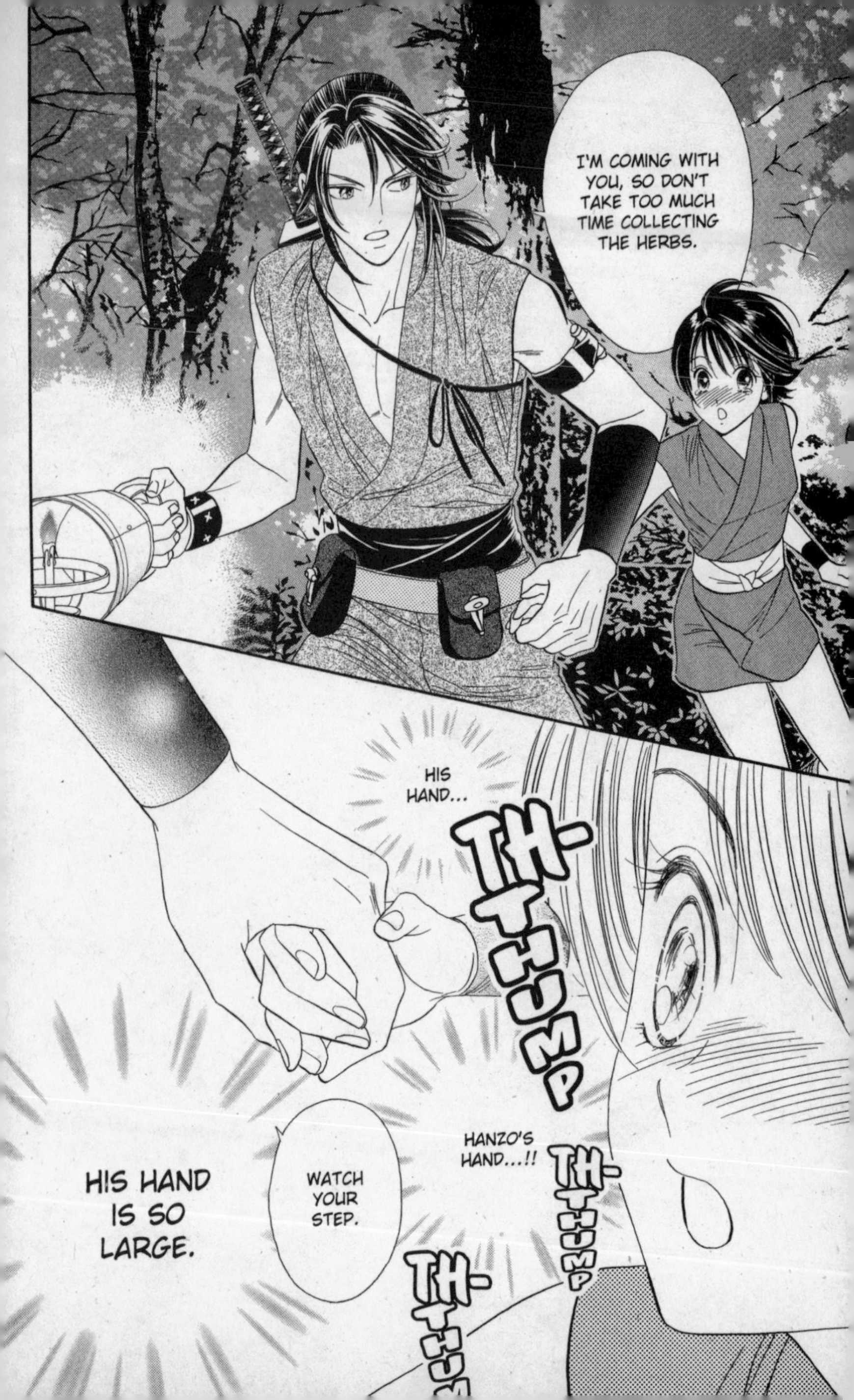

I'M COMING WITH YOU, SO DON'T TAKE TOO MUCH TIME COLLECTING THE HERBS.
TH-THUMP
HIS HAND...
HANZO'S HAND...!!
TH-THUMP
TH-THUM
WATCH YOUR STEP.
HIS HAND IS SO LARGE.

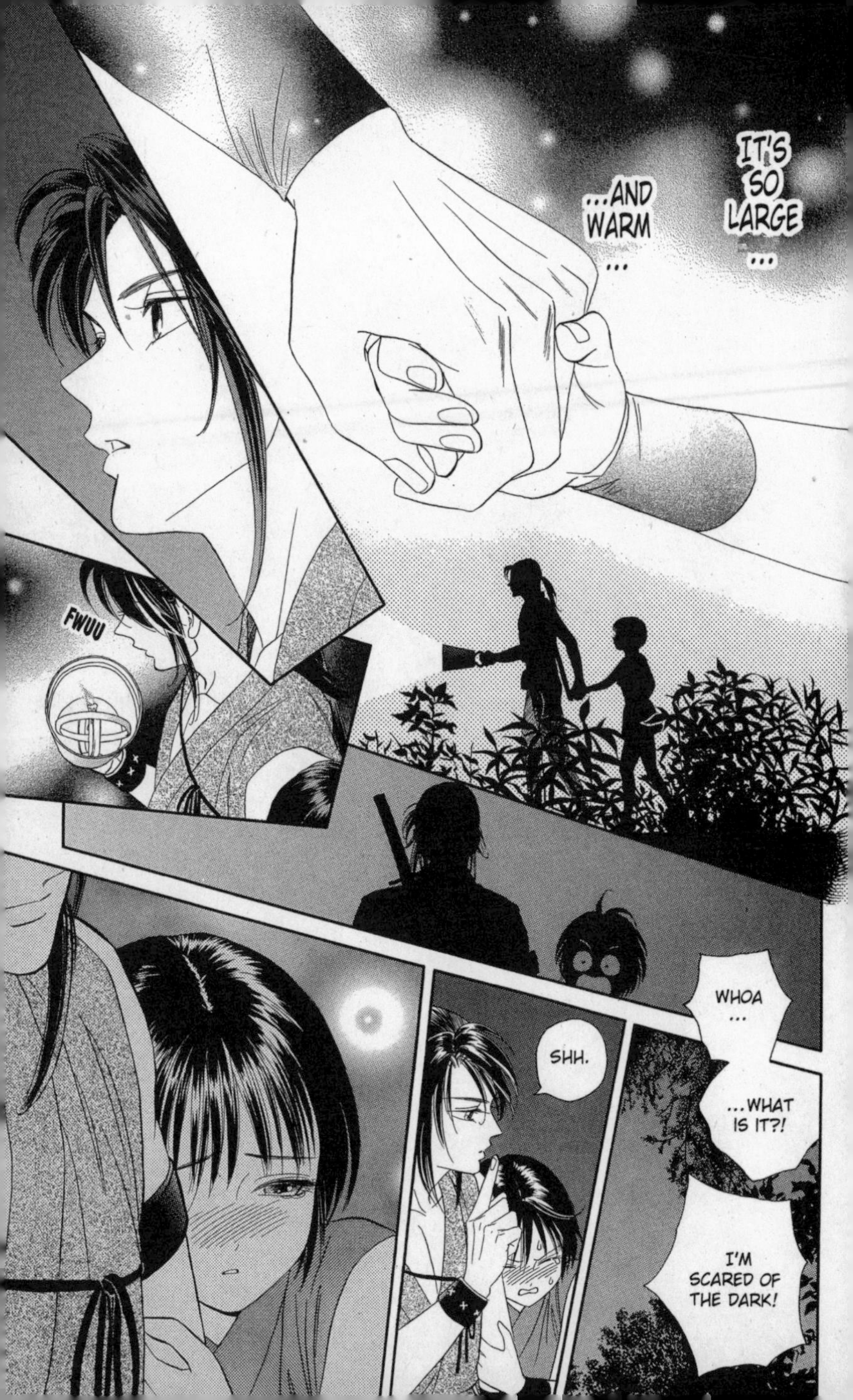
IT'S SO LARGE ...
...AND WARM ...
FWUU
WHOA ...
...WHAT IS IT?!
I'M SCARED OF THE DARK!
SHH.

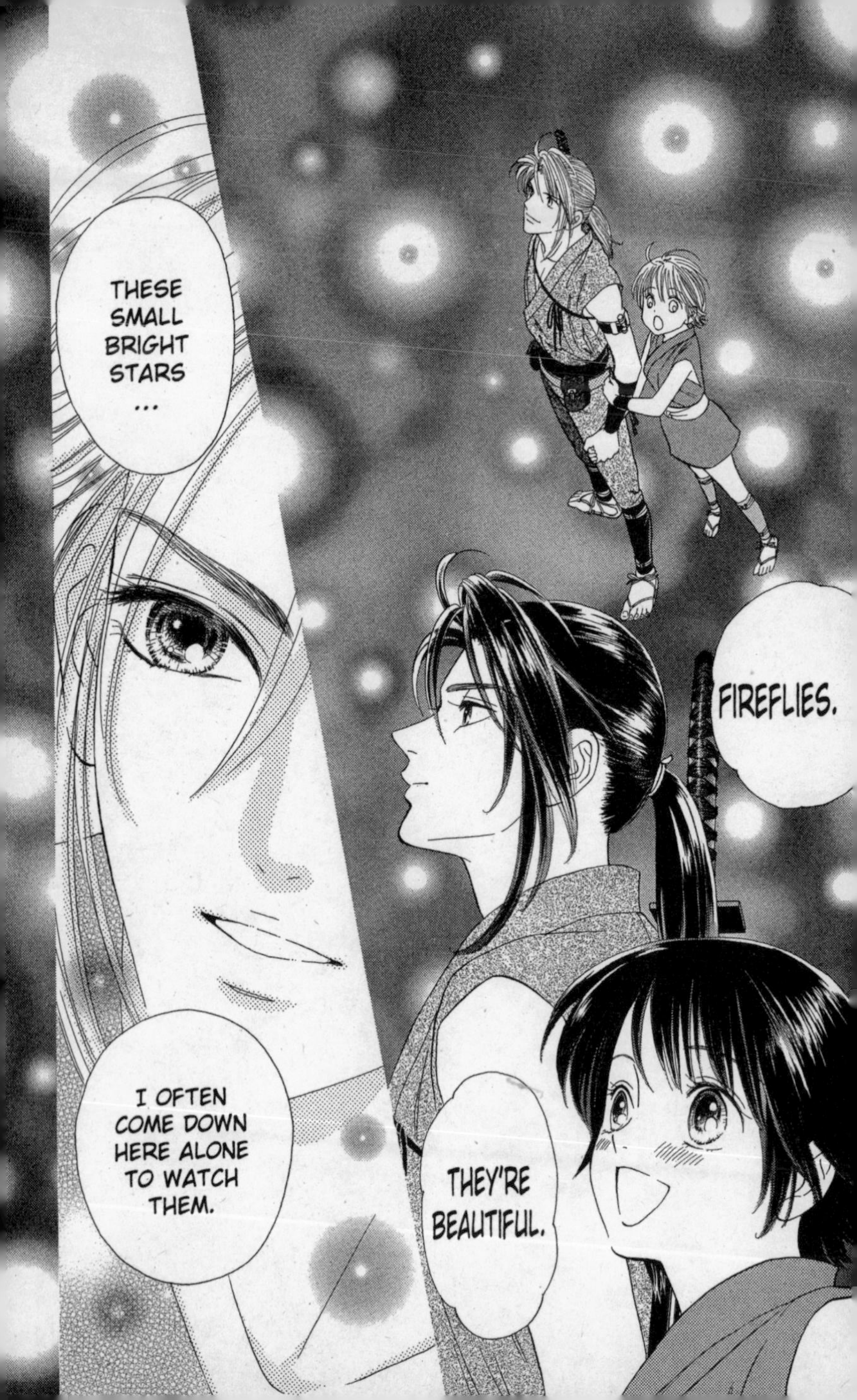
FIREFLIES.
THEY'RE BEAUTIFUL.
THESE SMALL BRIGHT STARS ...
I OFTEN COME DOWN HERE ALONE TO WATCH THEM.

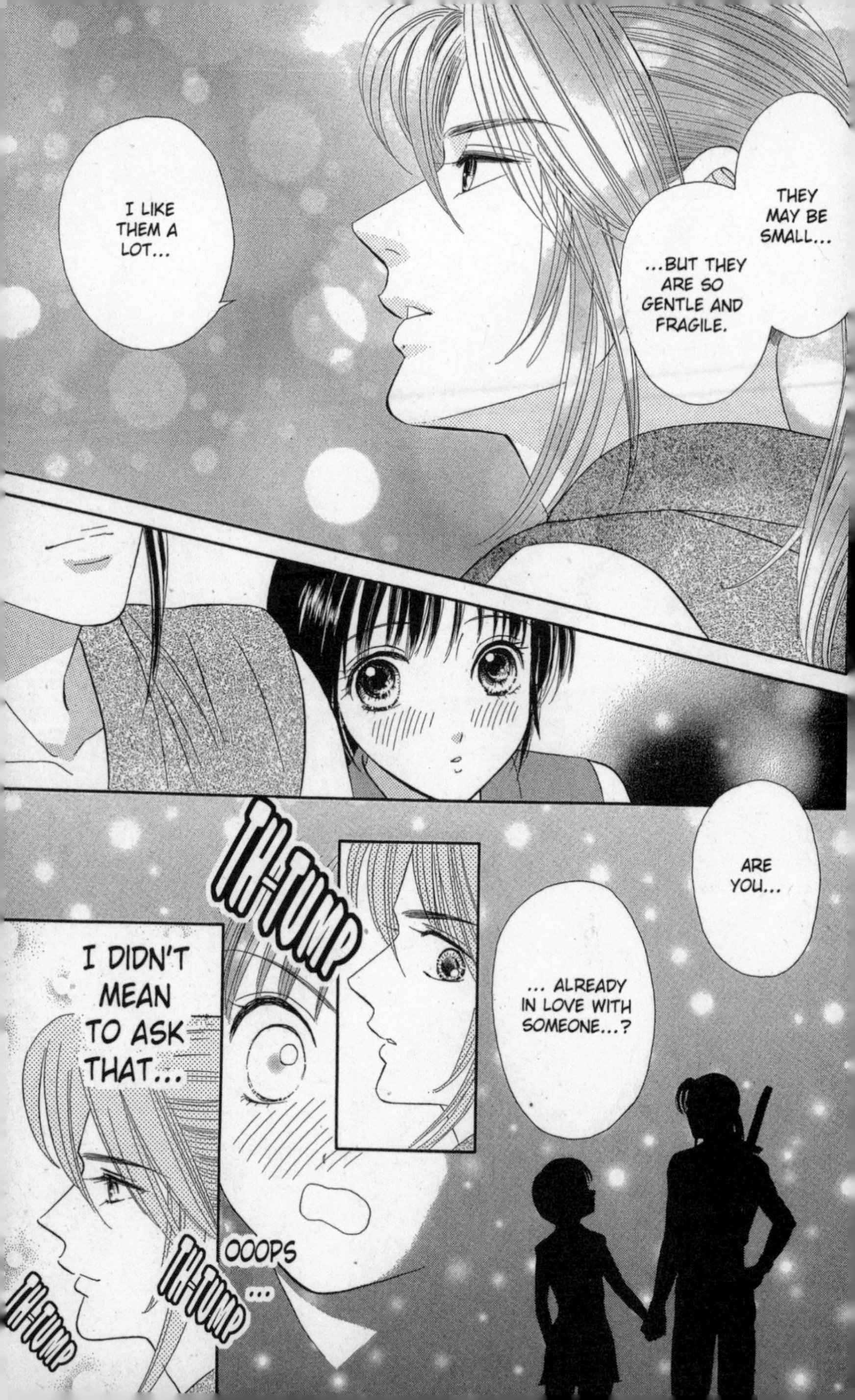
THEY MAY BE SMALL...
...BUT THEY ARE SO GENTLE AND FRAGILE.
I LIKE THEM A LOT...
ARE YOU...
... ALREADY IN LOVE WITH SOMEONE...?
TH-TUMP
I DIDN'T MEAN TO ASK THAT...
OOOPS ...
TH-TUMP
TH-TUMP

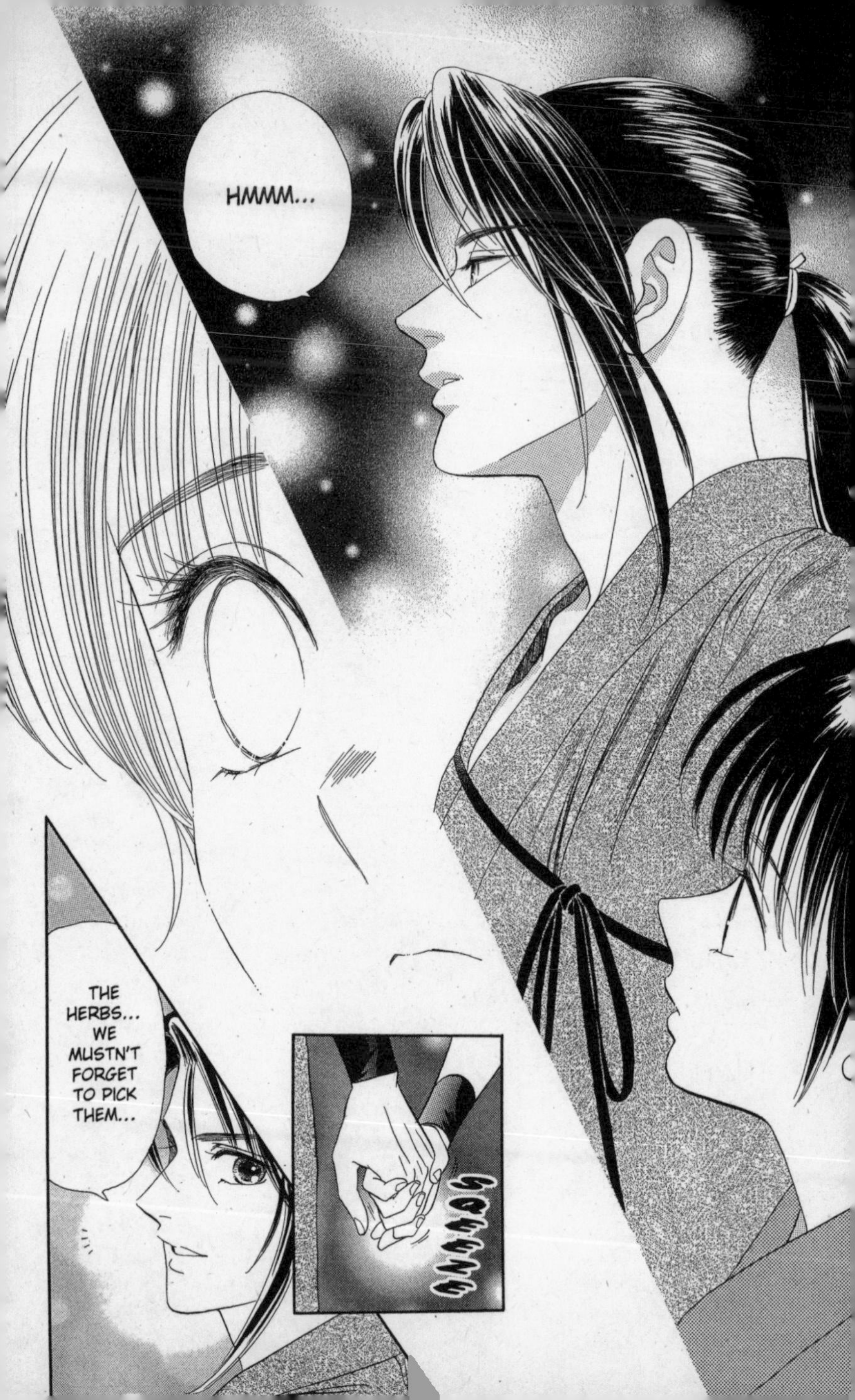
HMMM...
THE HERBS... WE MUSTN'T FORGET TO PICK THEM...

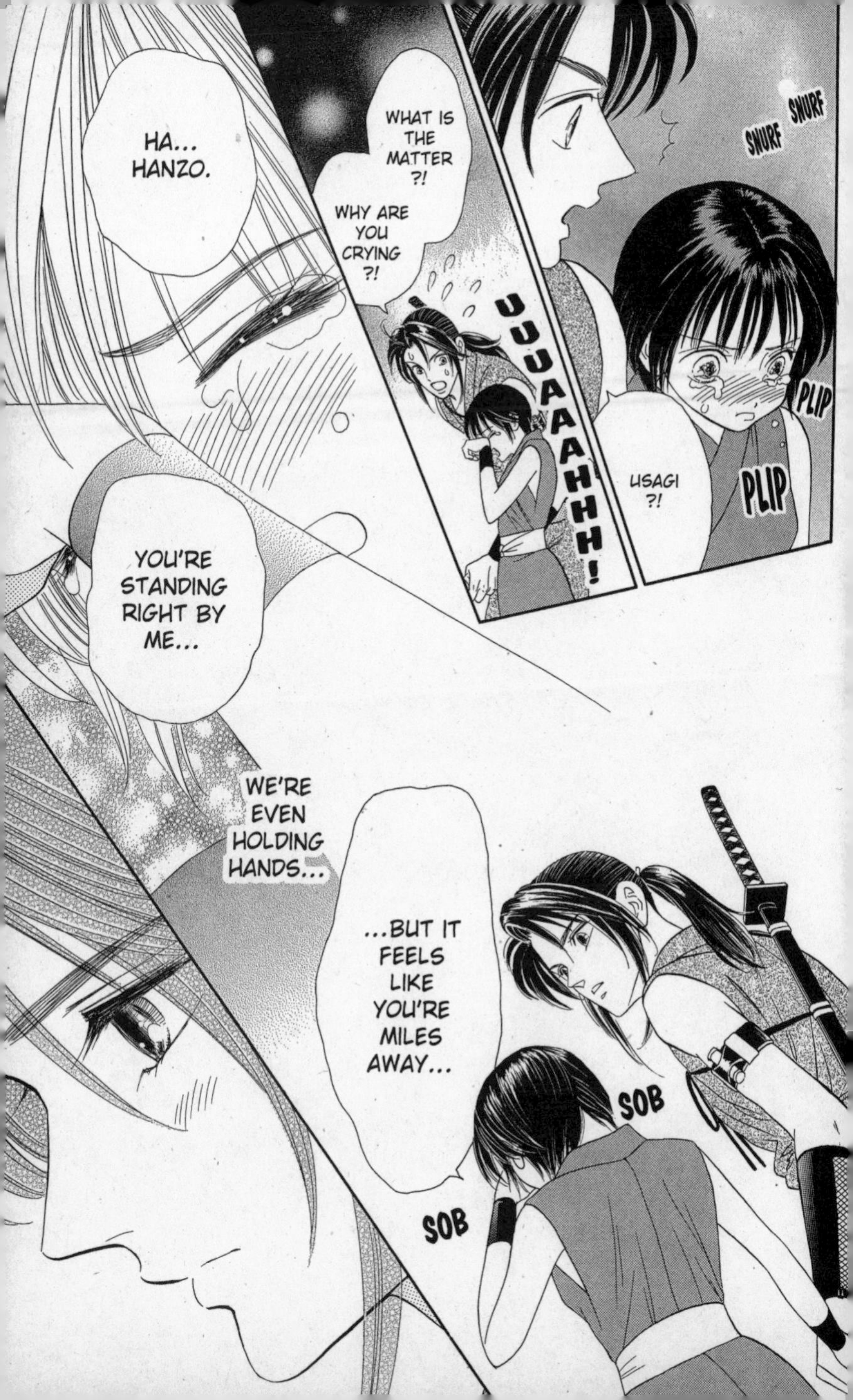
SNURF SNURF
PLIP
PLIP
USAGI ?!
WHAT IS THE MATTER ?!
WHY ARE YOU CRYING ?!
UUUAAAHHH!
HA... HANZO.
YOU'RE STANDING RIGHT BY ME...
WE'RE EVEN HOLDING HANDS...
...BUT IT FEELS LIKE YOU'RE MILES AWAY...
SOB
SOB

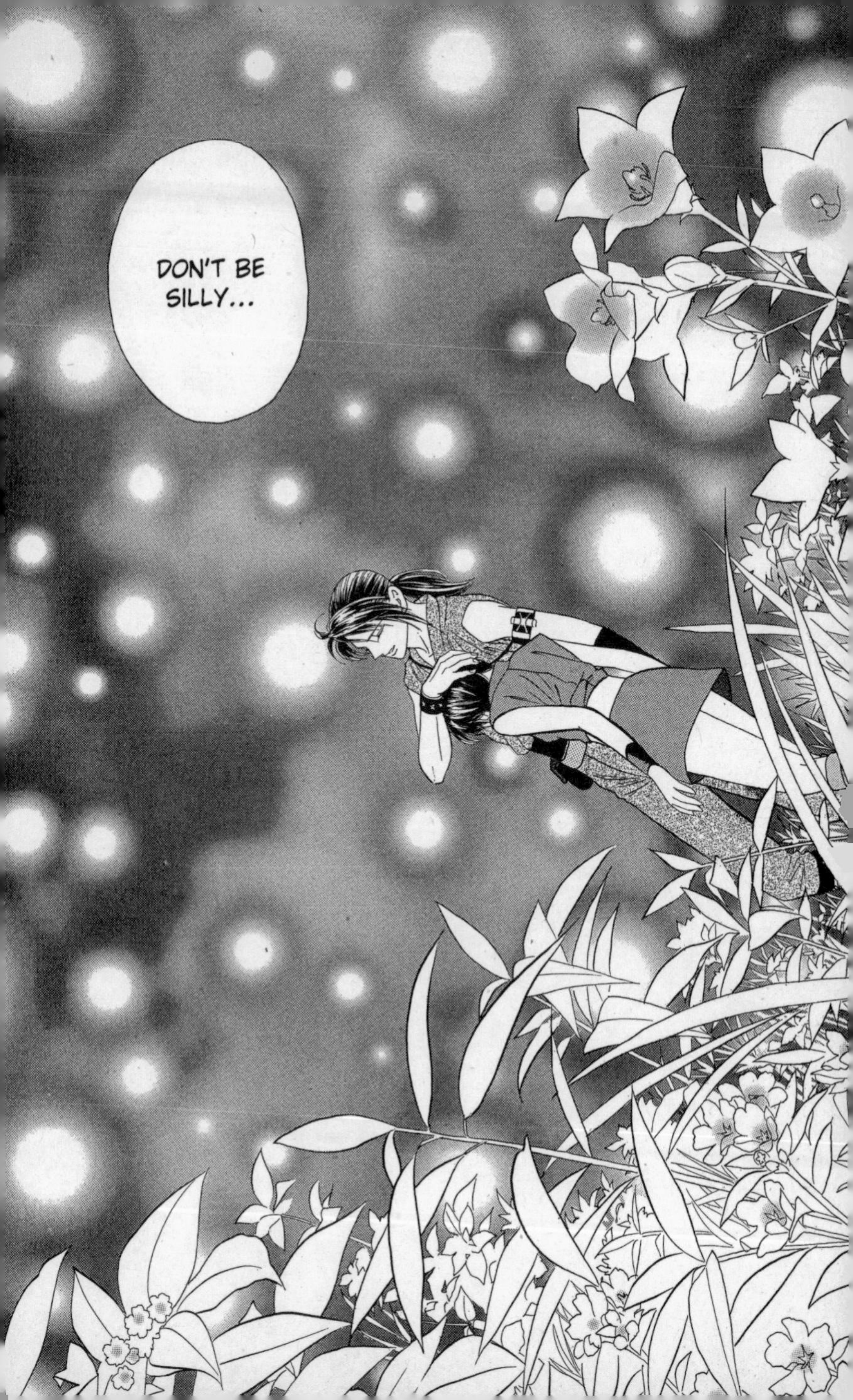
DON'T BE SILLY...

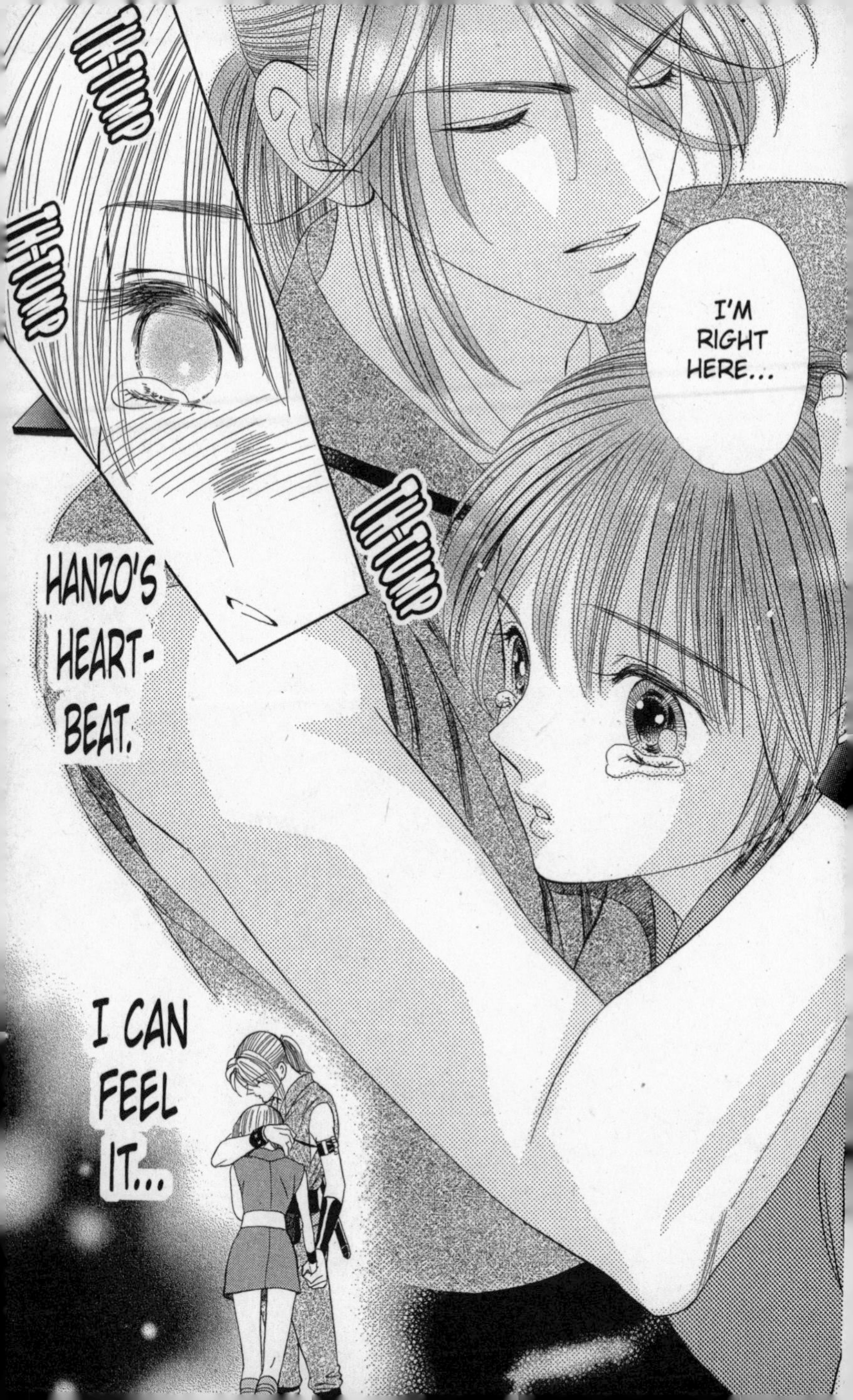
I'M RIGHT HERE...
TH-THUMP
TH-THUMP
TH-THUMP
HANZO'S HEART-BEAT.
I CAN FEEL IT...

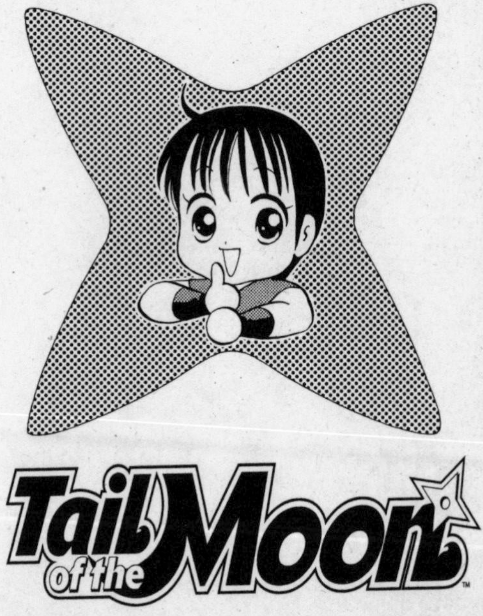

Tail of the Moon™

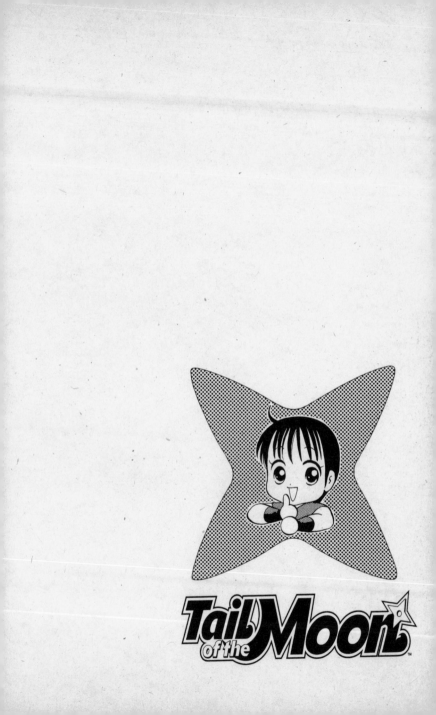

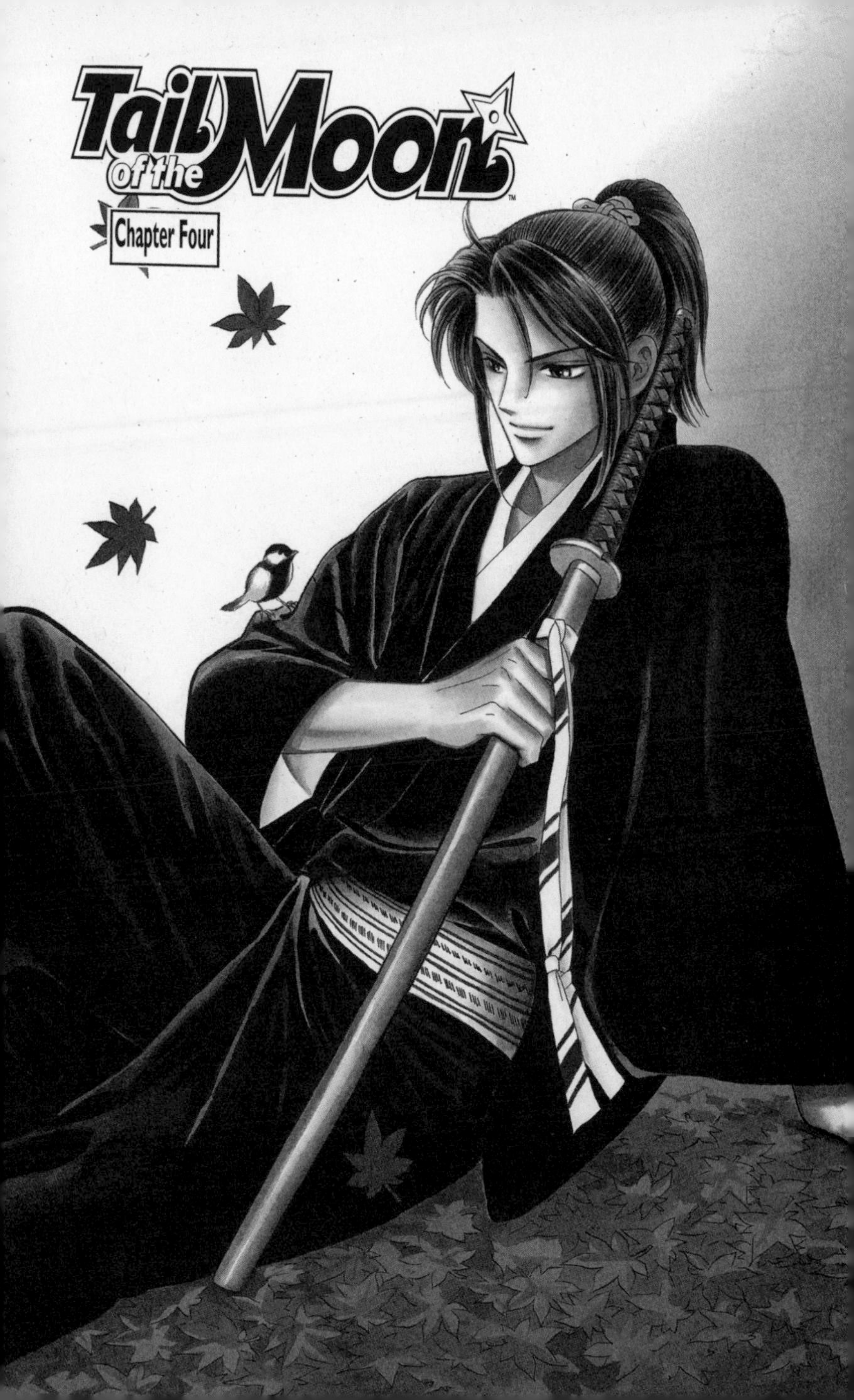
Tail of the Moon™
Chapter Four

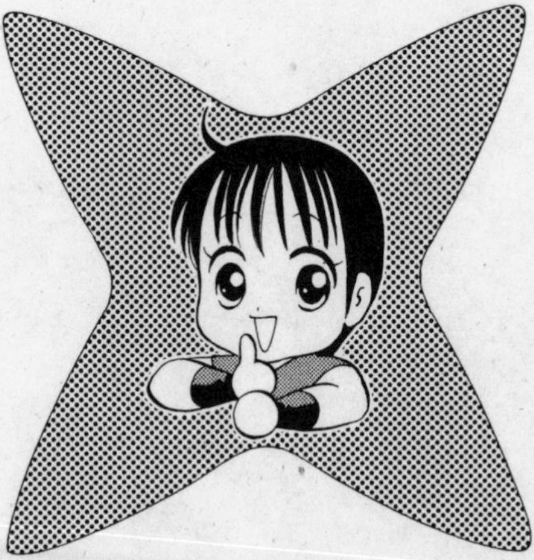

Tail of the Moon™

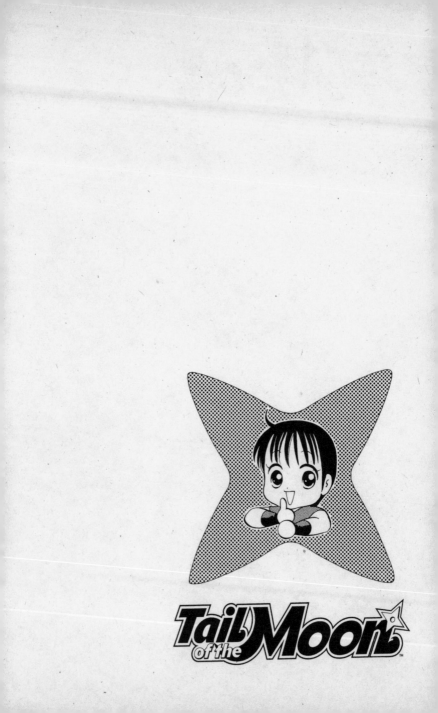

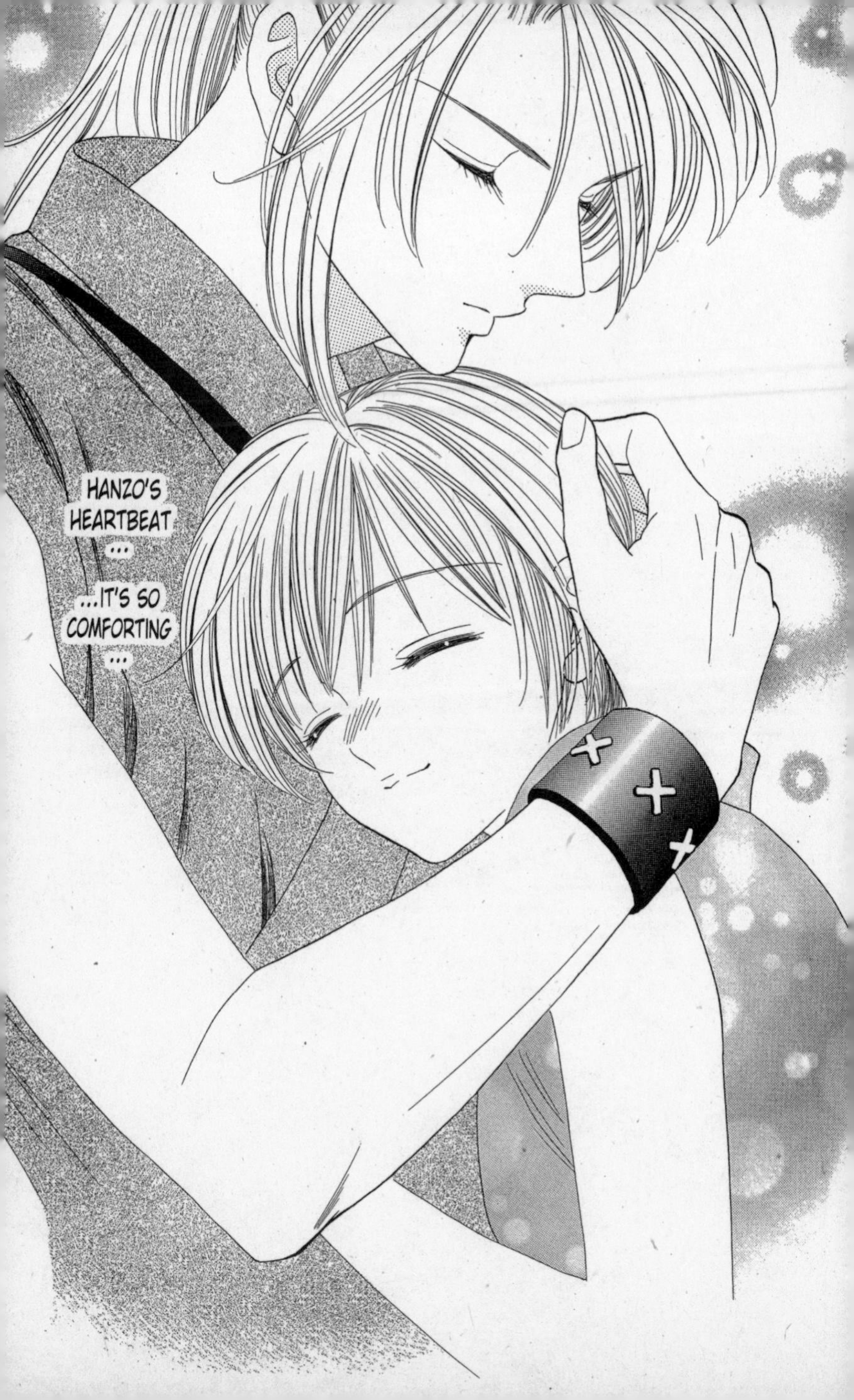
HANZO'S HEARTBEAT ...
...IT'S SO COMFORTING ...

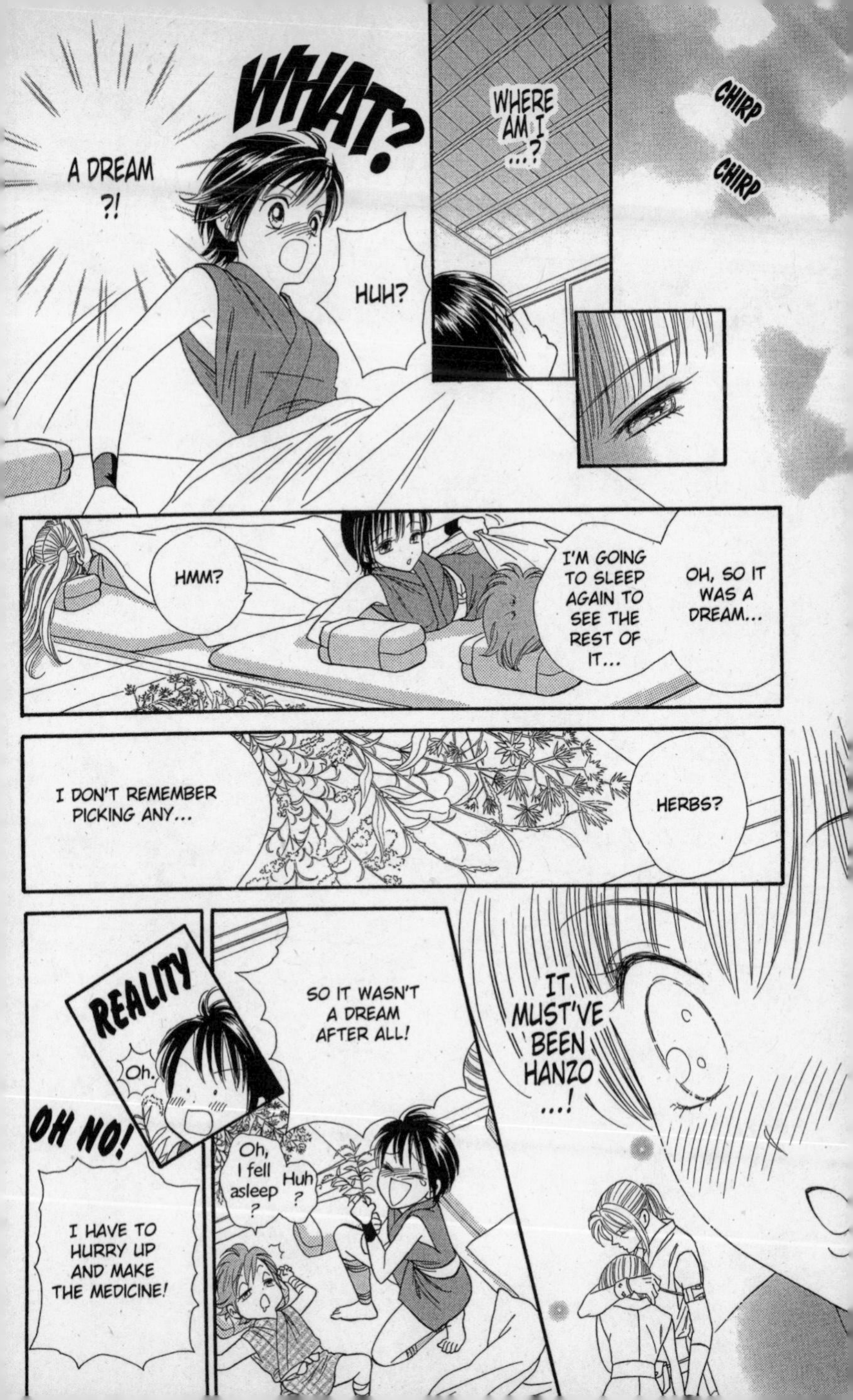

CHIRP
CHIRP
WHERE AM I ...?
WHAT?
A DREAM ?!
HUH?
OH, SO IT WAS A DREAM...
I'M GOING TO SLEEP AGAIN TO SEE THE REST OF IT...
HMM?
HERBS?
I DON'T REMEMBER PICKING ANY...
IT MUST'VE BEEN HANZO ...!
SO IT WASN'T A DREAM AFTER ALL!
Huh?
Oh, I fell asleep?
REALITY
Oh.
OH NO!
I HAVE TO HURRY UP AND MAKE THE MEDICINE!

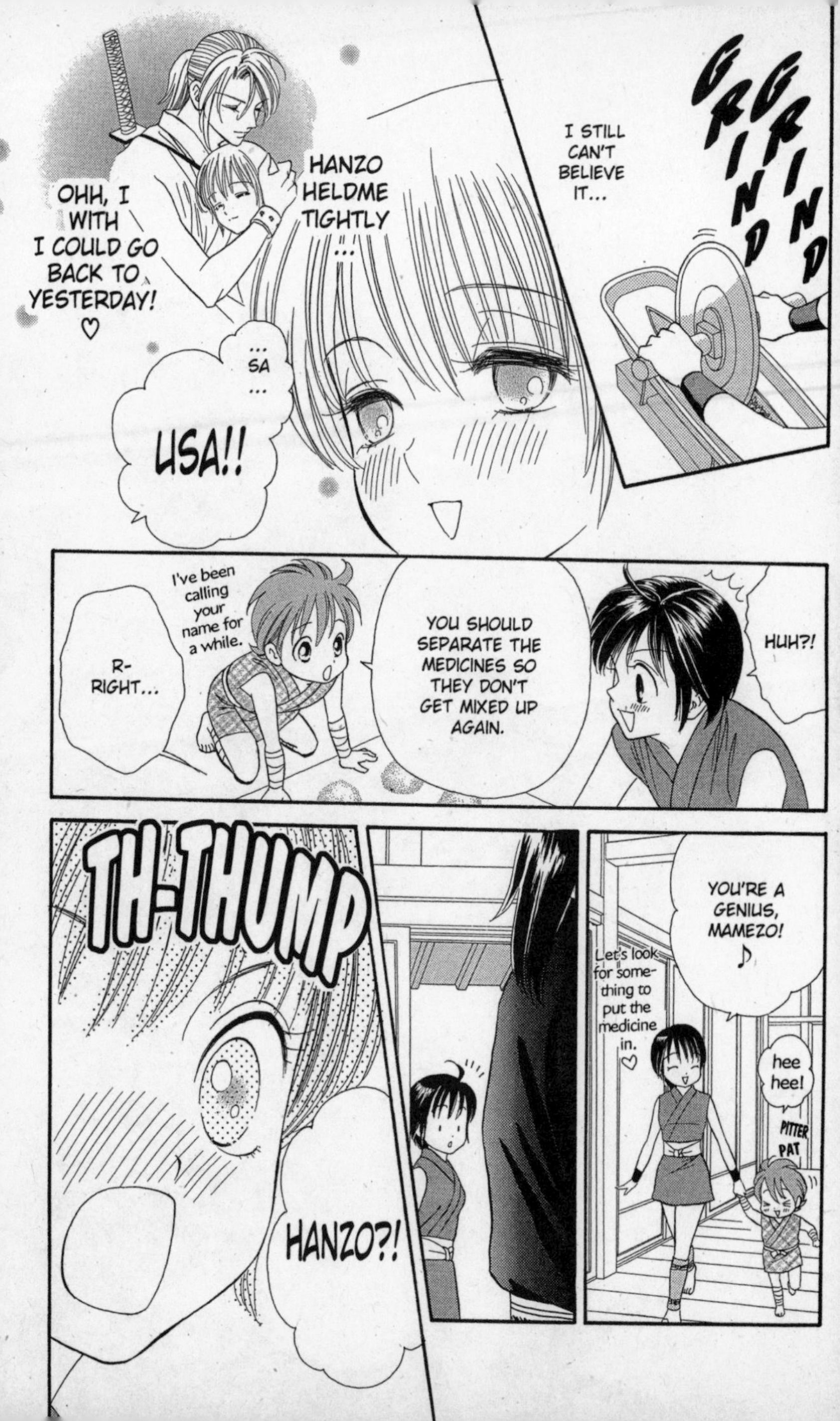
GRIND GRIND
I STILL CAN'T BELIEVE IT...
HANZO HELDME TIGHTLY ...
OHH, I WITH I COULD GO BACK TO YESTERDAY! ♡
... SA ...
USA!!
HUH?!
YOU SHOULD SEPARATE THE MEDICINES SO THEY DON'T GET MIXED UP AGAIN.
I've been calling your name for a while.
R-RIGHT...
YOU'RE A GENIUS, MAMEZO! ♪
Let's look for something to put the medicine in. ♡
hee hee!
PITTER PAT
TH-THUMP
HANZO?!

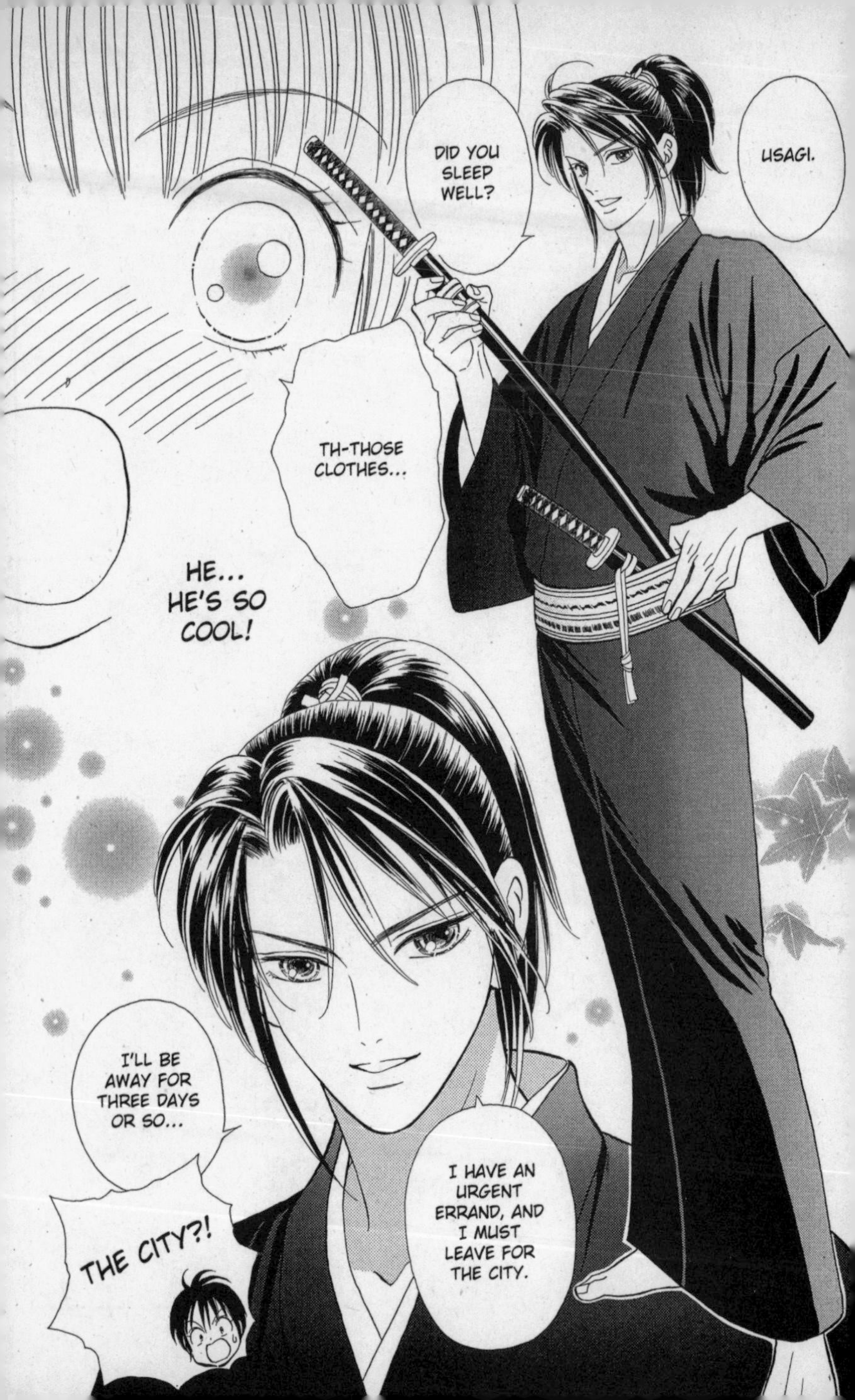
USAGI.
DID YOU SLEEP WELL?
TH-THOSE CLOTHES...
HE... HE'S SO COOL!
I HAVE AN URGENT ERRAND, AND I MUST LEAVE FOR THE CITY.
I'LL BE AWAY FOR THREE DAYS OR SO...
THE CITY?!

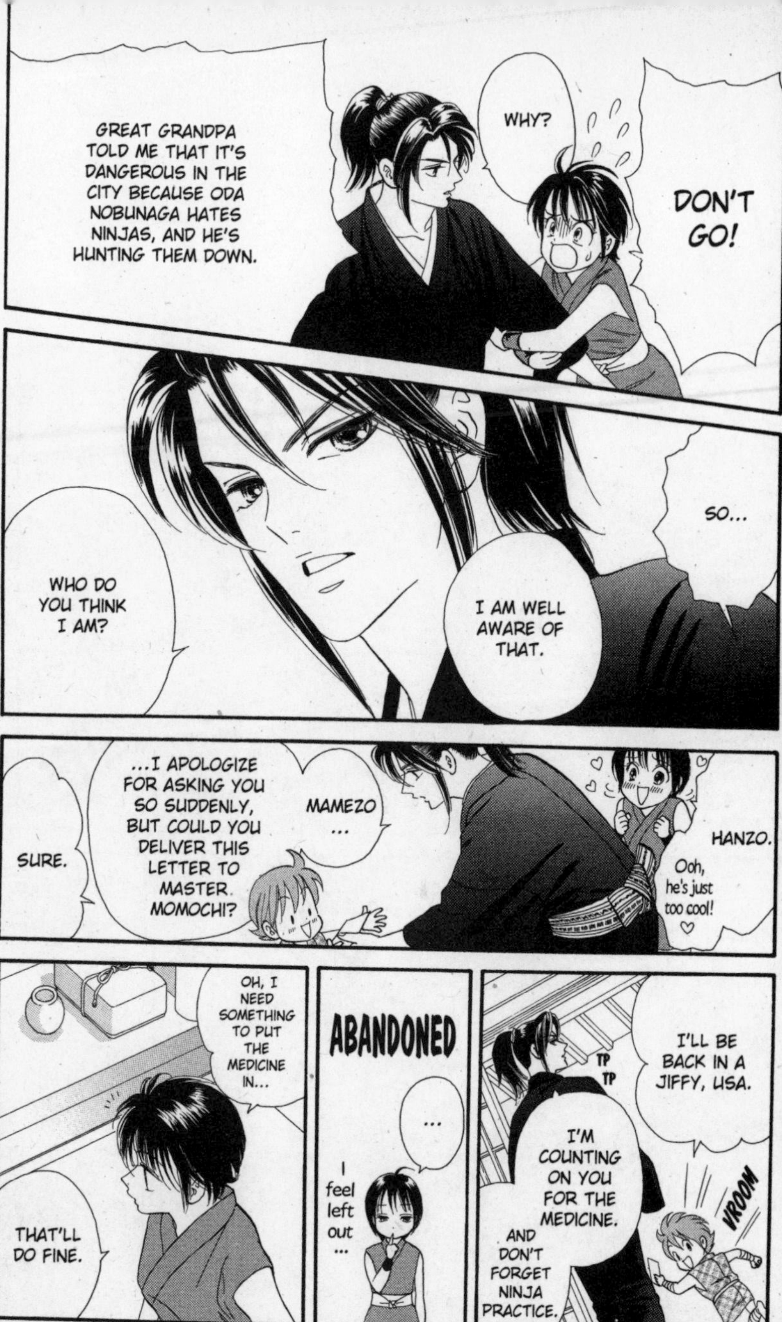

DON'T GO!
WHY?
GREAT GRANDPA TOLD ME THAT IT'S DANGEROUS IN THE CITY BECAUSE ODA NOBUNAGA HATES NINJAS, AND HE'S HUNTING THEM DOWN.
SO...
I AM WELL AWARE OF THAT.
WHO DO YOU THINK I AM?
HANZO.
Ooh, he's just too cool! ♡
MAMEZO...
...I APOLOGIZE FOR ASKING YOU SO SUDDENLY, BUT COULD YOU DELIVER THIS LETTER TO MASTER MOMOCHI?
SURE.
I'LL BE BACK IN A JIFFY, USA.
TP TP
I'M COUNTING ON YOU FOR THE MEDICINE.
AND DON'T FORGET NINJA PRACTICE.
VROOM
ABANDONED
...
I feel left out...
OH, I NEED SOMETHING TO PUT THE MEDICINE IN...
THAT'LL DO FINE.

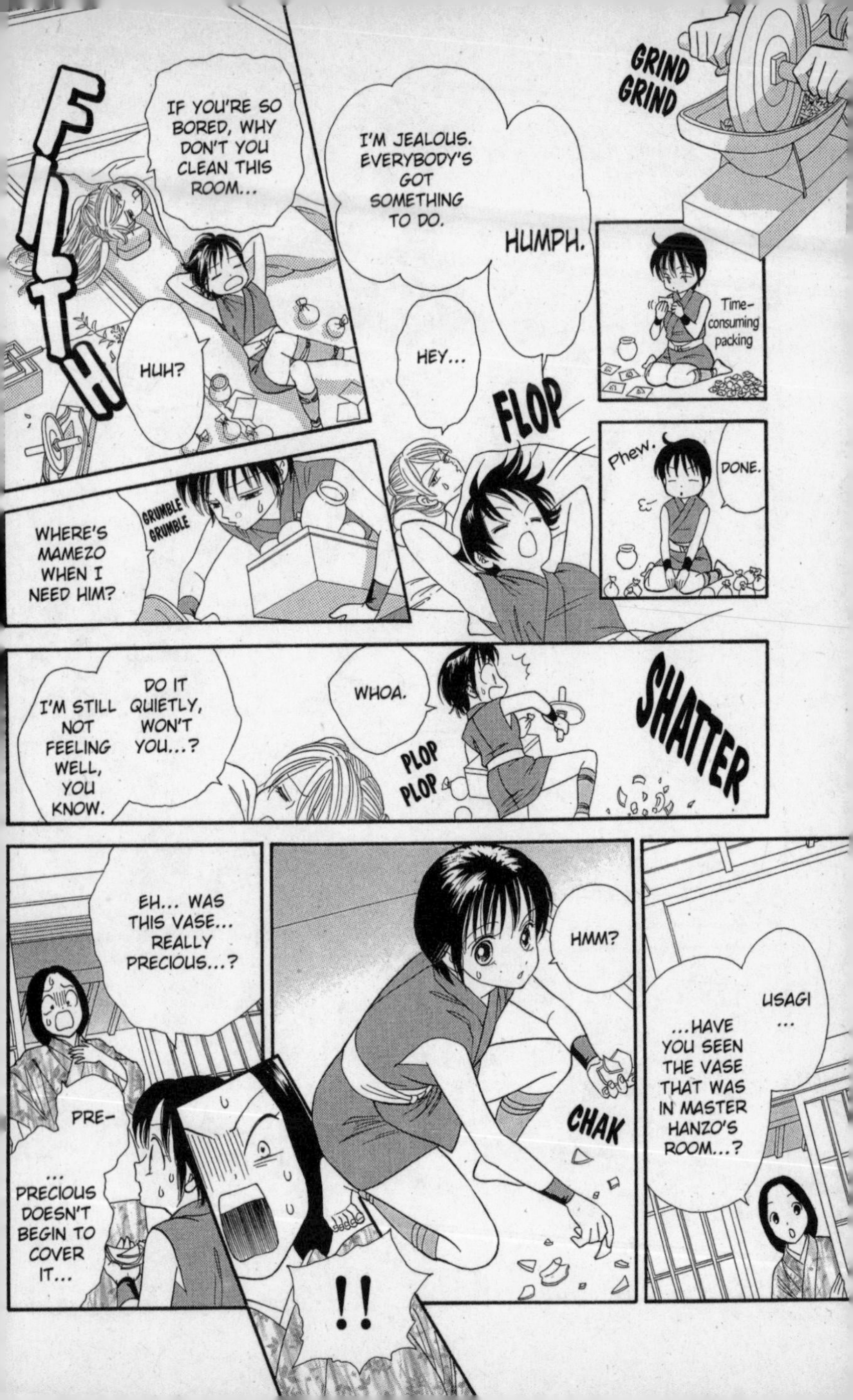
GRIND GRIND
Time-consuming packing
Phew.
DONE.
I'M JEALOUS. EVERYBODY'S GOT SOMETHING TO DO.
HUMPH.
HEY...
FLOP
IF YOU'RE SO BORED, WHY DON'T YOU CLEAN THIS ROOM...
HUH?
FILTH
GRUMBLE GRUMBLE
WHERE'S MAMEZO WHEN I NEED HIM?
SHATTER
WHOA.
PLOP PLOP
DO IT QUIETLY, WON'T YOU...?
I'M STILL NOT FEELING WELL, YOU KNOW.
USAGI...
...HAVE YOU SEEN THE VASE THAT WAS IN MASTER HANZO'S ROOM...?
HMM?
CHAK
EH... WAS THIS VASE... REALLY PRECIOUS...?
PRE-
...PRECIOUS DOESN'T BEGIN TO COVER IT...
!!

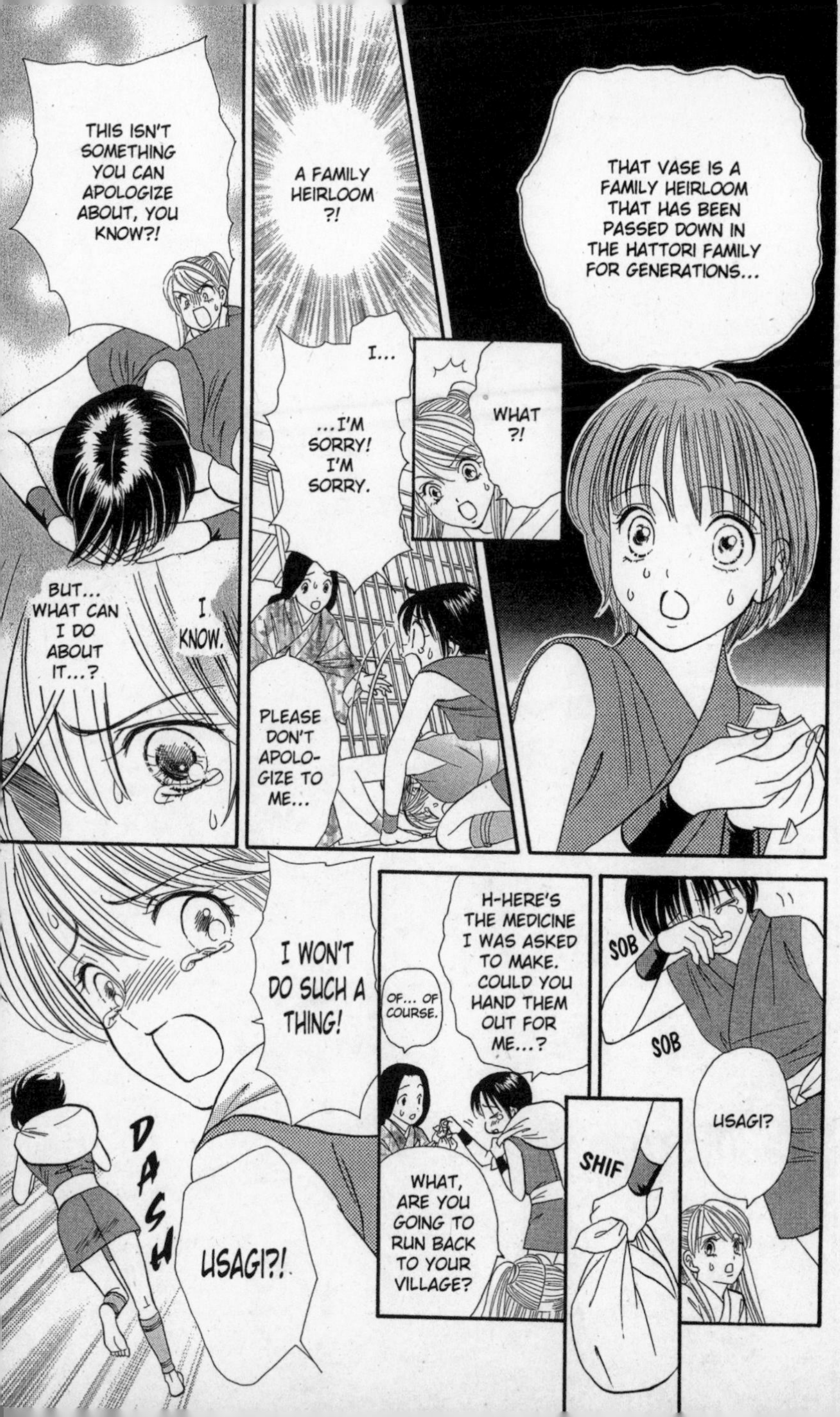
THAT VASE IS A FAMILY HEIRLOOM THAT HAS BEEN PASSED DOWN IN THE HATTORI FAMILY FOR GENERATIONS...
WHAT ?!
A FAMILY HEIRLOOM ?!
I...
...I'M SORRY! I'M SORRY.
PLEASE DON'T APOLOGIZE TO ME...
THIS ISN'T SOMETHING YOU CAN APOLOGIZE ABOUT, YOU KNOW?!
I KNOW.
BUT... WHAT CAN I DO ABOUT IT...?
SOB
SOB
USAGI?
SHIF
H-HERE'S THE MEDICINE I WAS ASKED TO MAKE. COULD YOU HAND THEM OUT FOR ME...?
OF... OF COURSE.
WHAT, ARE YOU GOING TO RUN BACK TO YOUR VILLAGE?
I WON'T DO SUCH A THING!
DASH
USAGI?!

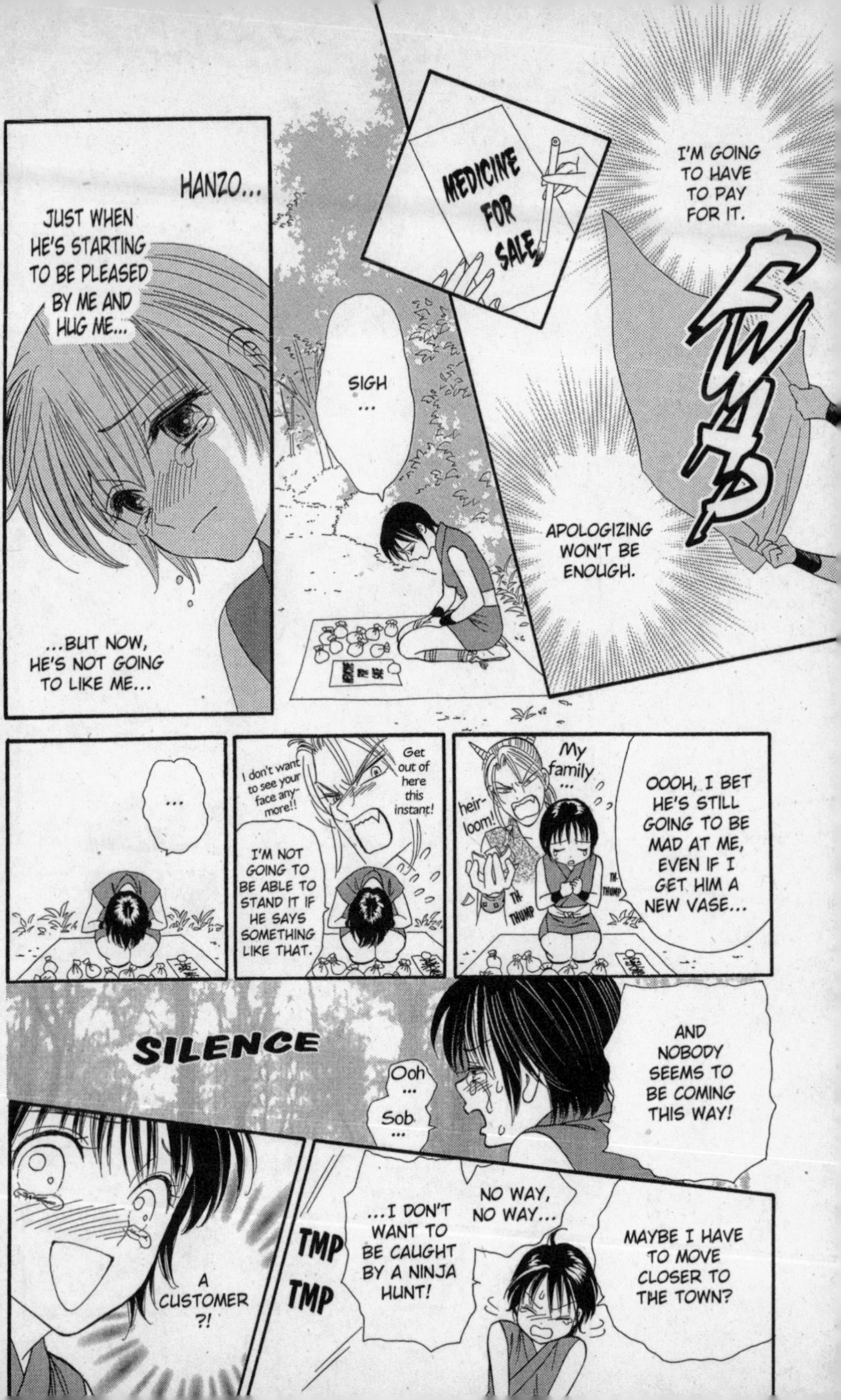
MEDICINE FOR SALE
I'M GOING TO HAVE TO PAY FOR IT.
WHAP
APOLOGIZING WON'T BE ENOUGH.
SIGH ...
HANZO...
JUST WHEN HE'S STARTING TO BE PLEASED BY ME AND HUG ME...
...BUT NOW, HE'S NOT GOING TO LIKE ME...
OOOH, I BET HE'S STILL GOING TO BE MAD AT ME, EVEN IF I GET HIM A NEW VASE...
My family ...
heir-loom!
TH-THUMP
TH-THUMP
Get out of here this instant!
I don't want to see your face any-more!!
I'M NOT GOING TO BE ABLE TO STAND IT IF HE SAYS SOMETHING LIKE THAT.
...
AND NOBODY SEEMS TO BE COMING THIS WAY!
Ooh ...
Sob ...
SILENCE
MAYBE I HAVE TO MOVE CLOSER TO THE TOWN?
NO WAY, NO WAY...
...I DON'T WANT TO BE CAUGHT BY A NINJA HUNT!
TMP
TMP
A CUSTOMER ?!

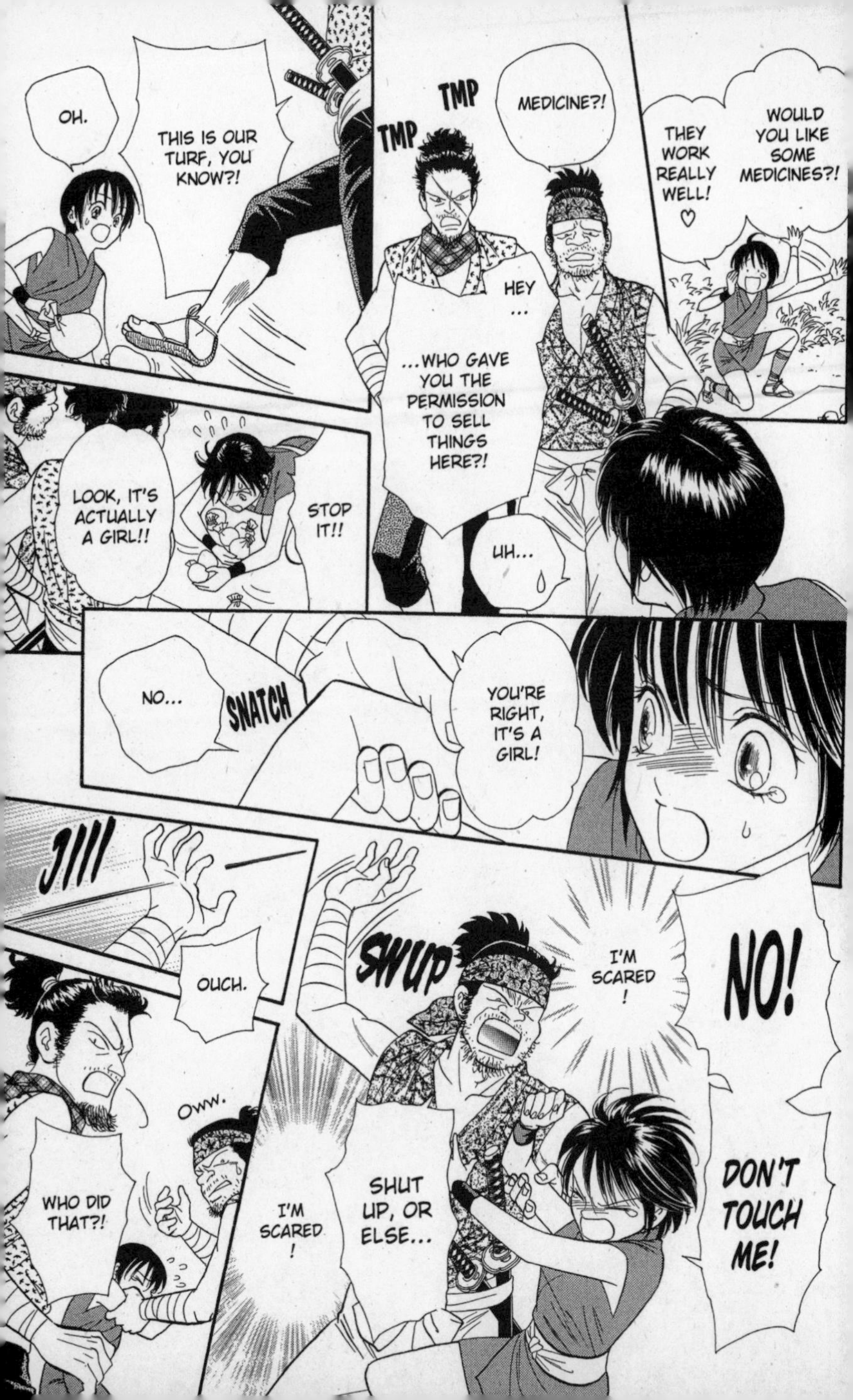
WOULD YOU LIKE SOME MEDICINES?!
THEY WORK REALLY WELL! ♡
TMP
TMP
MEDICINE?!
HEY ...
...WHO GAVE YOU THE PERMISSION TO SELL THINGS HERE?!
UH...
THIS IS OUR TURF, YOU KNOW?!
OH.
STOP IT!!
LOOK, IT'S ACTUALLY A GIRL!!
YOU'RE RIGHT, IT'S A GIRL!
SNATCH
NO...
NO!
I'M SCARED!
DON'T TOUCH ME!
SWUP
SHUT UP, OR ELSE...
I'M SCARED!
JI!!
OUCH.
OWW.
WHO DID THAT?!

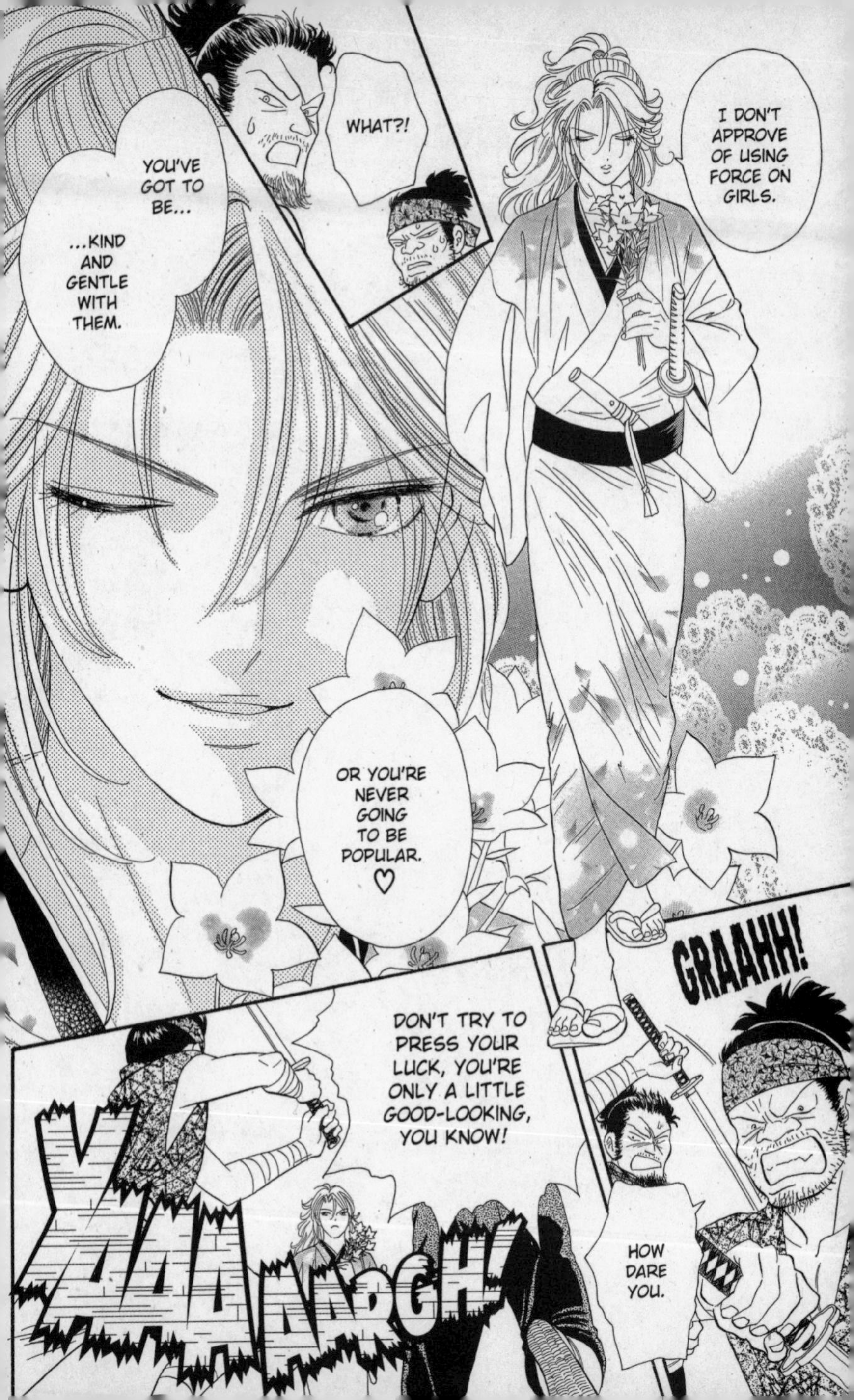
I DON'T APPROVE OF USING FORCE ON GIRLS.
WHAT?!
YOU'VE GOT TO BE...
...KIND AND GENTLE WITH THEM.
OR YOU'RE NEVER GOING TO BE POPULAR. ♡
GRAAHH!
HOW DARE YOU.
DON'T TRY TO PRESS YOUR LUCK, YOU'RE ONLY A LITTLE GOOD-LOOKING, YOU KNOW!

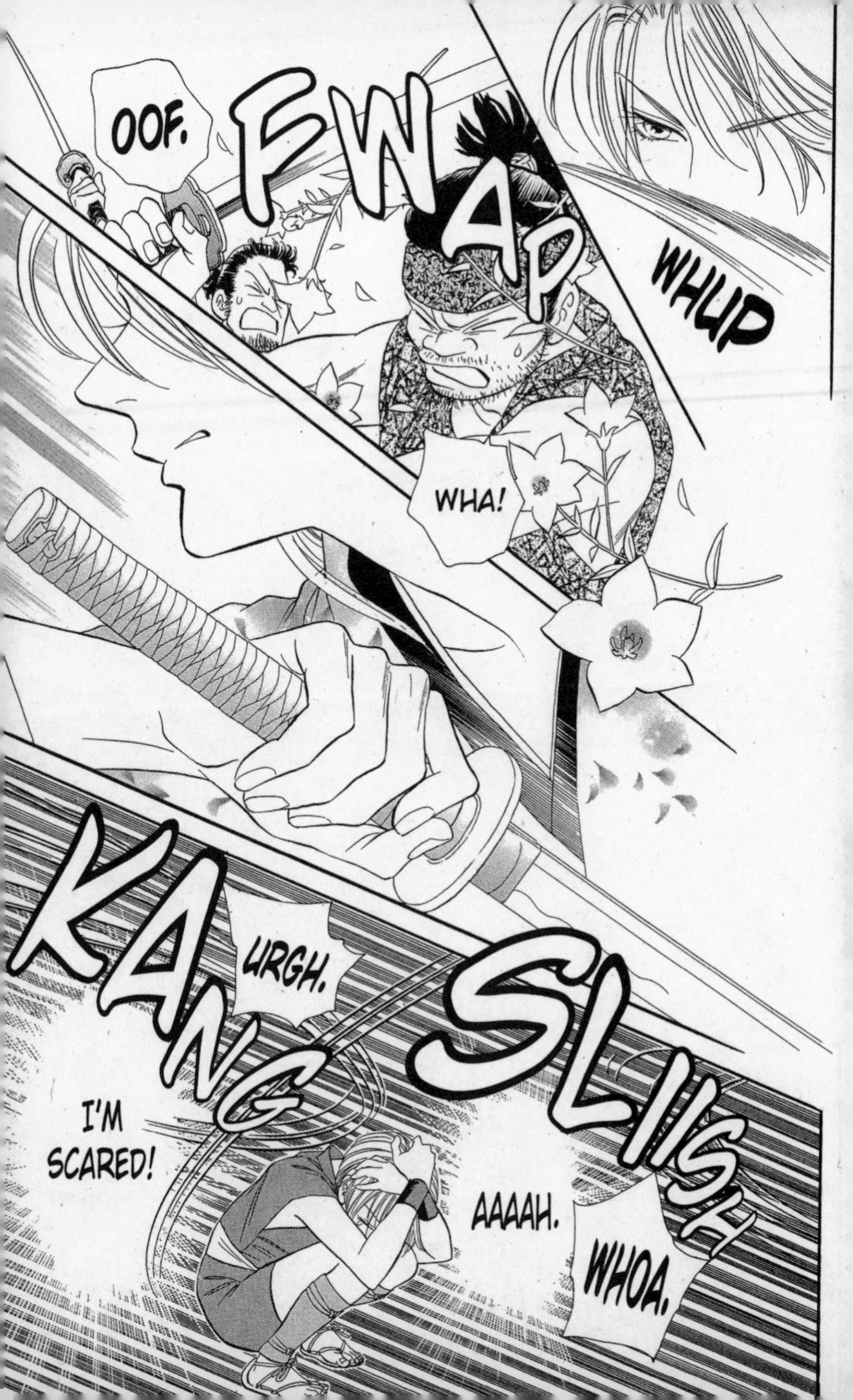
WHUP
FWAP
OOF.
WHA!
SLIISH
KANG
URGH.
AAAAH.
WHOA.
I'M SCARED!

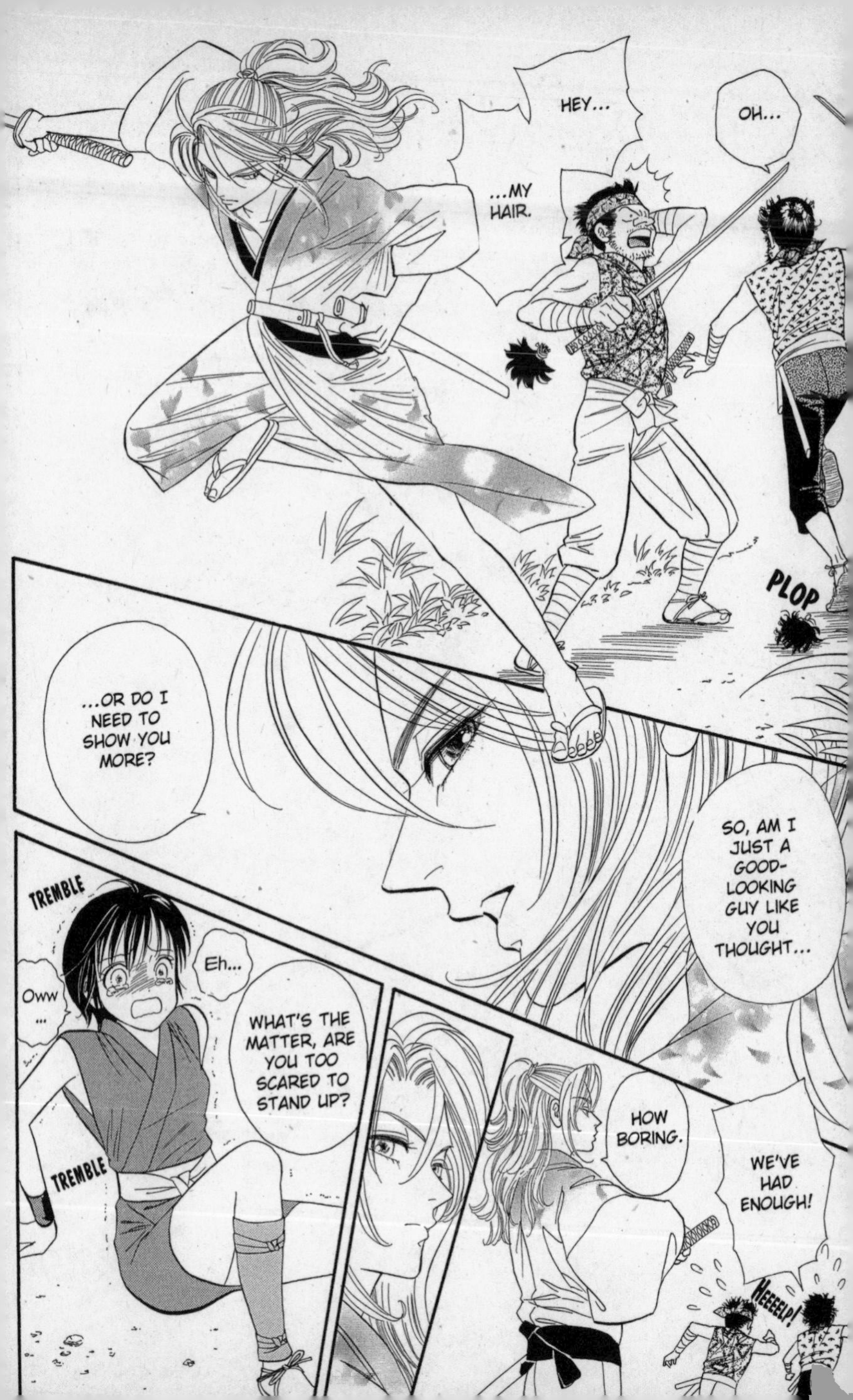
OH...
HEY...
...MY HAIR.
PLOP
SO, AM I JUST A GOOD-LOOKING GUY LIKE YOU THOUGHT...
...OR DO I NEED TO SHOW YOU MORE?
WE'VE HAD ENOUGH!
HEEEELP!
HOW BORING.
WHAT'S THE MATTER, ARE YOU TOO SCARED TO STAND UP?
Eh...
TREMBLE
Oww ...
TREMBLE

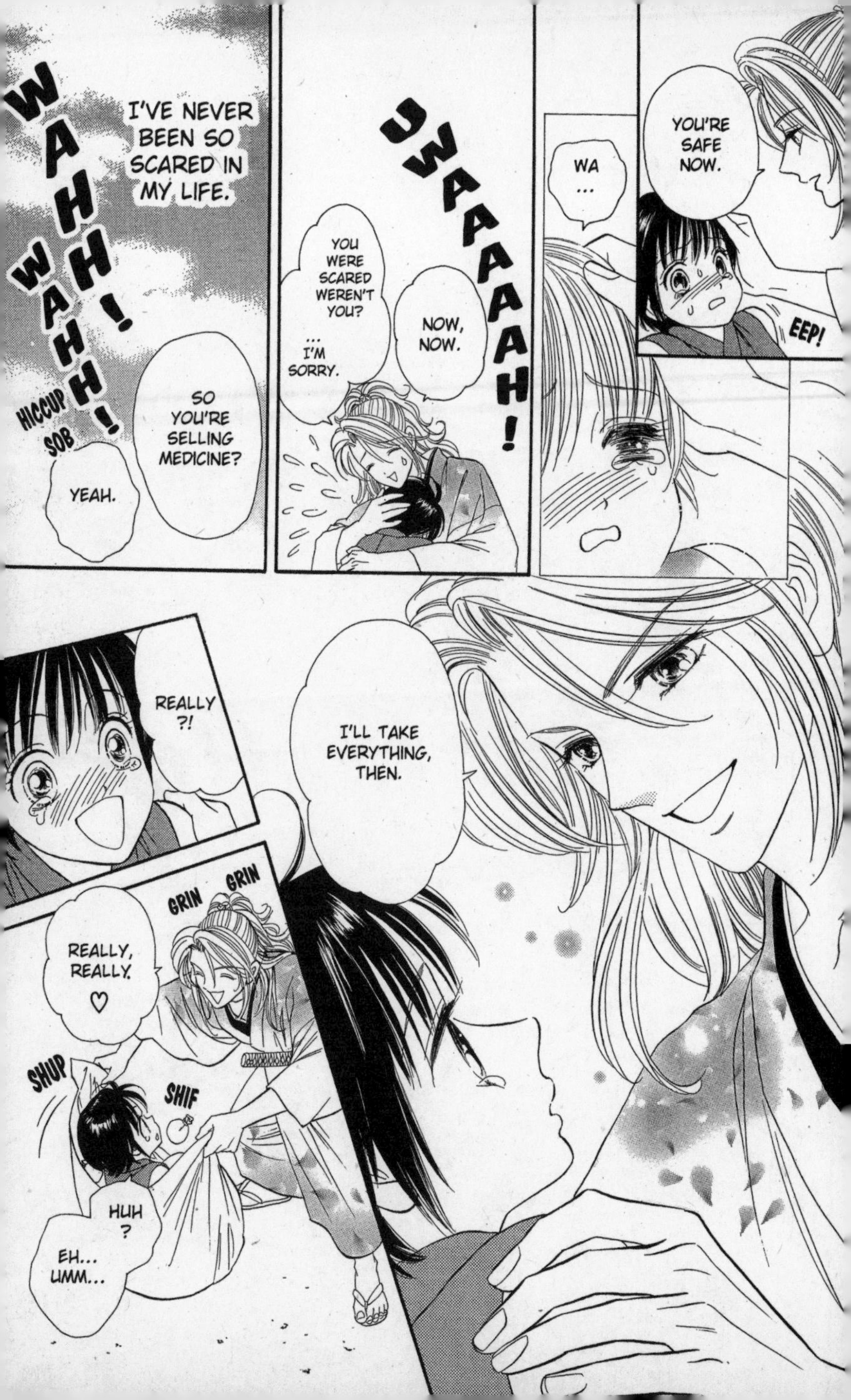
YOU'RE SAFE NOW.
EEP!
WA ...
UWAAAAAH!
NOW, NOW.
YOU WERE SCARED WEREN'T YOU?
... I'M SORRY.
WAHH! WAHH!
I'VE NEVER BEEN SO SCARED IN MY LIFE.
SO YOU'RE SELLING MEDICINE?
HICCUP
SOB
YEAH.
I'LL TAKE EVERYTHING, THEN.
REALLY ?!
GRIN GRIN
REALLY, REALLY. ♡
SHUP
SHIF
HUH ?
EH... UMM...

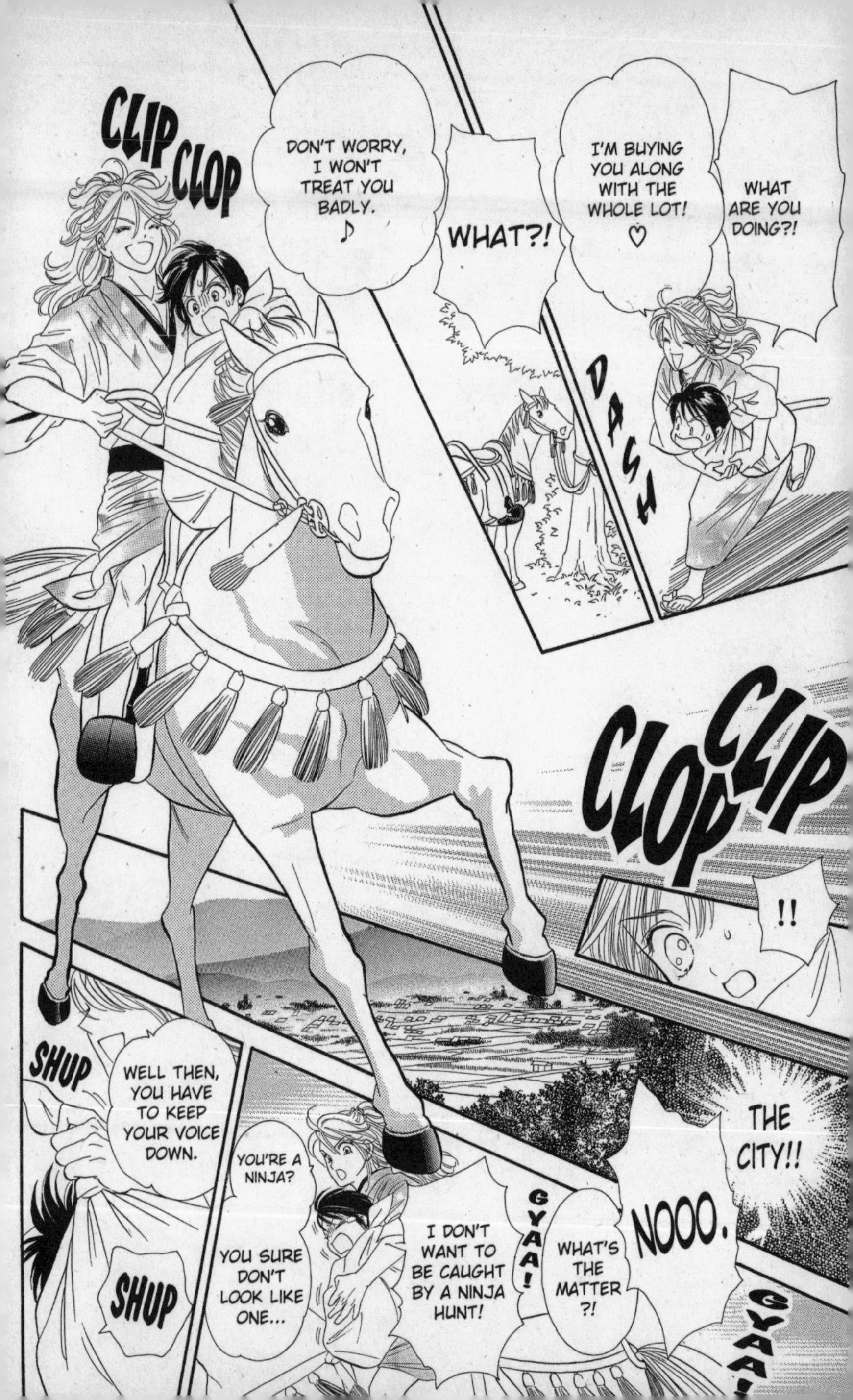
WHAT ARE YOU DOING?!
I'M BUYING YOU ALONG WITH THE WHOLE LOT! ♡
DASH
WHAT?!
DON'T WORRY, I WON'T TREAT YOU BADLY. ♪
CLIP CLOP
CLIP CLOP
!!
THE CITY!!
NOOO.
GYAAA!
WHAT'S THE MATTER?!
GYAAA!
I DON'T WANT TO BE CAUGHT BY A NINJA HUNT!
YOU'RE A NINJA?
YOU SURE DON'T LOOK LIKE ONE...
WELL THEN, YOU HAVE TO KEEP YOUR VOICE DOWN.
SHUP
SHUP

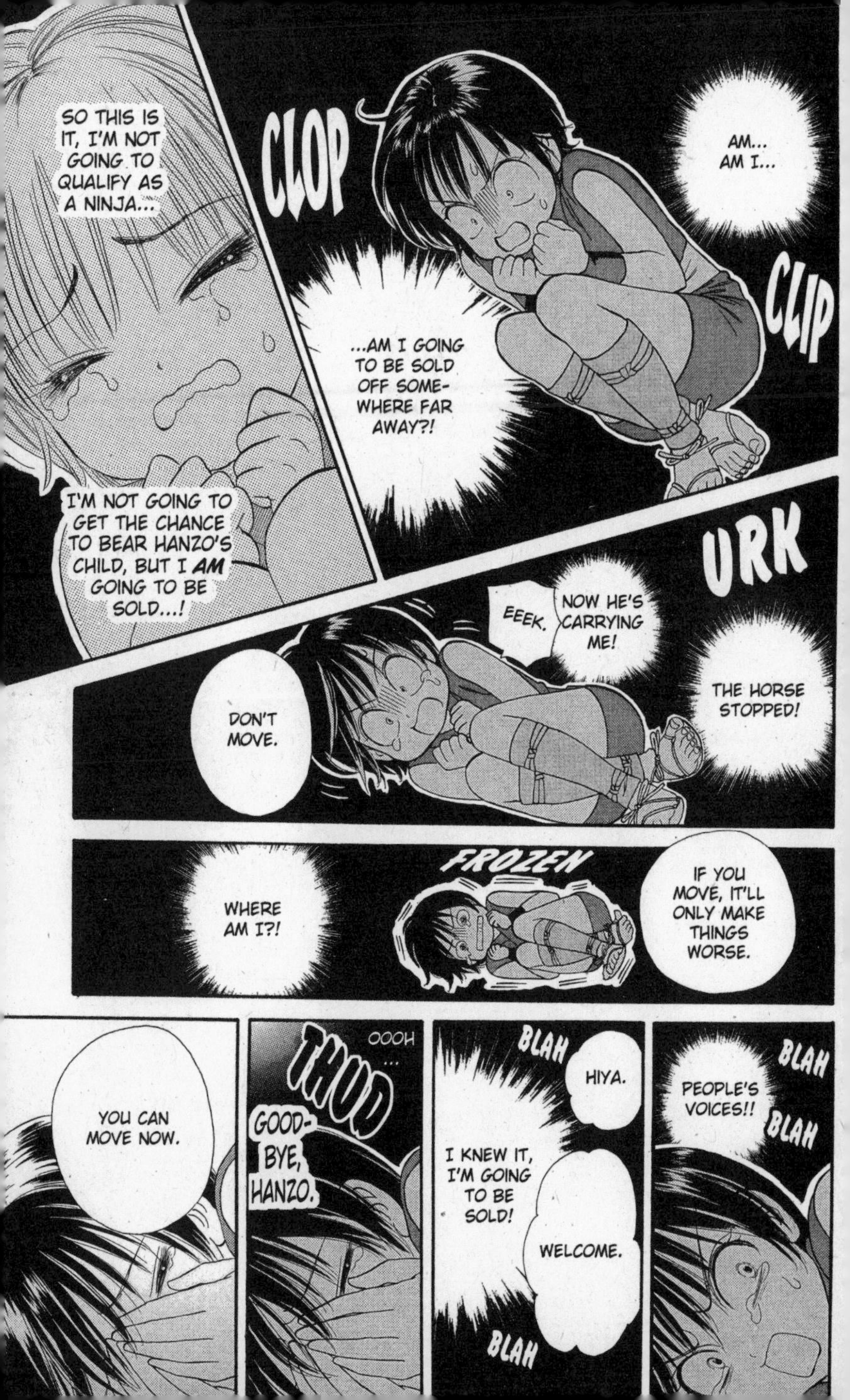
AM... AM I...
CLOP
CLIP
...AM I GOING TO BE SOLD OFF SOME-WHERE FAR AWAY?!
SO THIS IS IT, I'M NOT GOING TO QUALIFY AS A NINJA...
I'M NOT GOING TO GET THE CHANCE TO BEAR HANZO'S CHILD, BUT I ***AM*** GOING TO BE SOLD...!
URK
THE HORSE STOPPED!
NOW HE'S CARRYING ME!
EEEK.
DON'T MOVE.
IF YOU MOVE, IT'LL ONLY MAKE THINGS WORSE.
FROZEN
WHERE AM I?!
BLAH
BLAH
PEOPLE'S VOICES!!
BLAH
HIYA.
I KNEW IT, I'M GOING TO BE SOLD!
WELCOME.
BLAH
OOOH ...
THUD
GOOD-BYE, HANZO.
YOU CAN MOVE NOW.

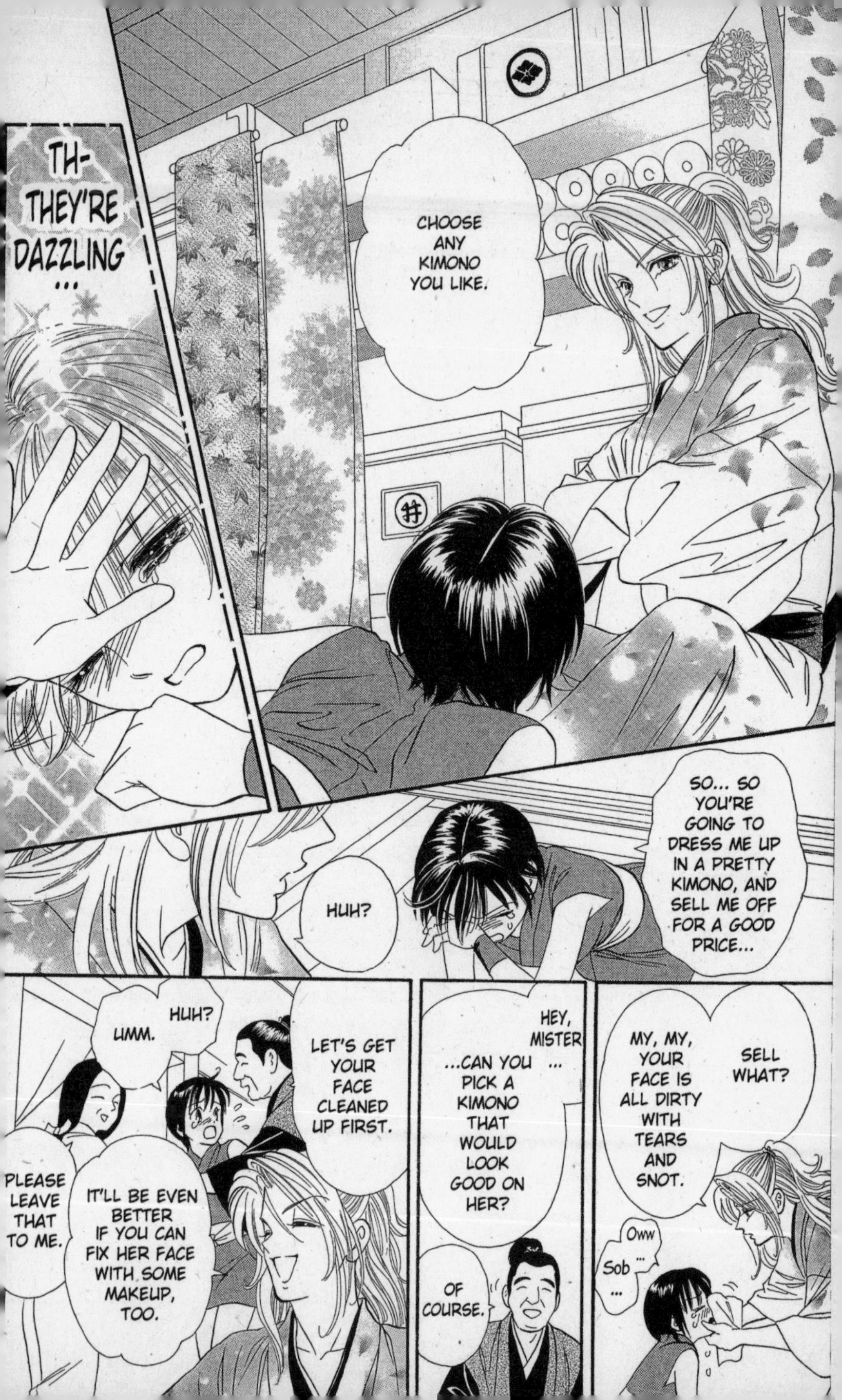
CHOOSE ANY KIMONO YOU LIKE.
TH- THEY'RE DAZZLING...
SO... SO YOU'RE GOING TO DRESS ME UP IN A PRETTY KIMONO, AND SELL ME OFF FOR A GOOD PRICE...
HUH?
SELL WHAT?
MY, MY, YOUR FACE IS ALL DIRTY WITH TEARS AND SNOT.
Oww...
Sob...
HEY, MISTER...
...CAN YOU PICK A KIMONO THAT WOULD LOOK GOOD ON HER?
OF COURSE.
LET'S GET YOUR FACE CLEANED UP FIRST.
HUH?
UMM.
IT'LL BE EVEN BETTER IF YOU CAN FIX HER FACE WITH SOME MAKEUP, TOO.
PLEASE LEAVE THAT TO ME.

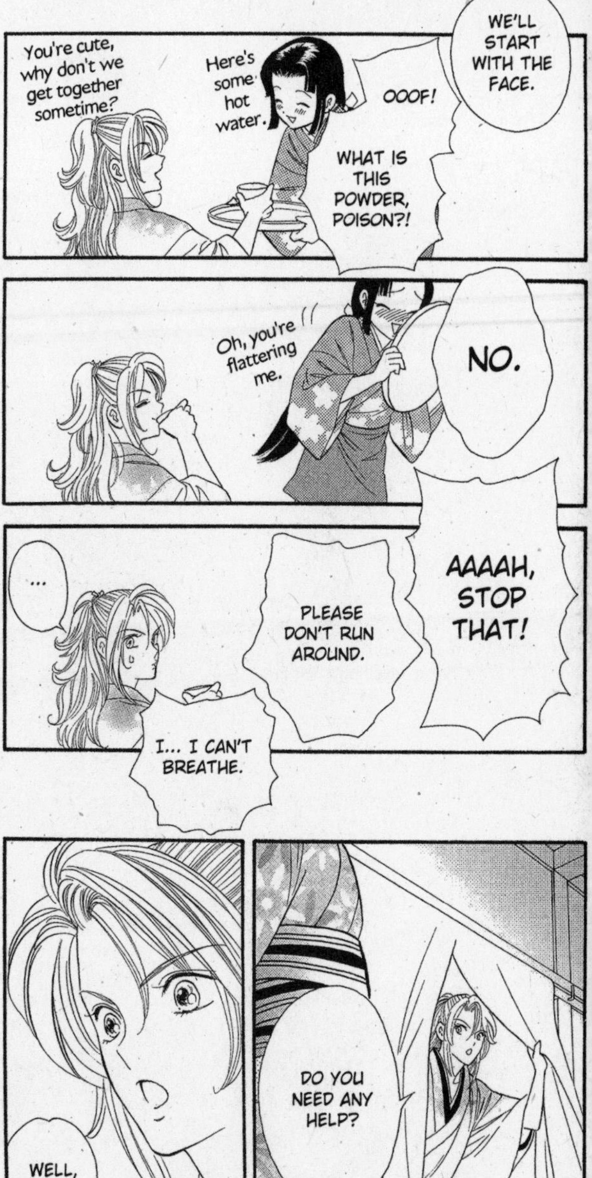
WE'LL START WITH THE FACE.
OOOF!
WHAT IS THIS POWDER, POISON?!
Here's some hot water.
You're cute, why don't we get together sometime?
NO.
Oh, you're flattering me.
AAAAH, STOP THAT!
PLEASE DON'T RUN AROUND.
...
I... I CAN'T BREATHE.
DO YOU NEED ANY HELP?
WELL, WELL.

This and that from the author 4

At the beginning of this series, even I was surprised at how much of a klutz Usagi really was. But the more the story unfolded, the more I began to see the cuteness within her.

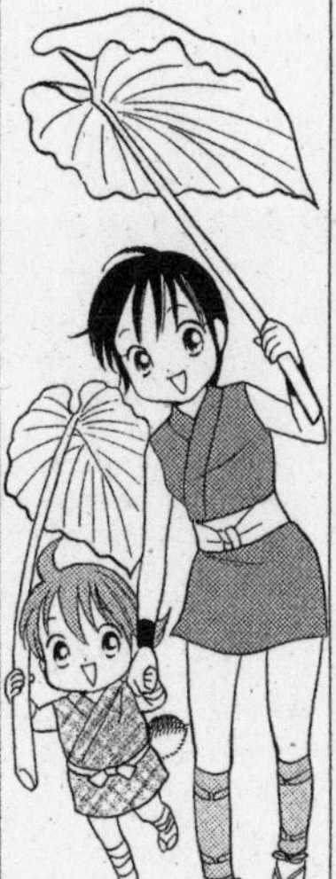

Mamezo and the piglet are cute, friendly characters, and I enjoy drawing them, too.

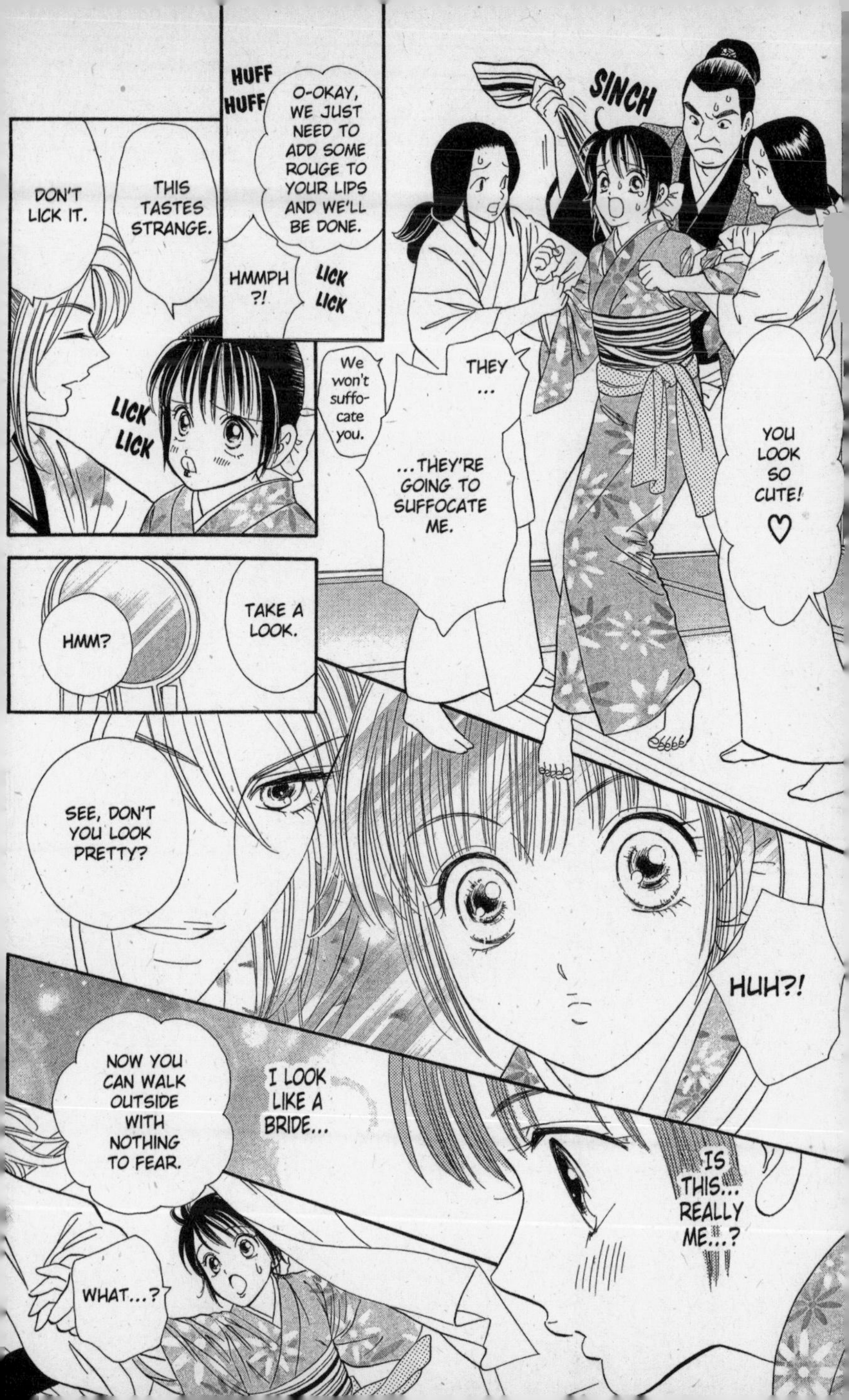
SINCH
YOU LOOK SO CUTE! ♥
THEY...
...THEY'RE GOING TO SUFFOCATE ME.
We won't suffo-cate you.
HUFF HUFF
O-OKAY, WE JUST NEED TO ADD SOME ROUGE TO YOUR LIPS AND WE'LL BE DONE.
LICK LICK
HMMPH ?!
THIS TASTES STRANGE.
DON'T LICK IT.
LICK LICK
TAKE A LOOK.
HMM?
SEE, DON'T YOU LOOK PRETTY?
HUH?!
I LOOK LIKE A BRIDE...
IS THIS... REALLY ME...?
NOW YOU CAN WALK OUTSIDE WITH NOTHING TO FEAR.
WHAT...?

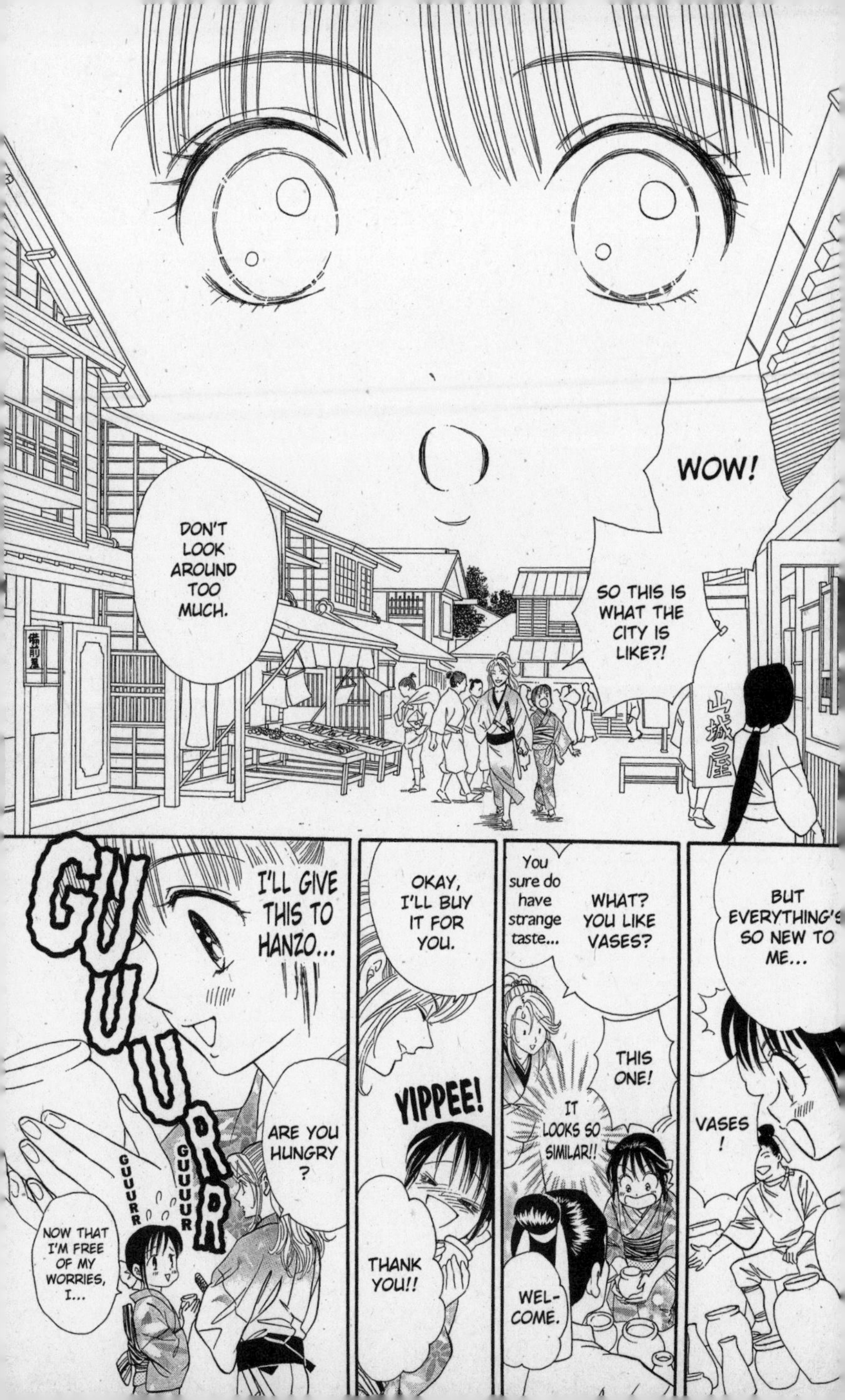
WOW!
SO THIS IS WHAT THE CITY IS LIKE?!
山城屋
DON'T LOOK AROUND TOO MUCH.
備前屋
BUT EVERYTHING'S SO NEW TO ME...
VASES!
WHAT? YOU LIKE VASES?
You sure do have strange taste...
THIS ONE!
IT LOOKS SO SIMILAR!!
WEL-COME.
OKAY, I'LL BUY IT FOR YOU.
YIPPEE!
THANK YOU!!
I'LL GIVE THIS TO HANZO...
GUUURRR
ARE YOU HUNGRY?
GUUUUR
GUUURR
NOW THAT I'M FREE OF MY WORRIES, I...

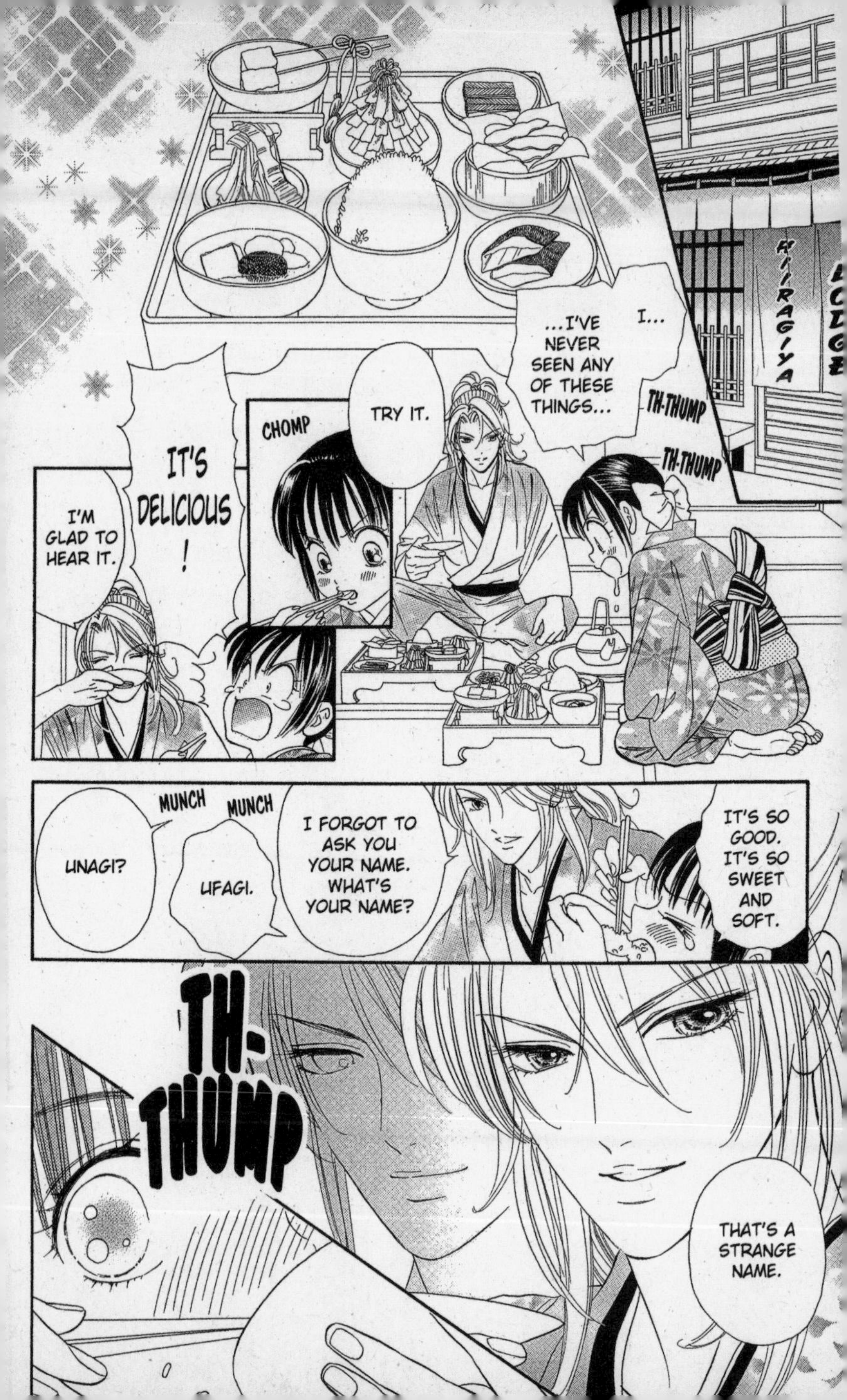

HIIRAGIYA
LODGE
I...
...I'VE NEVER SEEN ANY OF THESE THINGS...
TH-THUMP
TH-THUMP
TRY IT.
CHOMP
IT'S DELICIOUS!
I'M GLAD TO HEAR IT.
IT'S SO GOOD. IT'S SO SWEET AND SOFT.
I FORGOT TO ASK YOU YOUR NAME. WHAT'S YOUR NAME?
MUNCH
MUNCH
UFAGI.
UNAGI?
THAT'S A STRANGE NAME.
TH-THUMP

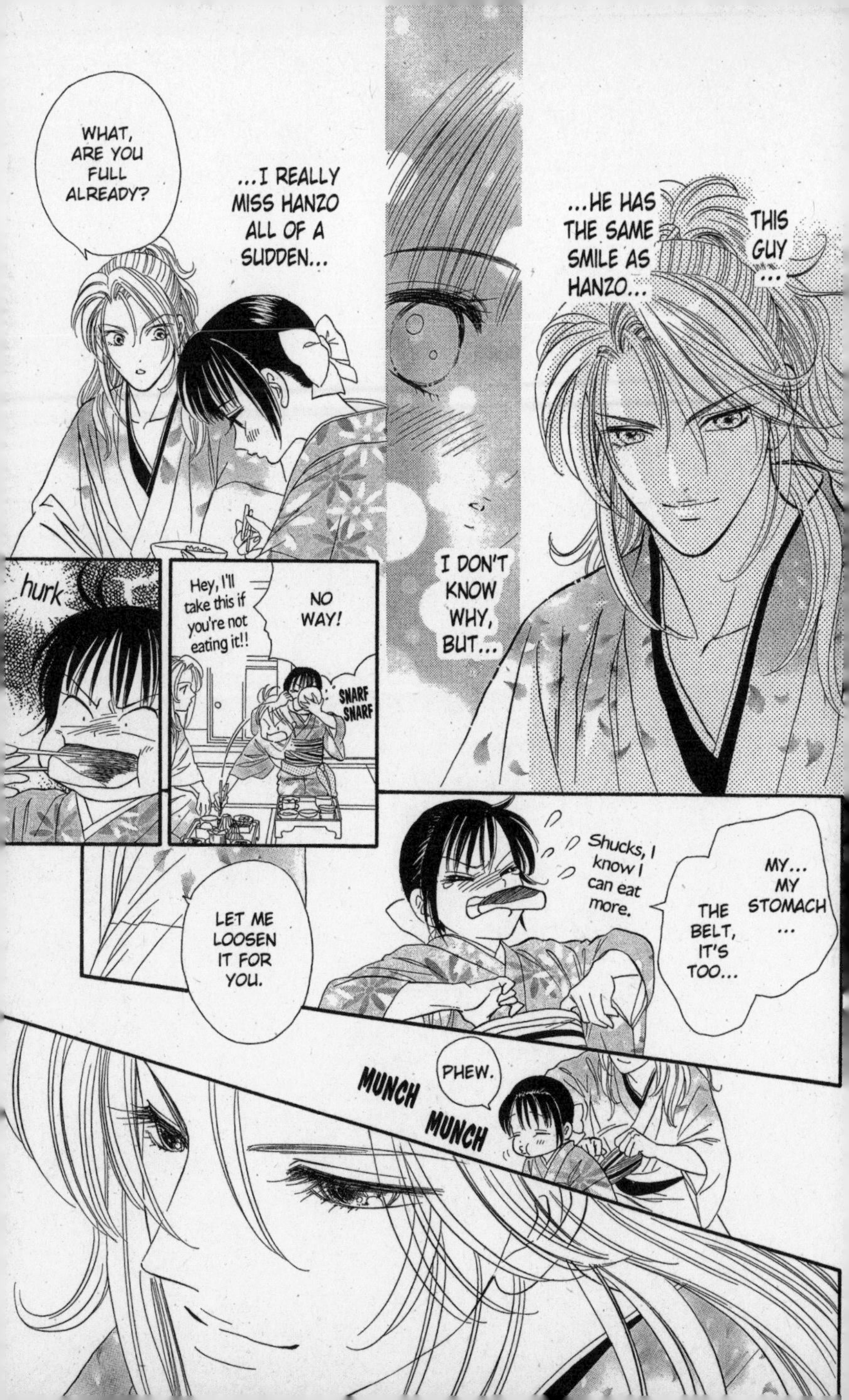
THIS GUY...
...HE HAS THE SAME SMILE AS HANZO...
I DON'T KNOW WHY, BUT...
...I REALLY MISS HANZO ALL OF A SUDDEN...
WHAT, ARE YOU FULL ALREADY?
NO WAY!
Hey, I'll take this if you're not eating it!!
SNARF SNARF
hurk
MY... MY STOMACH...
THE BELT, IT'S TOO...
Shucks, I know I can eat more.
LET ME LOOSEN IT FOR YOU.
PHEW.
MUNCH MUNCH

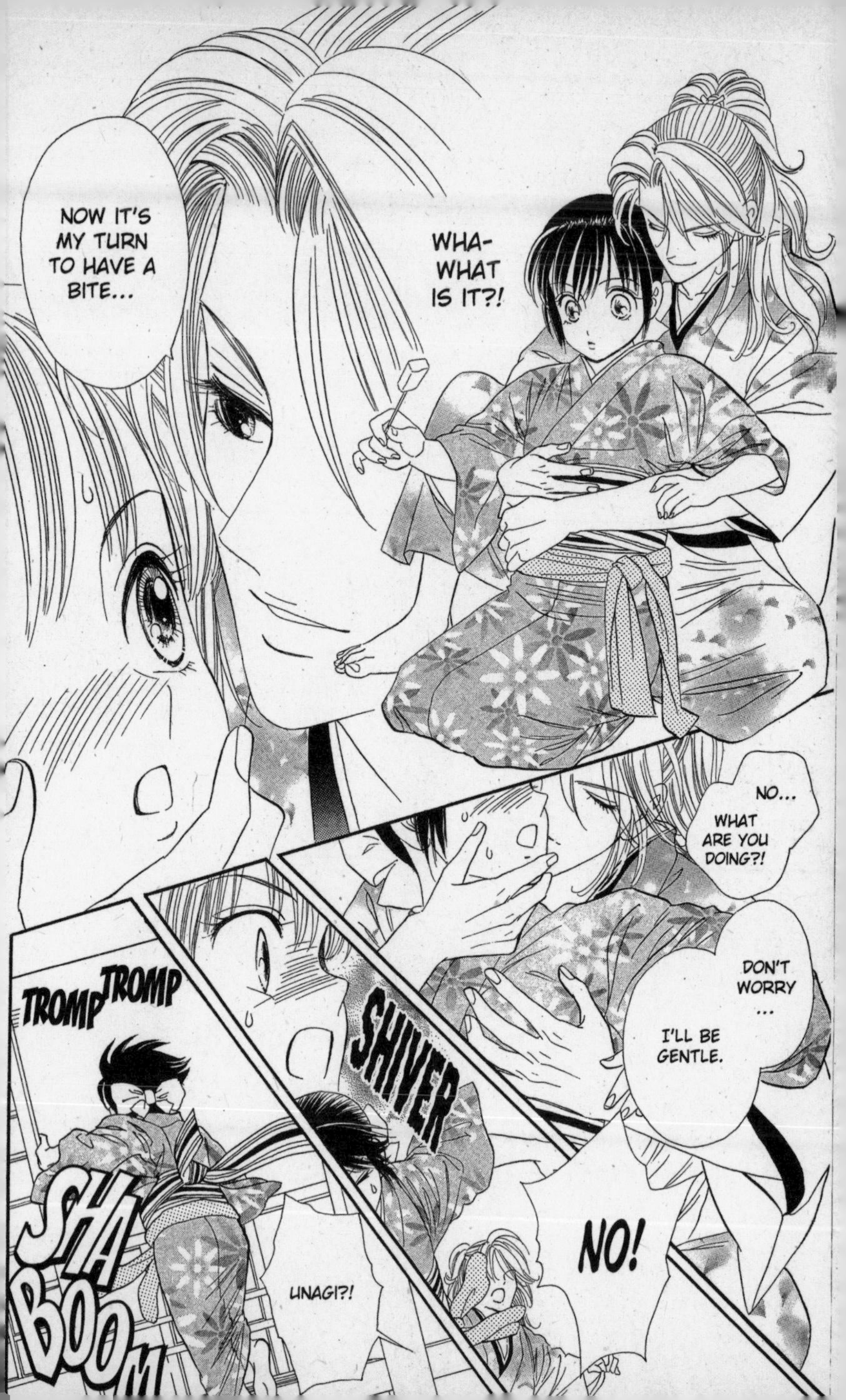
WHA- WHAT IS IT?!
NOW IT'S MY TURN TO HAVE A BITE...
NO... WHAT ARE YOU DOING?!
DON'T WORRY ... I'LL BE GENTLE.
SHIVER
NO!
UNAGI?!
TROMP TROMP
SHA BOOM

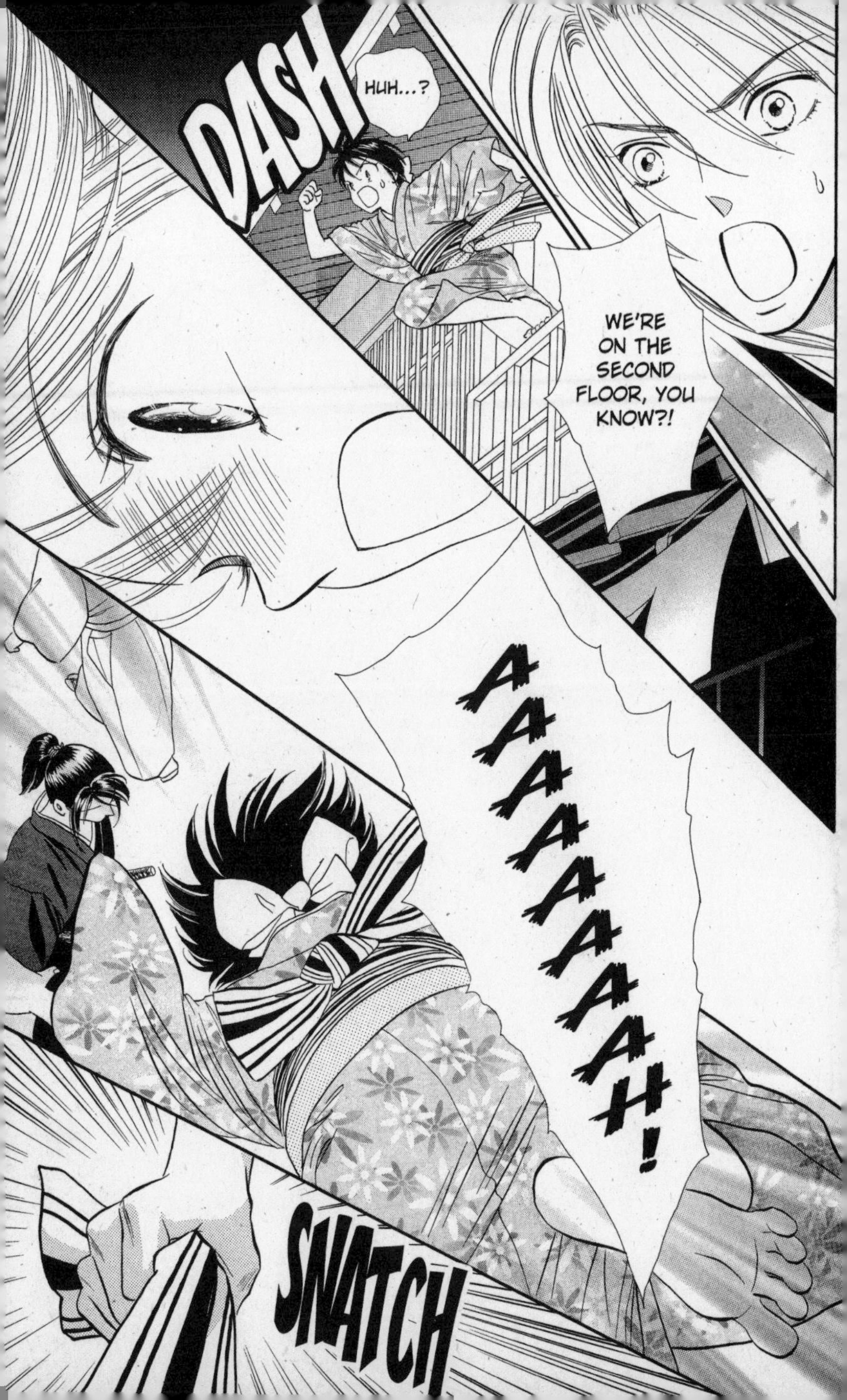
WE'RE ON THE SECOND FLOOR, YOU KNOW?!
DASH
HUH...?
AAAAAAAAH!
SNATCH

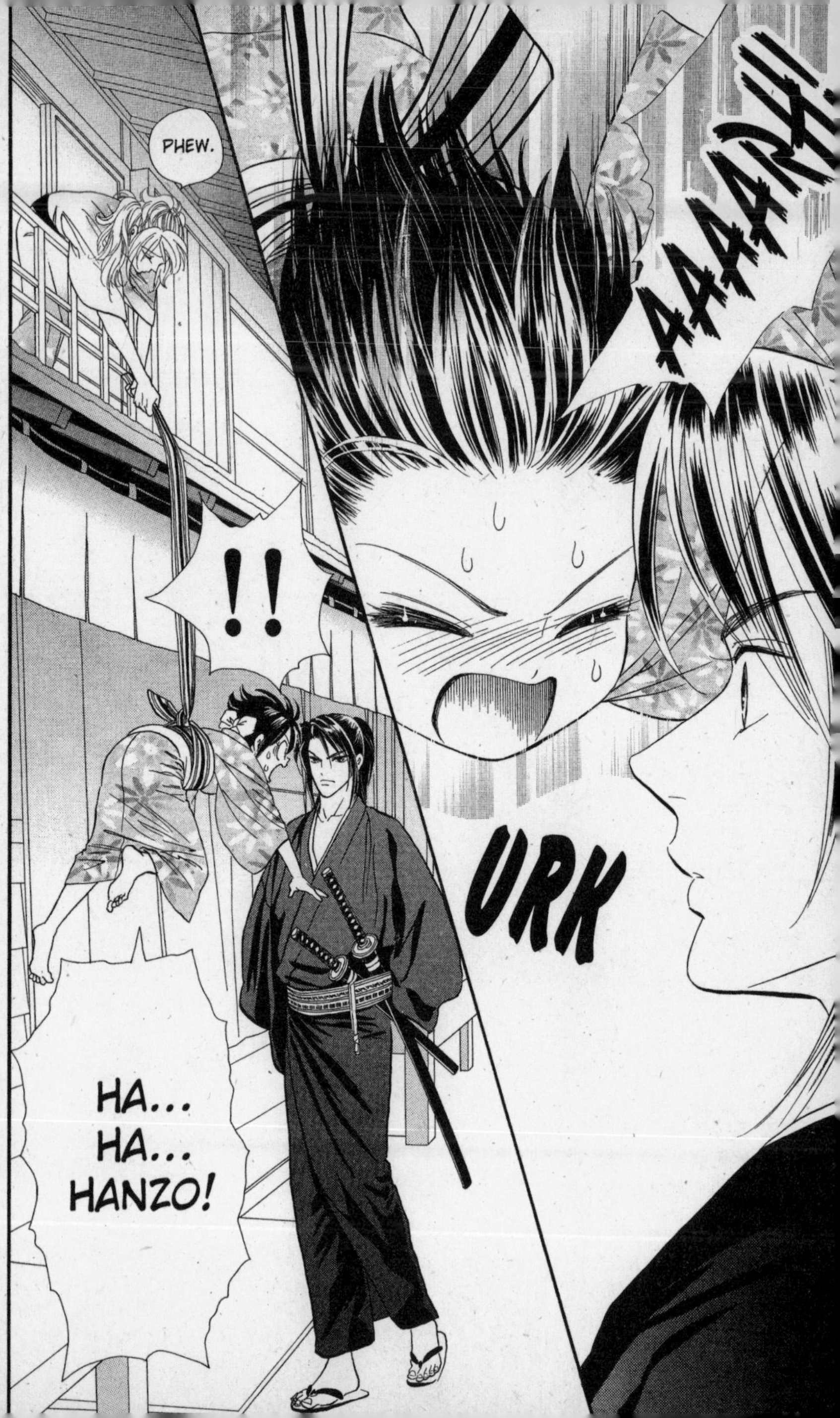
AAAARH!!
URK
PHEW.
!!
HA... HA... HANZO!

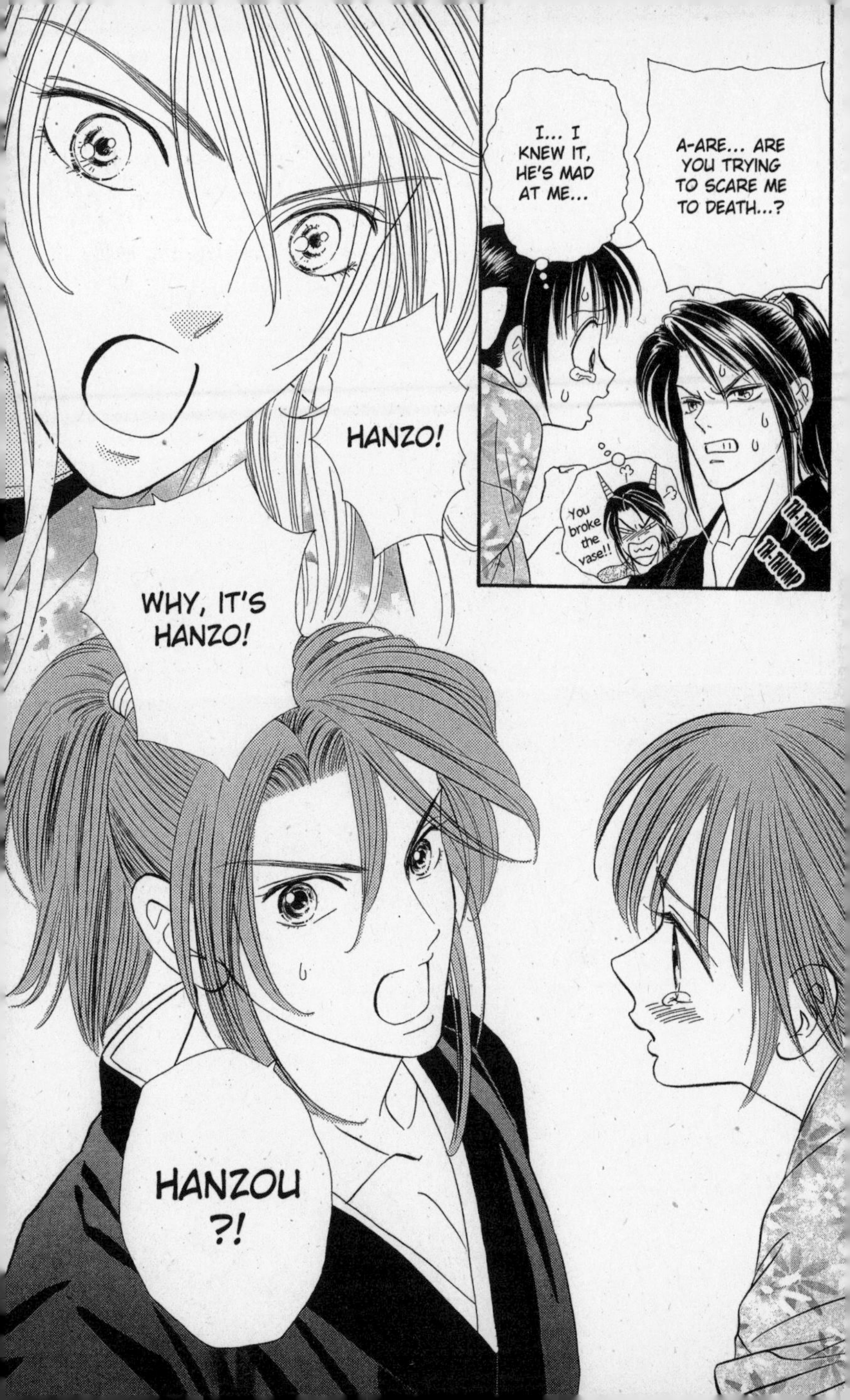
A-ARE... ARE YOU TRYING TO SCARE ME TO DEATH...?
I... I KNEW IT, HE'S MAD AT ME...
You broke the vase!!
TH-THUMP
TH-THUMP
HANZO!
WHY, IT'S HANZO!
HANZOU ?!

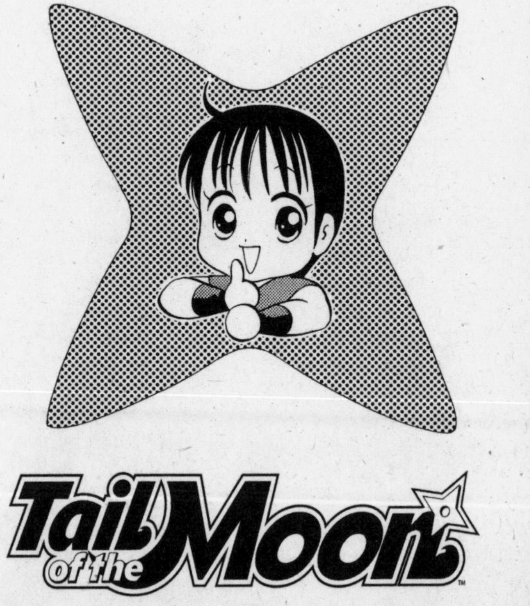

Tail of the Moon™

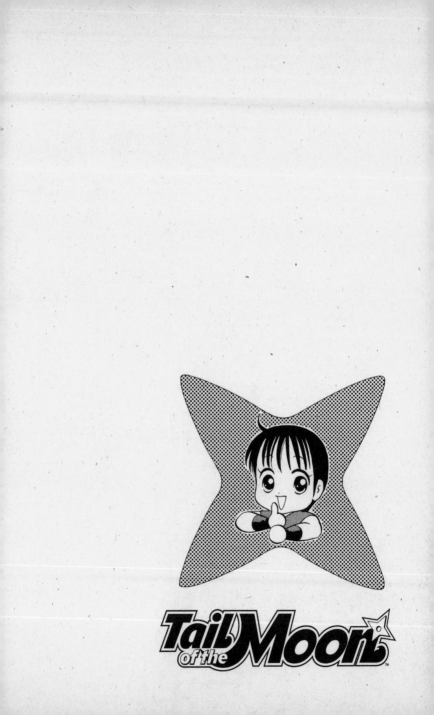

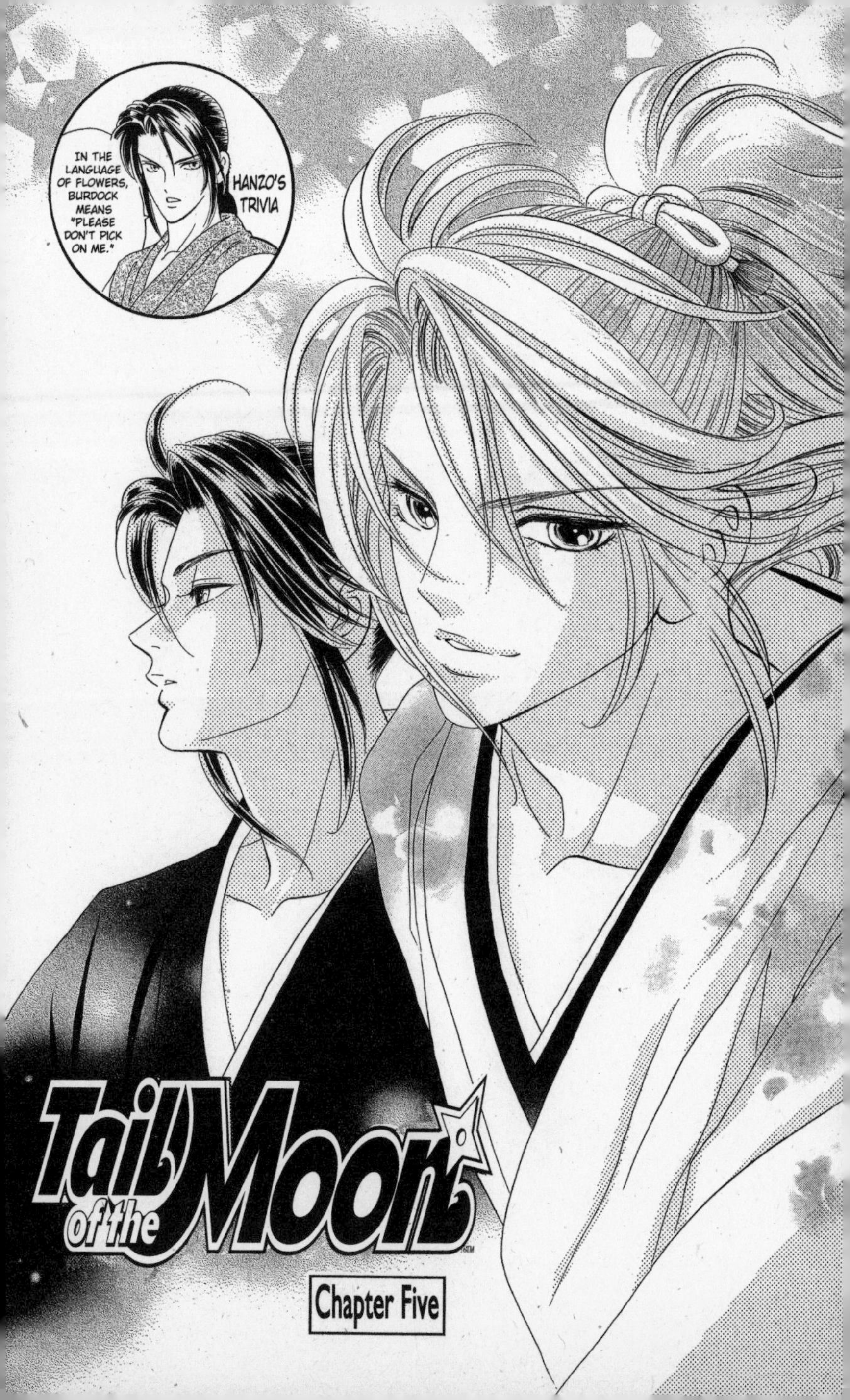
IN THE LANGUAGE OF FLOWERS, BURDOCK MEANS "PLEASE DON'T PICK ON ME."
HANZO'S TRIVIA
Tail of the Moon
Chapter Five

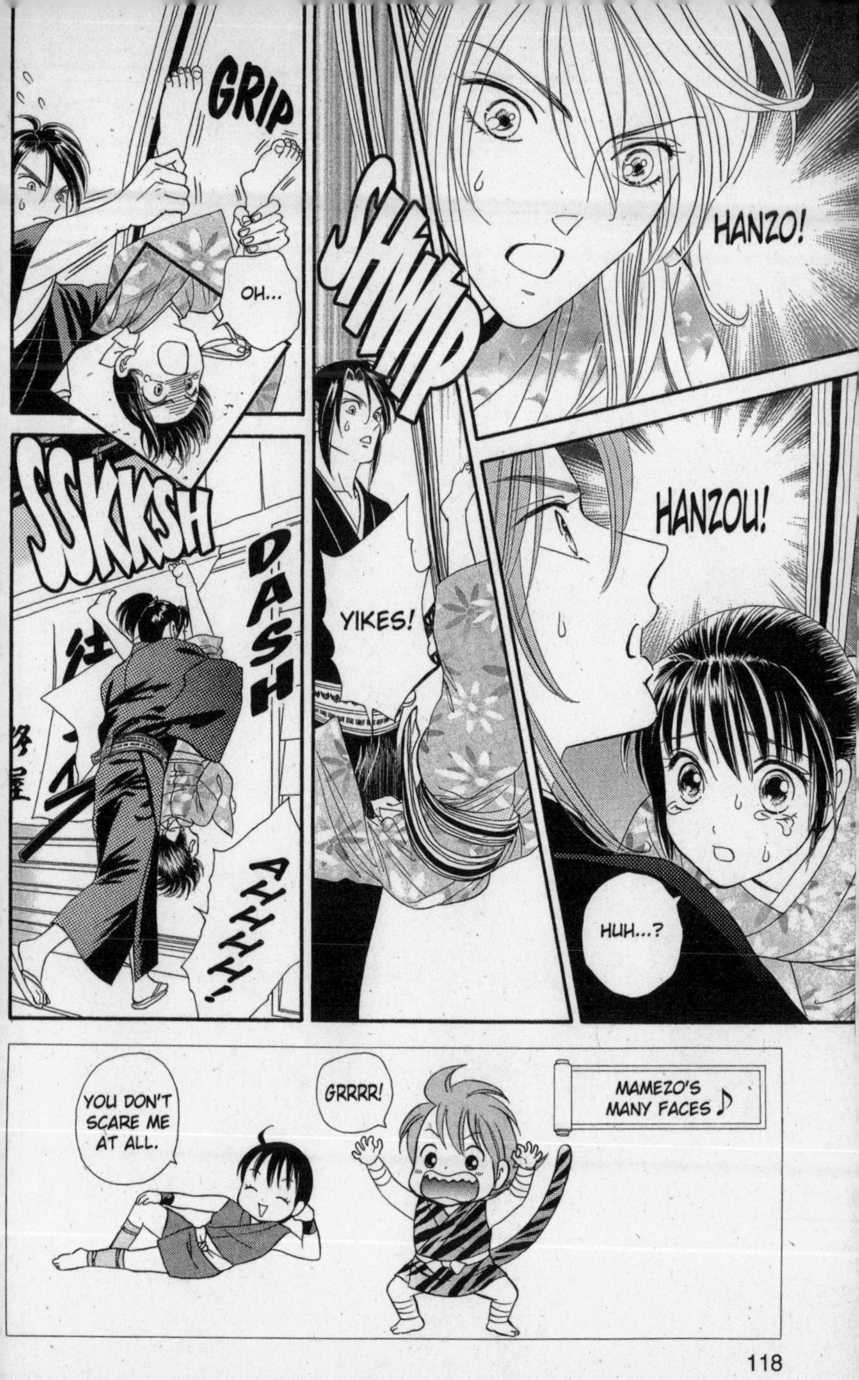
HANZO!
SHWIP
HANZOU!
HUH...?
YIKES!
GRIP
OH...
SSKKSH
DASH
AHHHHH!
MAMEZO'S MANY FACES ♪
GRRRR!
YOU DON'T SCARE ME AT ALL.

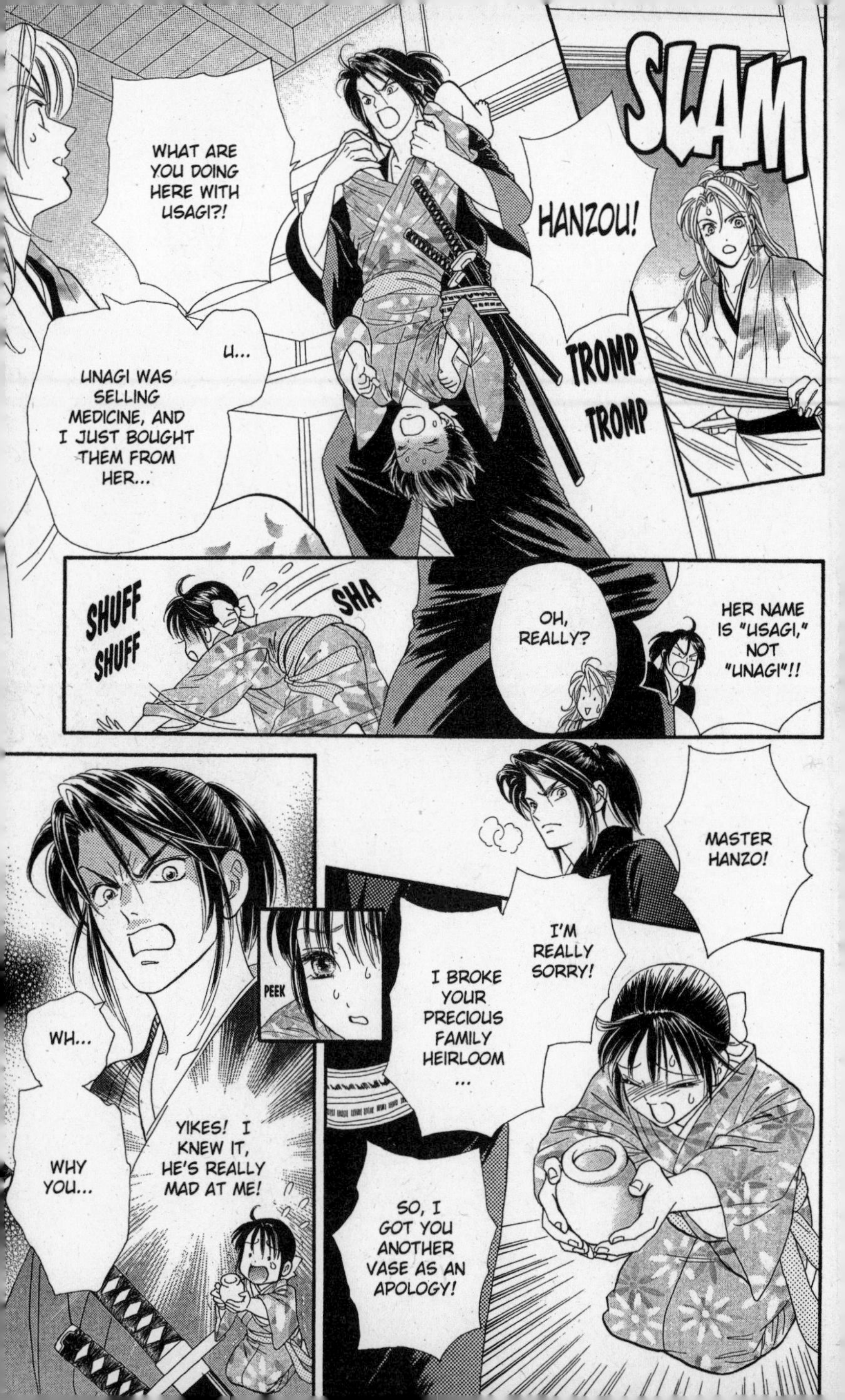
SLAM
HANZOU!
TROMP TROMP
WHAT ARE YOU DOING HERE WITH USAGI?!
U...
UNAGI WAS SELLING MEDICINE, AND I JUST BOUGHT THEM FROM HER...
HER NAME IS "USAGI," NOT "UNAGI"!!
OH, REALLY?
SHA
SHUFF SHUFF
MASTER HANZO!
I'M REALLY SORRY!
I BROKE YOUR PRECIOUS FAMILY HEIRLOOM ...
SO, I GOT YOU ANOTHER VASE AS AN APOLOGY!
PEEK
WH...
YIKES! I KNEW IT, HE'S REALLY MAD AT ME!
WHY YOU...

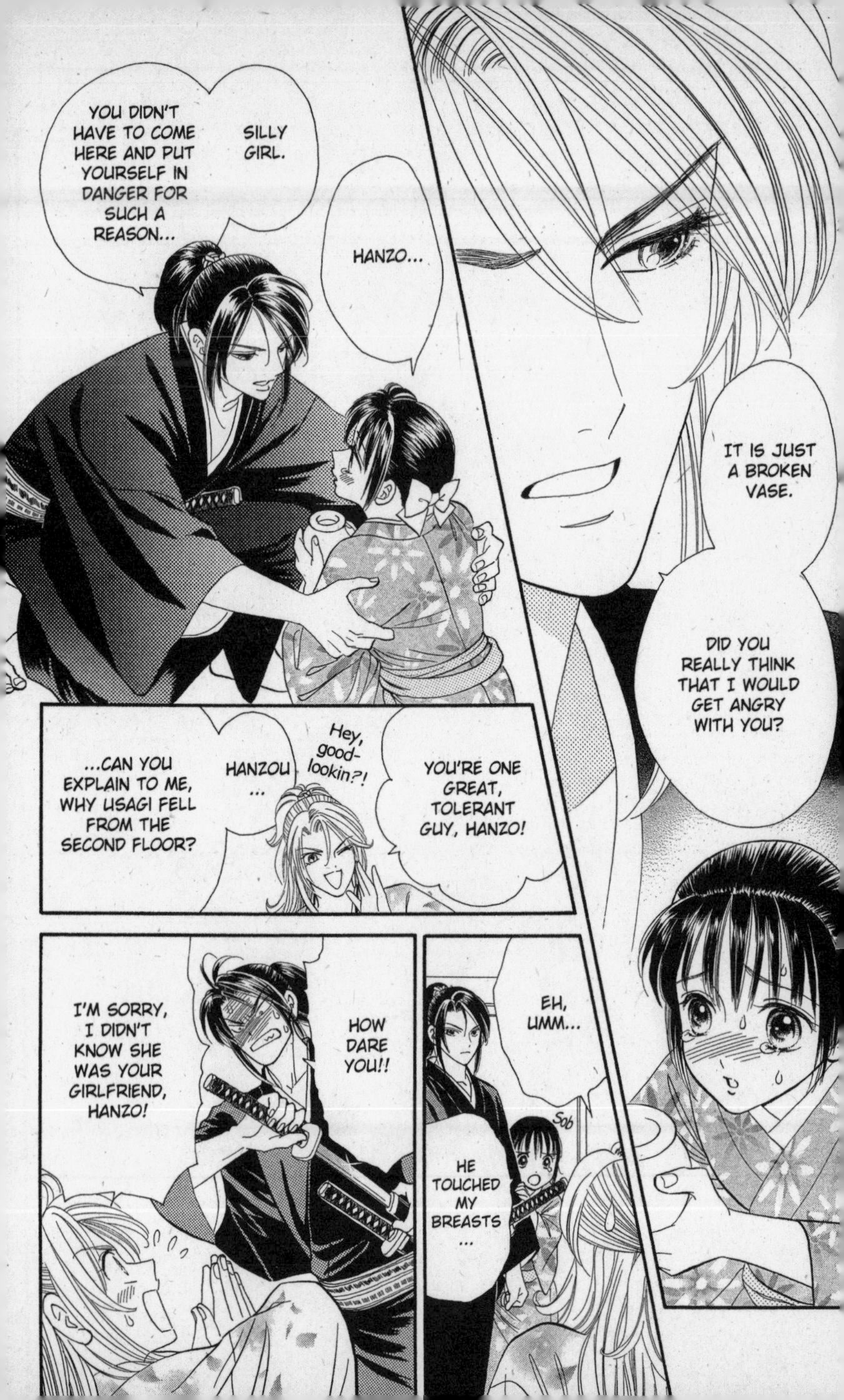
SILLY GIRL.
YOU DIDN'T HAVE TO COME HERE AND PUT YOURSELF IN DANGER FOR SUCH A REASON...
HANZO...
IT IS JUST A BROKEN VASE.
DID YOU REALLY THINK THAT I WOULD GET ANGRY WITH YOU?
YOU'RE ONE GREAT, TOLERANT GUY, HANZO!
Hey, good-lookin?!
HANZOU ...
...CAN YOU EXPLAIN TO ME, WHY USAGI FELL FROM THE SECOND FLOOR?
EH, UMM...
Sob
HE TOUCHED MY BREASTS ...
HOW DARE YOU!!
I'M SORRY, I DIDN'T KNOW SHE WAS YOUR GIRLFRIEND, HANZO!

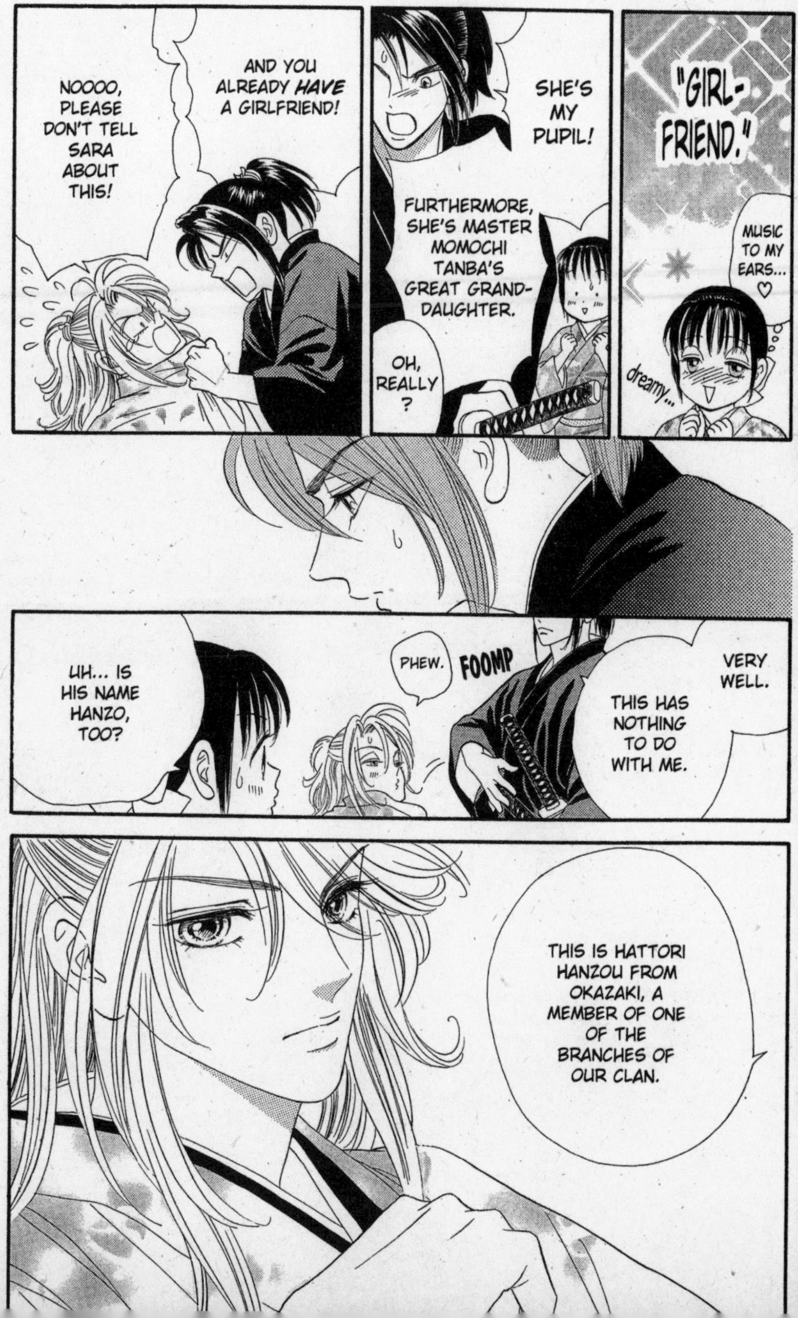
"GIRL-FRIEND."
MUSIC TO MY EARS... ♡
dreamy...
SHE'S MY PUPIL!
FURTHERMORE, SHE'S MASTER MOMOCHI TANBA'S GREAT GRAND-DAUGHTER.
OH, REALLY?
AND YOU ALREADY HAVE A GIRLFRIEND!
NOOOO, PLEASE DON'T TELL SARA ABOUT THIS!
VERY WELL.
THIS HAS NOTHING TO DO WITH ME.
FOOMP
PHEW.
UH... IS HIS NAME HANZO, TOO?
THIS IS HATTORI HANZOU FROM OKAZAKI, A MEMBER OF ONE OF THE BRANCHES OF OUR CLAN.

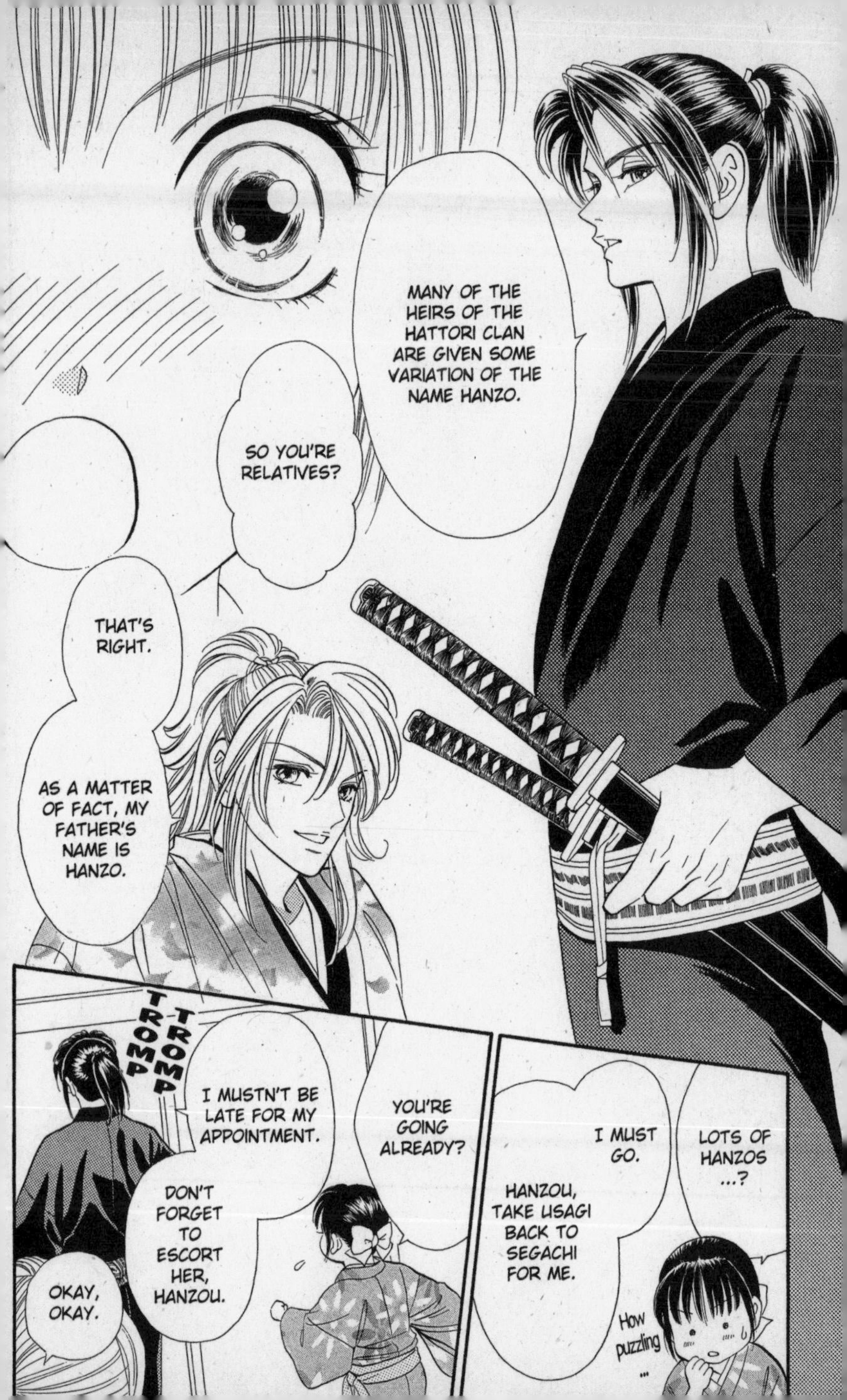
MANY OF THE HEIRS OF THE HATTORI CLAN ARE GIVEN SOME VARIATION OF THE NAME HANZO.
SO YOU'RE RELATIVES?
THAT'S RIGHT.
AS A MATTER OF FACT, MY FATHER'S NAME IS HANZO.
LOTS OF HANZOS ...?
I MUST GO.
HANZOU, TAKE USAGI BACK TO SEGACHI FOR ME.
How puzzling ...
YOU'RE GOING ALREADY?
I MUSTN'T BE LATE FOR MY APPOINTMENT.
TROMP TROMP
DON'T FORGET TO ESCORT HER, HANZOU.
OKAY, OKAY.

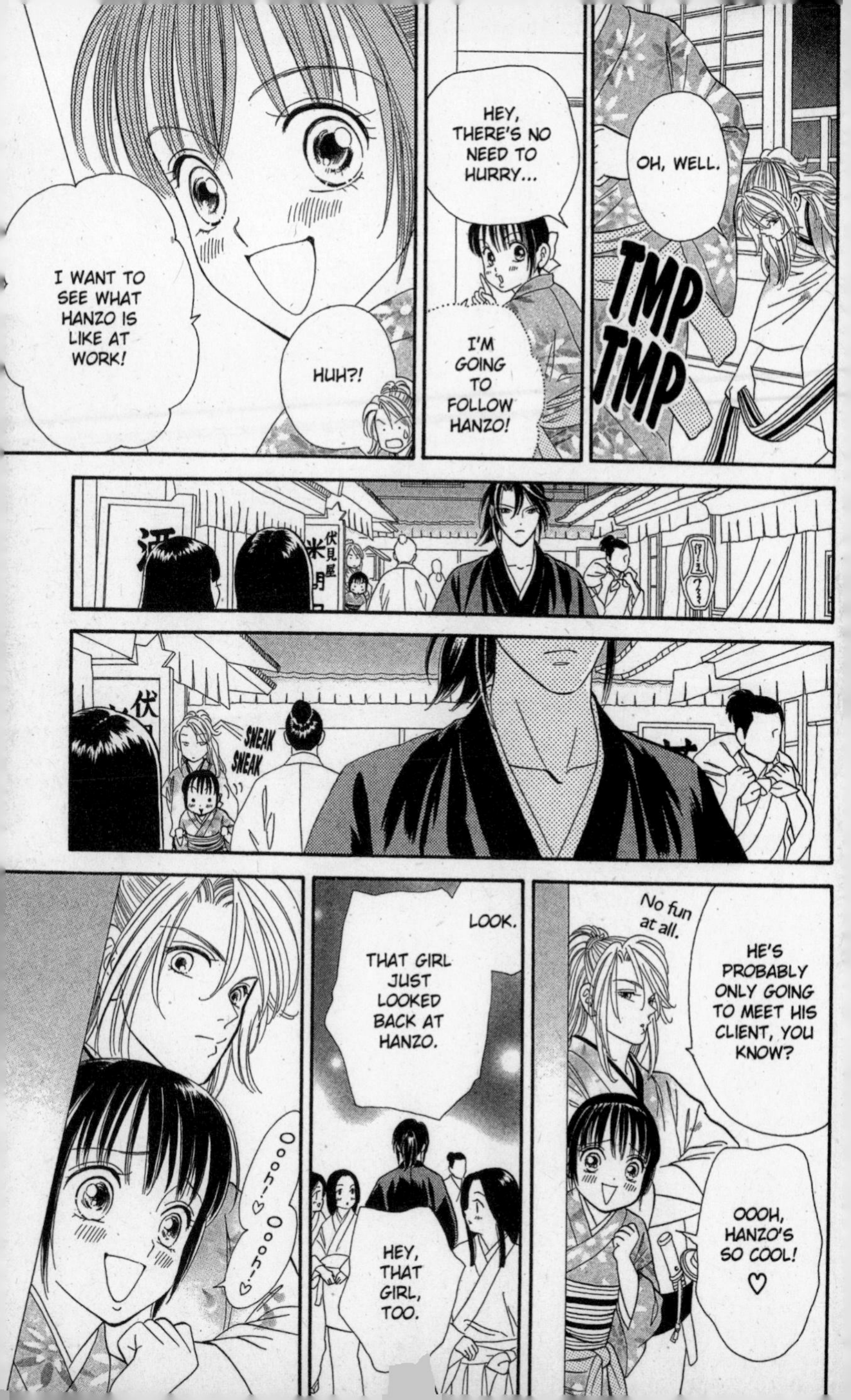
OH, WELL.
TMP TMP
HEY, THERE'S NO NEED TO HURRY...
I'M GOING TO FOLLOW HANZO!
HUH?!
I WANT TO SEE WHAT HANZO IS LIKE AT WORK!
伏見屋
SNEAK SNEAK
No fun at all.
HE'S PROBABLY ONLY GOING TO MEET HIS CLIENT, YOU KNOW?
OOOH, HANZO'S SO COOL! ♡
LOOK.
THAT GIRL JUST LOOKED BACK AT HANZO.
HEY, THAT GIRL, TOO.
Ooooh! ♡ Ooooh! ♡

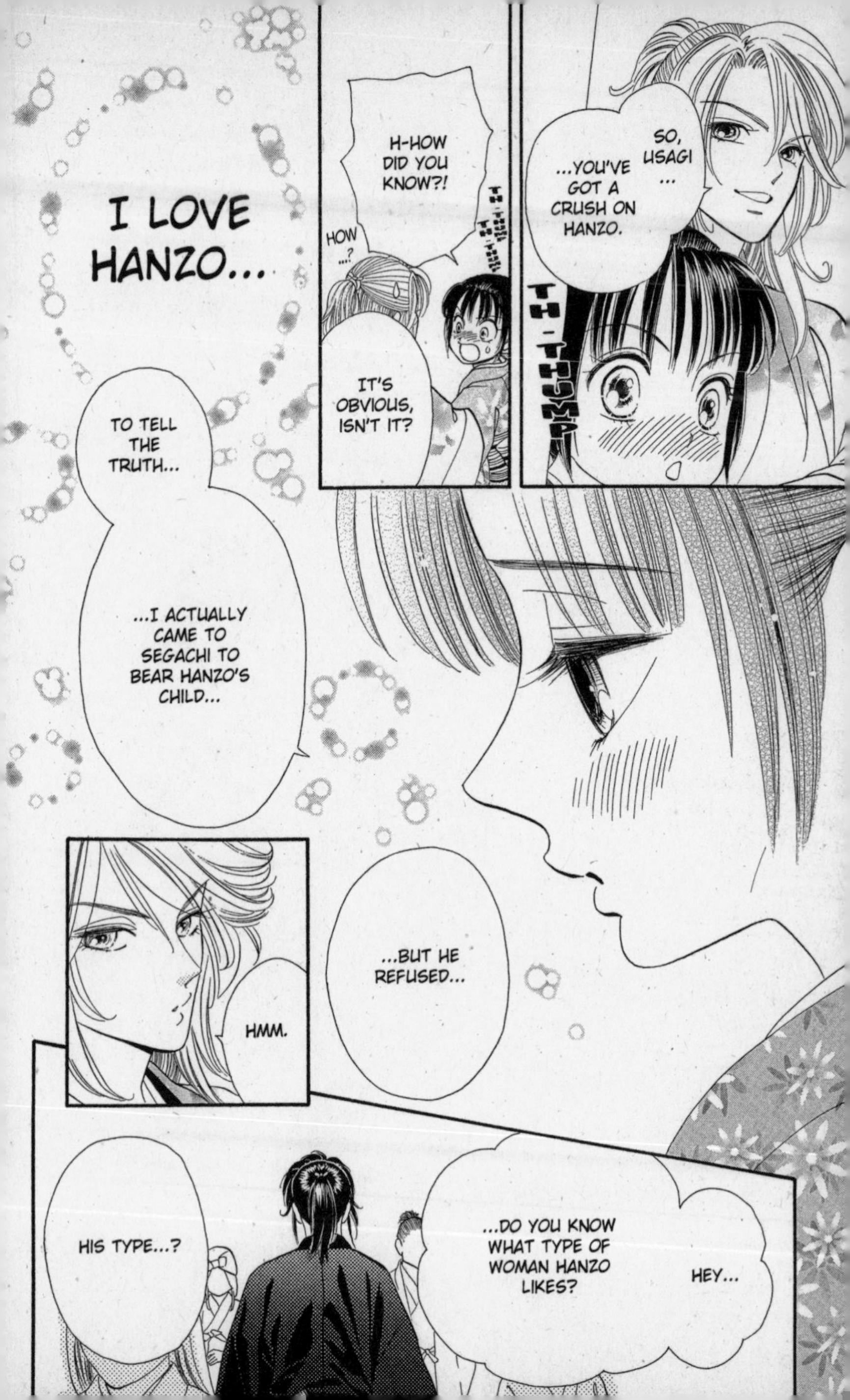

SO, USAGI...
...YOU'VE GOT A CRUSH ON HANZO.
TH-THUMP
H-HOW DID YOU KNOW?!
HOW ...?
IT'S OBVIOUS, ISN'T IT?
I LOVE HANZO...
TO TELL THE TRUTH...
...I ACTUALLY CAME TO SEGACHI TO BEAR HANZO'S CHILD...
...BUT HE REFUSED...
HMM.
HEY...
...DO YOU KNOW WHAT TYPE OF WOMAN HANZO LIKES?
HIS TYPE...?

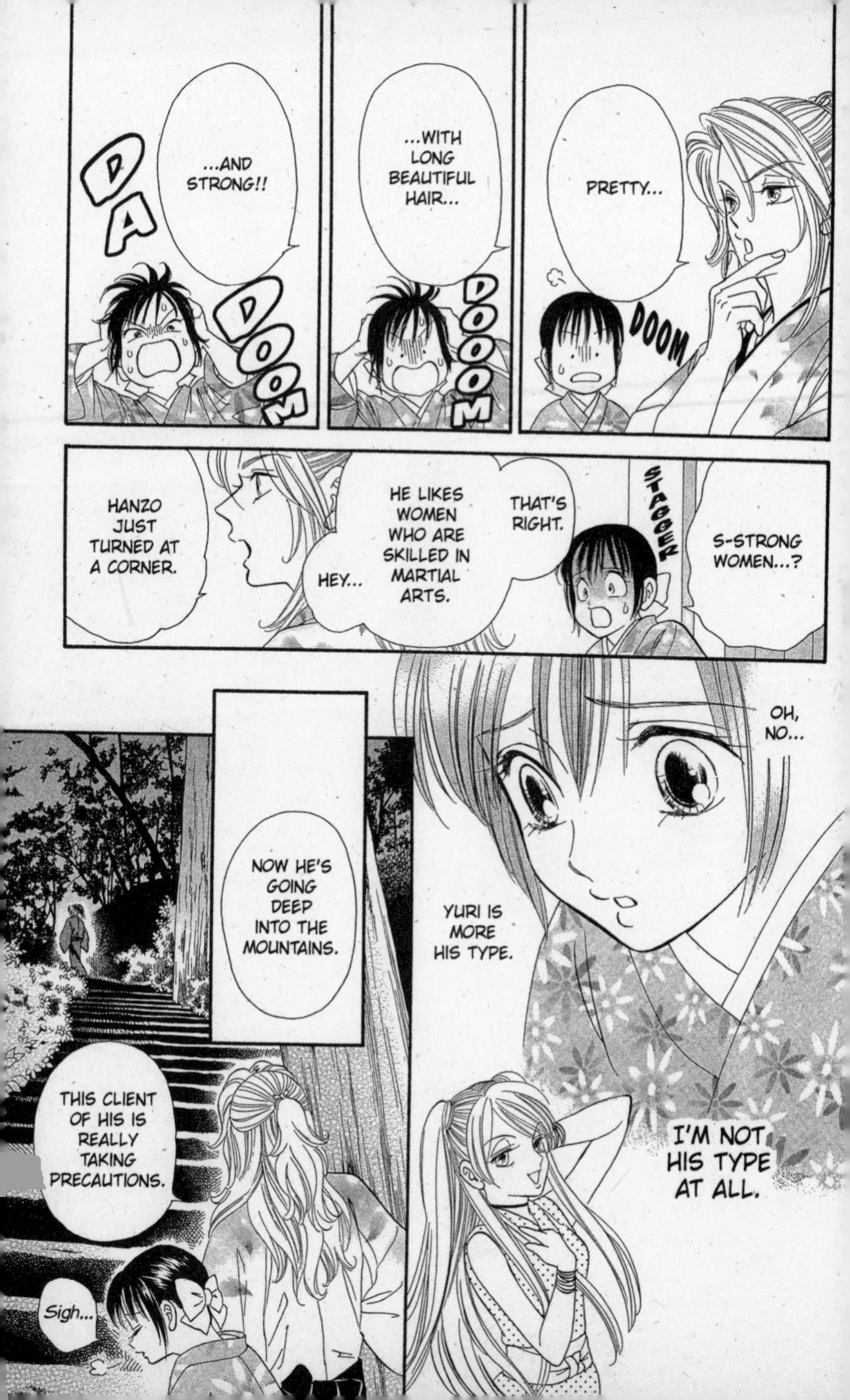
PRETTY...
DOOM
...WITH LONG BEAUTIFUL HAIR...
DOOOOM
...AND STRONG!!
DA
DOOM
S-STRONG WOMEN...?
STAGGER
THAT'S RIGHT.
HE LIKES WOMEN WHO ARE SKILLED IN MARTIAL ARTS.
HEY...
HANZO JUST TURNED AT A CORNER.
OH, NO...
YURI IS MORE HIS TYPE.
I'M NOT HIS TYPE AT ALL.
NOW HE'S GOING DEEP INTO THE MOUNTAINS.
THIS CLIENT OF HIS IS REALLY TAKING PRECAUTIONS.
Sigh...

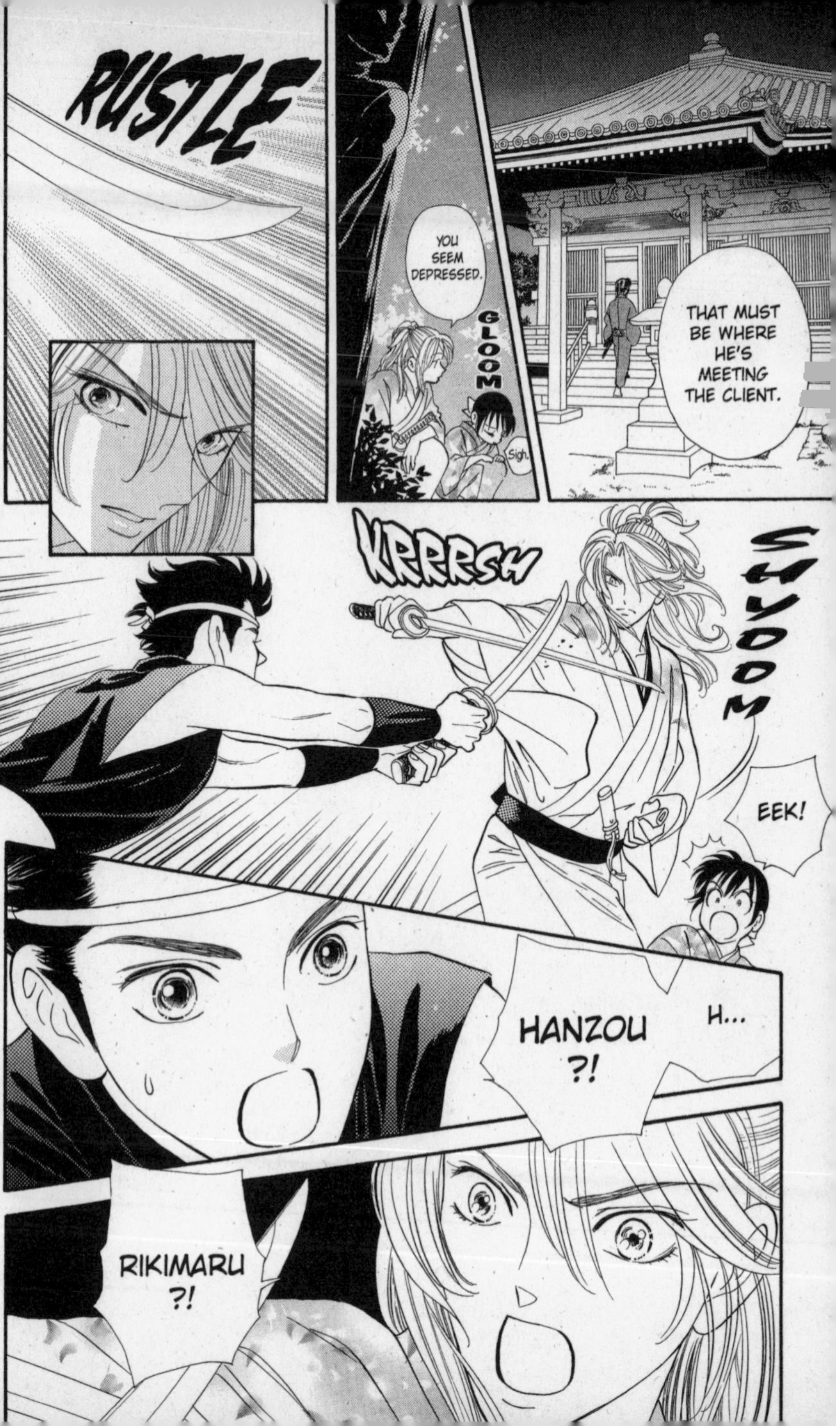
THAT MUST BE WHERE HE'S MEETING THE CLIENT.
YOU SEEM DEPRESSED.
GLOOM
Sigh.
RUSTLE
SHYOOM
KRRRSH
EEK!
H...
HANZOU ?!
RIKIMARU ?!

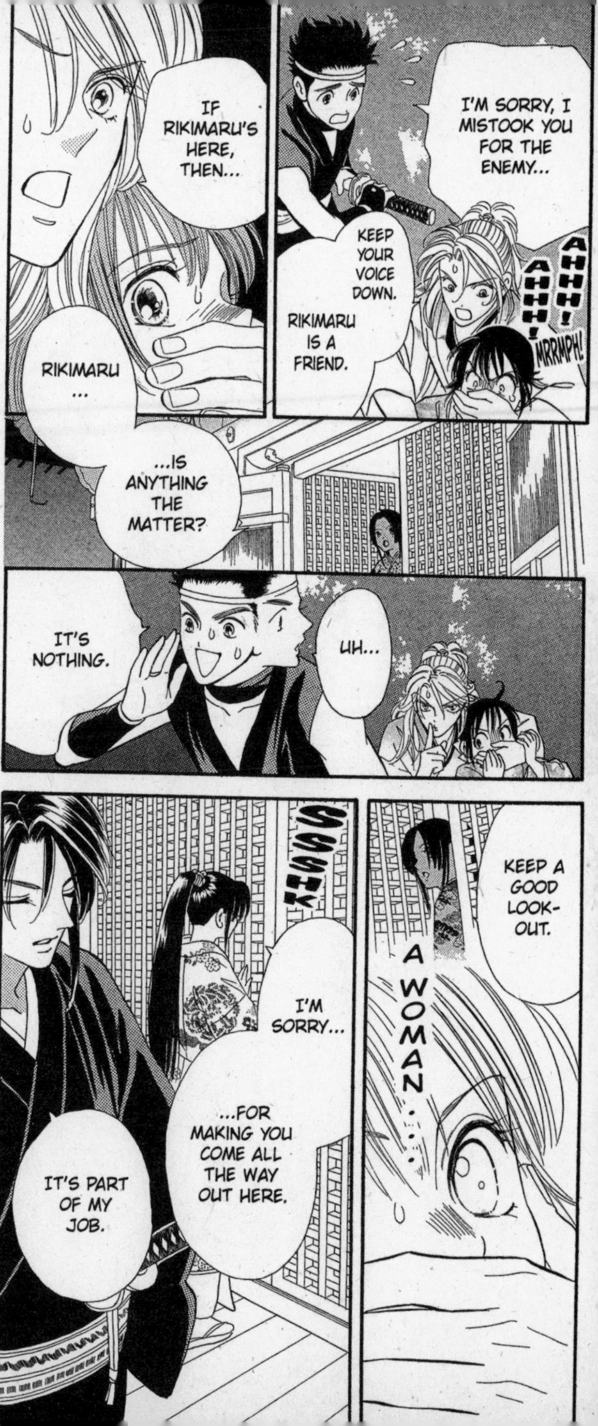
I'M SORRY, I MISTOOK YOU FOR THE ENEMY...
KEEP YOUR VOICE DOWN.
RIKIMARU IS A FRIEND.
AHHH!
AHHH!
MRRMPH!
IF RIKIMARU'S HERE, THEN...
RIKIMARU ...
...IS ANYTHING THE MATTER?
UH...
IT'S NOTHING.
KEEP A GOOD LOOK-OUT.
A WOMAN......
SSSHK
I'M SORRY...
...FOR MAKING YOU COME ALL THE WAY OUT HERE.
IT'S PART OF MY JOB.

This and that from the author 5

Before Tail of the Moon, all my stories tended to become very serious, the longer they ran. But for this story, it was easy to come up with cheerful stories...

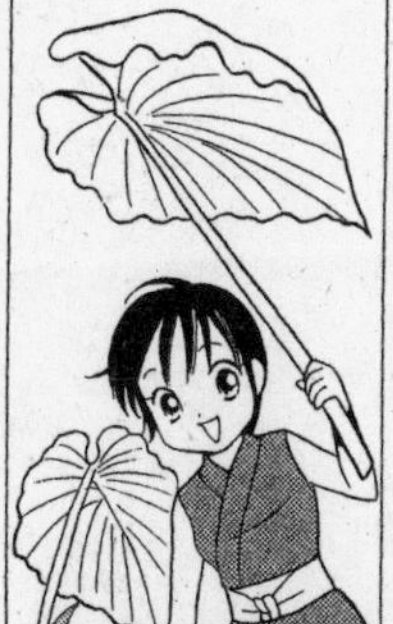

...and enjoy creating the manga every day.

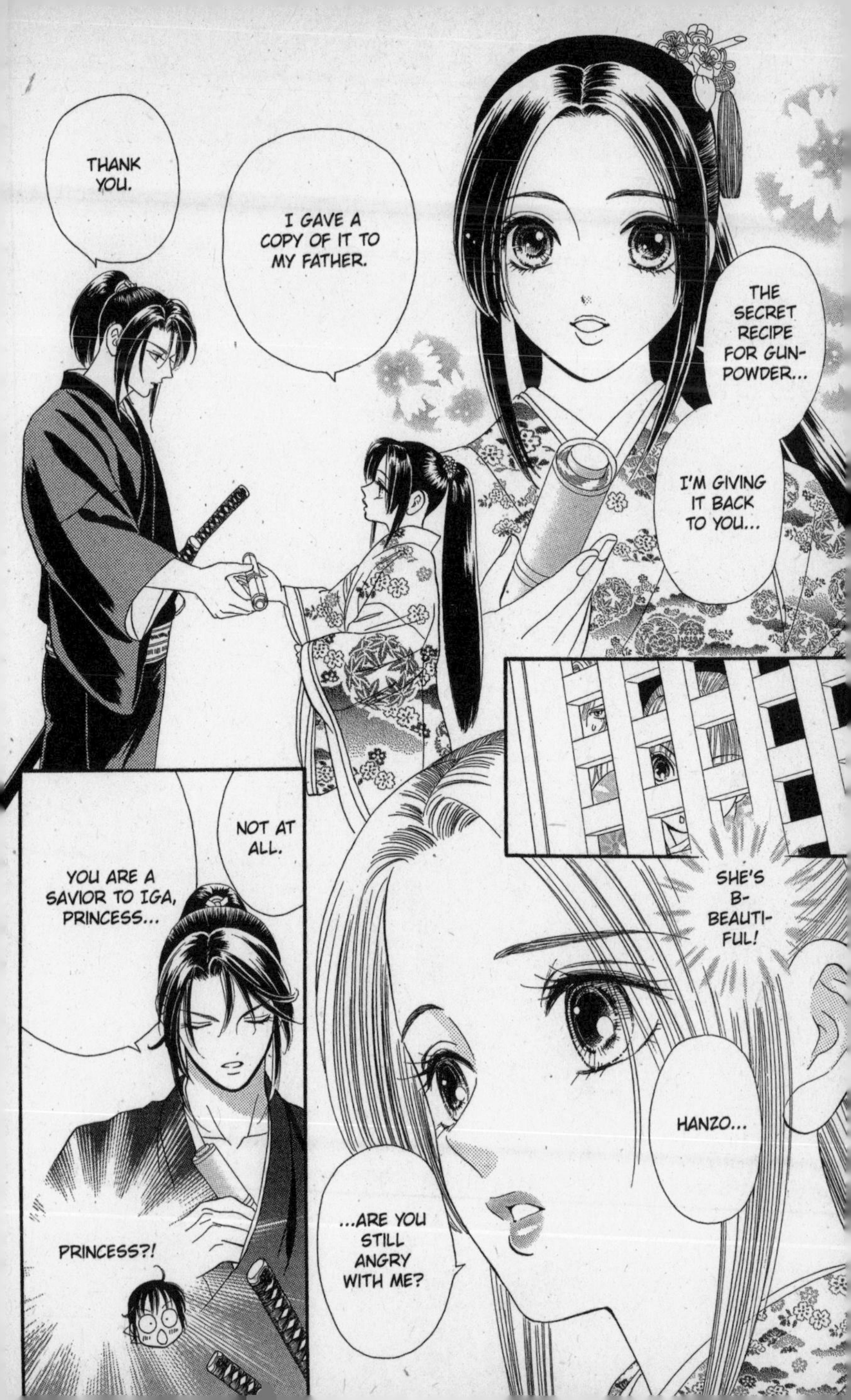
THE SECRET RECIPE FOR GUN-POWDER...
I'M GIVING IT BACK TO YOU...
I GAVE A COPY OF IT TO MY FATHER.
THANK YOU.
SHE'S B-BEAUTIFUL!
HANZO...
...ARE YOU STILL ANGRY WITH ME?
NOT AT ALL.
YOU ARE A SAVIOR TO IGA, PRINCESS...
PRINCESS?!

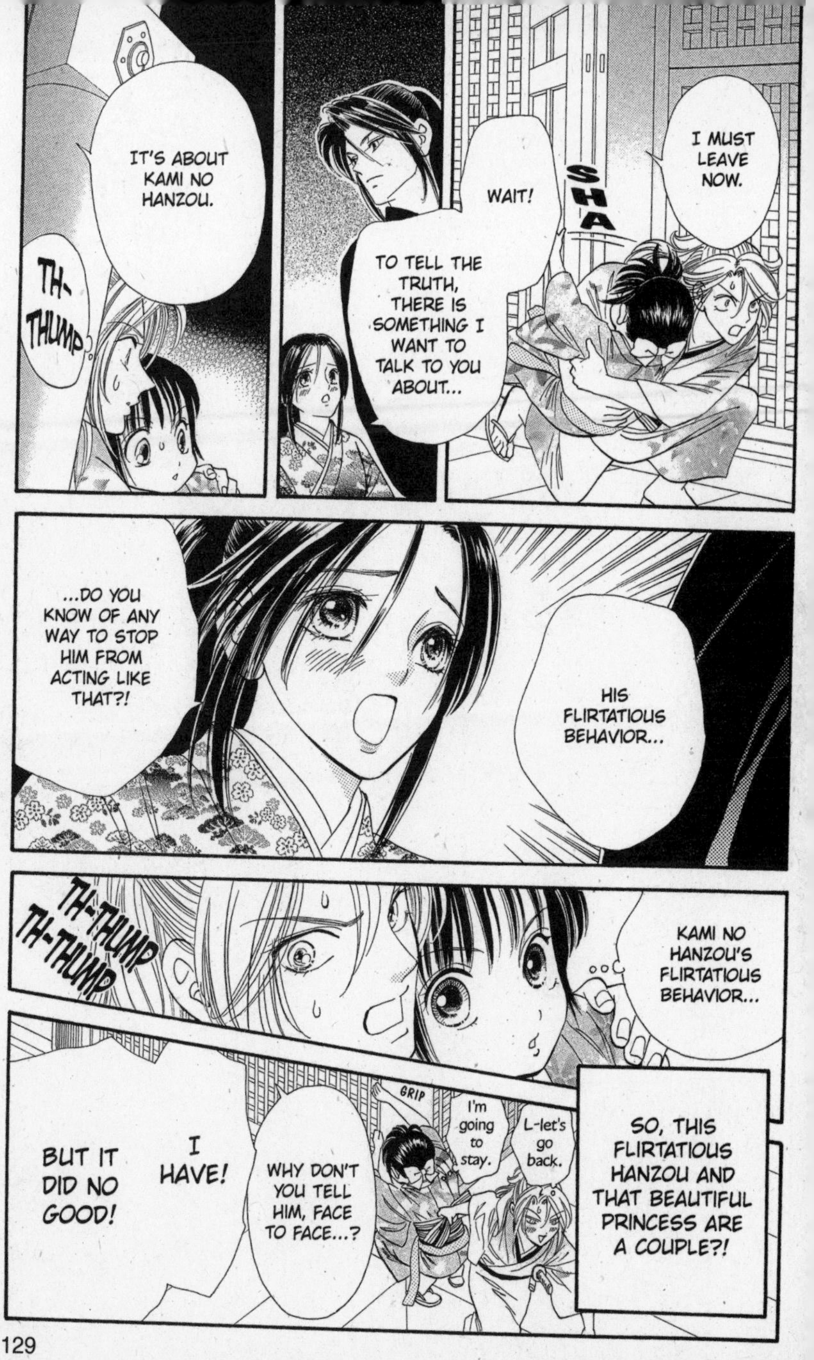
I MUST LEAVE NOW.
SHA
WAIT!
TO TELL THE TRUTH, THERE IS SOMETHING I WANT TO TALK TO YOU ABOUT...
IT'S ABOUT KAMI NO HANZOU.
TH-THUMP
HIS FLIRTATIOUS BEHAVIOR...
...DO YOU KNOW OF ANY WAY TO STOP HIM FROM ACTING LIKE THAT?!
KAMI NO HANZOU'S FLIRTATIOUS BEHAVIOR...
TH-THUMP TH-THUMP
SO, THIS FLIRTATIOUS HANZOU AND THAT BEAUTIFUL PRINCESS ARE A COUPLE?!
L-let's go back.
I'm going to stay.
GRIP
WHY DON'T YOU TELL HIM, FACE TO FACE...?
I HAVE!
BUT IT DID NO GOOD!

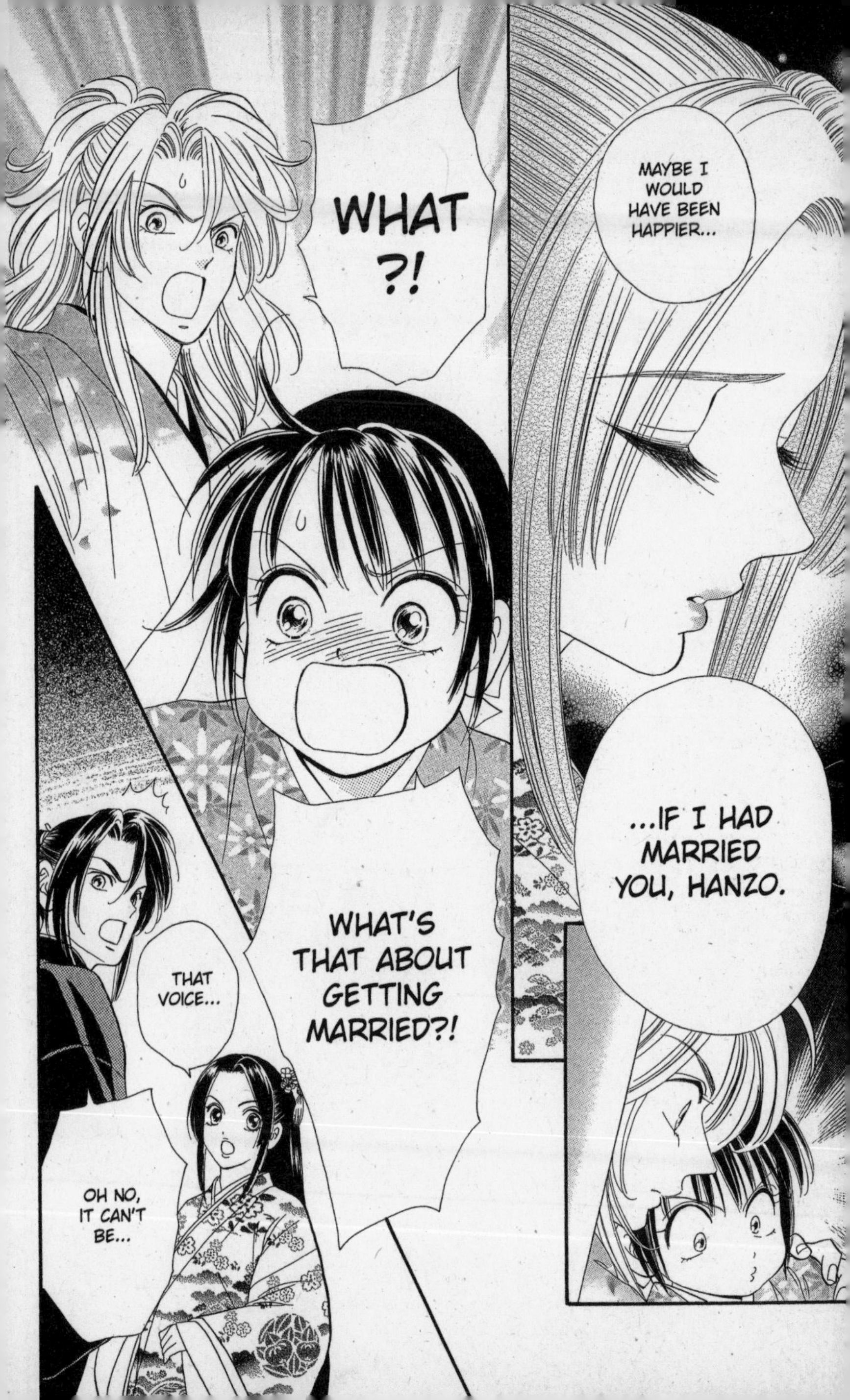
MAYBE I WOULD HAVE BEEN HAPPIER...
...IF I HAD MARRIED YOU, HANZO.
WHAT ?!
WHAT'S THAT ABOUT GETTING MARRIED?!
THAT VOICE...
OH NO, IT CAN'T BE...

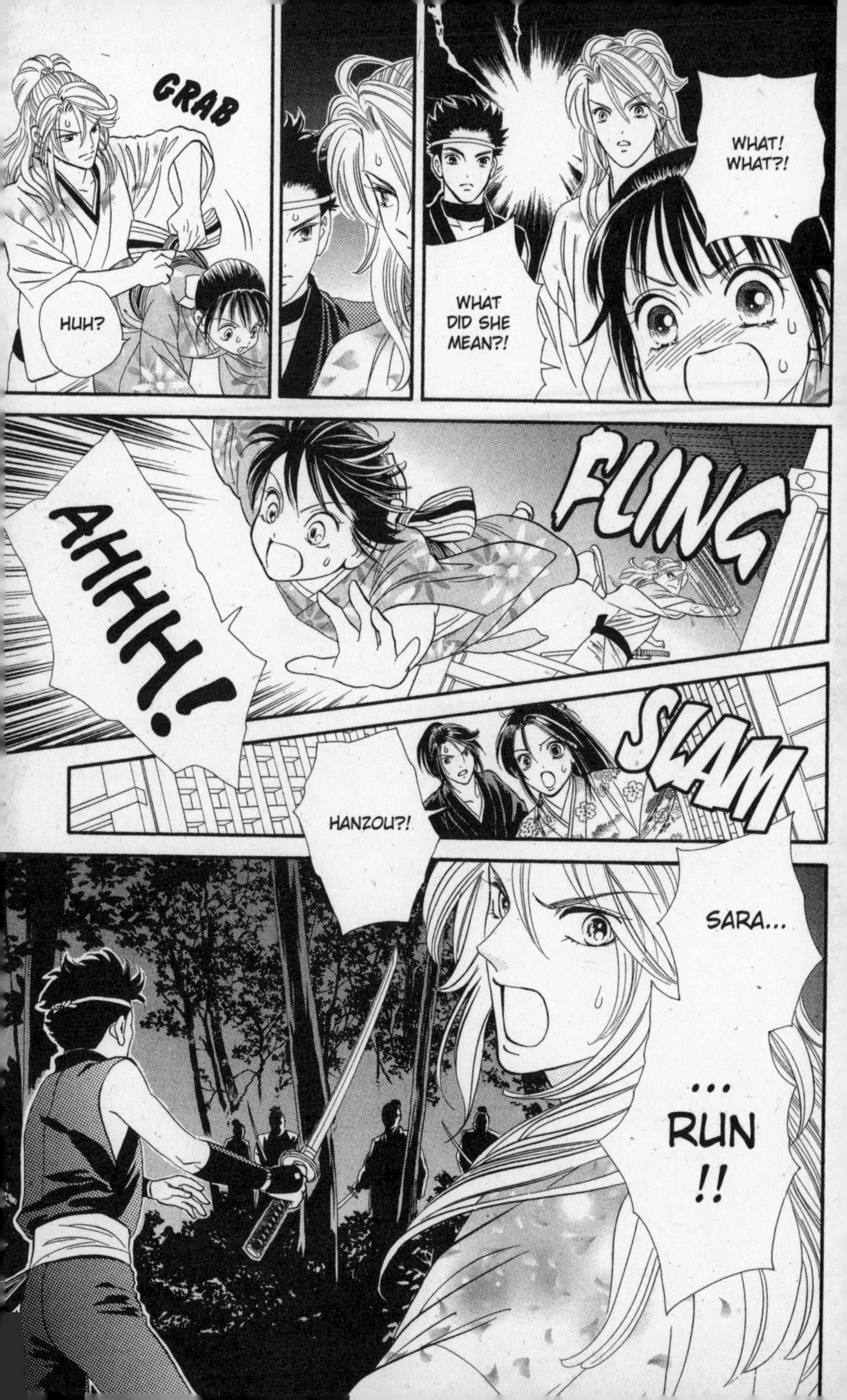
WHAT! WHAT?!
WHAT DID SHE MEAN?!
GRAB
HUH?
FLING
AHHHH!!
SLAM
HANZOU?!
SARA...
... RUN !!

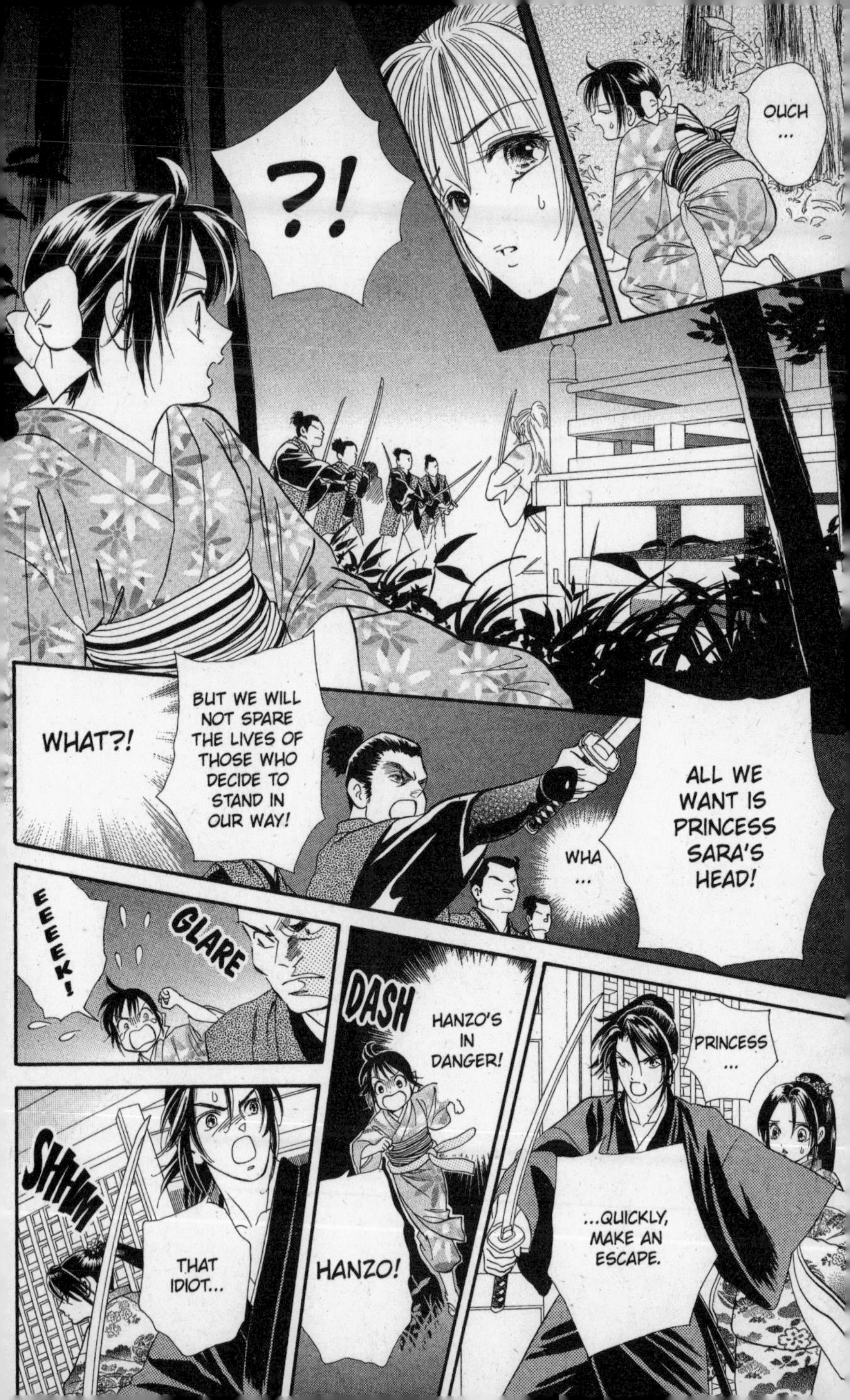

OUCH ...
?!
ALL WE WANT IS PRINCESS SARA'S HEAD!
WHA ...
BUT WE WILL NOT SPARE THE LIVES OF THOSE WHO DECIDE TO STAND IN OUR WAY!
WHAT?!
PRINCESS ...
...QUICKLY, MAKE AN ESCAPE.
DASH
HANZO'S IN DANGER!
HANZO!
GLARE
EEEEK!
SHHM
THAT IDIOT...

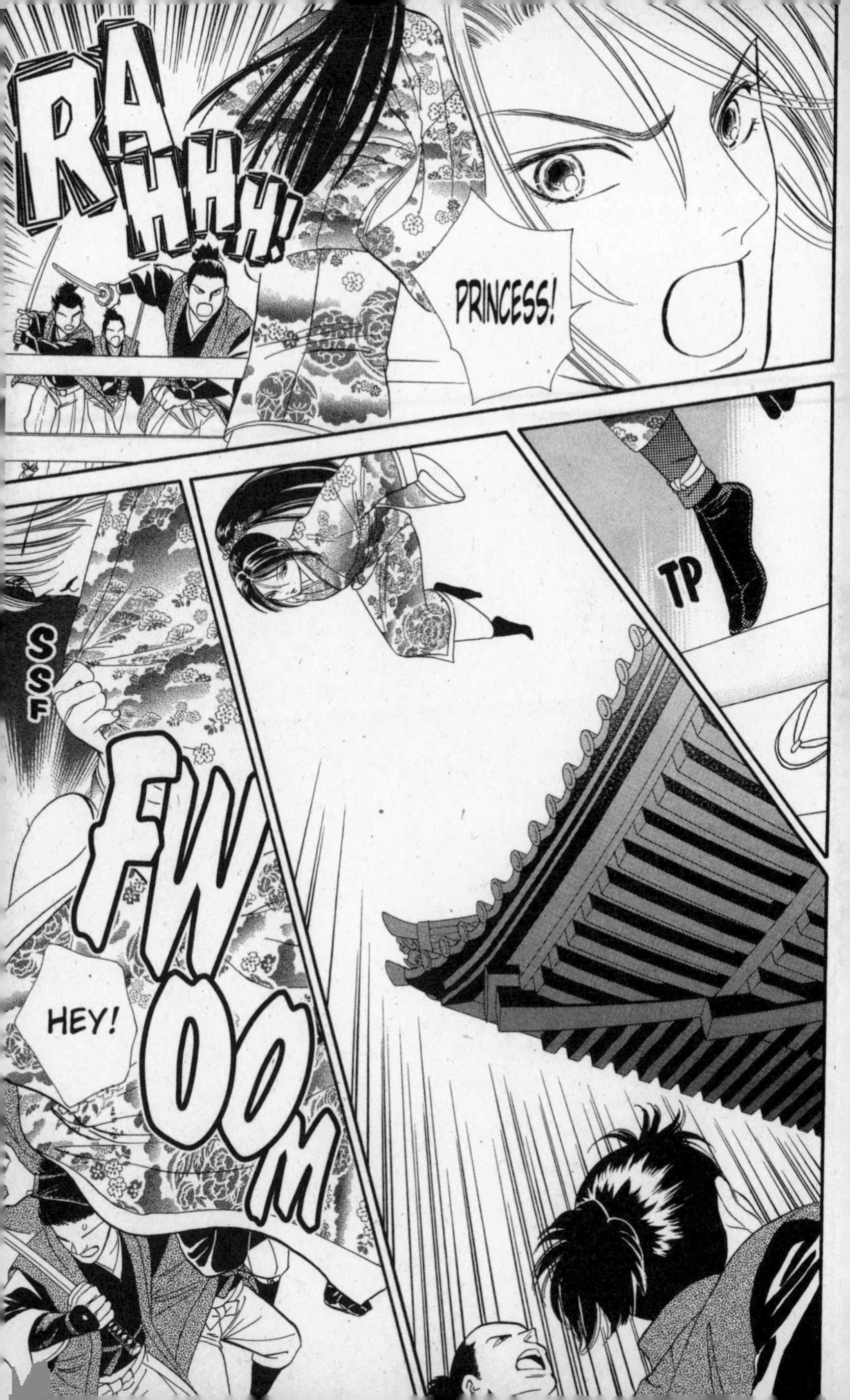
PRINCESS!
RAHHH!
TP
SSF
FWOOM
HEY!

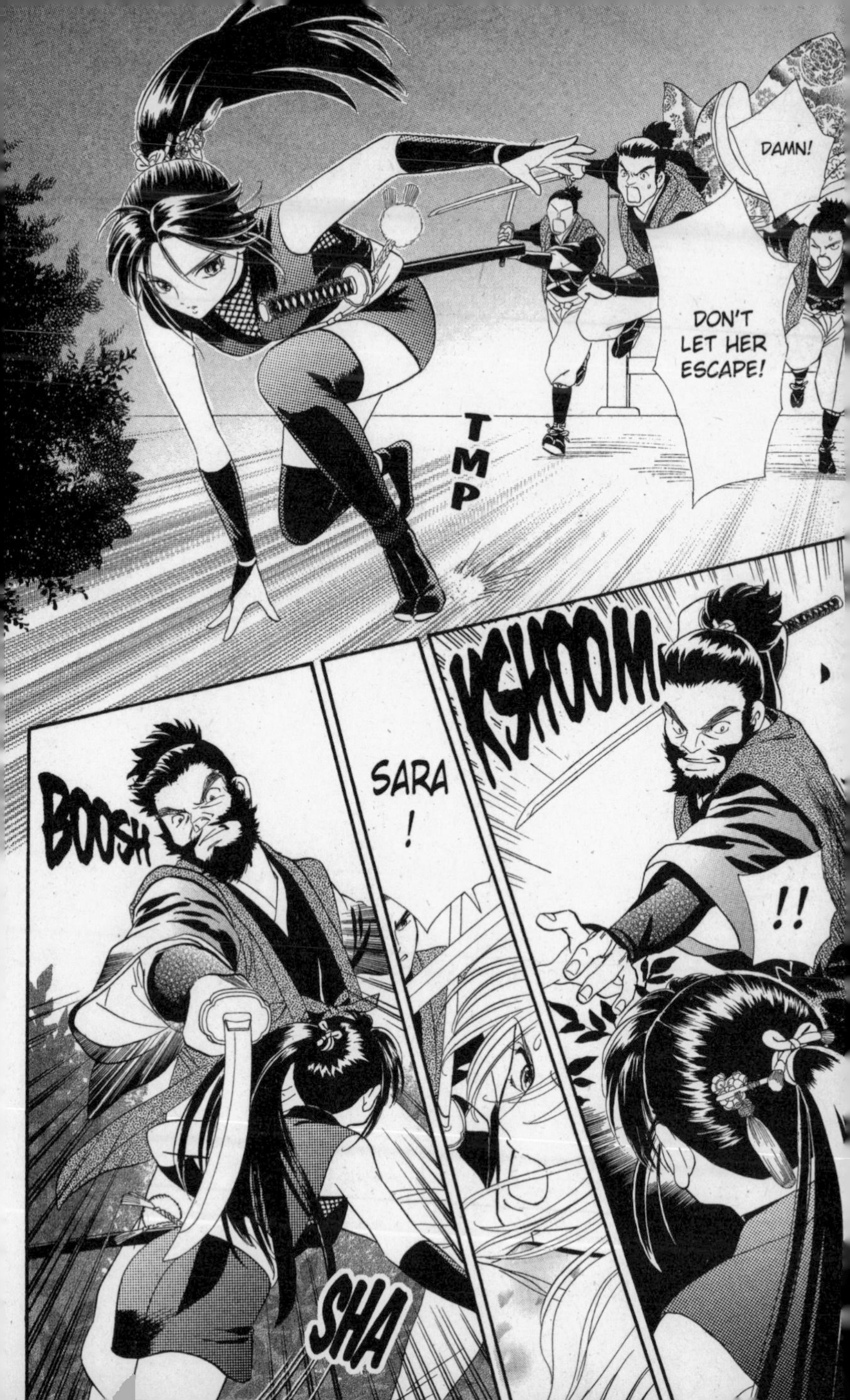
DAMN!
DON'T LET HER ESCAPE!
TMP
KSHOOM
!!
SARA!
BOOSH
SHA

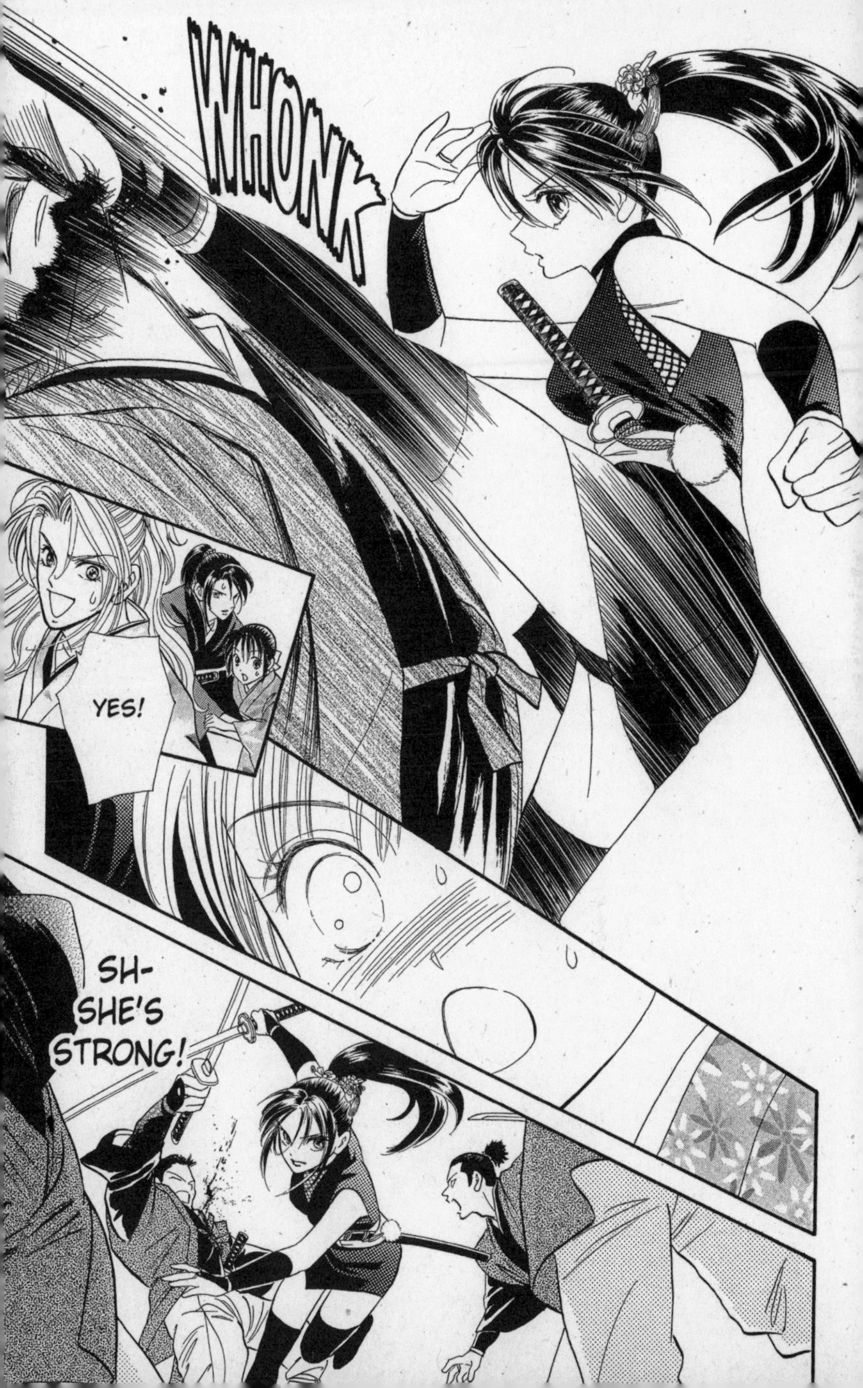
WHONK
YES!
SH-SHE'S STRONG!

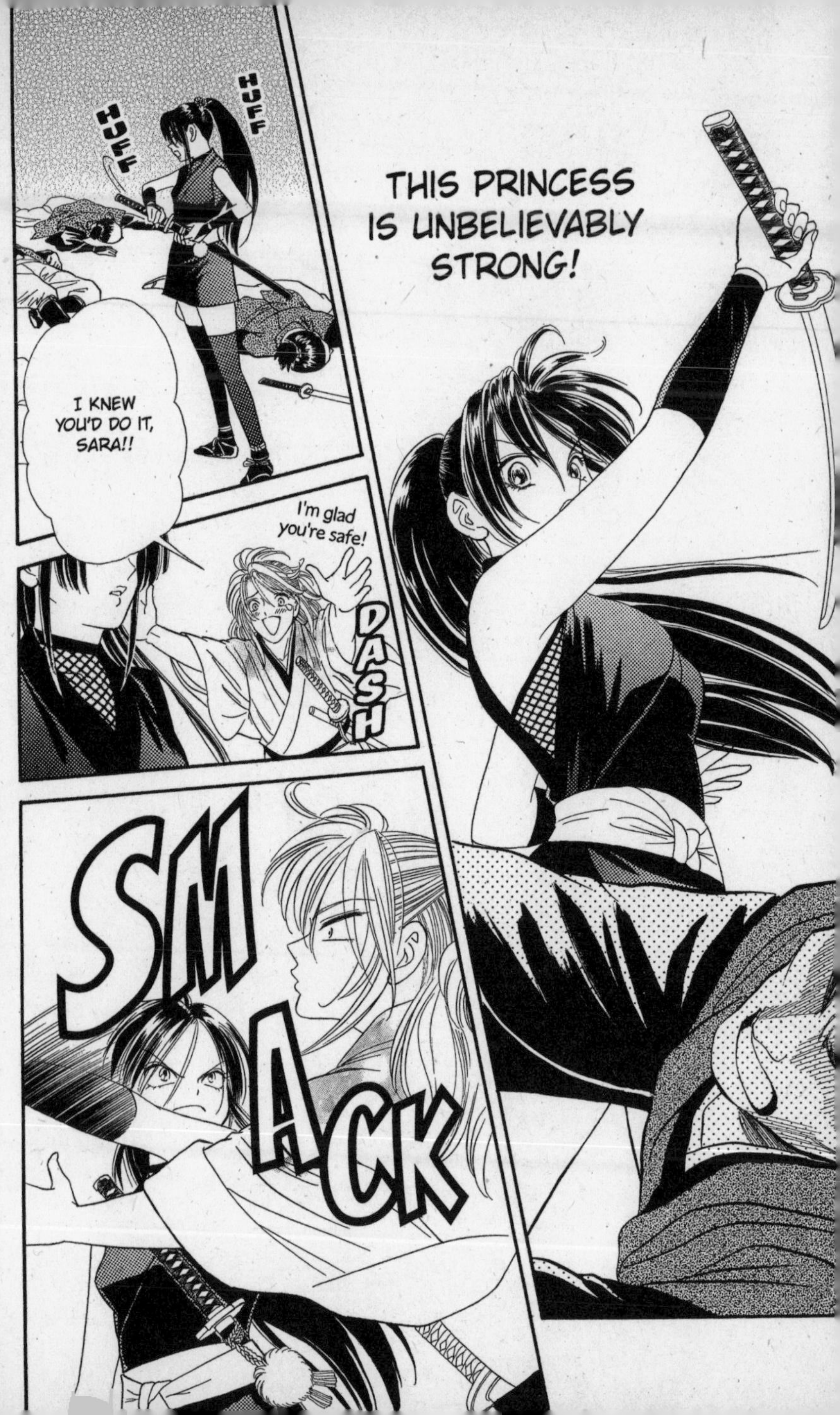
THIS PRINCESS IS UNBELIEVABLY STRONG!
HUFF
HUFF
I KNEW YOU'D DO IT, SARA!!
I'm glad you're safe!
DASH
SMACK

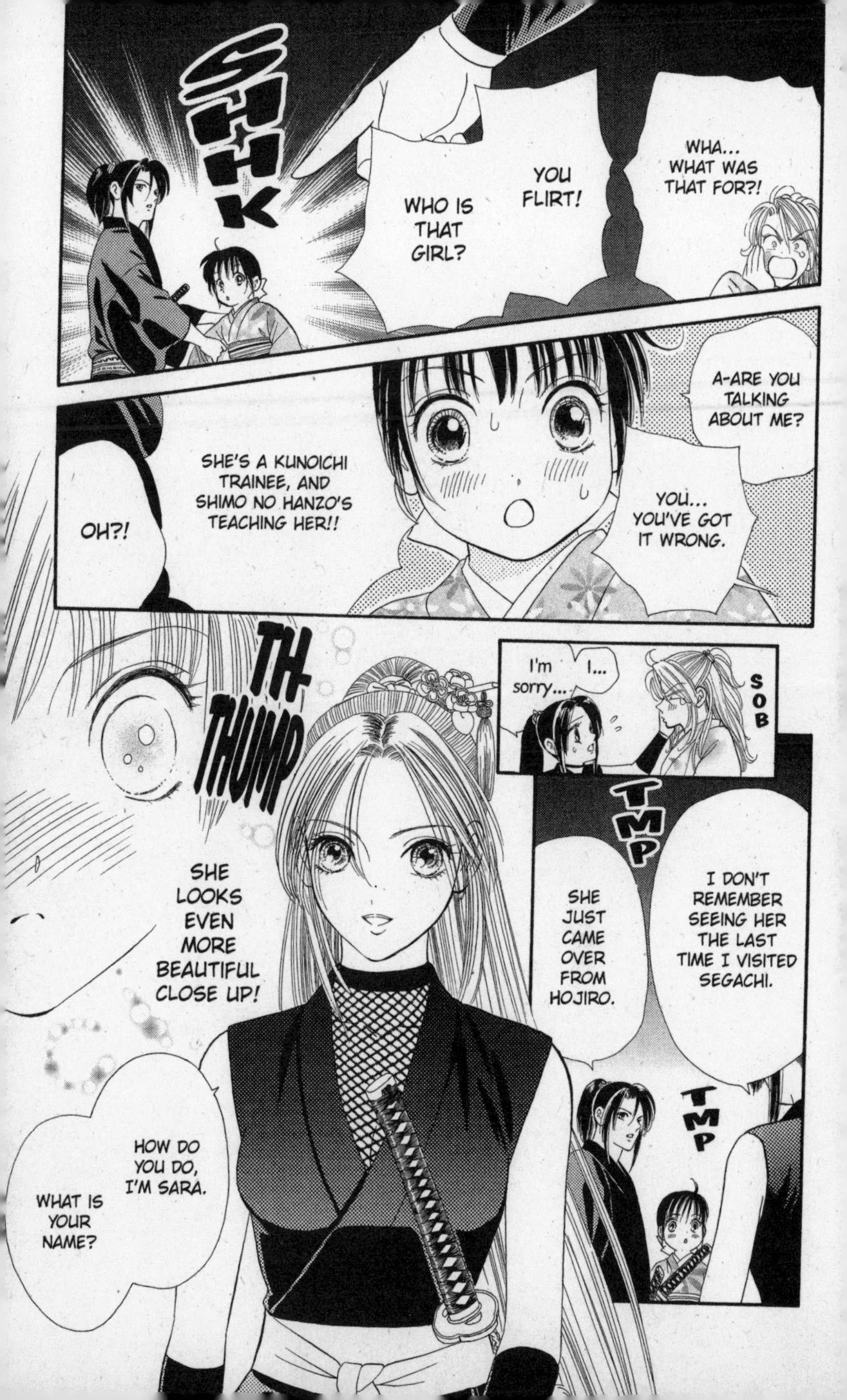
WHA... WHAT WAS THAT FOR?!
YOU FLIRT!
WHO IS THAT GIRL?
SHHK
A-ARE YOU TALKING ABOUT ME?
YOU... YOU'VE GOT IT WRONG.
SHE'S A KUNOICHI TRAINEE, AND SHIMO NO HANZO'S TEACHING HER!!
OH?!
SOB
I...
I'm sorry...
TMP
I DON'T REMEMBER SEEING HER THE LAST TIME I VISITED SEGACHI.
SHE JUST CAME OVER FROM HOJIRO.
TMP
TH-THUMP
SHE LOOKS EVEN MORE BEAUTIFUL CLOSE UP!
HOW DO YOU DO, I'M SARA.
WHAT IS YOUR NAME?

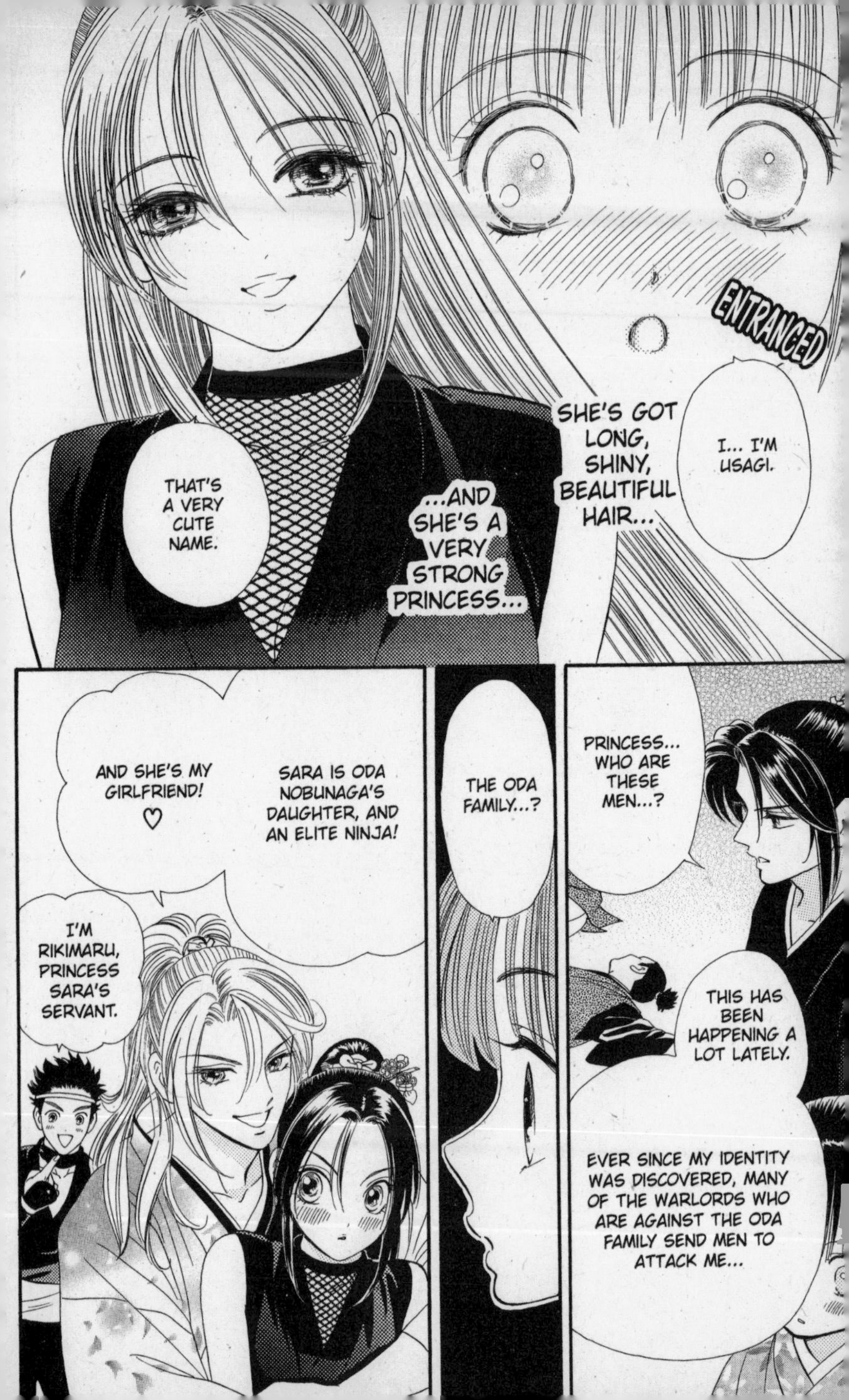
ENTRANCED
I... I'M USAGI.
SHE'S GOT LONG, SHINY, BEAUTIFUL HAIR...
...AND SHE'S A VERY STRONG PRINCESS...
THAT'S A VERY CUTE NAME.
PRINCESS... WHO ARE THESE MEN...?
THIS HAS BEEN HAPPENING A LOT LATELY.
EVER SINCE MY IDENTITY WAS DISCOVERED, MANY OF THE WARLORDS WHO ARE AGAINST THE ODA FAMILY SEND MEN TO ATTACK ME...
THE ODA FAMILY...?
SARA IS ODA NOBUNAGA'S DAUGHTER, AND AN ELITE NINJA!
AND SHE'S MY GIRLFRIEND! ♡
I'M RIKIMARU, PRINCESS SARA'S SERVANT.

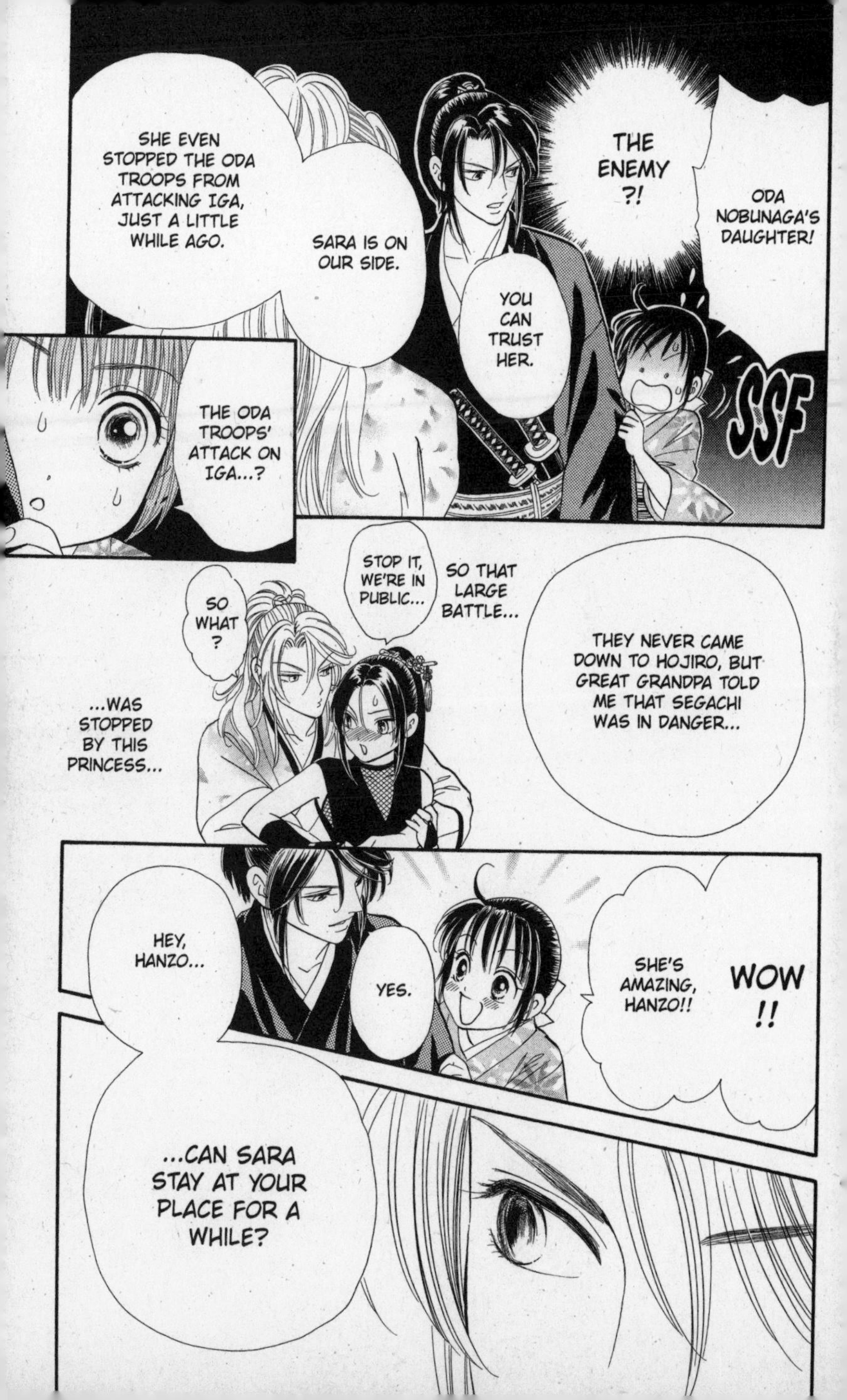
ODA NOBUNAGA'S DAUGHTER!
THE ENEMY ?!
SSF
YOU CAN TRUST HER.
SARA IS ON OUR SIDE.
SHE EVEN STOPPED THE ODA TROOPS FROM ATTACKING IGA, JUST A LITTLE WHILE AGO.
THE ODA TROOPS' ATTACK ON IGA...?
THEY NEVER CAME DOWN TO HOJIRO, BUT GREAT GRANDPA TOLD ME THAT SEGACHI WAS IN DANGER...
SO THAT LARGE BATTLE...
...WAS STOPPED BY THIS PRINCESS...
STOP IT, WE'RE IN PUBLIC...
SO WHAT ?
WOW !!
SHE'S AMAZING, HANZO!!
YES.
HEY, HANZO...
...CAN SARA STAY AT YOUR PLACE FOR A WHILE?

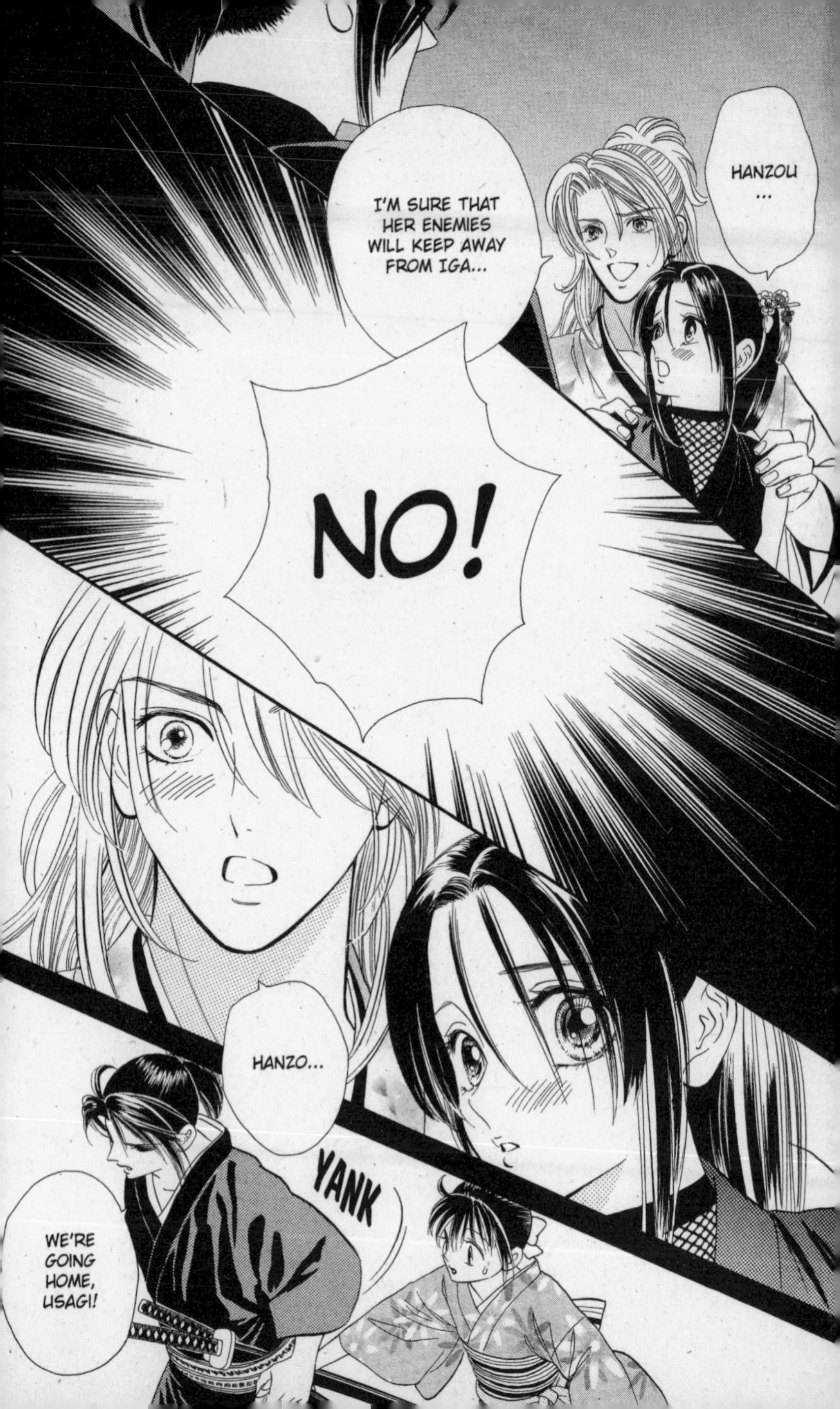
HANZOU ...
I'M SURE THAT HER ENEMIES WILL KEEP AWAY FROM IGA...
NO!
HANZO...
YANK
WE'RE GOING HOME, USAGI!

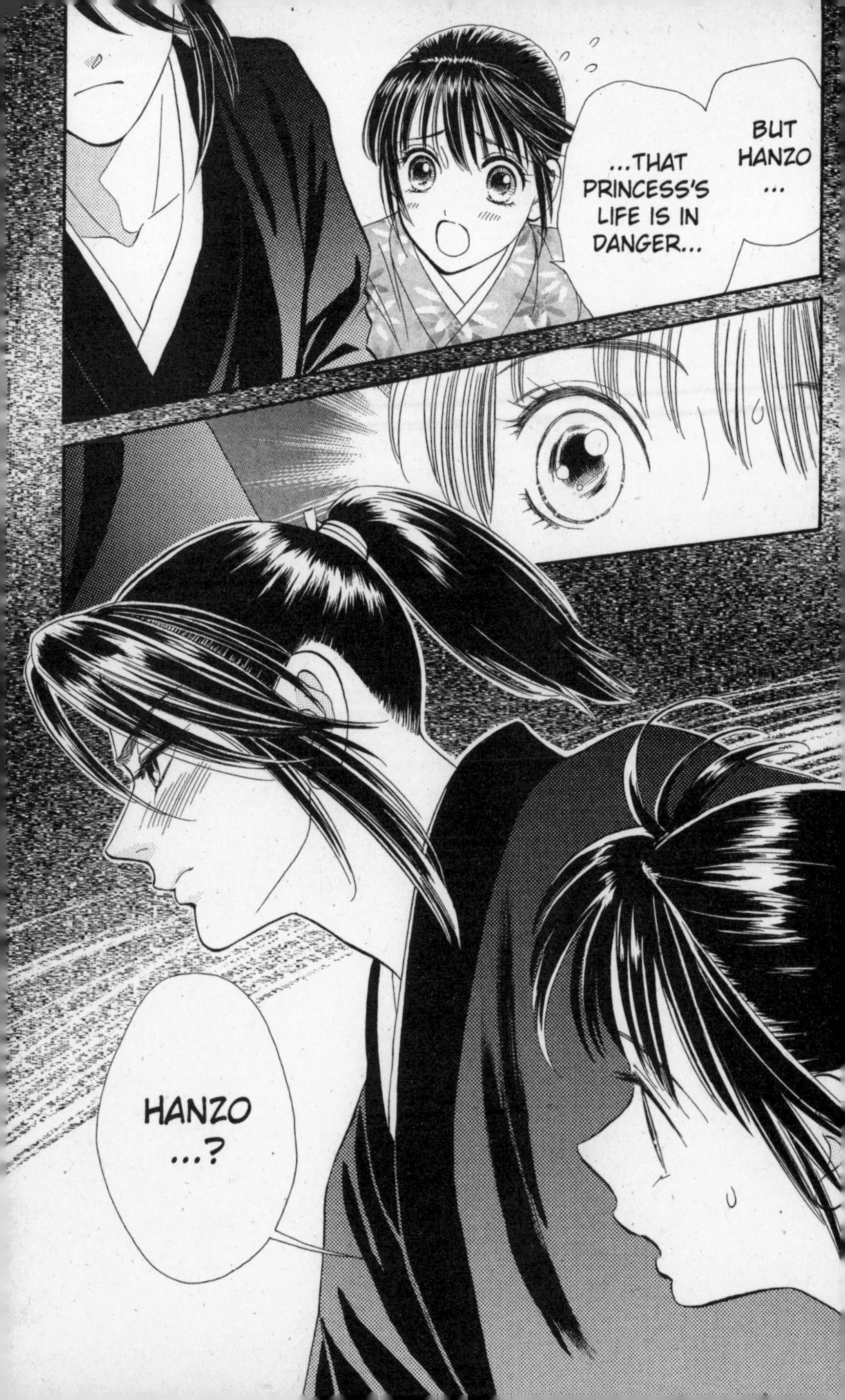
BUT HANZO ...
...THAT PRINCESS'S LIFE IS IN DANGER...
HANZO ...?

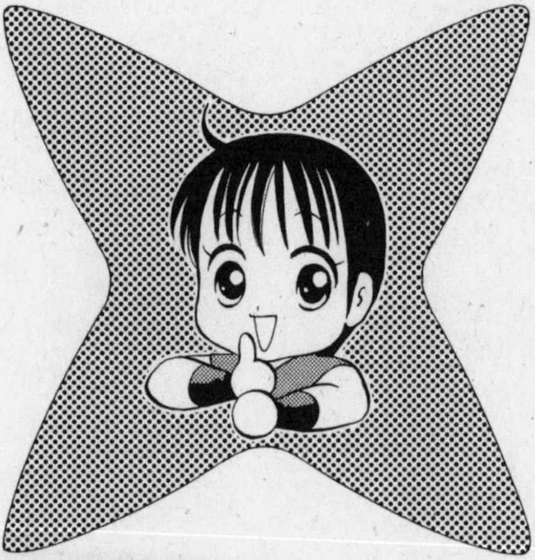

Tail of the Moon™

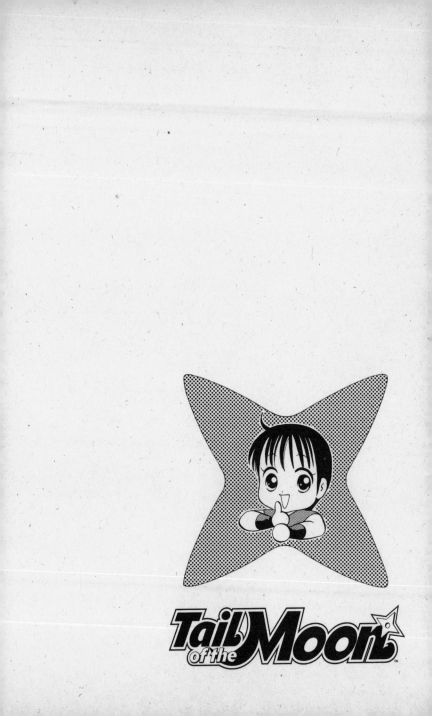

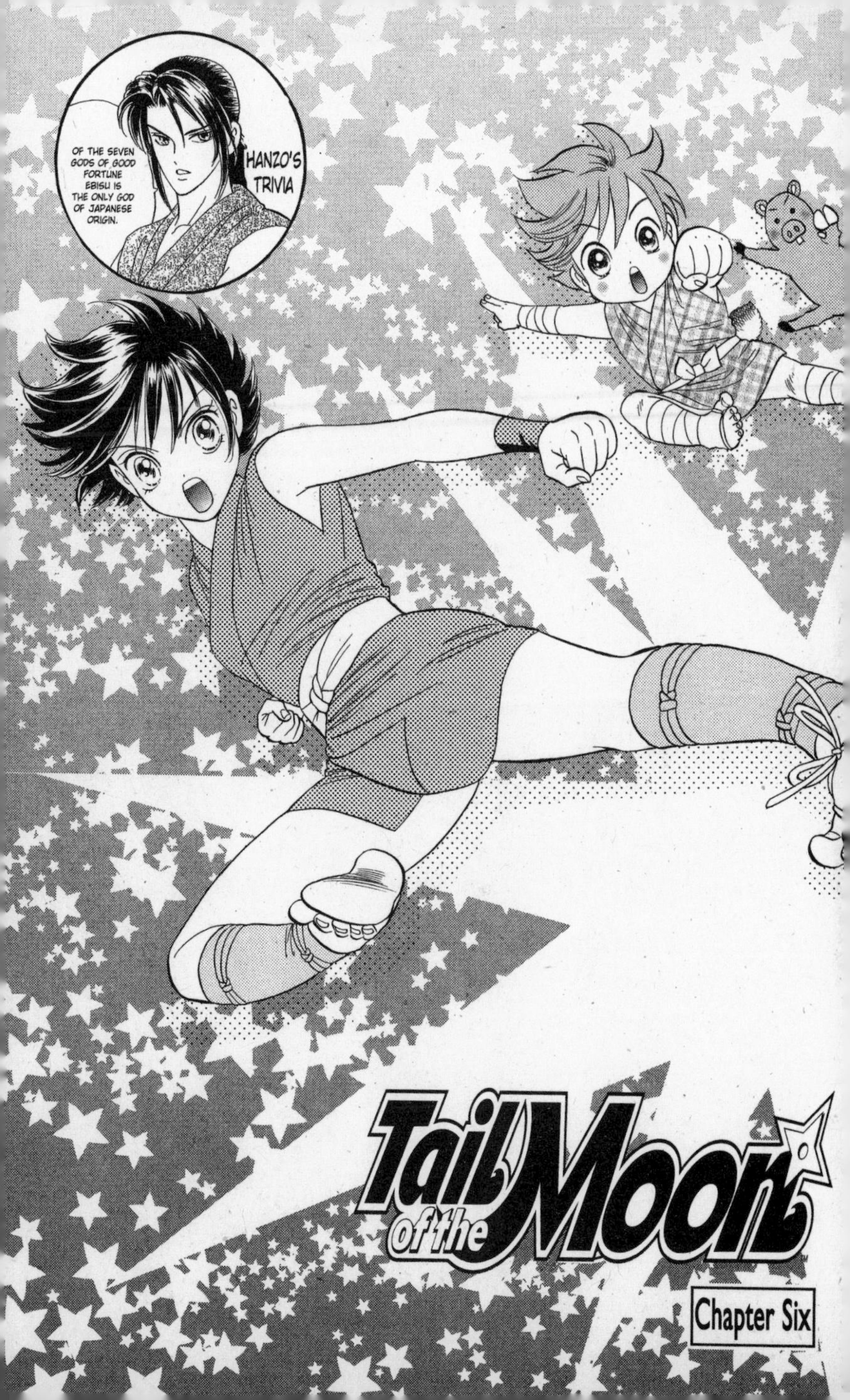
HANZO'S TRIVIA
OF THE SEVEN GODS OF GOOD FORTUNE EBISU IS THE ONLY GOD OF JAPANESE ORIGIN.
Tail of the Moon
Chapter Six

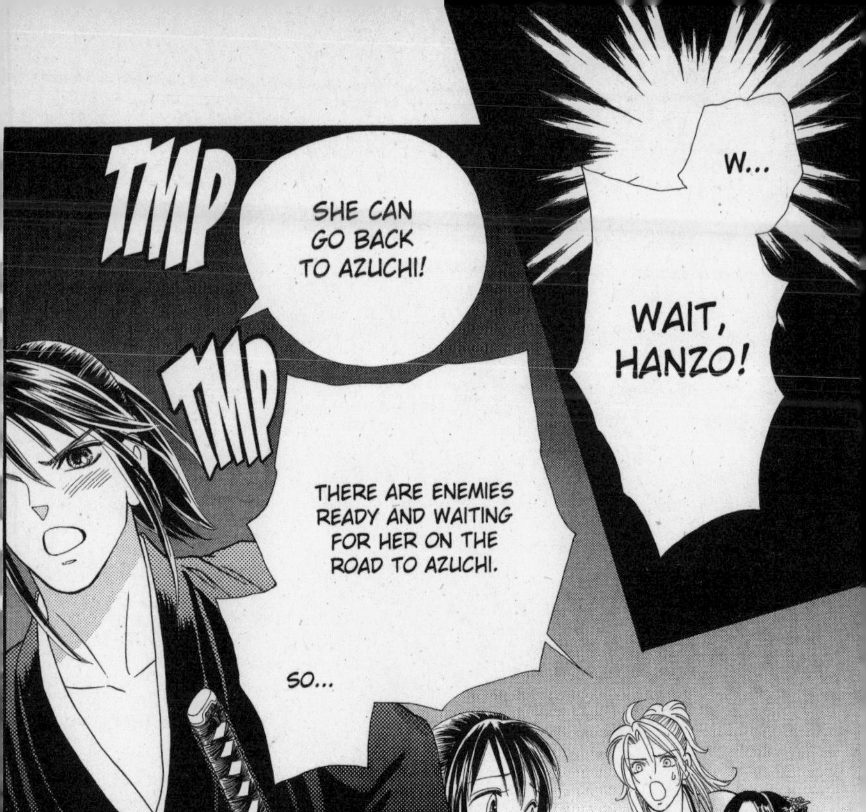
W...
WAIT, HANZO!
TMP
SHE CAN GO BACK TO AZUCHI!
TMP
THERE ARE ENEMIES READY AND WAITING FOR HER ON THE ROAD TO AZUCHI.
SO...
IT'S OKAY, HANZOU...

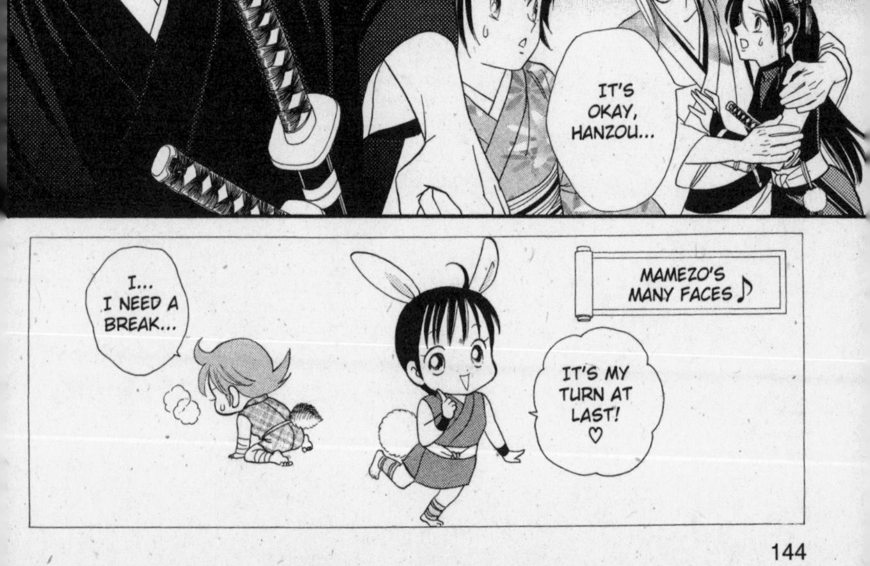
MAMEZO'S MANY FACES ♪
IT'S MY TURN AT LAST! ♡
I... I NEED A BREAK...

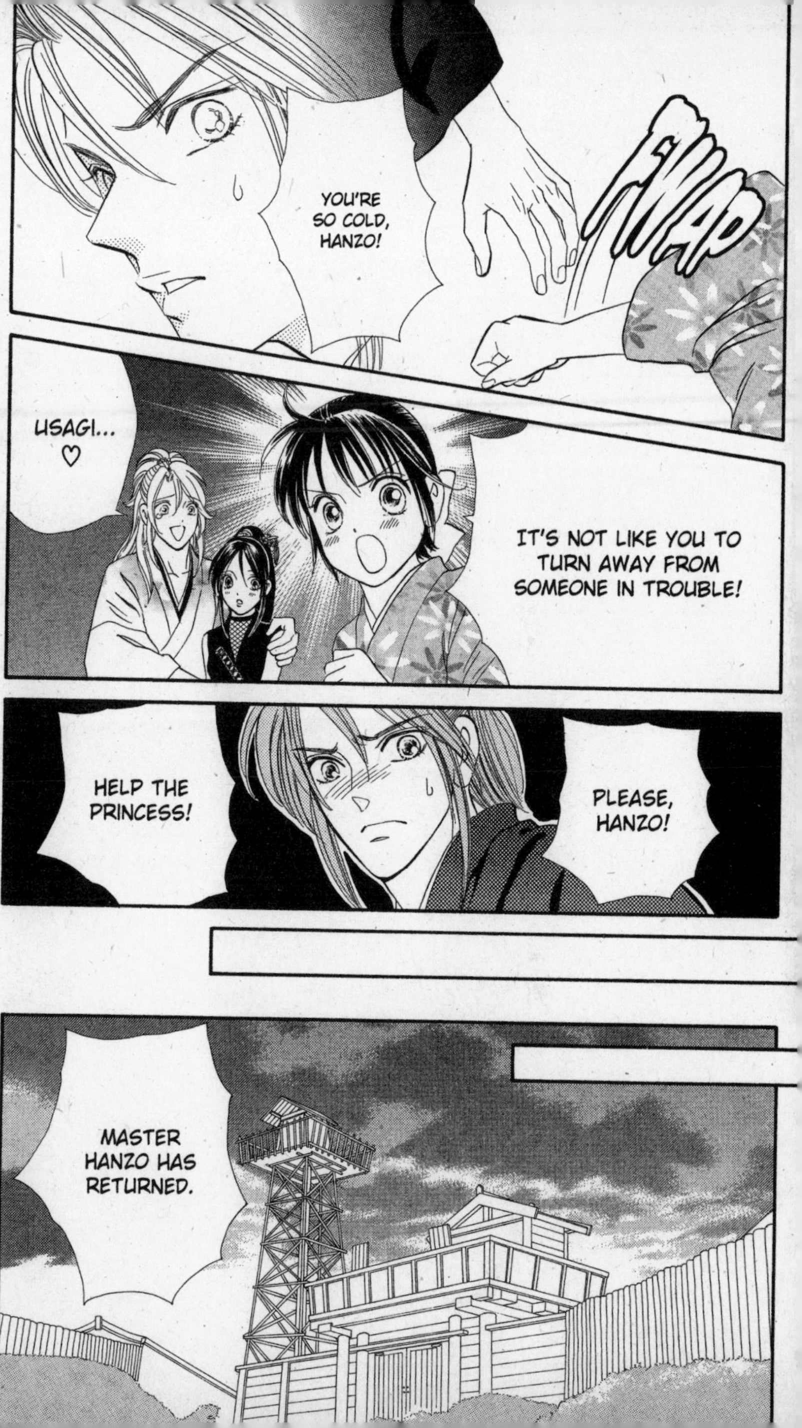
FWAP
YOU'RE SO COLD, HANZO!
IT'S NOT LIKE YOU TO TURN AWAY FROM SOMEONE IN TROUBLE!
USAGI... ♡
PLEASE, HANZO!
HELP THE PRINCESS!
MASTER HANZO HAS RETURNED.

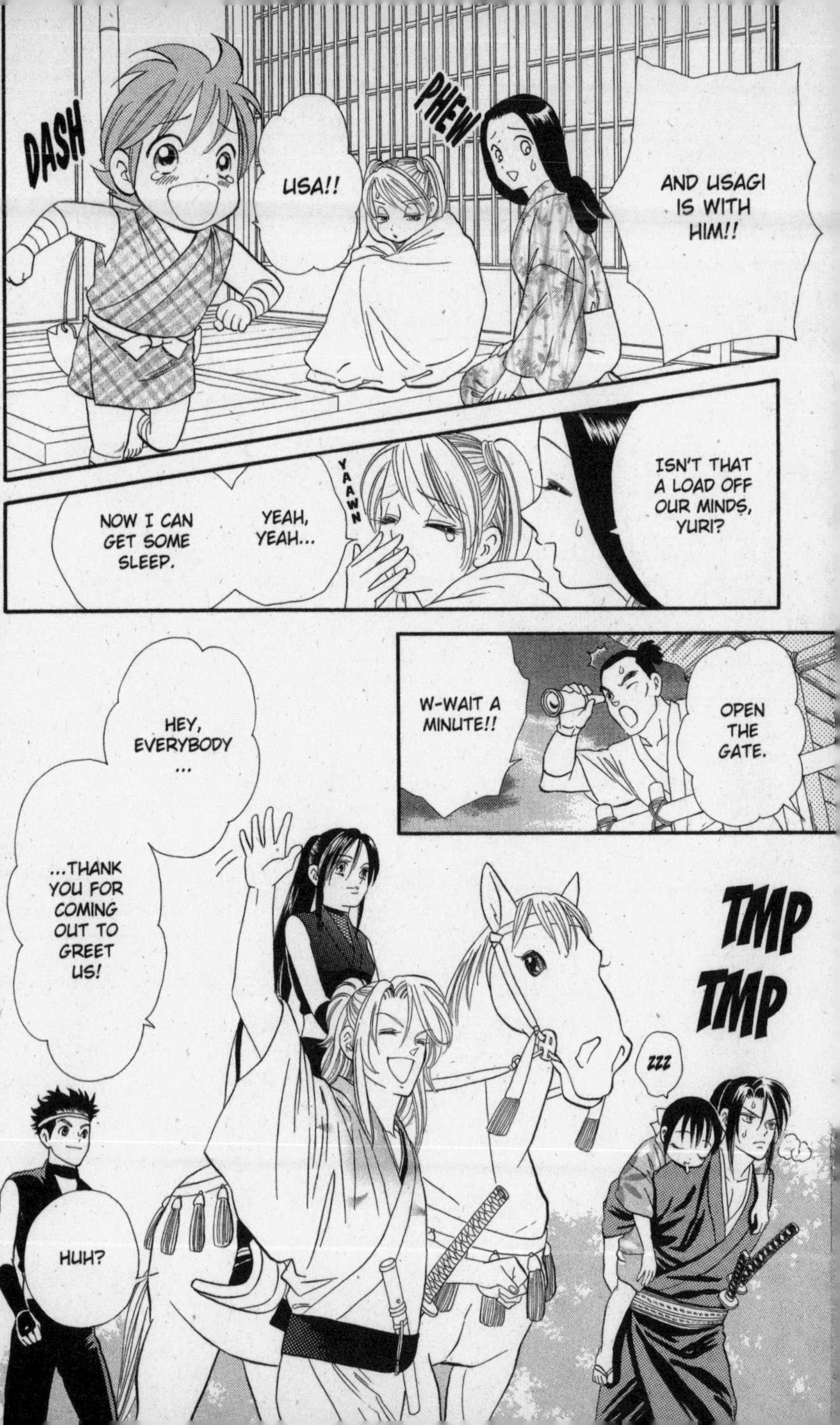
AND USAGI IS WITH HIM!!
PHEW
USA!!
DASH
ISN'T THAT A LOAD OFF OUR MINDS, YURI?
YAAWN
YEAH, YEAH...
NOW I CAN GET SOME SLEEP.
OPEN THE GATE.
W-WAIT A MINUTE!!
TMP TMP
ZZZ
HEY, EVERYBODY ...
...THANK YOU FOR COMING OUT TO GREET US!
HUH?

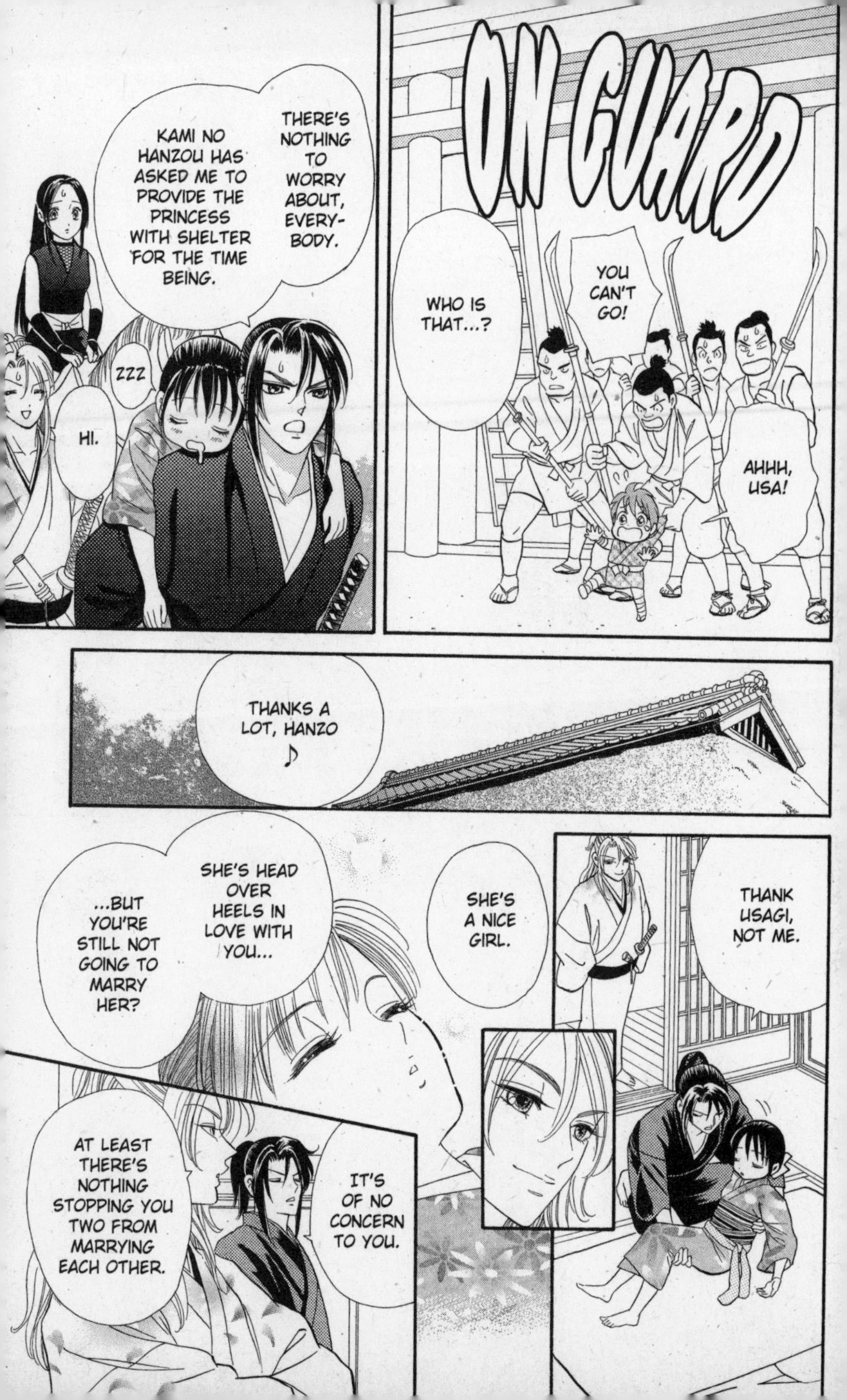
ON GUARD
YOU CAN'T GO!
WHO IS THAT...?
AHHH, USA!
THERE'S NOTHING TO WORRY ABOUT, EVERY-BODY.
KAMI NO HANZOU HAS ASKED ME TO PROVIDE THE PRINCESS WITH SHELTER FOR THE TIME BEING.
ZZZ
HI.
THANKS A LOT, HANZO ♪
THANK USAGI, NOT ME.
SHE'S A NICE GIRL.
SHE'S HEAD OVER HEELS IN LOVE WITH YOU...
...BUT YOU'RE STILL NOT GOING TO MARRY HER?
IT'S OF NO CONCERN TO YOU.
AT LEAST THERE'S NOTHING STOPPING YOU TWO FROM MARRYING EACH OTHER.

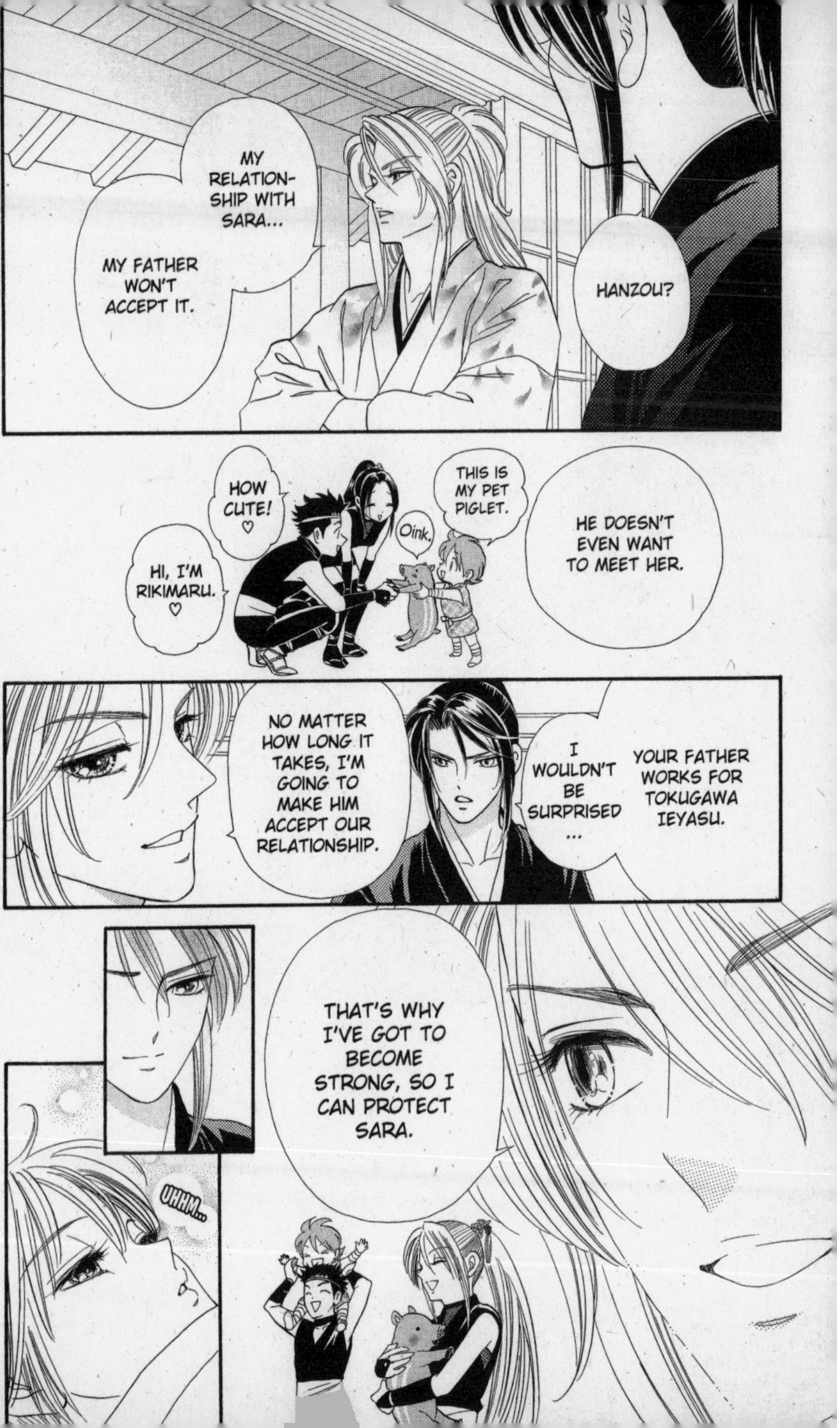
HANZOU?
MY RELATIONSHIP WITH SARA...
MY FATHER WON'T ACCEPT IT.
HE DOESN'T EVEN WANT TO MEET HER.
THIS IS MY PET PIGLET.
Oink.
HOW CUTE! ♡
HI, I'M RIKIMARU. ♡
YOUR FATHER WORKS FOR TOKUGAWA IEYASU.
I WOULDN'T BE SURPRISED ...
NO MATTER HOW LONG IT TAKES, I'M GOING TO MAKE HIM ACCEPT OUR RELATIONSHIP.
THAT'S WHY I'VE GOT TO BECOME STRONG, SO I CAN PROTECT SARA.
UHHM...

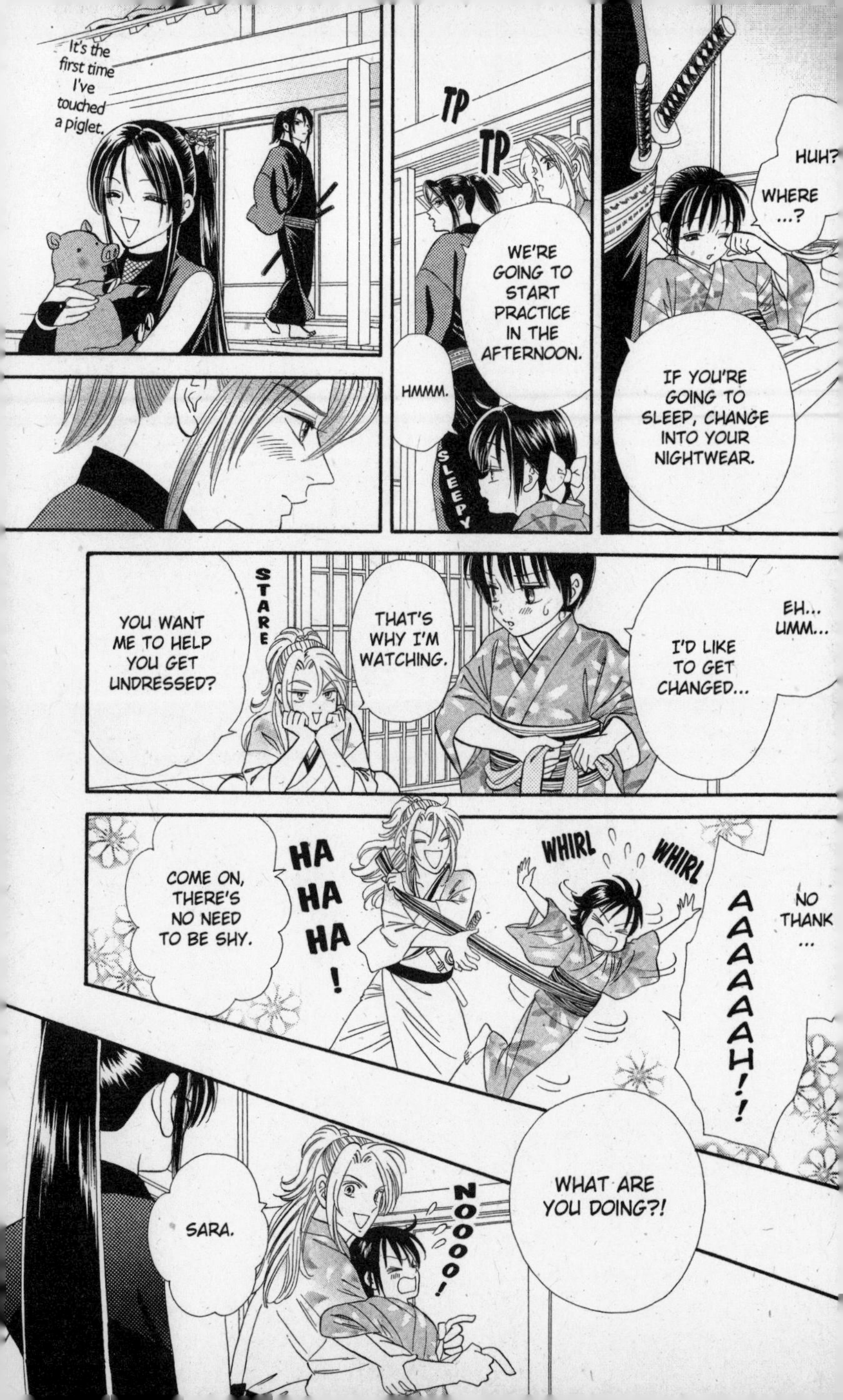
HUH?
WHERE ...?
IF YOU'RE GOING TO SLEEP, CHANGE INTO YOUR NIGHTWEAR.
TP
TP
WE'RE GOING TO START PRACTICE IN THE AFTERNOON.
HMMM.
SLEEPY
It's the first time I've touched a piglet.
EH... UMM...
I'D LIKE TO GET CHANGED...
THAT'S WHY I'M WATCHING.
STARE
YOU WANT ME TO HELP YOU GET UNDRESSED?
NO THANK...
AAAAAAAH!!
WHIRL
WHIRL
HA HA HA!
COME ON, THERE'S NO NEED TO BE SHY.
WHAT ARE YOU DOING?!
NOOOO!
SARA.

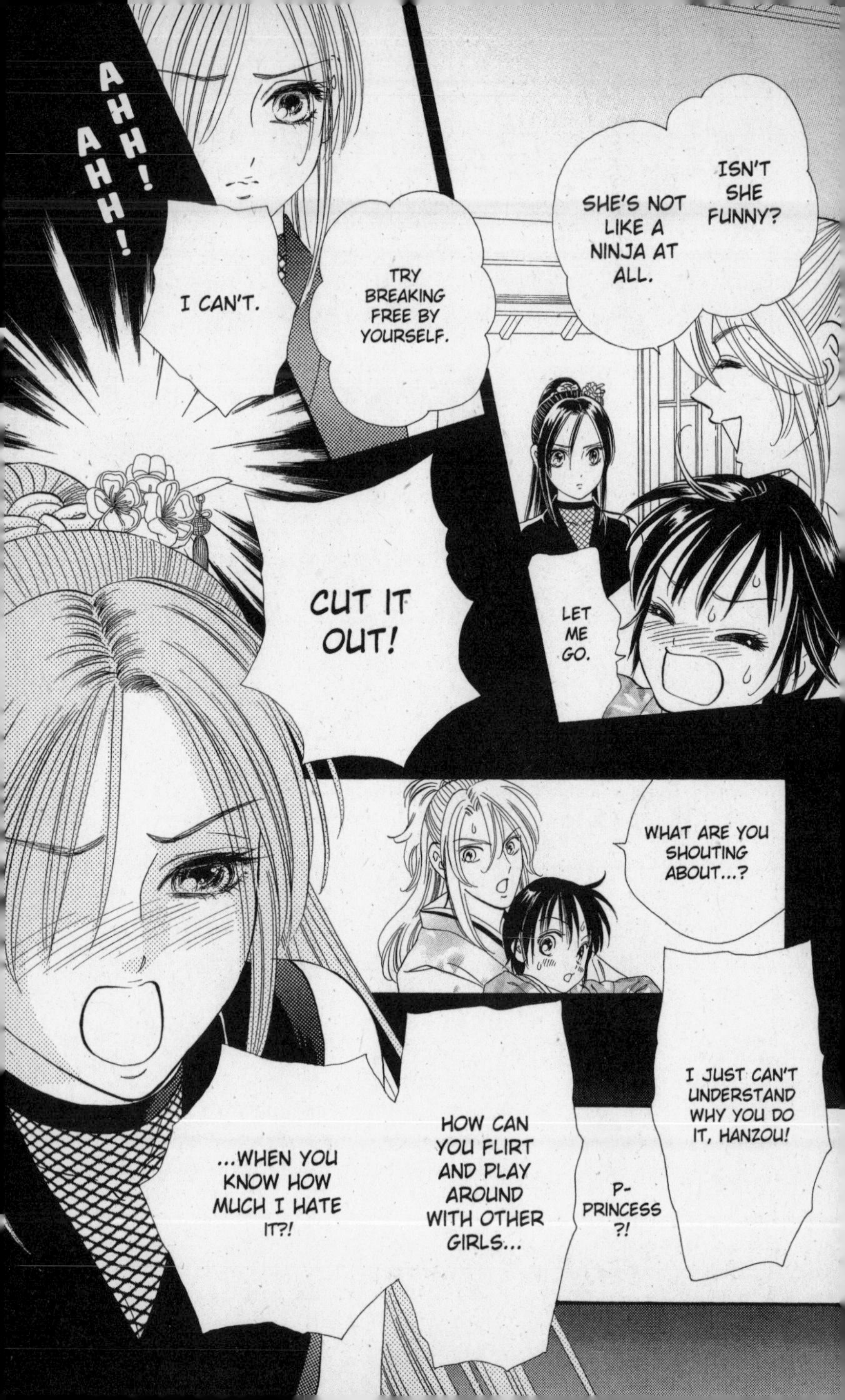
ISN'T SHE FUNNY?
SHE'S NOT LIKE A NINJA AT ALL.
LET ME GO.
AHH! AHH!
TRY BREAKING FREE BY YOURSELF.
I CAN'T.
CUT IT OUT!
WHAT ARE YOU SHOUTING ABOUT...?
I JUST CAN'T UNDERSTAND WHY YOU DO IT, HANZOU!
P-PRINCESS?!
HOW CAN YOU FLIRT AND PLAY AROUND WITH OTHER GIRLS...
...WHEN YOU KNOW HOW MUCH I HATE IT?!

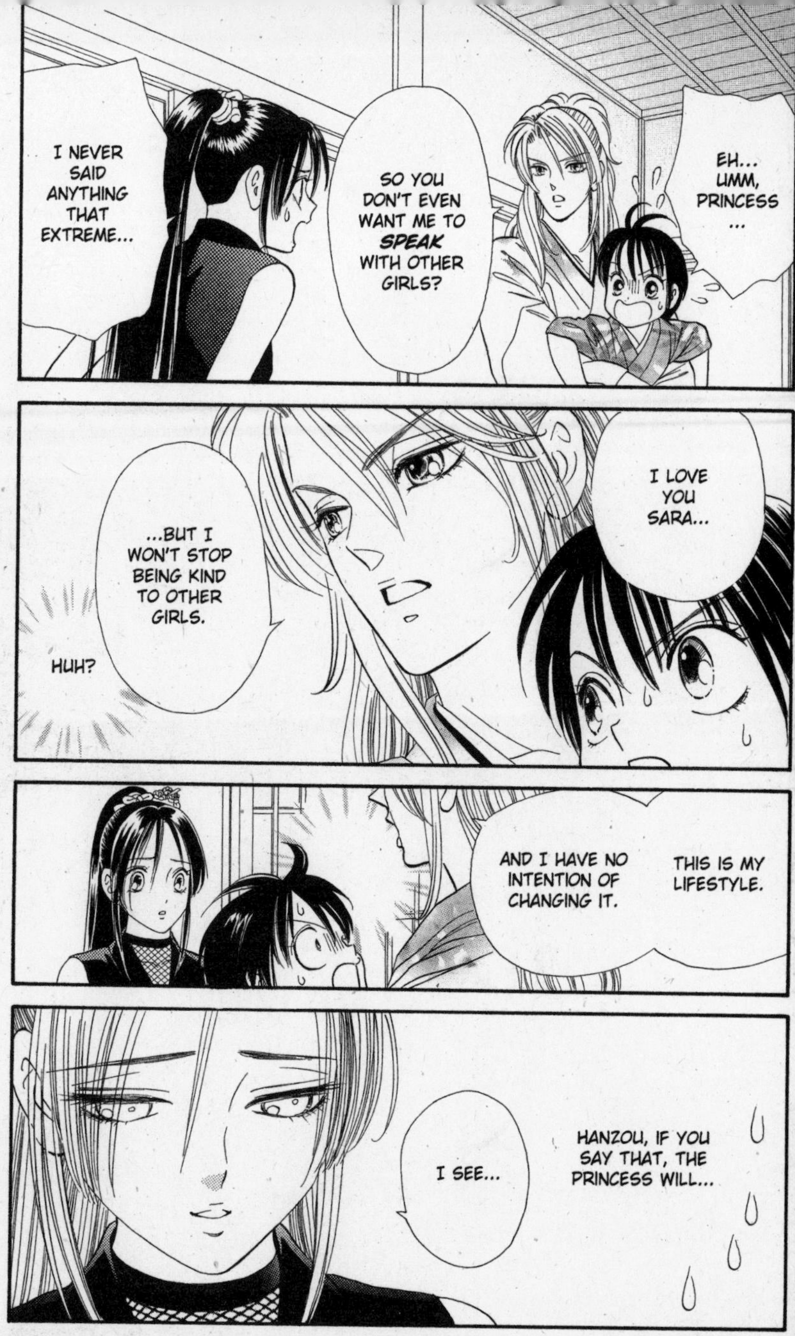
EH... UMM, PRINCESS...
SO YOU DON'T EVEN WANT ME TO **SPEAK** WITH OTHER GIRLS?
I NEVER SAID ANYTHING THAT EXTREME...
I LOVE YOU SARA...
...BUT I WON'T STOP BEING KIND TO OTHER GIRLS.
HUH?
THIS IS MY LIFESTYLE.
AND I HAVE NO INTENTION OF CHANGING IT.
HANZOU, IF YOU SAY THAT, THE PRINCESS WILL...
I SEE...

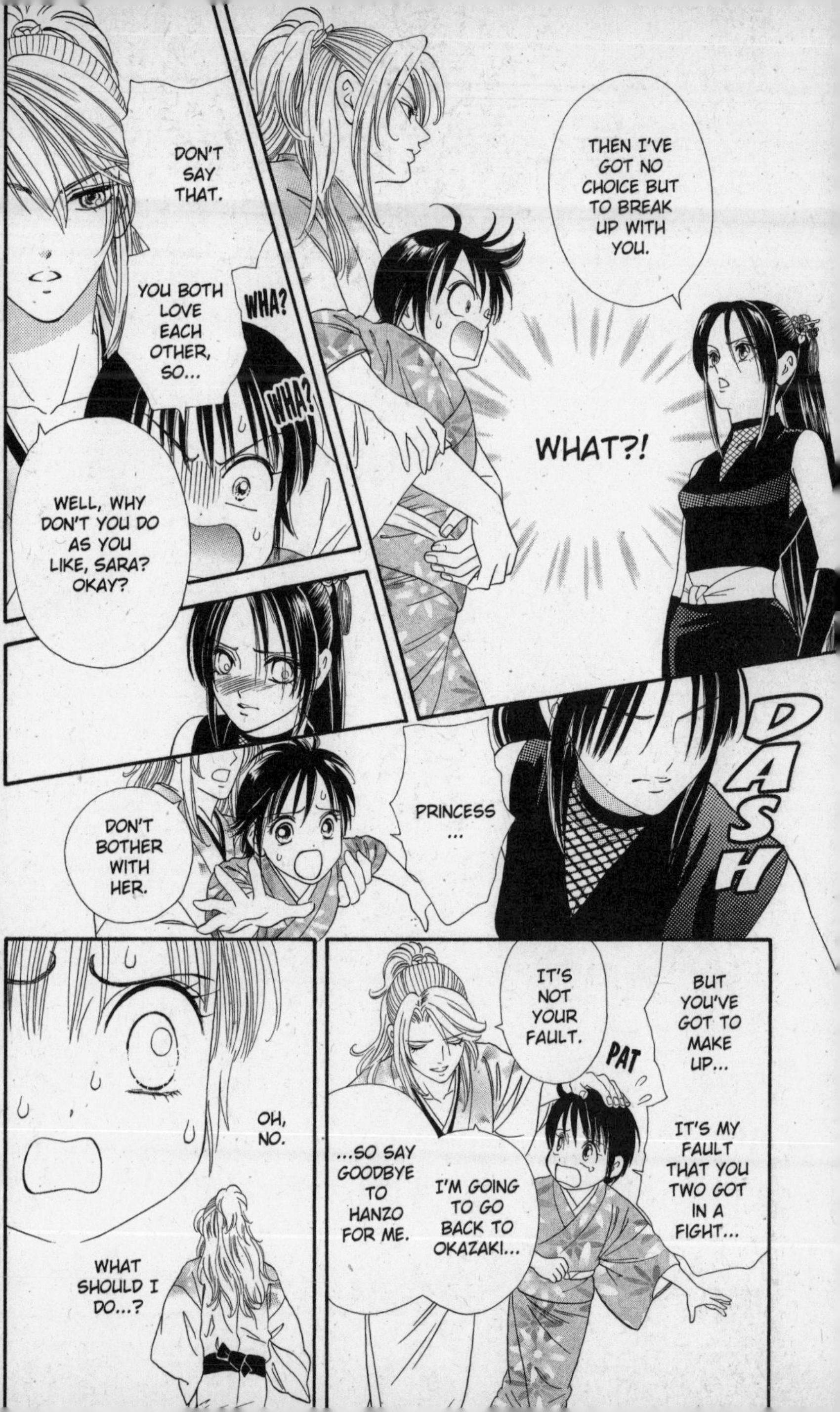
THEN I'VE GOT NO CHOICE BUT TO BREAK UP WITH YOU.
WHAT?!
WHA?
DON'T SAY THAT.
YOU BOTH LOVE EACH OTHER, SO...
WHA?
WELL, WHY DON'T YOU DO AS YOU LIKE, SARA? OKAY?
DASH
PRINCESS...
DON'T BOTHER WITH HER.
BUT YOU'VE GOT TO MAKE UP...
IT'S NOT YOUR FAULT.
PAT
IT'S MY FAULT THAT YOU TWO GOT IN A FIGHT...
I'M GOING TO GO BACK TO OKAZAKI...
...SO SAY GOODBYE TO HANZO FOR ME.
OH, NO.
WHAT SHOULD I DO...?

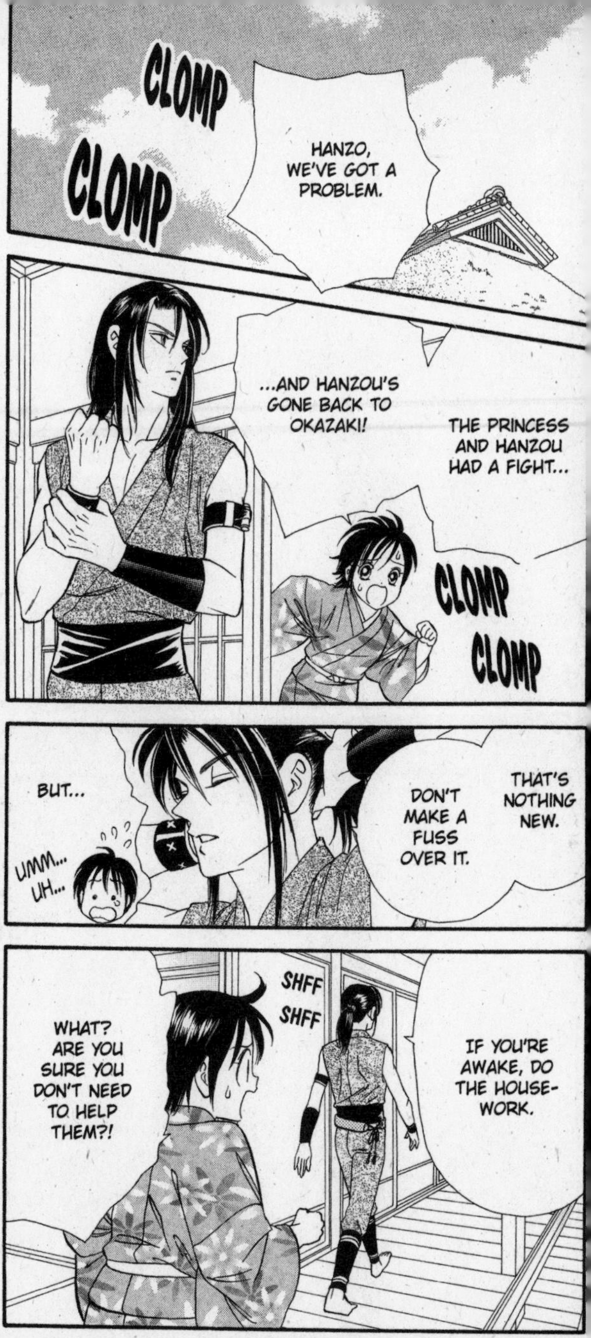
HANZO, WE'VE GOT A PROBLEM.
CLOMP
CLOMP
THE PRINCESS AND HANZOU HAD A FIGHT...
...AND HANZOU'S GONE BACK TO OKAZAKI!
CLOMP
CLOMP
THAT'S NOTHING NEW.
DON'T MAKE A FUSS OVER IT.
BUT...
UMM... UH...
IF YOU'RE AWAKE, DO THE HOUSE-WORK.
SHFF
SHFF
WHAT? ARE YOU SURE YOU DON'T NEED TO HELP THEM?!

This and that from the author 6

I read every letter I get from all of my readers gratefully. Thank you very much!!
I have never actually seen anybody reading my manga...

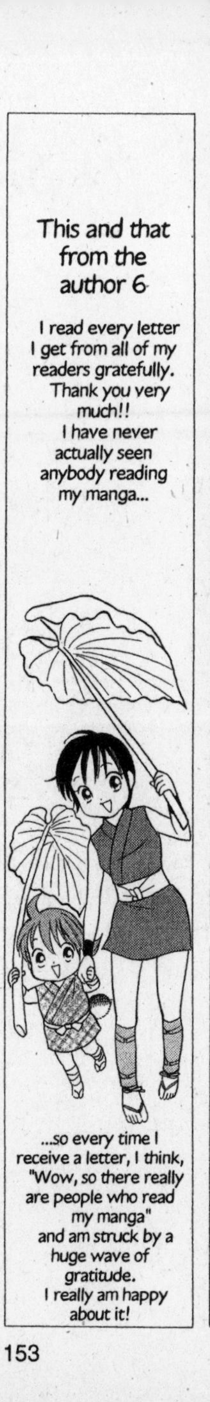

...so every time I receive a letter, I think, "Wow, so there really are people who read my manga" and am struck by a huge wave of gratitude.
I really am happy about it!

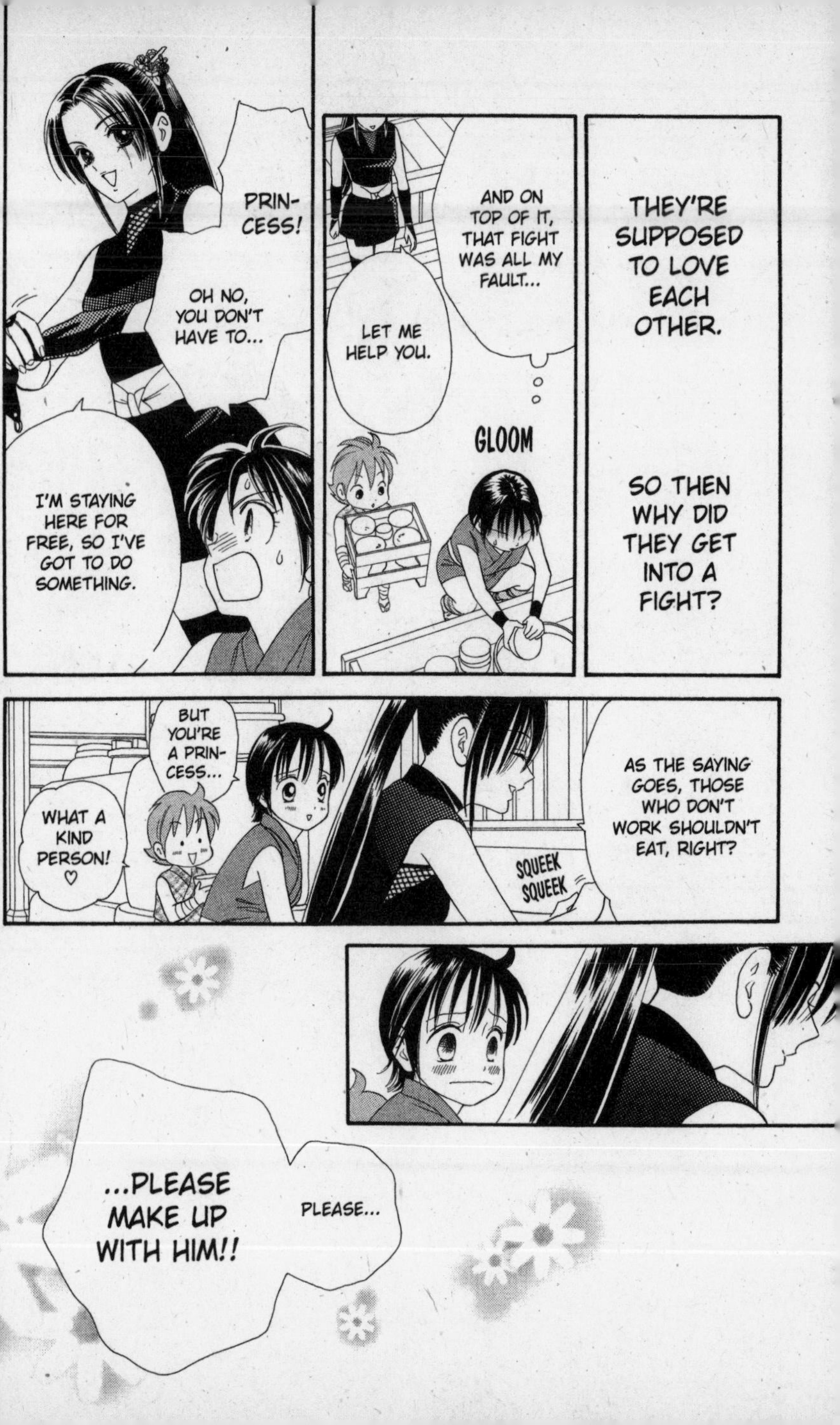
THEY'RE SUPPOSED TO LOVE EACH OTHER.
SO THEN WHY DID THEY GET INTO A FIGHT?
AND ON TOP OF IT, THAT FIGHT WAS ALL MY FAULT...
GLOOM
LET ME HELP YOU.
PRIN-CESS!
OH NO, YOU DON'T HAVE TO...
I'M STAYING HERE FOR FREE, SO I'VE GOT TO DO SOMETHING.
AS THE SAYING GOES, THOSE WHO DON'T WORK SHOULDN'T EAT, RIGHT?
SQUEEK SQUEEK
BUT YOU'RE A PRIN-CESS...
WHAT A KIND PERSON! ♡
PLEASE...
...PLEASE MAKE UP WITH HIM!!

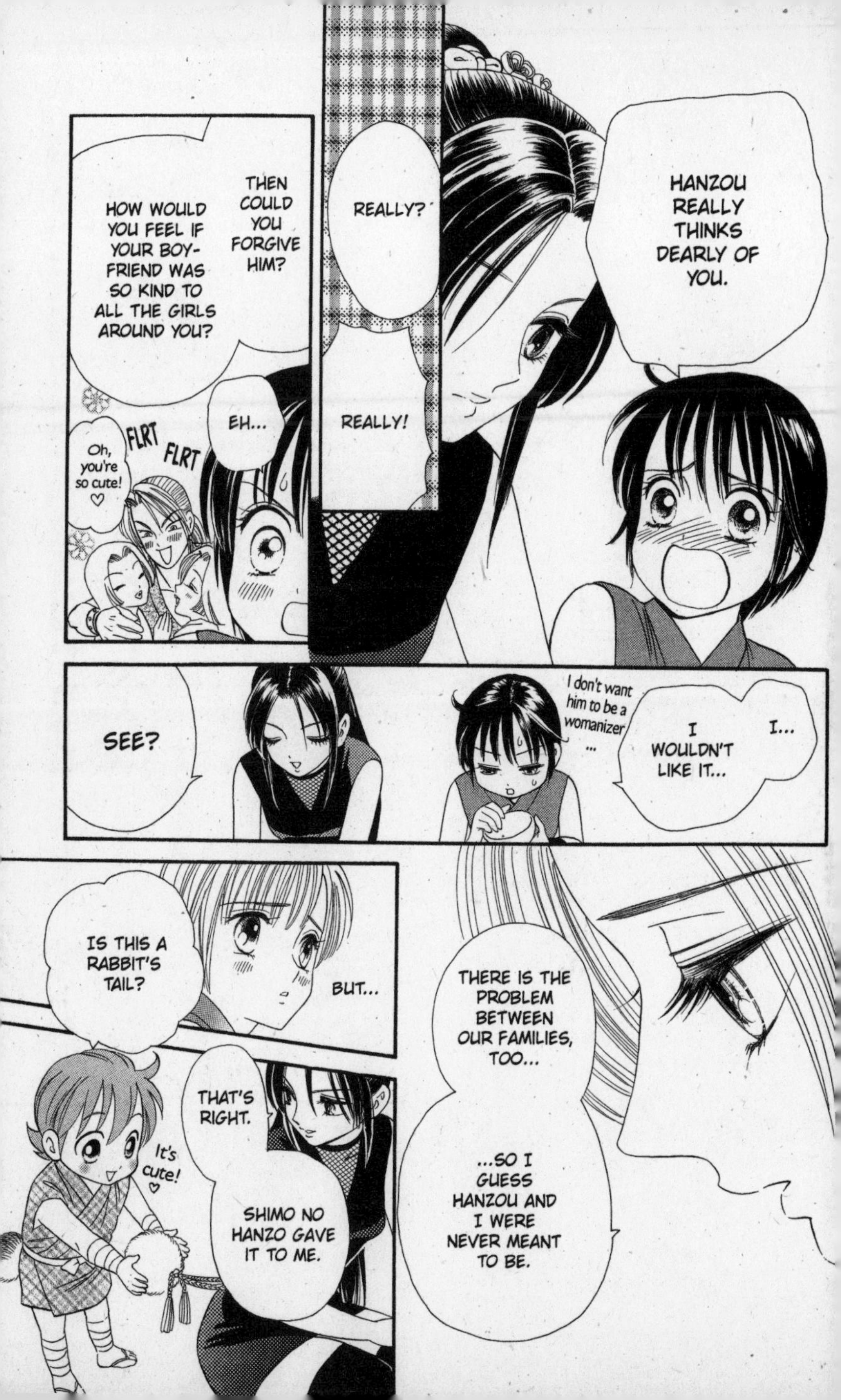
HANZOU REALLY THINKS DEARLY OF YOU.
REALLY?
REALLY!
THEN COULD YOU FORGIVE HIM?
HOW WOULD YOU FEEL IF YOUR BOY-FRIEND WAS SO KIND TO ALL THE GIRLS AROUND YOU?
EH...
FLRT FLRT
Oh, you're so cute! ♡
I...
I WOULDN'T LIKE IT...
I don't want him to be a womanizer...
SEE?
THERE IS THE PROBLEM BETWEEN OUR FAMILIES, TOO...
...SO I GUESS HANZOU AND I WERE NEVER MEANT TO BE.
BUT...
IS THIS A RABBIT'S TAIL?
THAT'S RIGHT.
SHIMO NO HANZO GAVE IT TO ME.
It's cute! ♡

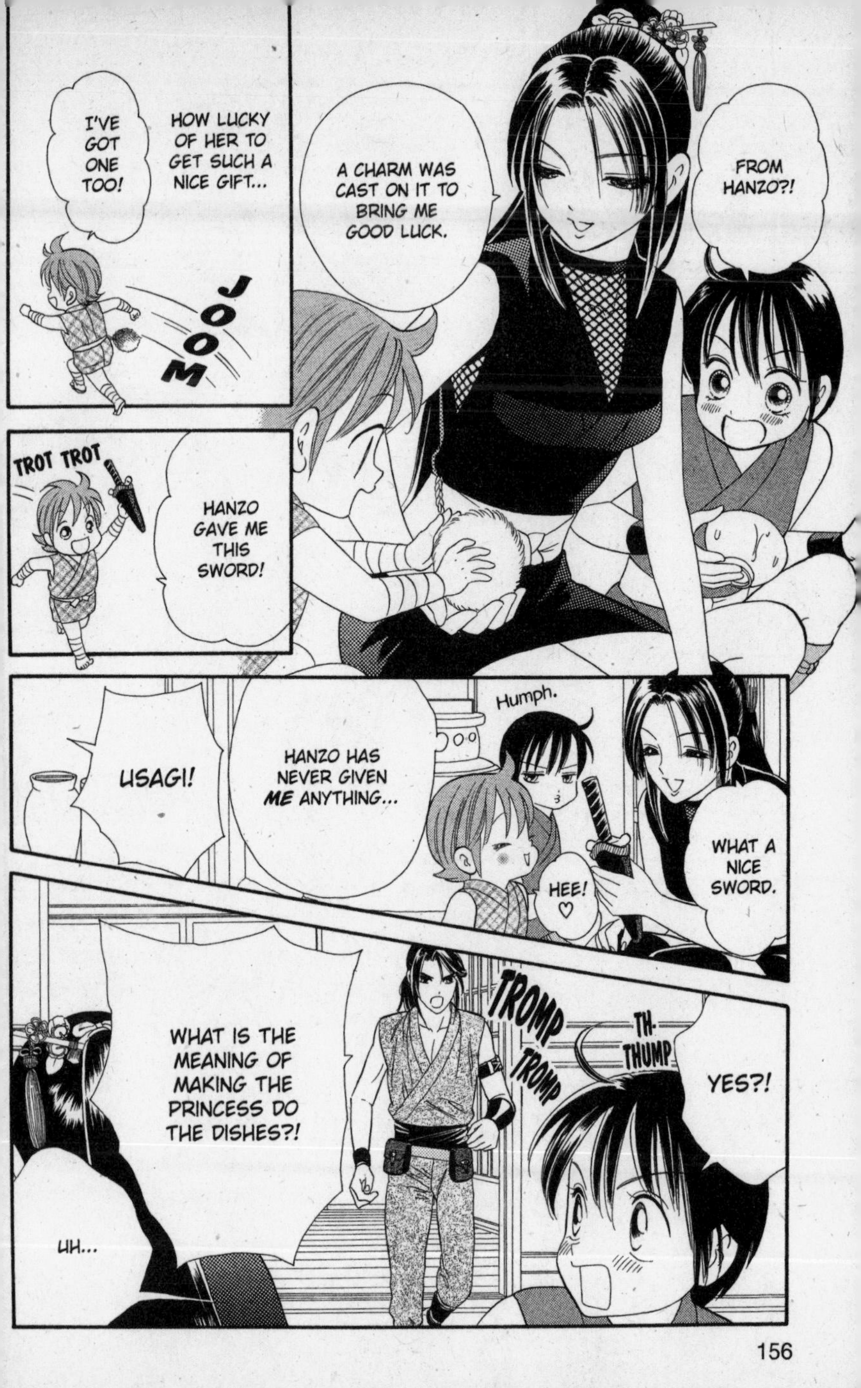

FROM HANZO?!
A CHARM WAS CAST ON IT TO BRING ME GOOD LUCK.
HOW LUCKY OF HER TO GET SUCH A NICE GIFT...
I'VE GOT ONE TOO!
JOOM
HANZO GAVE ME THIS SWORD!
TROT TROT
Humph.
WHAT A NICE SWORD.
HEE! ♡
HANZO HAS NEVER GIVEN *ME* ANYTHING...
USAGI!
YES?!
TH-THUMP
TROMP TROMP
WHAT IS THE MEANING OF MAKING THE PRINCESS DO THE DISHES?!
UH...

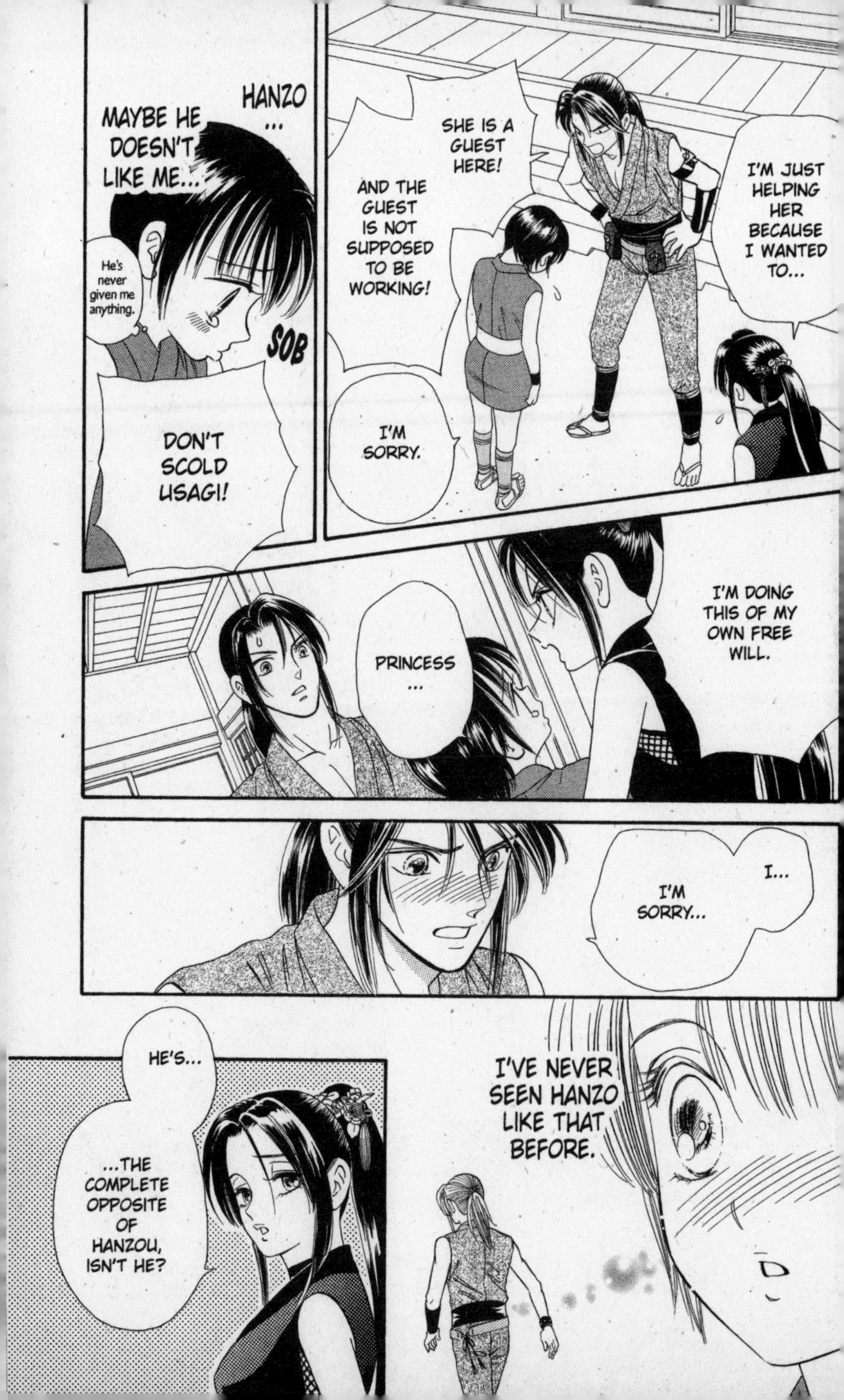
SHE IS A GUEST HERE!
AND THE GUEST IS NOT SUPPOSED TO BE WORKING!
I'M JUST HELPING HER BECAUSE I WANTED TO...
I'M SORRY.
HANZO ...
MAYBE HE DOESN'T LIKE ME...
He's never given me anything.
SOB
DON'T SCOLD USAGI!
I'M DOING THIS OF MY OWN FREE WILL.
PRINCESS ...
I...
I'M SORRY...
I'VE NEVER SEEN HANZO LIKE THAT BEFORE.
HE'S...
...THE COMPLETE OPPOSITE OF HANZOU, ISN'T HE?

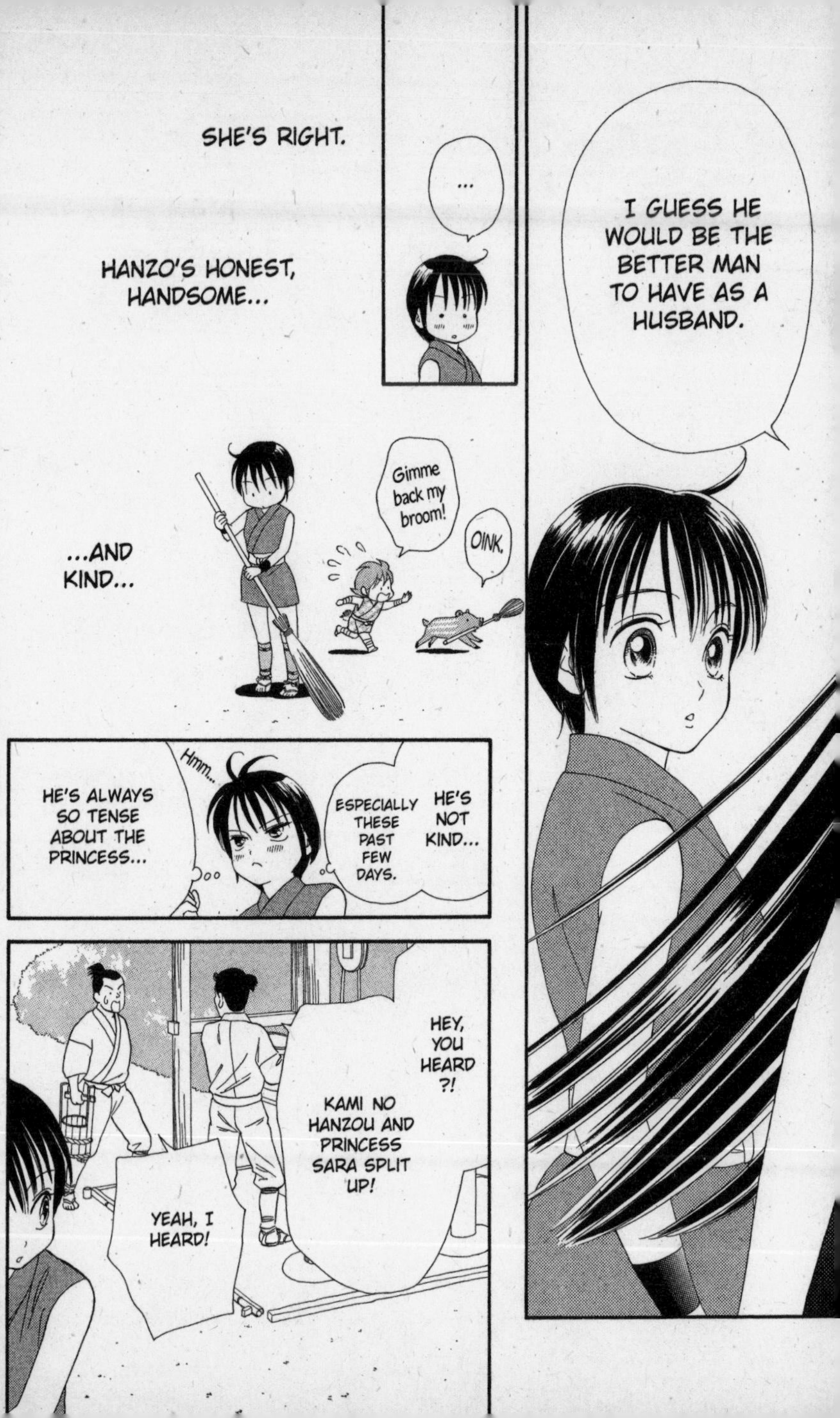
I GUESS HE WOULD BE THE BETTER MAN TO HAVE AS A HUSBAND.
...
SHE'S RIGHT.
HANZO'S HONEST, HANDSOME...
OINK.
Gimme back my broom!
...AND KIND...
HE'S NOT KIND...
ESPECIALLY THESE PAST FEW DAYS.
Hmm...
HE'S ALWAYS SO TENSE ABOUT THE PRINCESS...
HEY, YOU HEARD ?!
KAMI NO HANZOU AND PRINCESS SARA SPLIT UP!
YEAH, I HEARD!

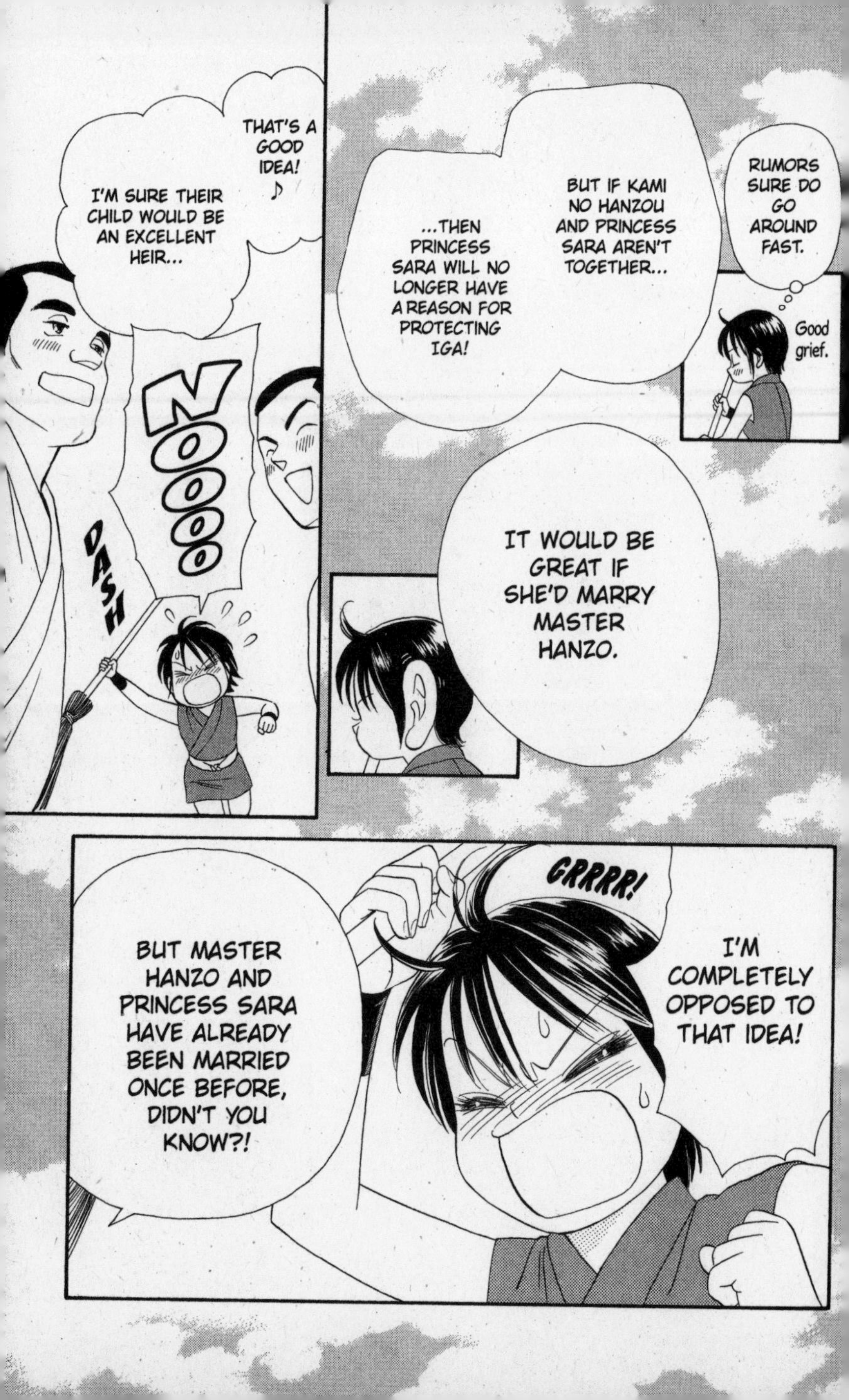
RUMORS SURE DO GO AROUND FAST.
Good grief.
BUT IF KAMI NO HANZOU AND PRINCESS SARA AREN'T TOGETHER...
...THEN PRINCESS SARA WILL NO LONGER HAVE A REASON FOR PROTECTING IGA!
IT WOULD BE GREAT IF SHE'D MARRY MASTER HANZO.
THAT'S A GOOD IDEA! ♪
I'M SURE THEIR CHILD WOULD BE AN EXCELLENT HEIR...
NOOOOO
DASH
GRRRR!
I'M COMPLETELY OPPOSED TO THAT IDEA!
BUT MASTER HANZO AND PRINCESS SARA HAVE ALREADY BEEN MARRIED ONCE BEFORE, DIDN'T YOU KNOW?!

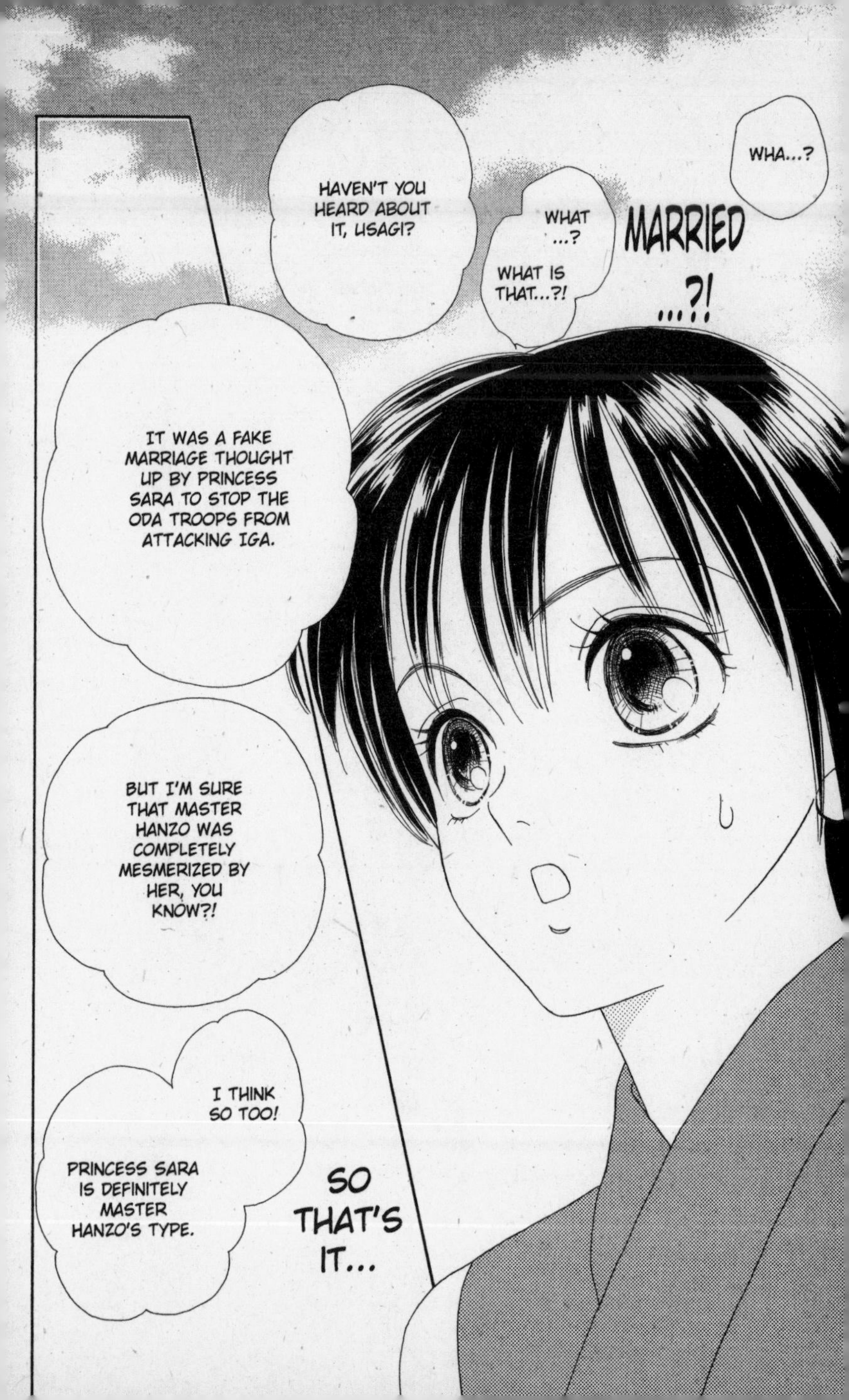
WHA...?
MARRIED ...?!
WHAT ...? WHAT IS THAT...?!
HAVEN'T YOU HEARD ABOUT IT, USAGI?
IT WAS A FAKE MARRIAGE THOUGHT UP BY PRINCESS SARA TO STOP THE ODA TROOPS FROM ATTACKING IGA.
BUT I'M SURE THAT MASTER HANZO WAS COMPLETELY MESMERIZED BY HER, YOU KNOW?!
I THINK SO TOO!
PRINCESS SARA IS DEFINITELY MASTER HANZO'S TYPE.
SO THAT'S IT...

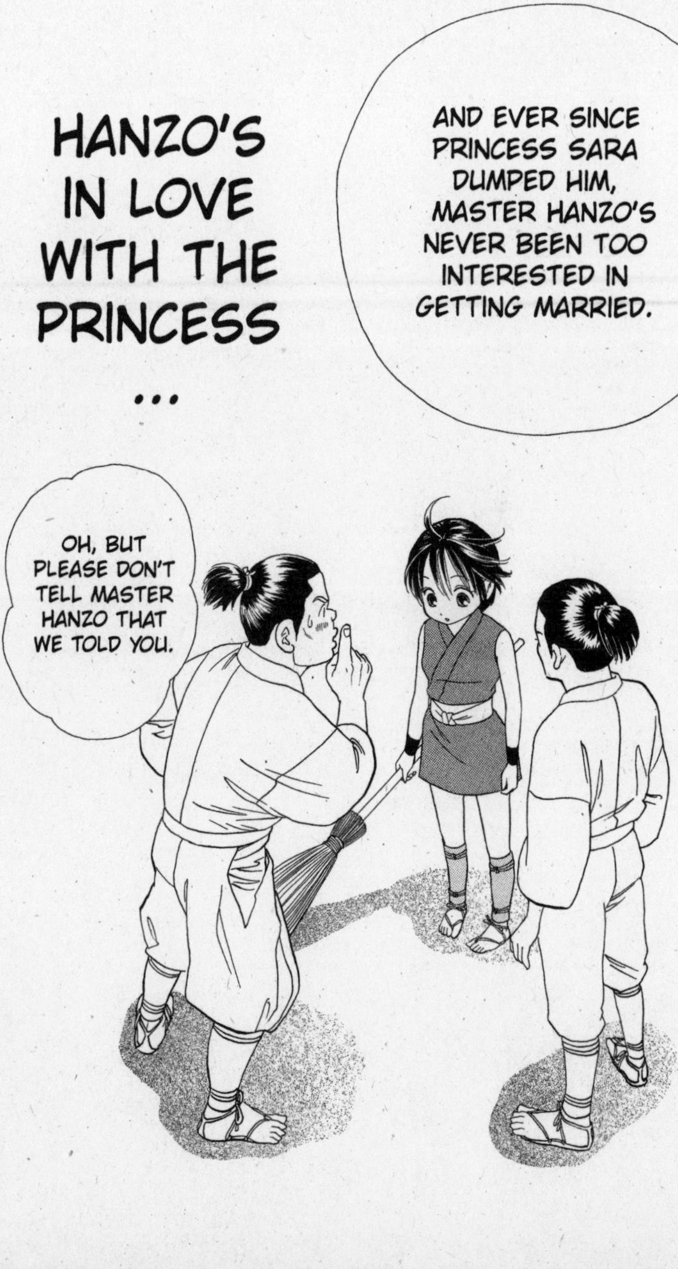
AND EVER SINCE PRINCESS SARA DUMPED HIM, MASTER HANZO'S NEVER BEEN TOO INTERESTED IN GETTING MARRIED.
HANZO'S IN LOVE WITH THE PRINCESS...
OH, BUT PLEASE DON'T TELL MASTER HANZO THAT WE TOLD YOU.

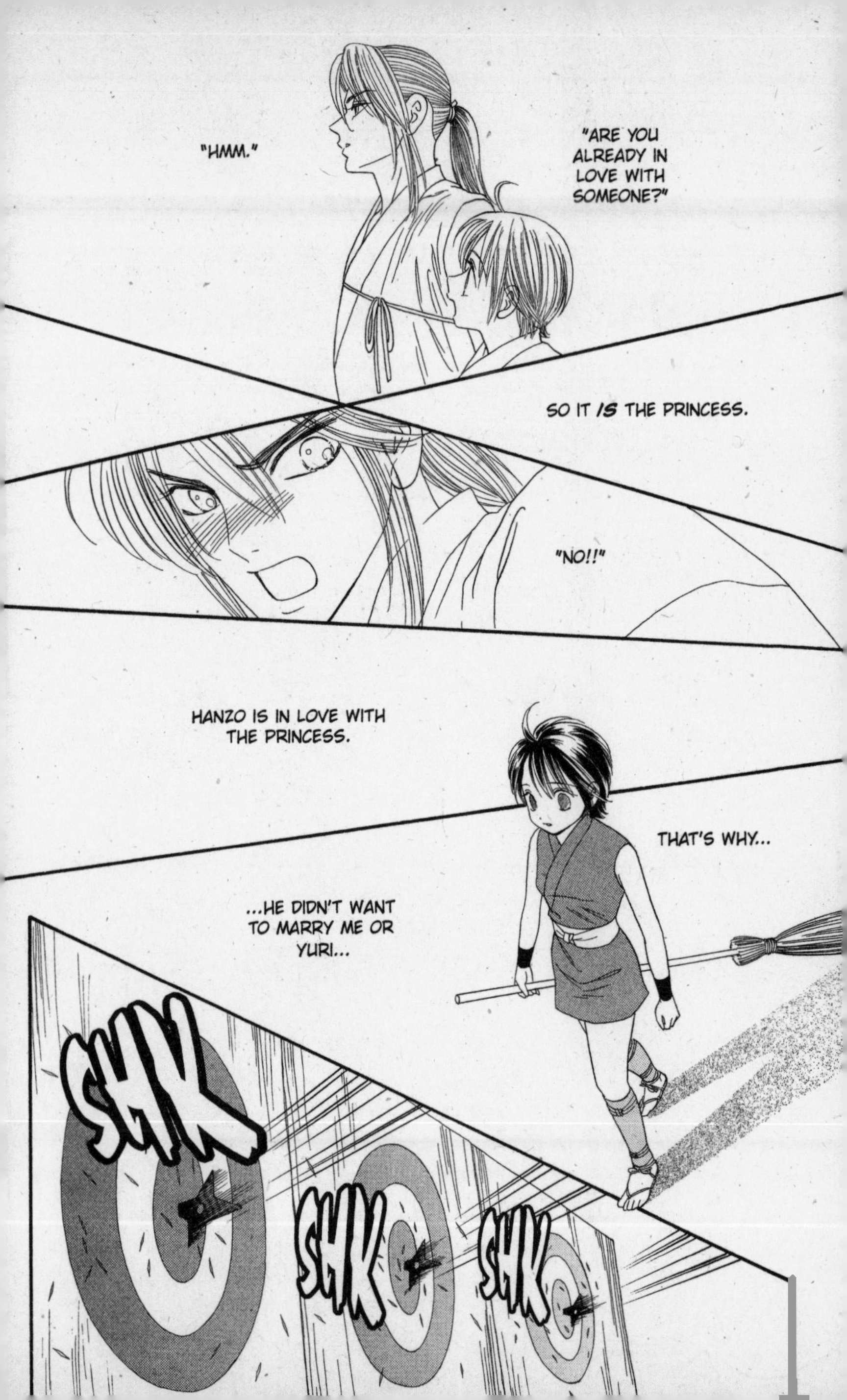
"ARE YOU ALREADY IN LOVE WITH SOMEONE?"
"HMM."
SO IT *IS* THE PRINCESS.
"NO!!"
HANZO IS IN LOVE WITH THE PRINCESS.
THAT'S WHY...
...HE DIDN'T WANT TO MARRY ME OR YURI...
SHK
SHK
SHK

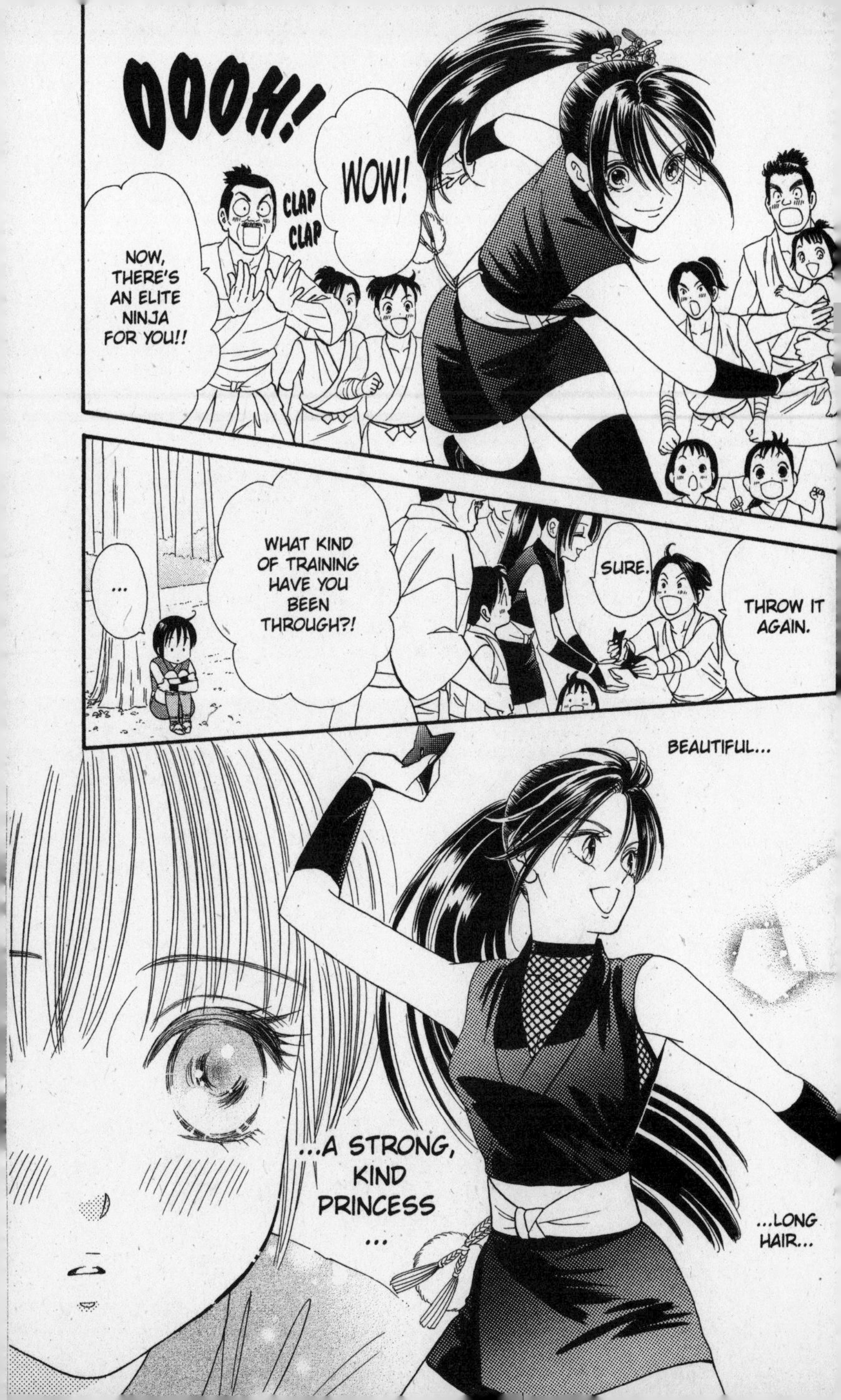
OOOH!
WOW!
CLAP CLAP
NOW, THERE'S AN ELITE NINJA FOR YOU!!
THROW IT AGAIN.
SURE.
WHAT KIND OF TRAINING HAVE YOU BEEN THROUGH?!
...
BEAUTIFUL...
...LONG HAIR...
...A STRONG, KIND PRINCESS ...

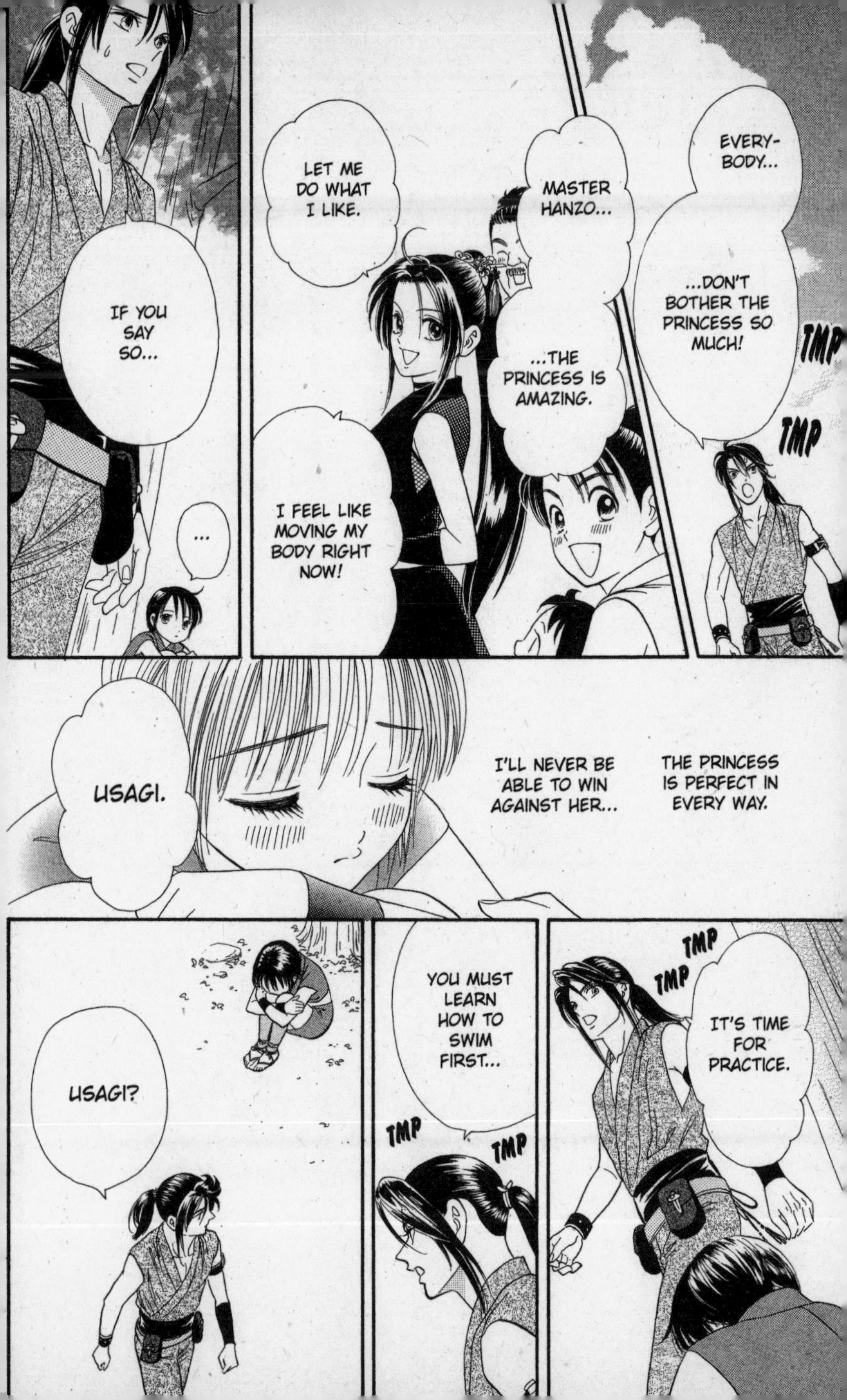
EVERY-BODY...
...DON'T BOTHER THE PRINCESS SO MUCH!
TMP
TMP
MASTER HANZO...
...THE PRINCESS IS AMAZING.
LET ME DO WHAT I LIKE.
I FEEL LIKE MOVING MY BODY RIGHT NOW!
IF YOU SAY SO...
...
THE PRINCESS IS PERFECT IN EVERY WAY.
I'LL NEVER BE ABLE TO WIN AGAINST HER...
USAGI.
TMP
TMP
IT'S TIME FOR PRACTICE.
YOU MUST LEARN HOW TO SWIM FIRST...
TMP
TMP
USAGI?

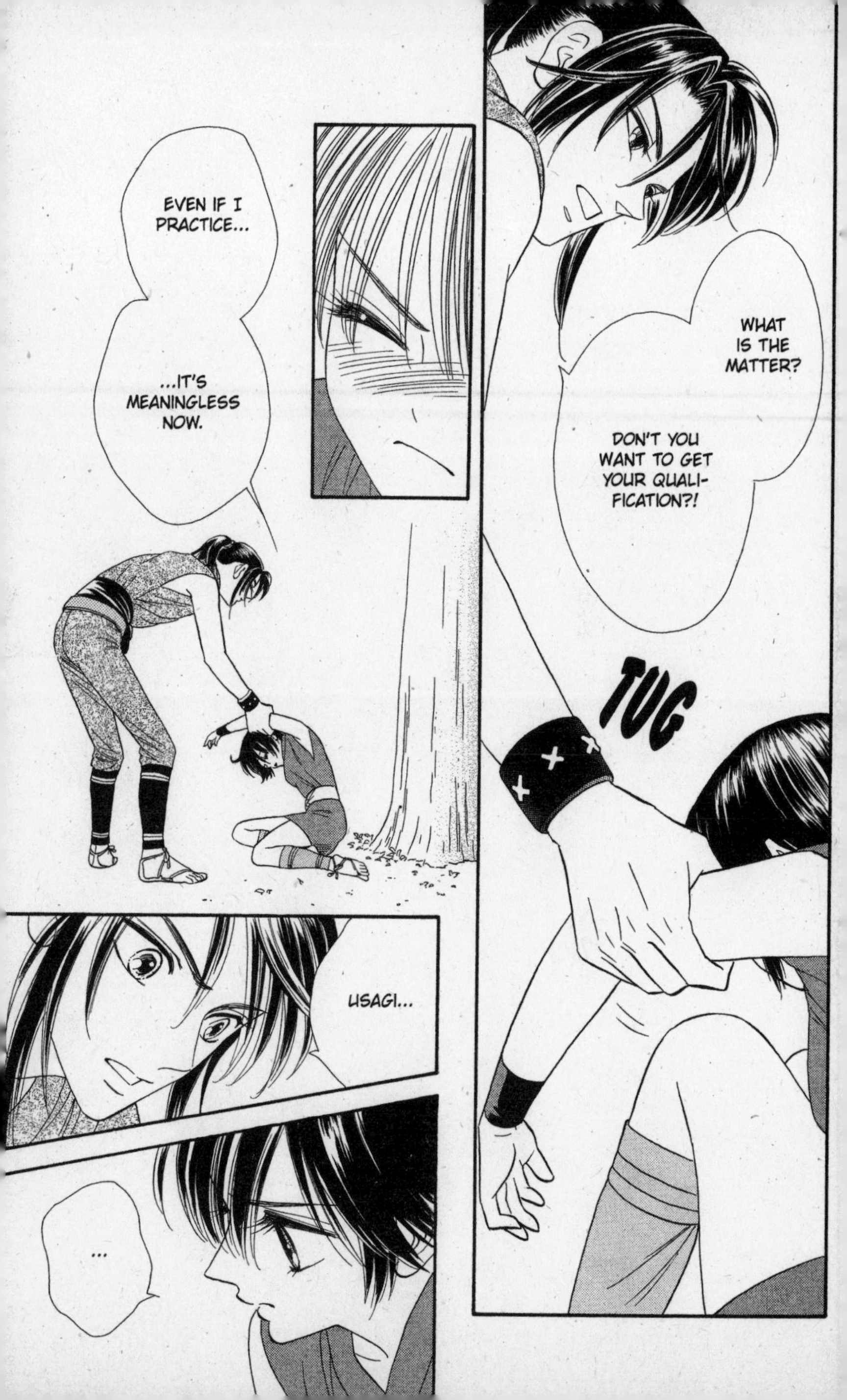
WHAT IS THE MATTER?
DON'T YOU WANT TO GET YOUR QUALI-FICATION?!
TUG
EVEN IF I PRACTICE...
...IT'S MEANINGLESS NOW.
USAGI...
...

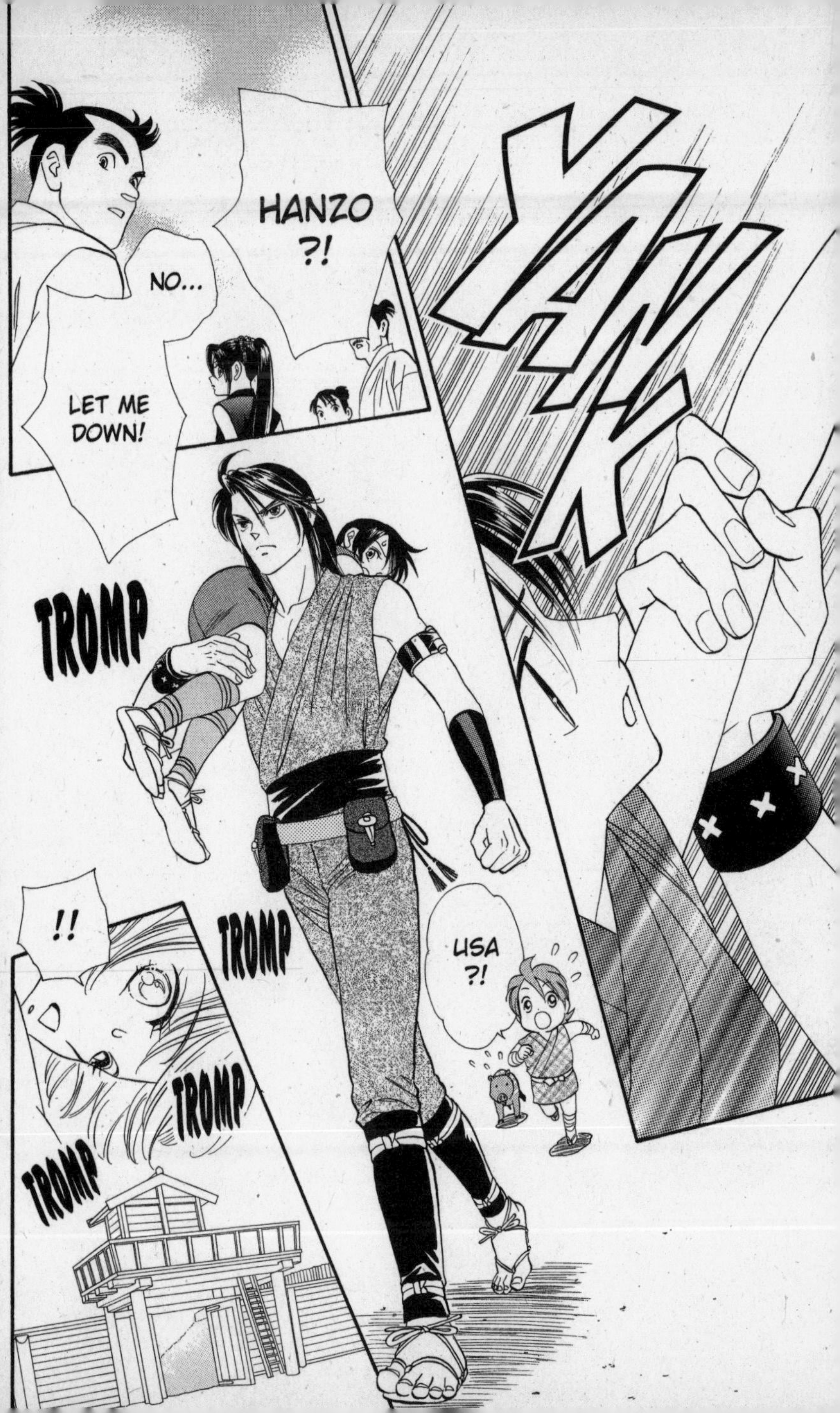
YANK
HANZO ?!
NO...
LET ME DOWN!
TROMP
TROMP
USA ?!
!!
TROMP
TROMP

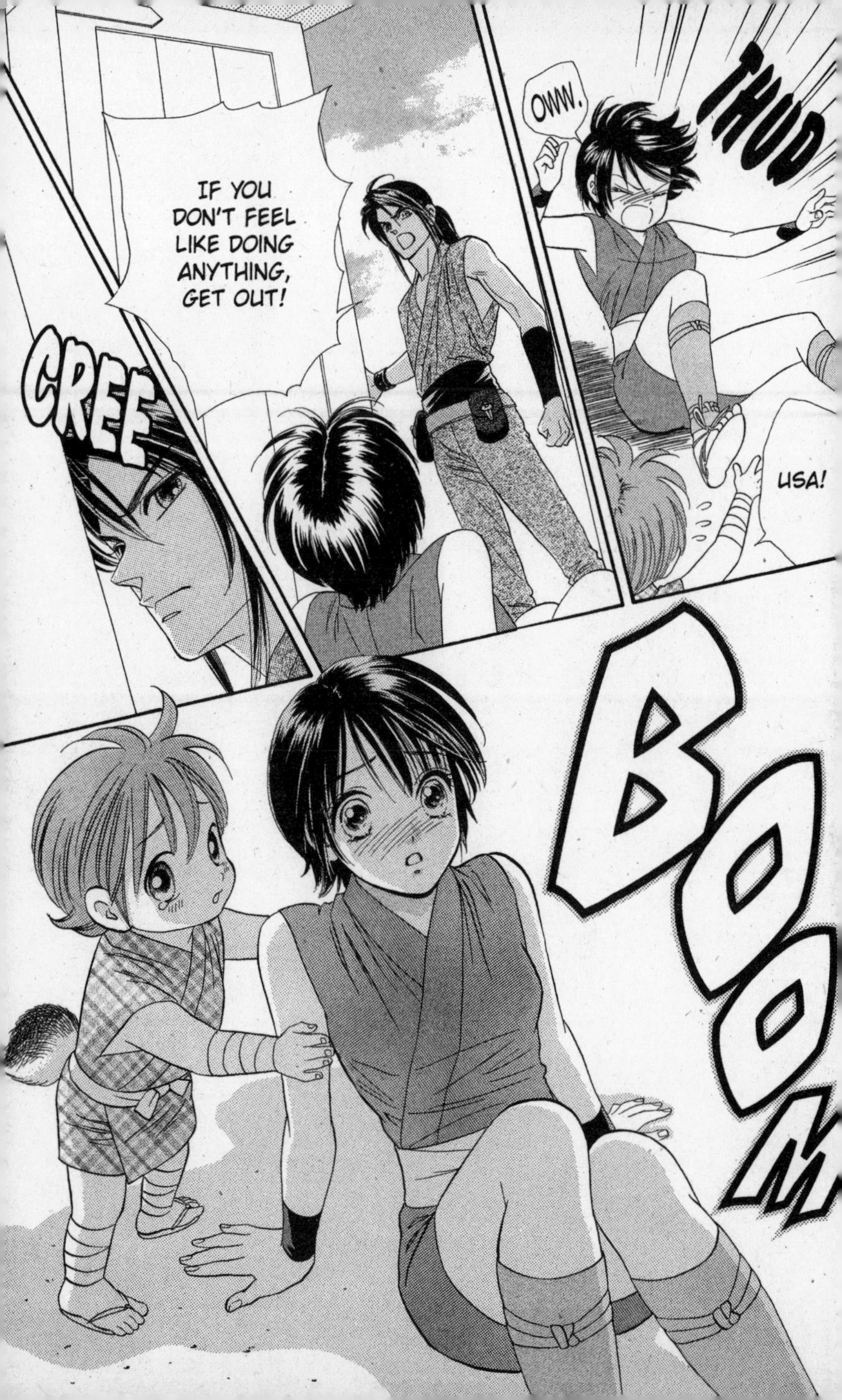
THUD
OWW.
USA!
IF YOU DON'T FEEL LIKE DOING ANYTHING, GET OUT!
CREE
BOOM

Please, My Dear Tanba!♬#1

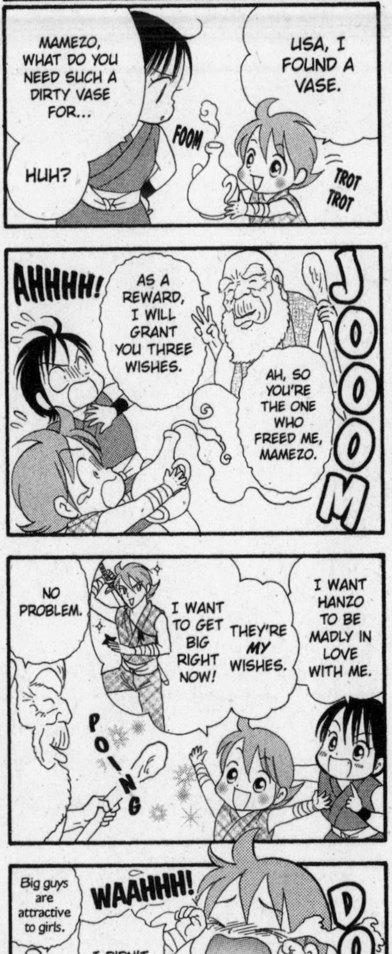
USA, I FOUND A VASE.
MAMEZO, WHAT DO YOU NEED SUCH A DIRTY VASE FOR...
TROT TROT
FOOM
HUH?
JOOOM
AH, SO YOU'RE THE ONE WHO FREED ME, MAMEZO.
AS A REWARD, I WILL GRANT YOU THREE WISHES.
AHHHH!
I WANT HANZO TO BE MADLY IN LOVE WITH ME.
THEY'RE MY WISHES.
I WANT TO GET BIG RIGHT NOW!
NO PROBLEM.
POING
DOOM
WAAHHH!
Big guys are attractive to girls.
I DIDN'T WANT TO BE THIS BIG!
I, I'm drowning!
STOP CRYING, MAMEZO!

Please, My Dear Tanba!♬#2

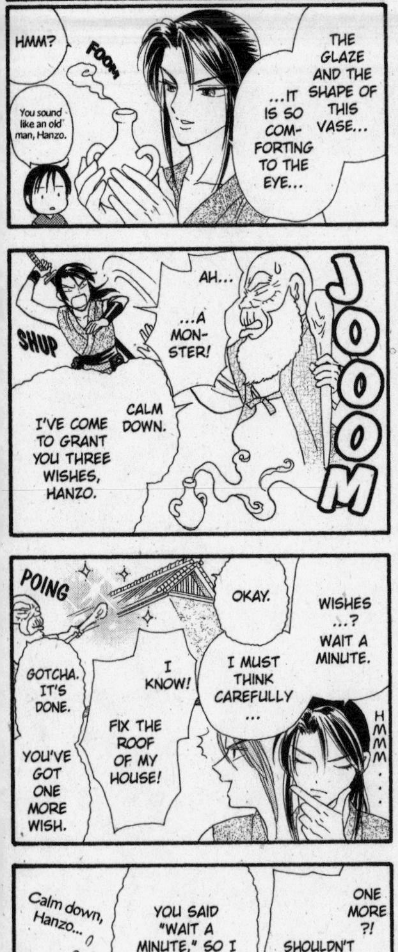
THE GLAZE AND THE SHAPE OF THIS VASE...
...IT IS SO COMFORTING TO THE EYE...
FOOM
HMM?
You sound like an old man, Hanzo.
JOOOM
AH...
...A MONSTER!
CALM DOWN.
I'VE COME TO GRANT YOU THREE WISHES, HANZO.
SHUP
WISHES...? WAIT A MINUTE.
HMMM...
OKAY.
I MUST THINK CAREFULLY...
I KNOW!
FIX THE ROOF OF MY HOUSE!
POING
GOTCHA. IT'S DONE.
YOU'VE GOT ONE MORE WISH.
ONE MORE?!
SHOULDN'T IT BE TWO MORE?!
YOU SAID "WAIT A MINUTE," SO I WAITED FOR YOU, DIDN'T I? SO THAT'S...
Calm down, Hanzo...
H-how dare you!!

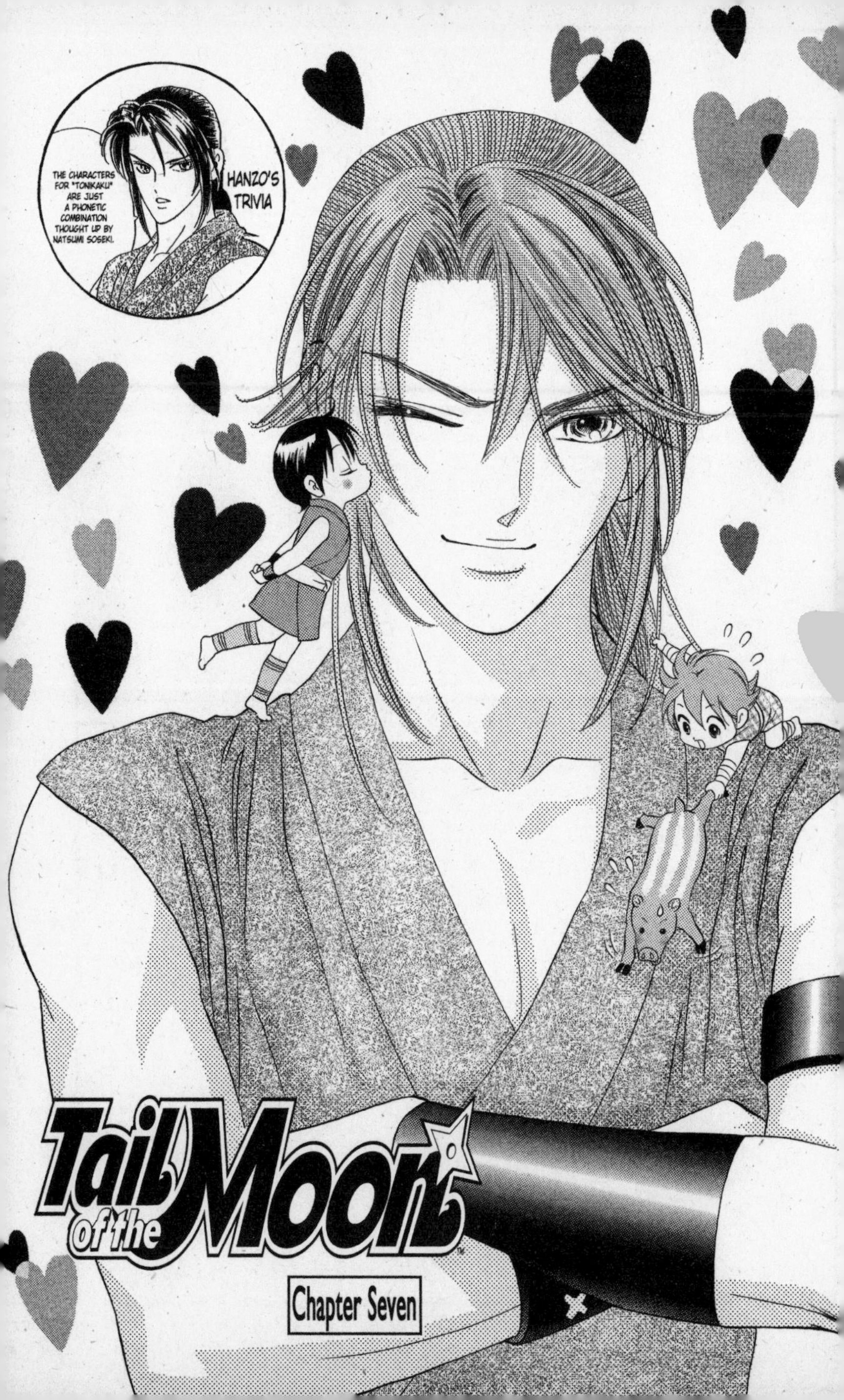

HANZO'S TRIVIA
THE CHARACTERS FOR "TONIKAKU" ARE JUST A PHONETIC COMBINATION THOUGHT UP BY NATSUMI SOSEKI.
Tail of the Moon
Chapter Seven

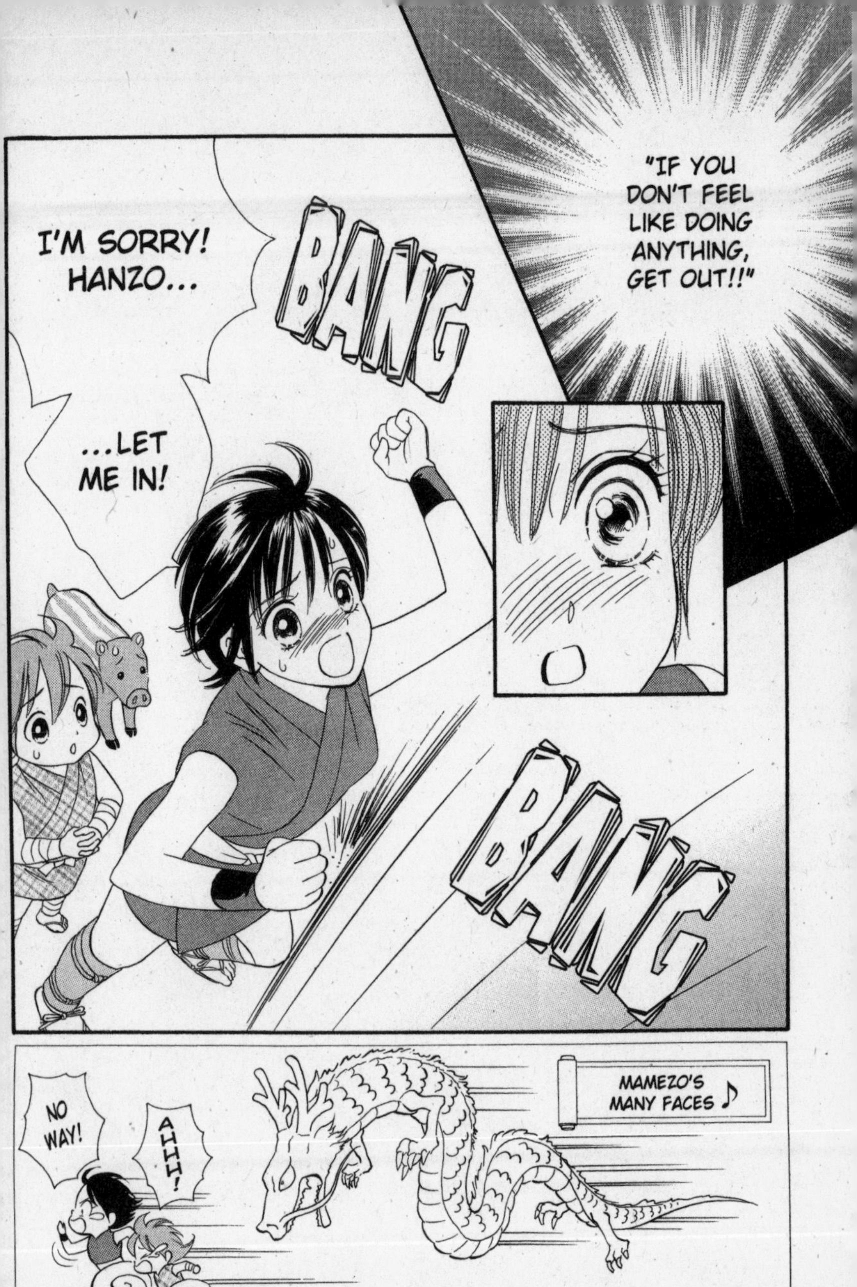
"IF YOU DON'T FEEL LIKE DOING ANYTHING, GET OUT!!"
BANG
I'M SORRY! HANZO...
...LET ME IN!
BANG
MAMEZO'S MANY FACES ♪
AHHH!
NO WAY!
CONTINUED IN VOLUME 2!

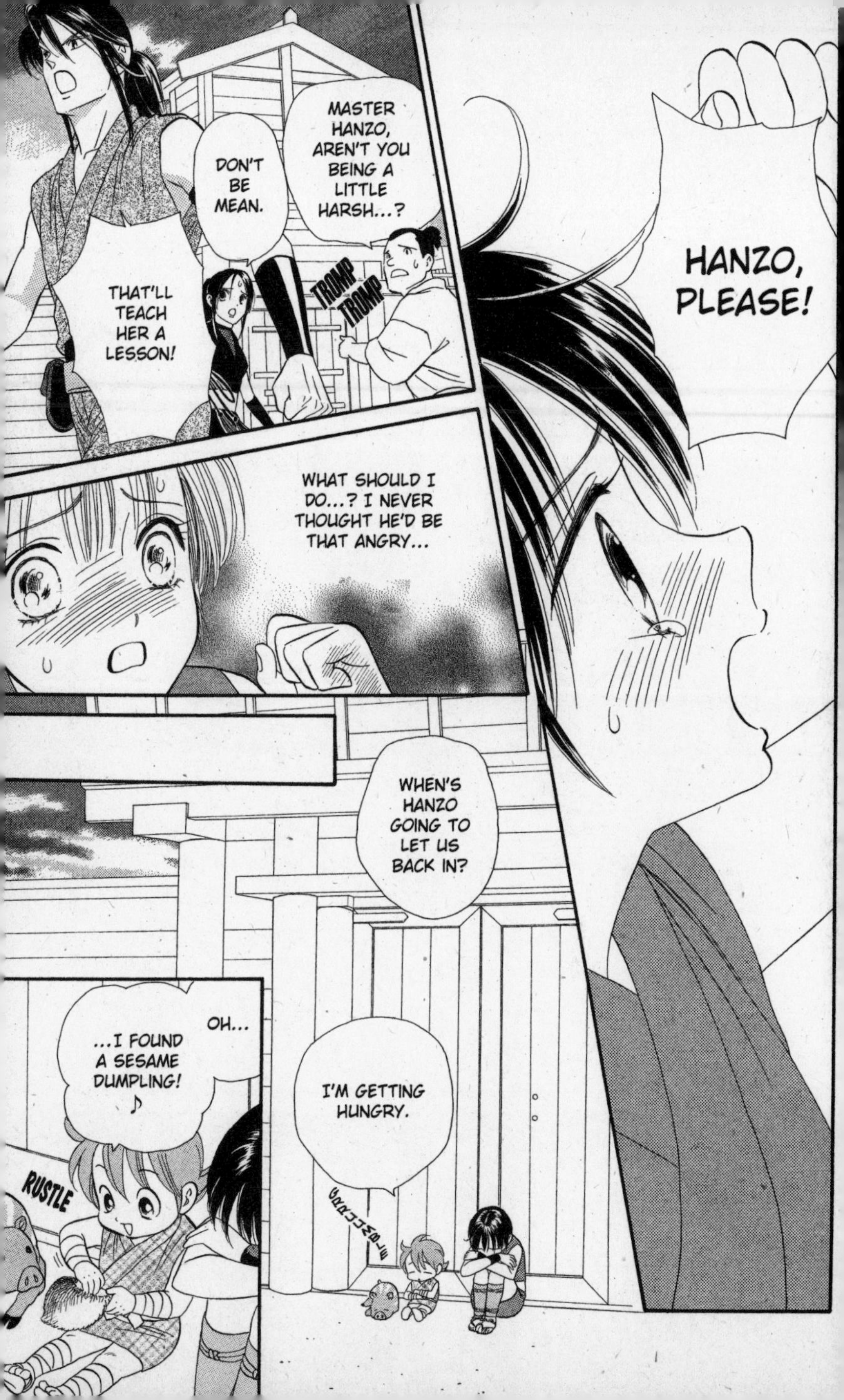
HANZO, PLEASE!
MASTER HANZO, AREN'T YOU BEING A LITTLE HARSH...?
DON'T BE MEAN.
TROMP TROMP
THAT'LL TEACH HER A LESSON!
WHAT SHOULD I DO...? I NEVER THOUGHT HE'D BE THAT ANGRY...
WHEN'S HANZO GOING TO LET US BACK IN?
I'M GETTING HUNGRY.
GRUMBLE
OH...
...I FOUND A SESAME DUMPLING! ♪
RUSTLE

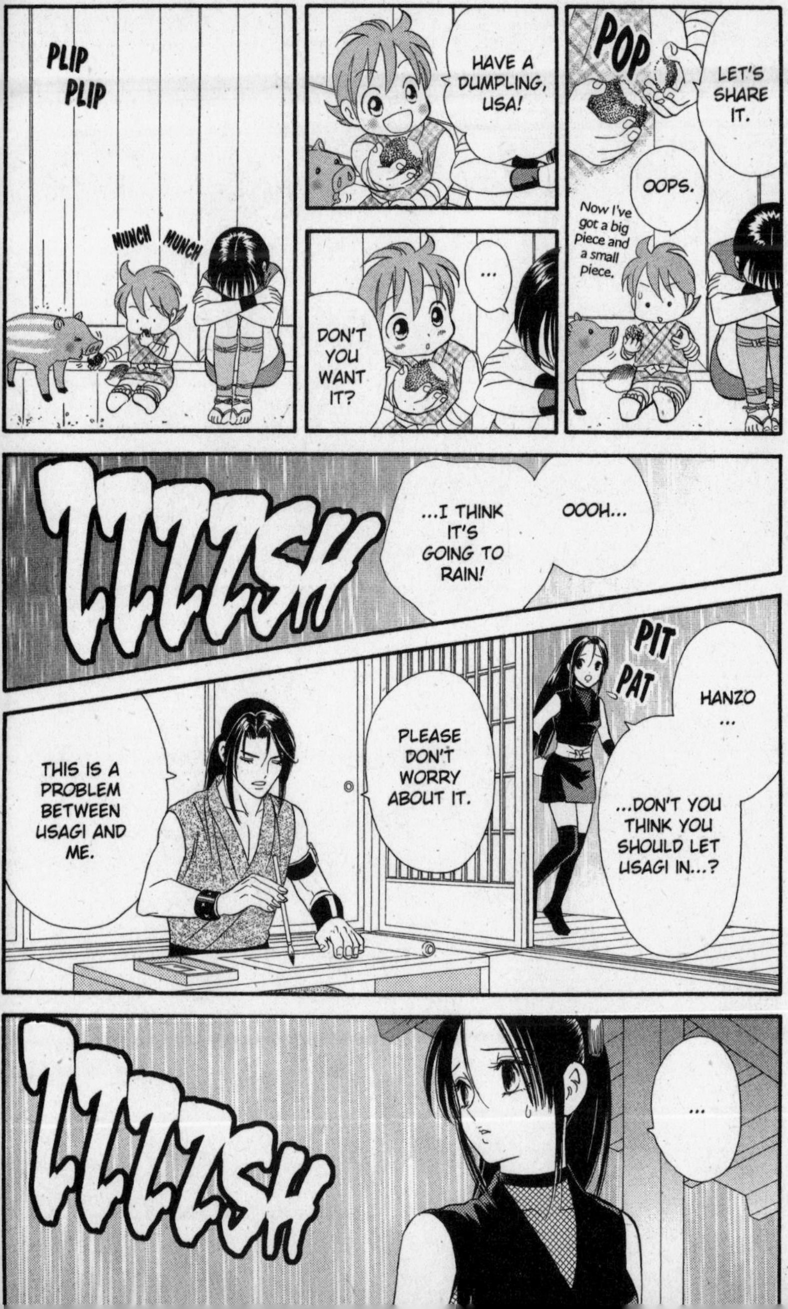
POP
LET'S SHARE IT.
OOPS.
Now I've got a big piece and a small piece.
HAVE A DUMPLING, USA!
...
DON'T YOU WANT IT?
PLIP PLIP
MUNCH MUNCH
OOOH...
...I THINK IT'S GOING TO RAIN!
ZZZZSH
PIT PAT
HANZO ...
...DON'T YOU THINK YOU SHOULD LET USAGI IN...?
PLEASE DON'T WORRY ABOUT IT.
THIS IS A PROBLEM BETWEEN USAGI AND ME.
...
ZZZZZSH

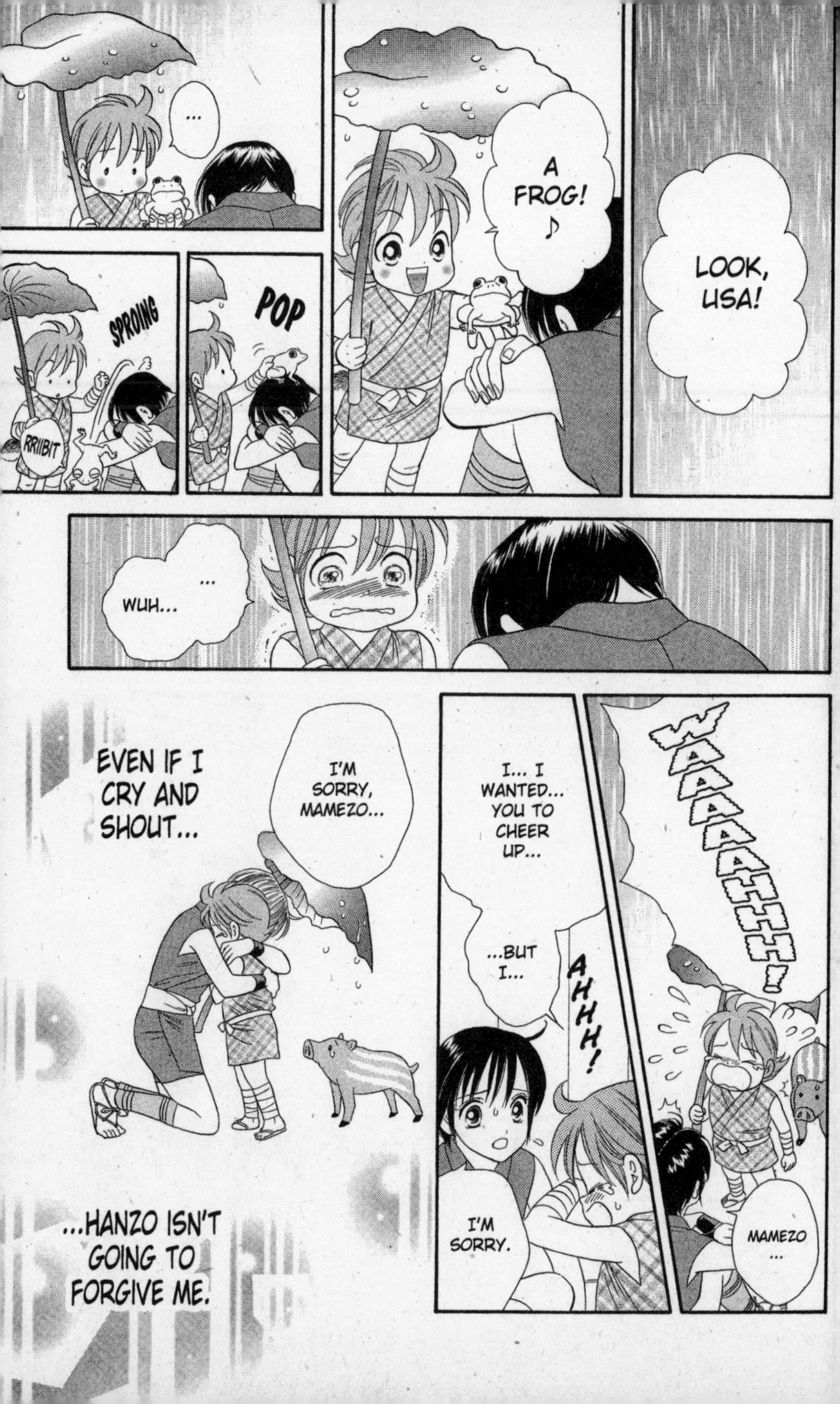
LOOK, USA!
A FROG! ♪
...
POP
SPROING
RRIIBIT
... WUH...
WAAAAAHHH!
MAMEZO ...
I... I WANTED... YOU TO CHEER UP...
...BUT I...
AHHH!
I'M SORRY.
I'M SORRY, MAMEZO...
EVEN IF I CRY AND SHOUT...
...HANZO ISN'T GOING TO FORGIVE ME.

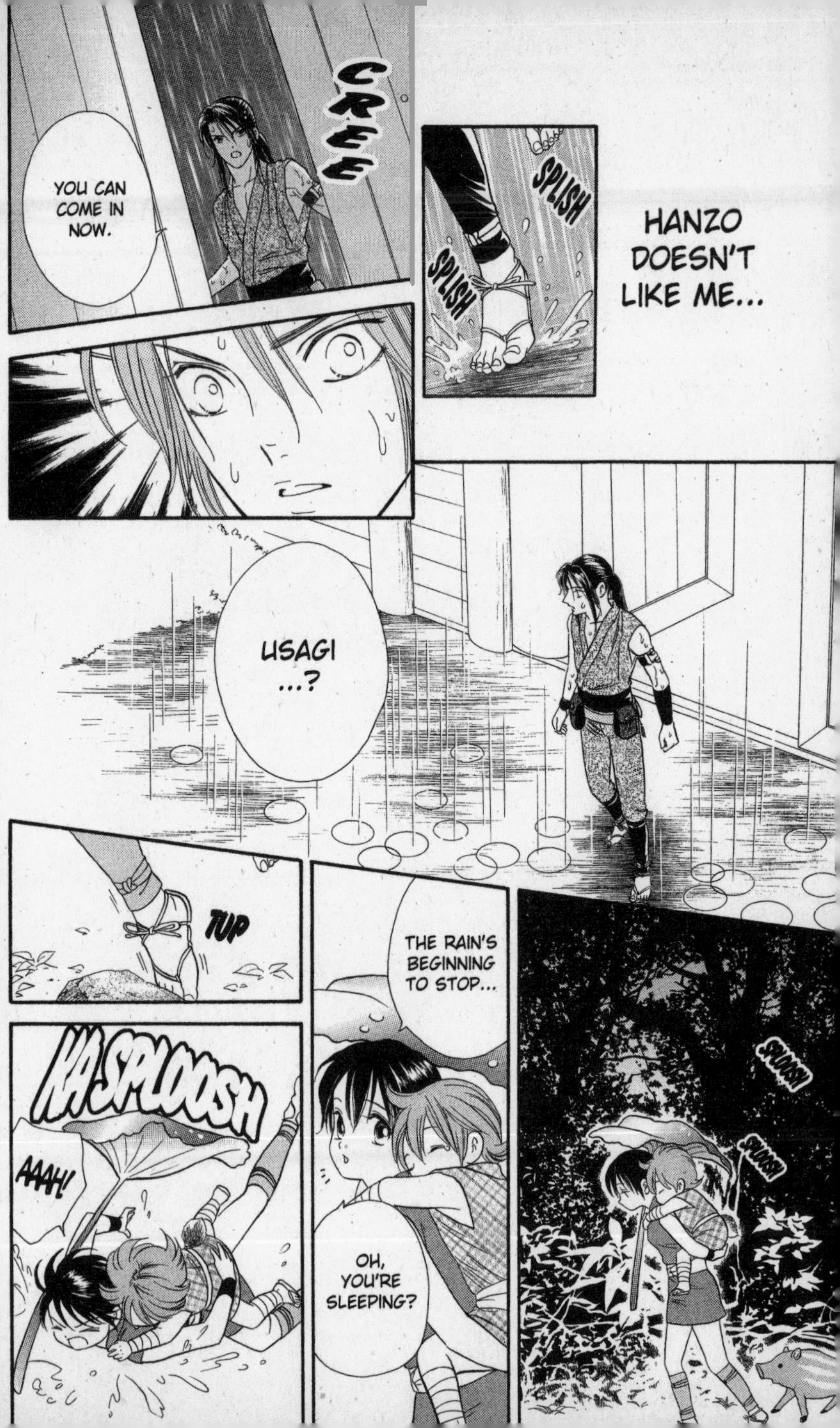
HANZO DOESN'T LIKE ME...
SPLISH
SPLISH
CREE
YOU CAN COME IN NOW.
USAGI ...?
SPLOOSH
SPLOOSH
THE RAIN'S BEGINNING TO STOP...
OH, YOU'RE SLEEPING?
TUP
KA-SPLOOSH
AAAH!

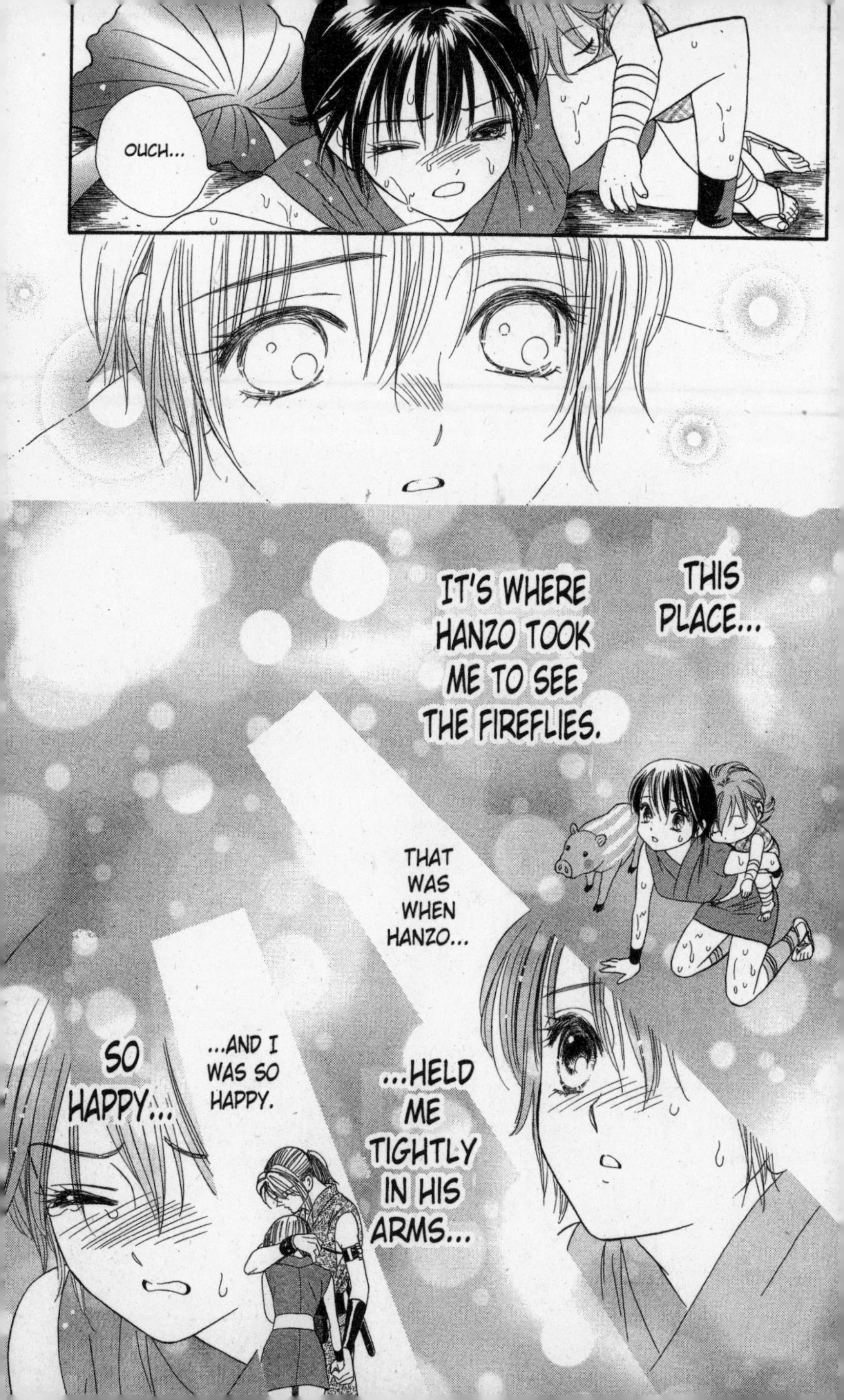
OUCH...
THIS PLACE...
IT'S WHERE HANZO TOOK ME TO SEE THE FIREFLIES.
THAT WAS WHEN HANZO...
...HELD ME TIGHTLY IN HIS ARMS...
...AND I WAS SO HAPPY.
SO HAPPY...

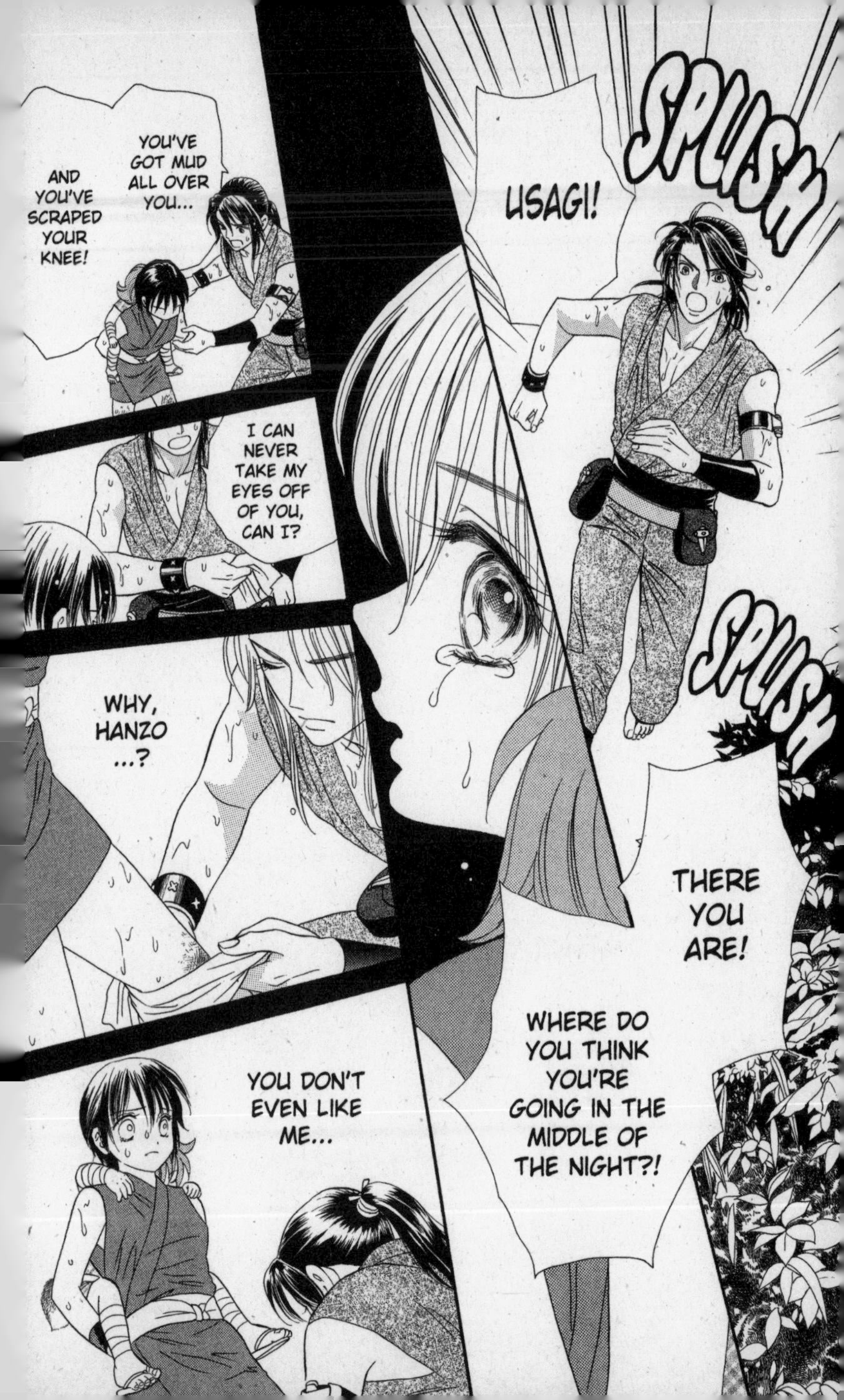
SPLISH
USAGI!
SPLISH
THERE YOU ARE!
WHERE DO YOU THINK YOU'RE GOING IN THE MIDDLE OF THE NIGHT?!
YOU'VE GOT MUD ALL OVER YOU...
AND YOU'VE SCRAPED YOUR KNEE!
I CAN NEVER TAKE MY EYES OFF OF YOU, CAN I?
WHY, HANZO ...?
YOU DON'T EVEN LIKE ME...

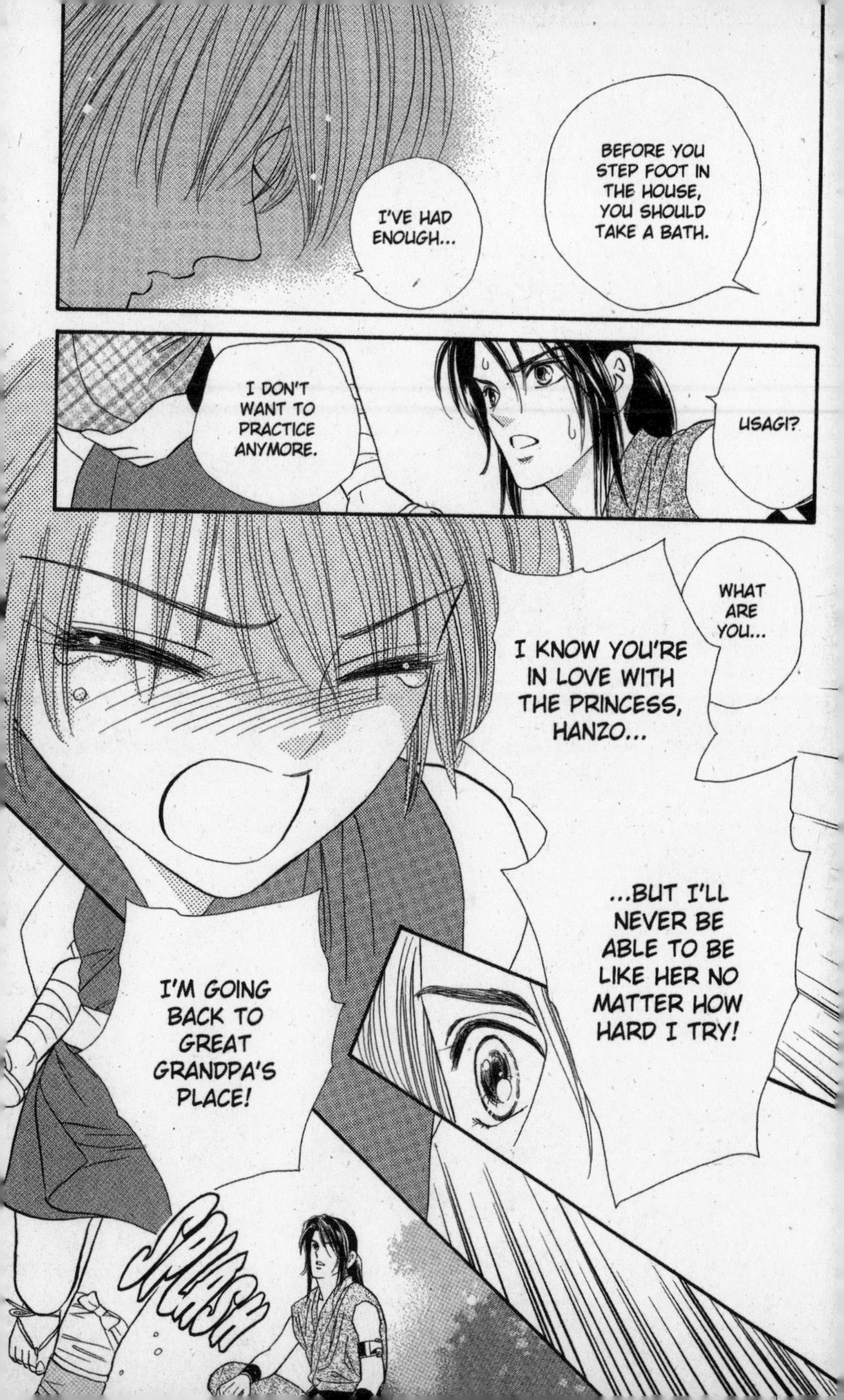
BEFORE YOU STEP FOOT IN THE HOUSE, YOU SHOULD TAKE A BATH.
I'VE HAD ENOUGH...
USAGI?
I DON'T WANT TO PRACTICE ANYMORE.
WHAT ARE YOU...
I KNOW YOU'RE IN LOVE WITH THE PRINCESS, HANZO...
...BUT I'LL NEVER BE ABLE TO BE LIKE HER NO MATTER HOW HARD I TRY!
I'M GOING BACK TO GREAT GRANDPA'S PLACE!
SPLASH

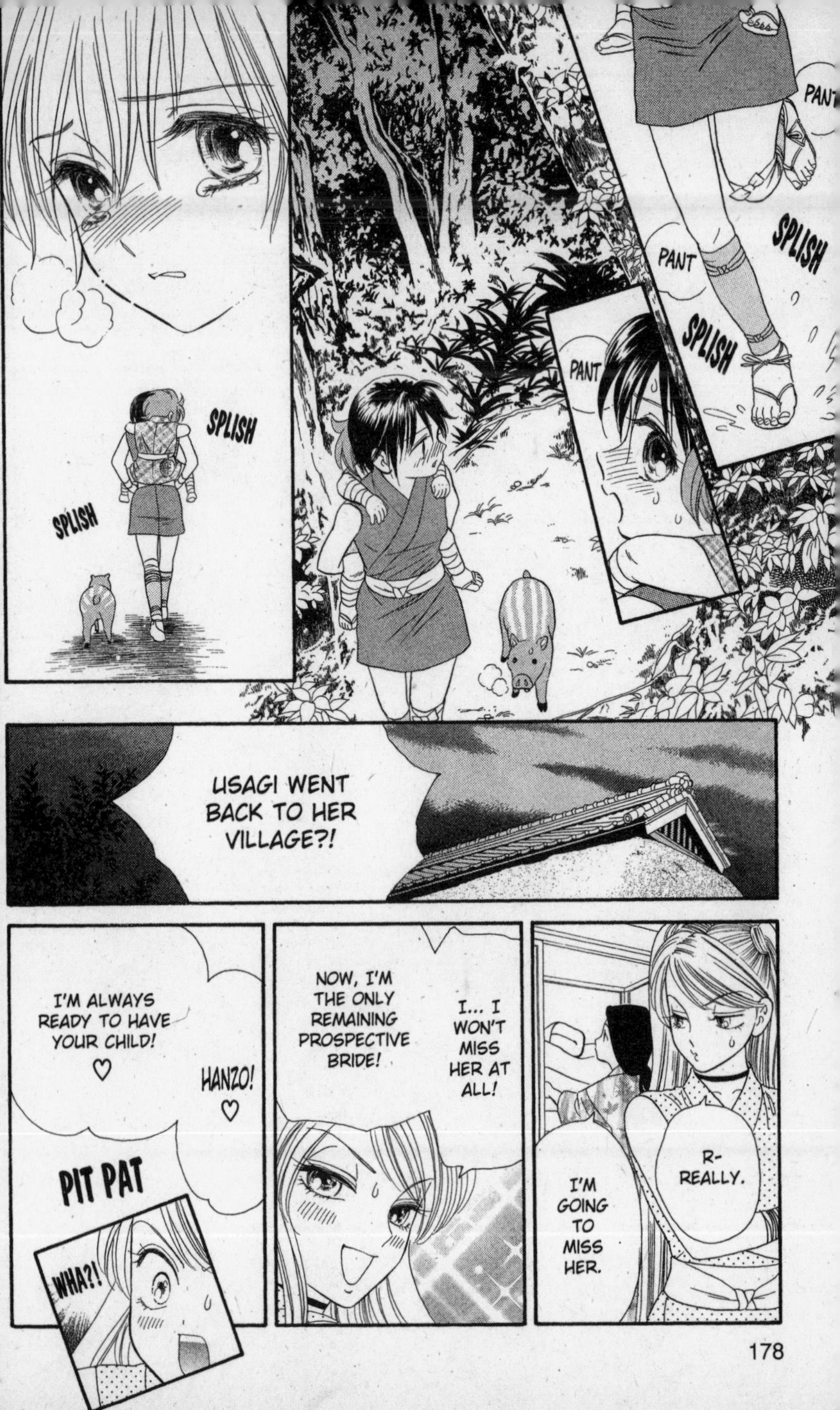
PANT
PANT
SPLISH
SPLISH
PANT
SPLISH
SPLISH
USAGI WENT BACK TO HER VILLAGE?!
R- REALLY.
I'M GOING TO MISS HER.
I... I WON'T MISS HER AT ALL!
NOW, I'M THE ONLY REMAINING PROSPECTIVE BRIDE!
HANZO! ♡
I'M ALWAYS READY TO HAVE YOUR CHILD! ♡
PIT PAT
WHA?!

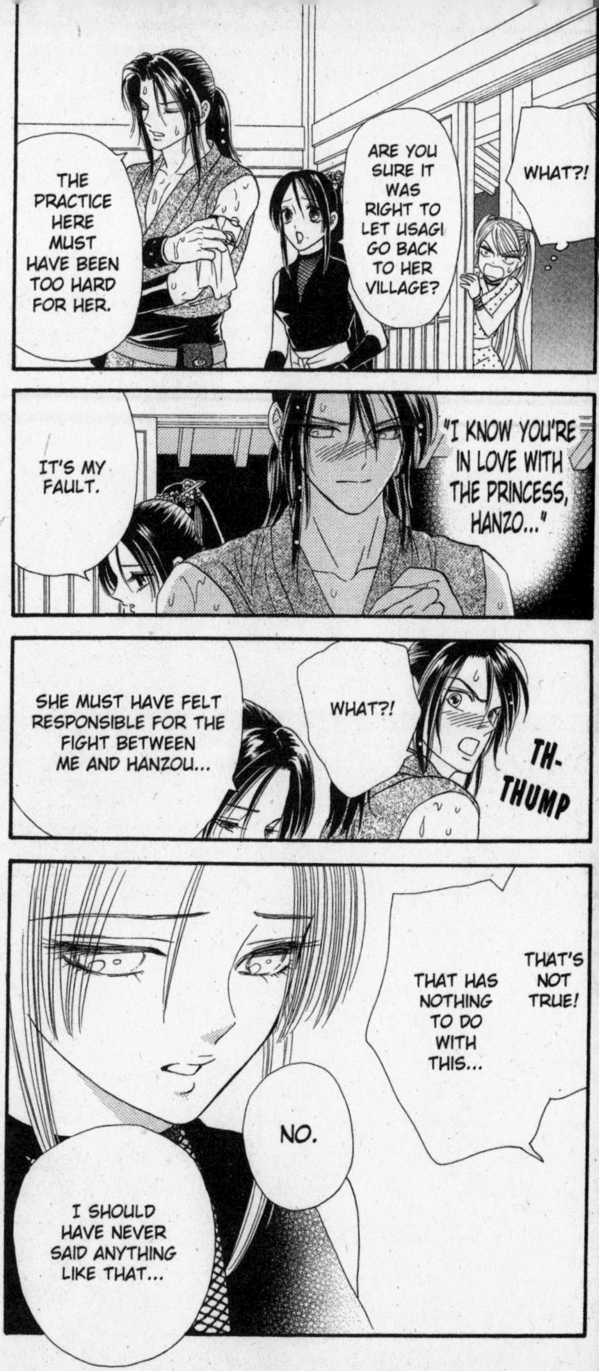
WHAT?!
ARE YOU SURE IT WAS RIGHT TO LET USAGI GO BACK TO HER VILLAGE?
THE PRACTICE HERE MUST HAVE BEEN TOO HARD FOR HER.
"I KNOW YOU'RE IN LOVE WITH THE PRINCESS, HANZO..."
IT'S MY FAULT.
TH-THUMP
WHAT?!
SHE MUST HAVE FELT RESPONSIBLE FOR THE FIGHT BETWEEN ME AND HANZOU...
THAT'S NOT TRUE!
THAT HAS NOTHING TO DO WITH THIS...
NO.
I SHOULD HAVE NEVER SAID ANYTHING LIKE THAT...

This and that from the author 7

If you've got any remarks or requests, please let me know about them. The address is:

Tail of the Moon
c/o
VIZ Media
P.O. Box 77010
San Francisco,
CA 94133

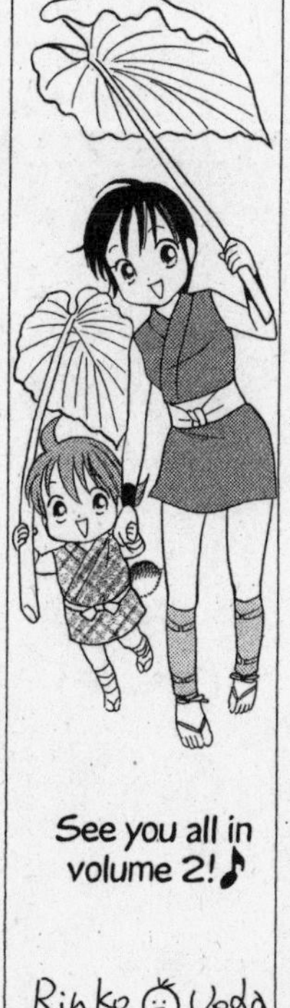

See you all in volume 2!♪

Rinko Ueda

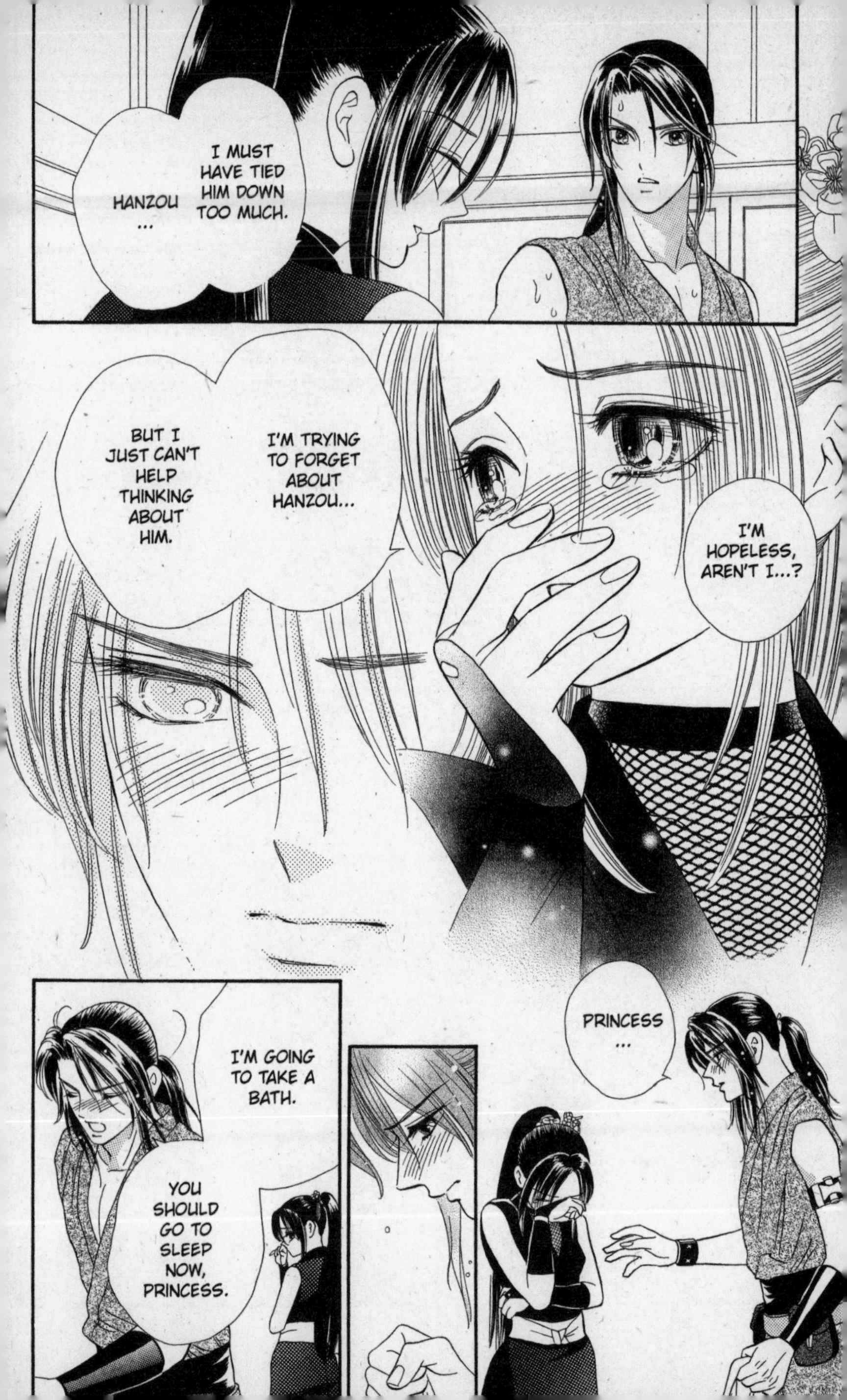
I MUST HAVE TIED HIM DOWN TOO MUCH.
HANZOU ...
I'M HOPELESS, AREN'T I...?
I'M TRYING TO FORGET ABOUT HANZOU...
BUT I JUST CAN'T HELP THINKING ABOUT HIM.
PRINCESS ...
I'M GOING TO TAKE A BATH.
YOU SHOULD GO TO SLEEP NOW, PRINCESS.

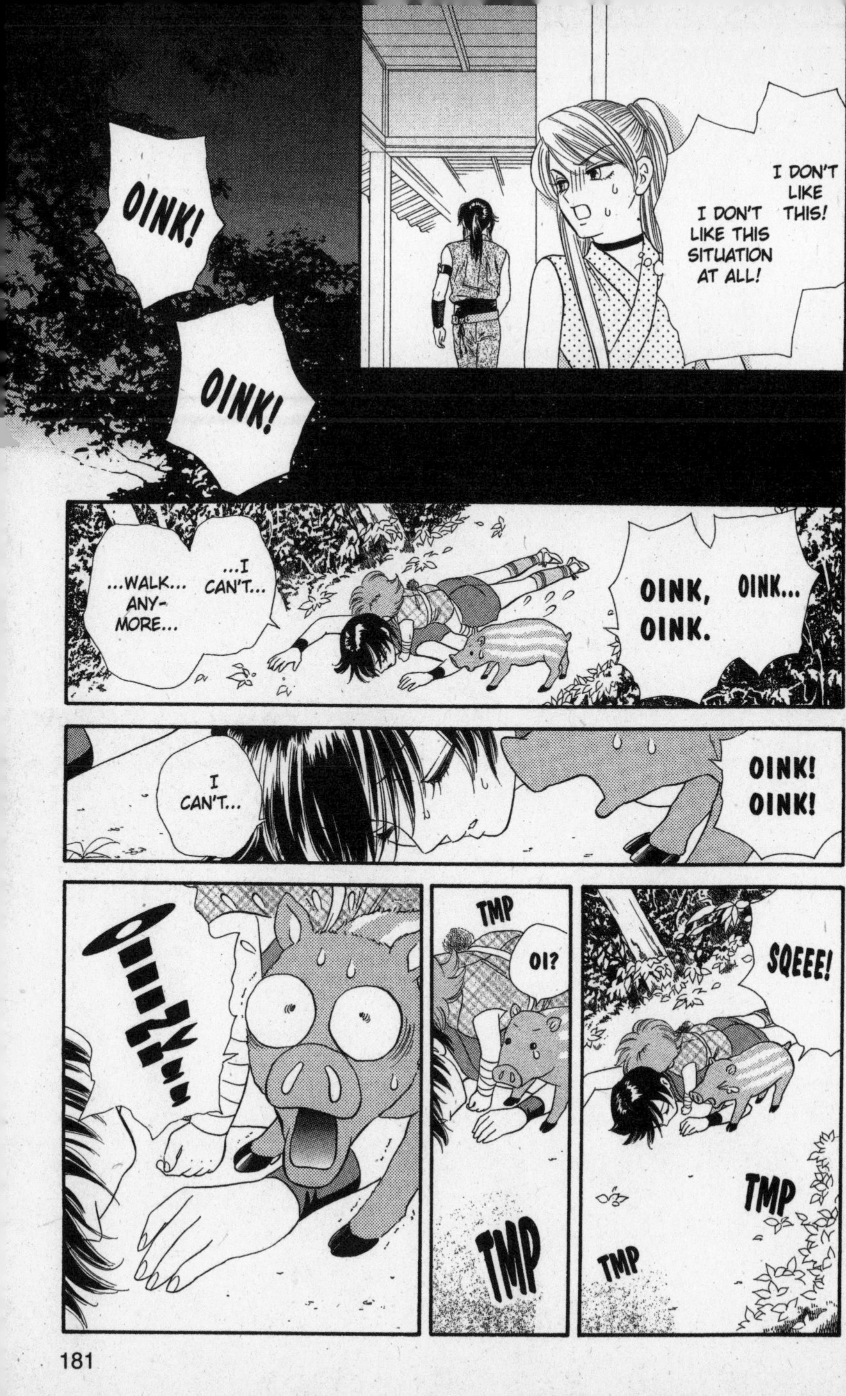
I DON'T LIKE THIS!
I DON'T LIKE THIS SITUATION AT ALL!
OINK!
OINK!
OINK...
OINK, OINK.
...I CAN'T...
...WALK... ANY-MORE...
OINK! OINK!
I CAN'T...
SQEEE!
TMP
TMP
TMP
OI?
TMP

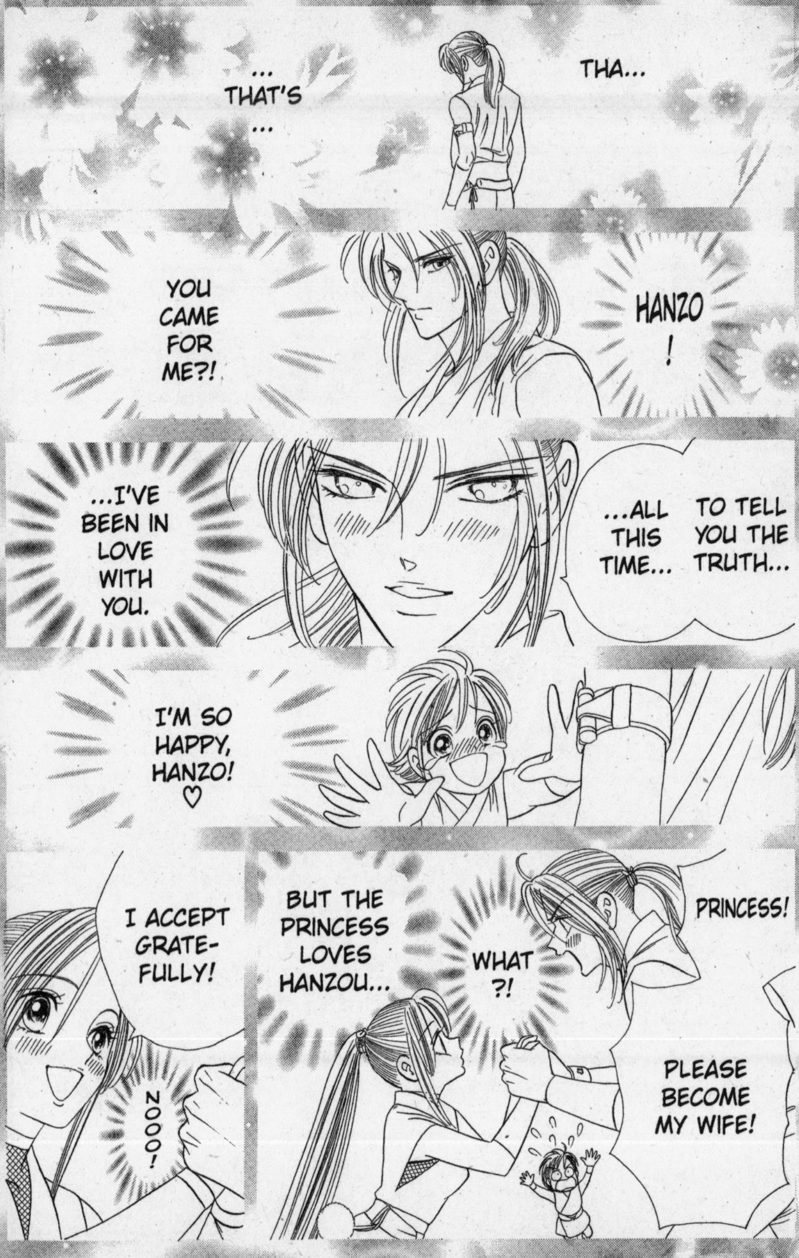
THA...
... THAT'S ...
HANZO!
YOU CAME FOR ME?!
TO TELL YOU THE TRUTH...
...ALL THIS TIME...
...I'VE BEEN IN LOVE WITH YOU.
I'M SO HAPPY, HANZO! ♡
PRINCESS!
PLEASE BECOME MY WIFE!
WHAT ?!
BUT THE PRINCESS LOVES HANZOU...
I ACCEPT GRATE-FULLY!
NOOOO!

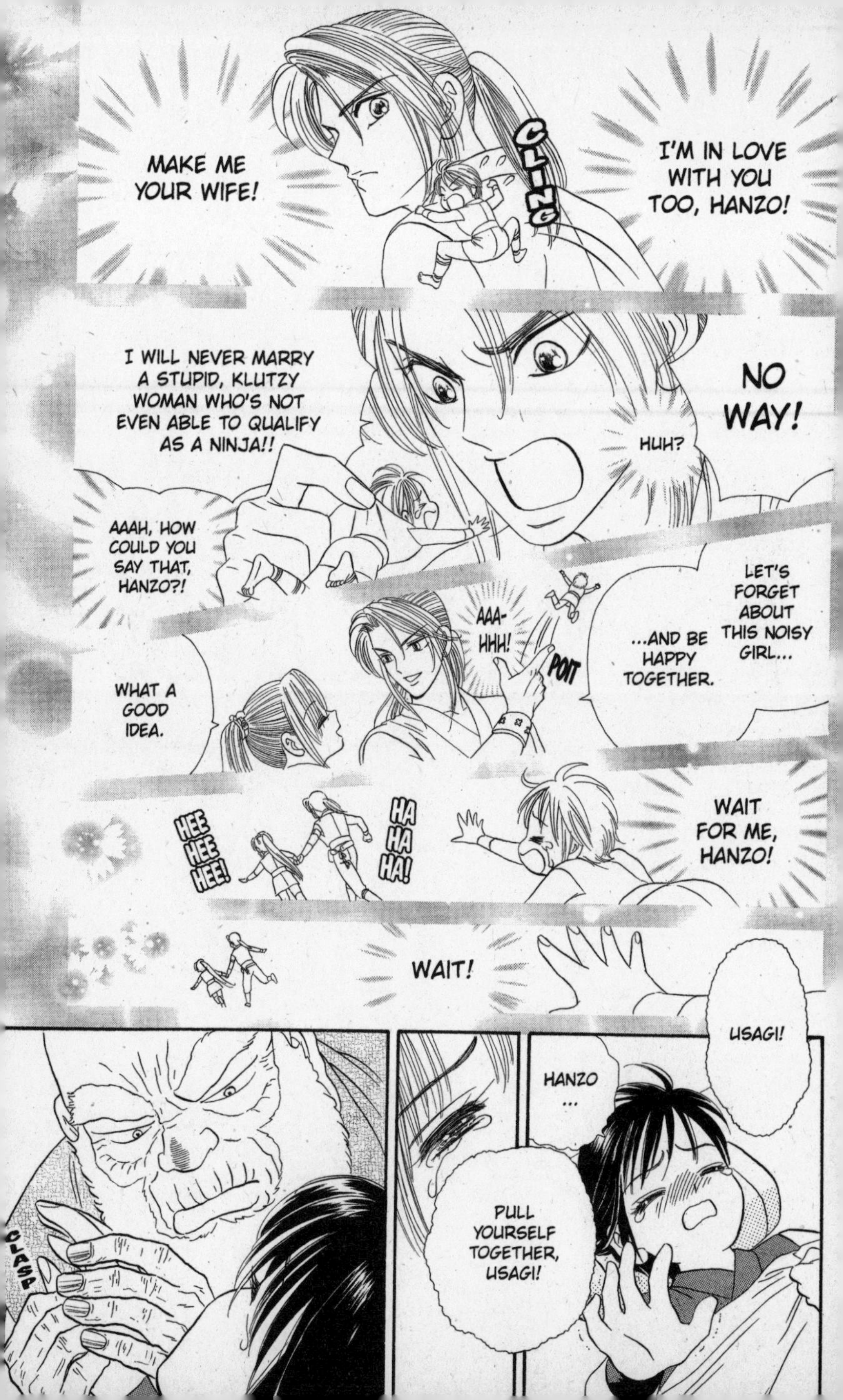
I'M IN LOVE WITH YOU TOO, HANZO!
CLING
MAKE ME YOUR WIFE!
NO WAY!
HUH?
I WILL NEVER MARRY A STUPID, KLUTZY WOMAN WHO'S NOT EVEN ABLE TO QUALIFY AS A NINJA!!
AAAH, HOW COULD YOU SAY THAT, HANZO?!
LET'S FORGET ABOUT THIS NOISY GIRL...
...AND BE HAPPY TOGETHER.
POIT
AAA-HHH!
WHAT A GOOD IDEA.
WAIT FOR ME, HANZO!
HA HA HA!
HEE HEE HEE!
WAIT!
USAGI!
HANZO ...
PULL YOURSELF TOGETHER, USAGI!
CLASP

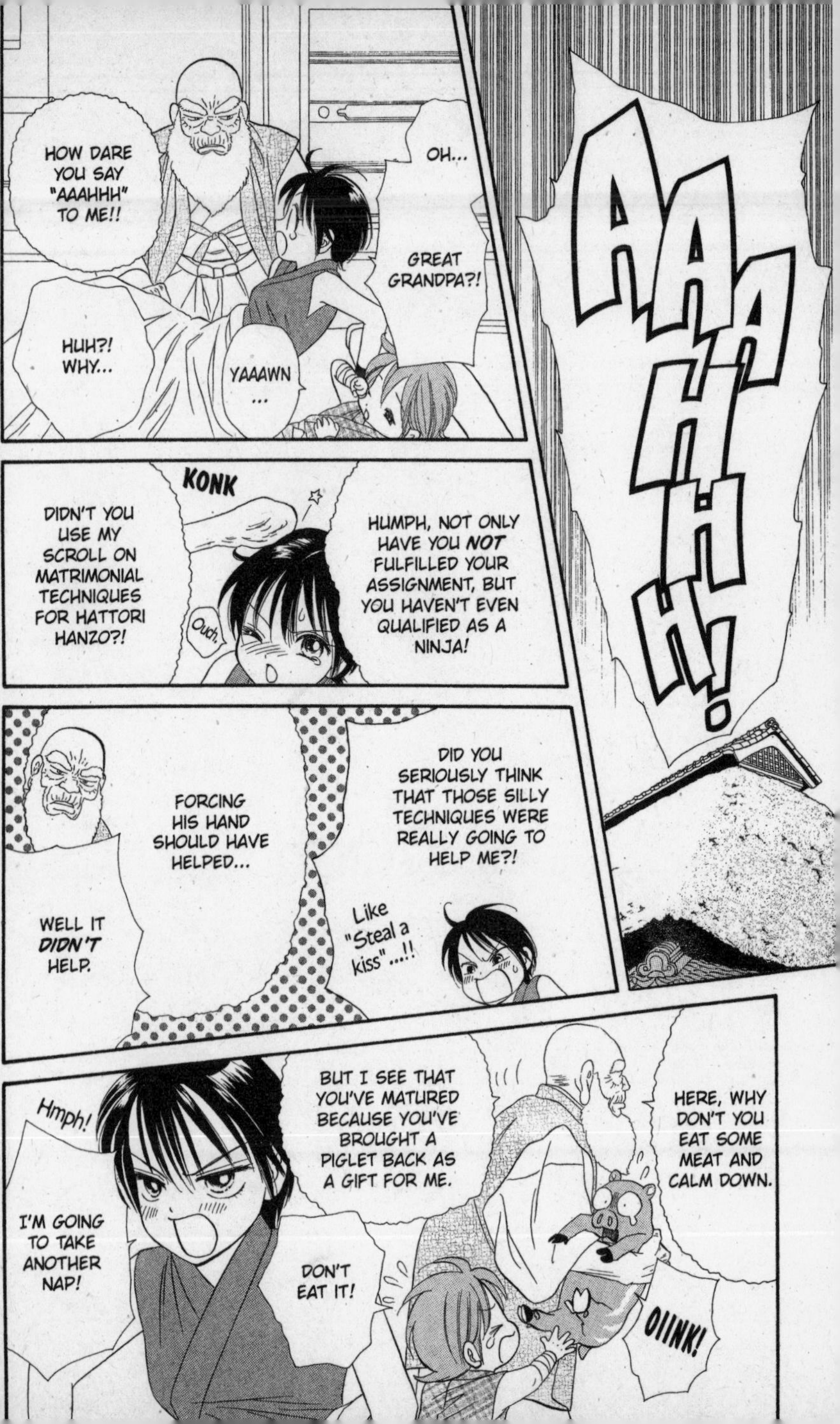
AAAHHH!
OH...
GREAT GRANDPA?!
HOW DARE YOU SAY "AAAHHH" TO ME!!
YAAAWN ...
HUH?! WHY...
KONK
HUMPH, NOT ONLY HAVE YOU *NOT* FULFILLED YOUR ASSIGNMENT, BUT YOU HAVEN'T EVEN QUALIFIED AS A NINJA!
Ouch.
DIDN'T YOU USE MY SCROLL ON MATRIMONIAL TECHNIQUES FOR HATTORI HANZO?!
DID YOU SERIOUSLY THINK THAT THOSE SILLY TECHNIQUES WERE REALLY GOING TO HELP ME?!
Like "Steal a kiss"...!!
FORCING HIS HAND SHOULD HAVE HELPED...
WELL IT *DIDN'T* HELP.
HERE, WHY DON'T YOU EAT SOME MEAT AND CALM DOWN.
BUT I SEE THAT YOU'VE MATURED BECAUSE YOU'VE BROUGHT A PIGLET BACK AS A GIFT FOR ME.
OIINK!
DON'T EAT IT!
Hmph!
I'M GOING TO TAKE ANOTHER NAP!

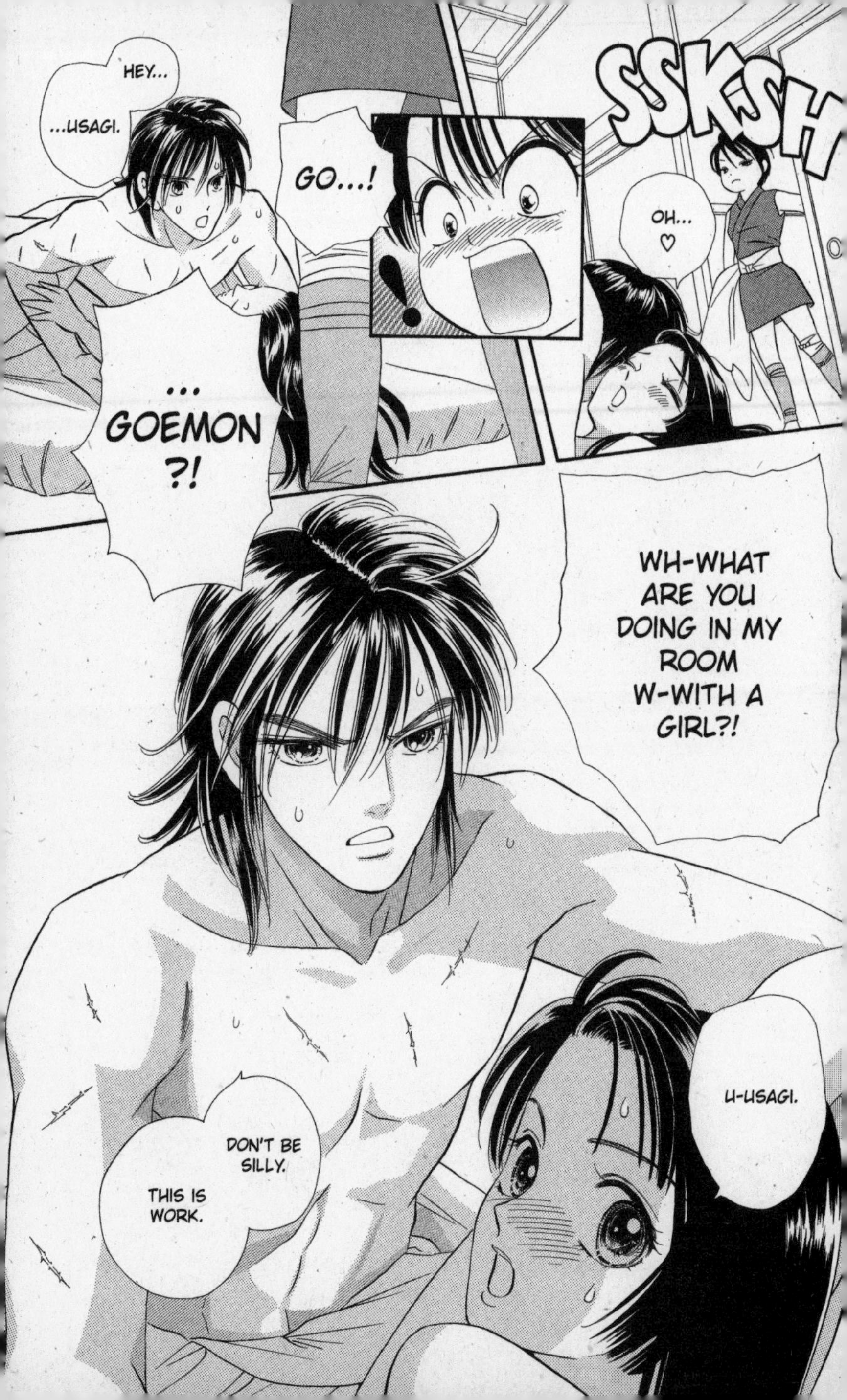
SSKSH
OH... ♥
GO...!
HEY...
...USAGI.
... GOEMON ?!
WH-WHAT ARE YOU DOING IN MY ROOM W-WITH A GIRL?!
U-USAGI.
DON'T BE SILLY.
THIS IS WORK.

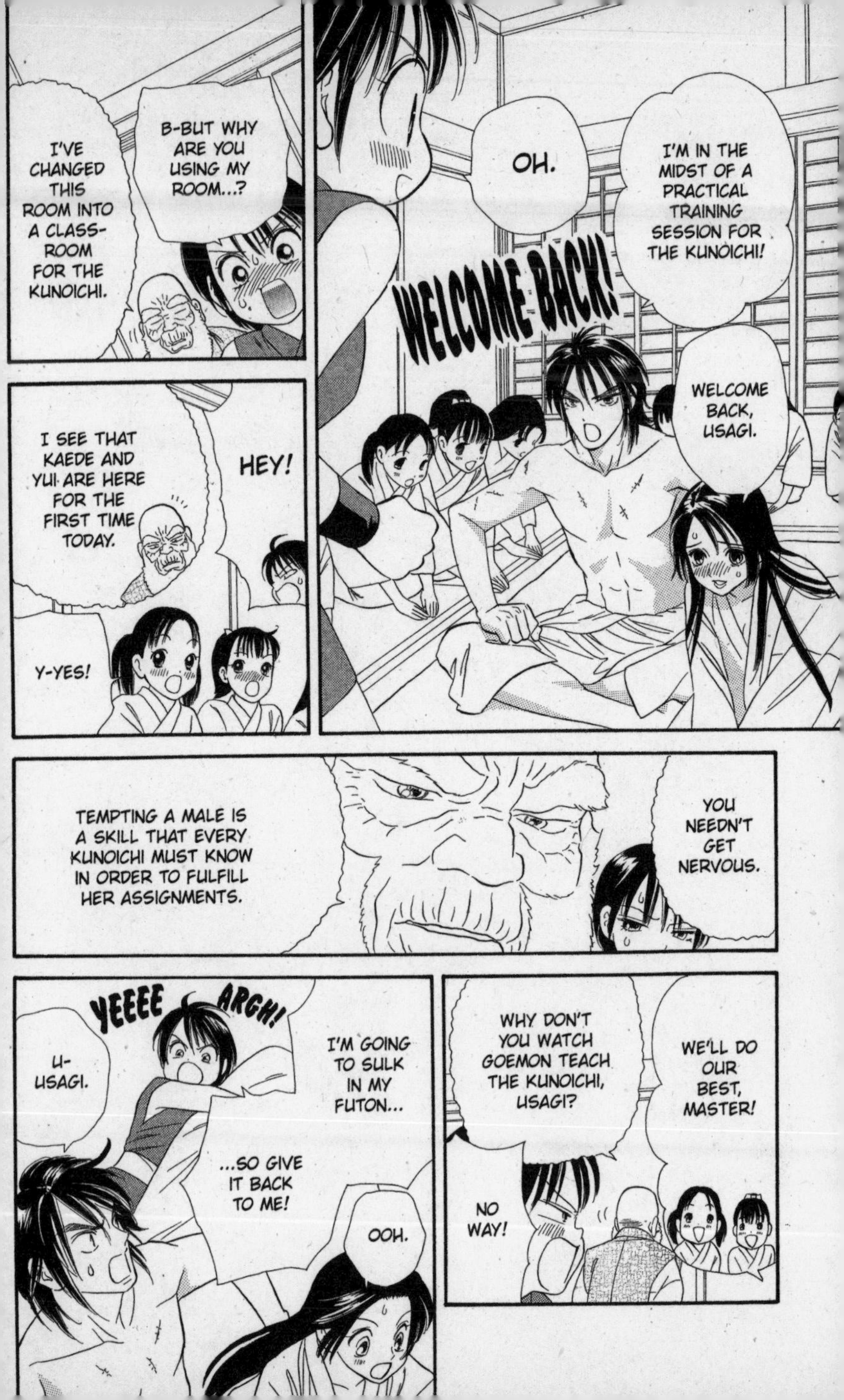
I'M IN THE MIDST OF A PRACTICAL TRAINING SESSION FOR THE KUNOICHI!
OH.
WELCOME BACK!
WELCOME BACK, USAGI.
B-BUT WHY ARE YOU USING MY ROOM...?
I'VE CHANGED THIS ROOM INTO A CLASS-ROOM FOR THE KUNOICHI.
HEY!
I SEE THAT KAEDE AND YUI ARE HERE FOR THE FIRST TIME TODAY.
Y-YES!
YOU NEEDN'T GET NERVOUS.
TEMPTING A MALE IS A SKILL THAT EVERY KUNOICHI MUST KNOW IN ORDER TO FULFILL HER ASSIGNMENTS.
WE'LL DO OUR BEST, MASTER!
WHY DON'T YOU WATCH GOEMON TEACH THE KUNOICHI, USAGI?
NO WAY!
YEEEE ARGH!
I'M GOING TO SULK IN MY FUTON...
U-USAGI.
...SO GIVE IT BACK TO ME!
OOH.

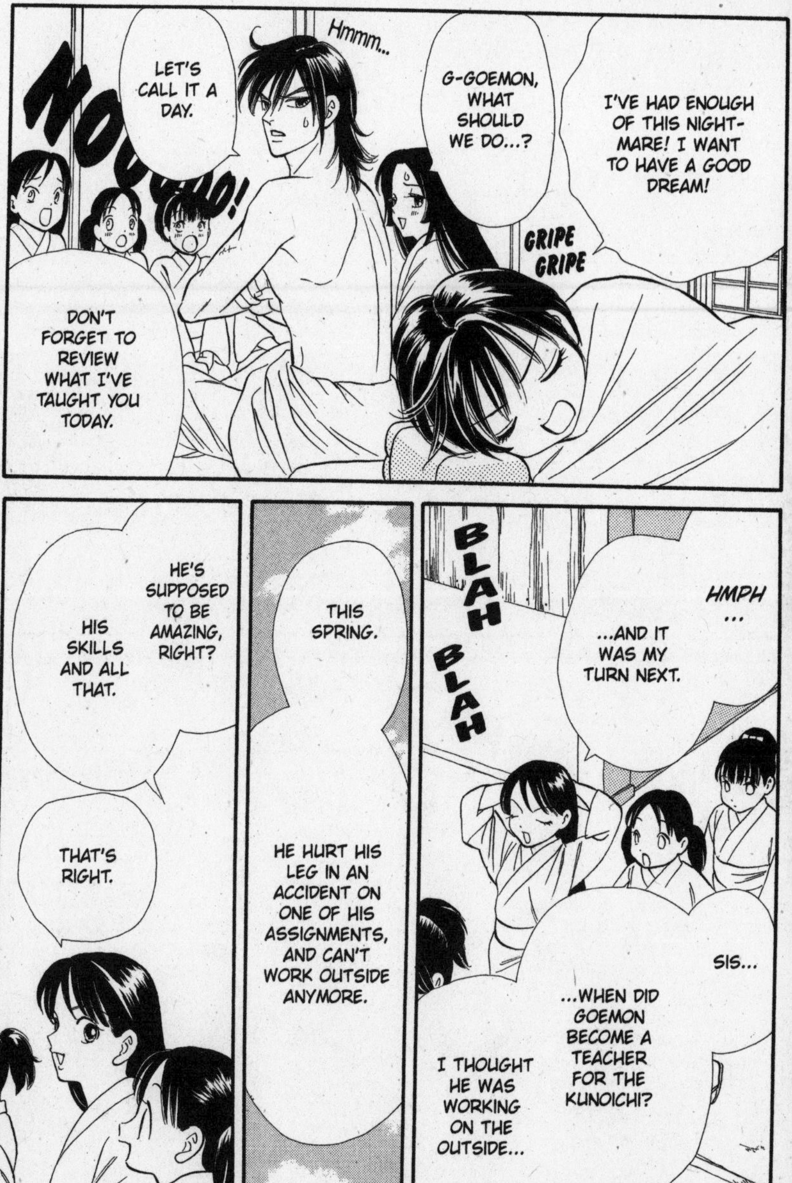
I'VE HAD ENOUGH OF THIS NIGHTMARE! I WANT TO HAVE A GOOD DREAM!
GRIPE GRIPE
G-GOEMON, WHAT SHOULD WE DO...?
Hmmm...
LET'S CALL IT A DAY.
DON'T FORGET TO REVIEW WHAT I'VE TAUGHT YOU TODAY.
HMPH ...
...AND IT WAS MY TURN NEXT.
BLAH BLAH
SIS...
...WHEN DID GOEMON BECOME A TEACHER FOR THE KUNOICHI?
I THOUGHT HE WAS WORKING ON THE OUTSIDE...
THIS SPRING.
HE HURT HIS LEG IN AN ACCIDENT ON ONE OF HIS ASSIGNMENTS, AND CAN'T WORK OUTSIDE ANYMORE.
HE'S SUPPOSED TO BE AMAZING, RIGHT?
HIS SKILLS AND ALL THAT.
THAT'S RIGHT.

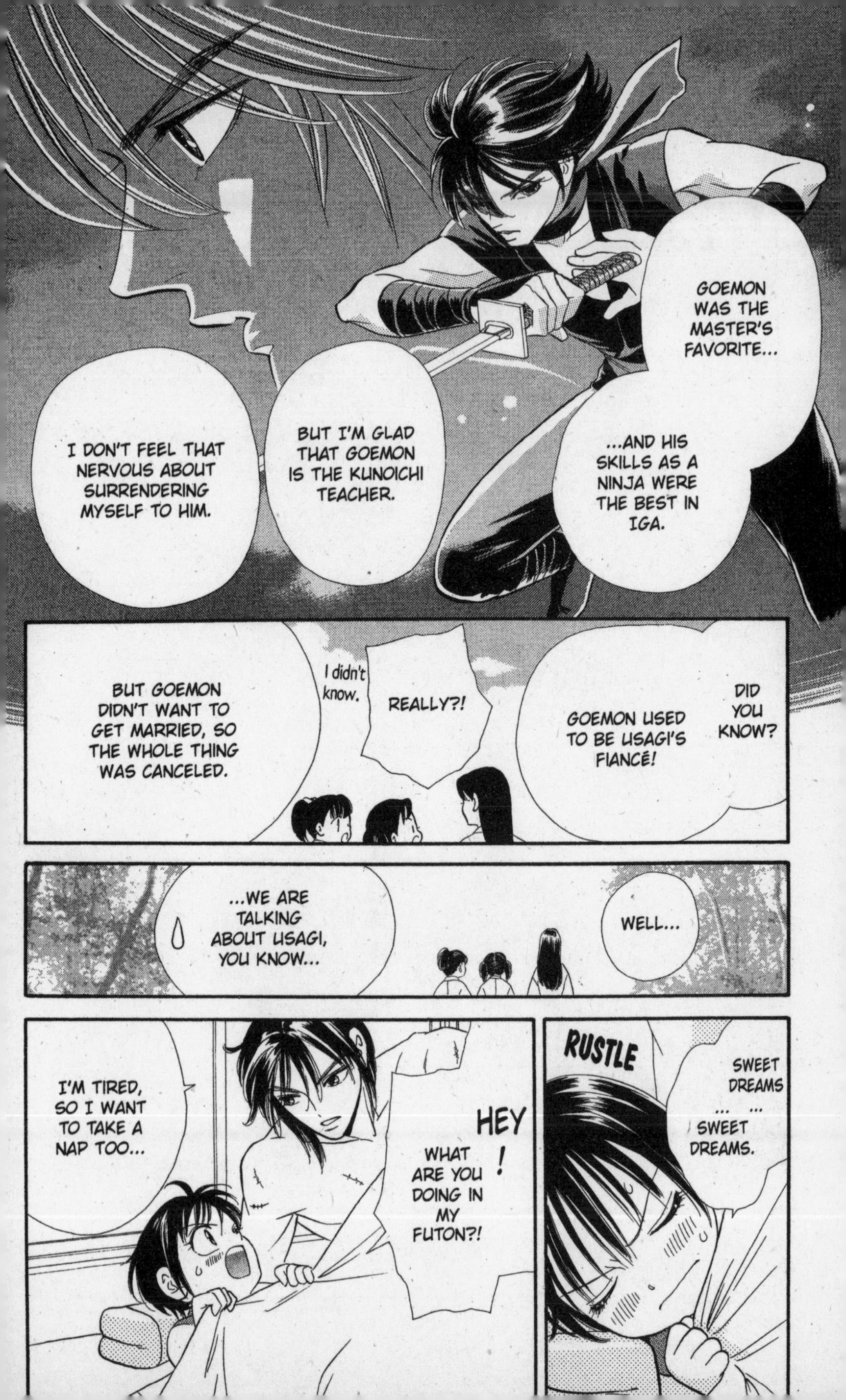
GOEMON WAS THE MASTER'S FAVORITE...
...AND HIS SKILLS AS A NINJA WERE THE BEST IN IGA.
BUT I'M GLAD THAT GOEMON IS THE KUNOICHI TEACHER.
I DON'T FEEL THAT NERVOUS ABOUT SURRENDERING MYSELF TO HIM.
DID YOU KNOW?
GOEMON USED TO BE USAGI'S FIANCÉ!
REALLY?!
I didn't know.
BUT GOEMON DIDN'T WANT TO GET MARRIED, SO THE WHOLE THING WAS CANCELED.
WELL...
...WE ARE TALKING ABOUT USAGI, YOU KNOW...
RUSTLE
SWEET DREAMS... ...SWEET DREAMS.
HEY!
WHAT ARE YOU DOING IN MY FUTON?!
I'M TIRED, SO I WANT TO TAKE A NAP TOO...

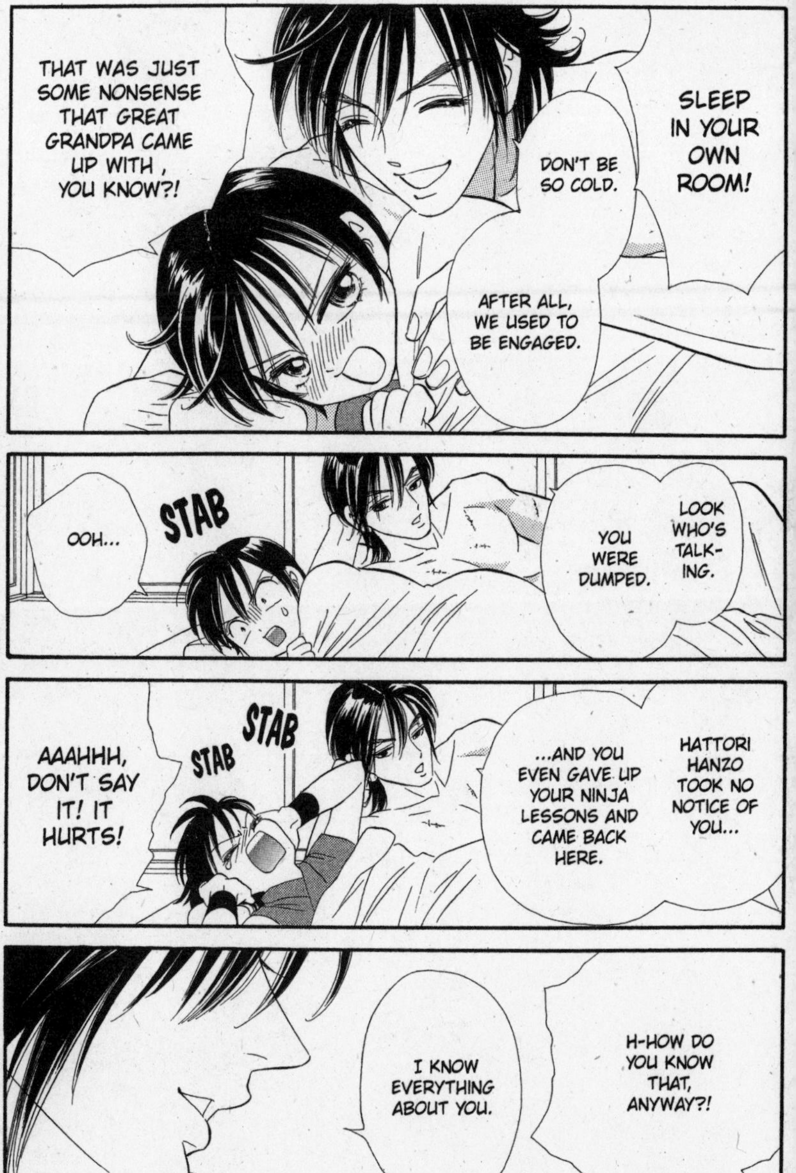
SLEEP IN YOUR OWN ROOM!
DON'T BE SO COLD.
AFTER ALL, WE USED TO BE ENGAGED.
THAT WAS JUST SOME NONSENSE THAT GREAT GRANDPA CAME UP WITH , YOU KNOW?!
LOOK WHO'S TALK- ING.
YOU WERE DUMPED.
STAB
OOH...
HATTORI HANZO TOOK NO NOTICE OF YOU...
...AND YOU EVEN GAVE UP YOUR NINJA LESSONS AND CAME BACK HERE.
STAB
STAB
AAAHHH, DON'T SAY IT! IT HURTS!
H-HOW DO YOU KNOW THAT, ANYWAY?!
I KNOW EVERYTHING ABOUT YOU.

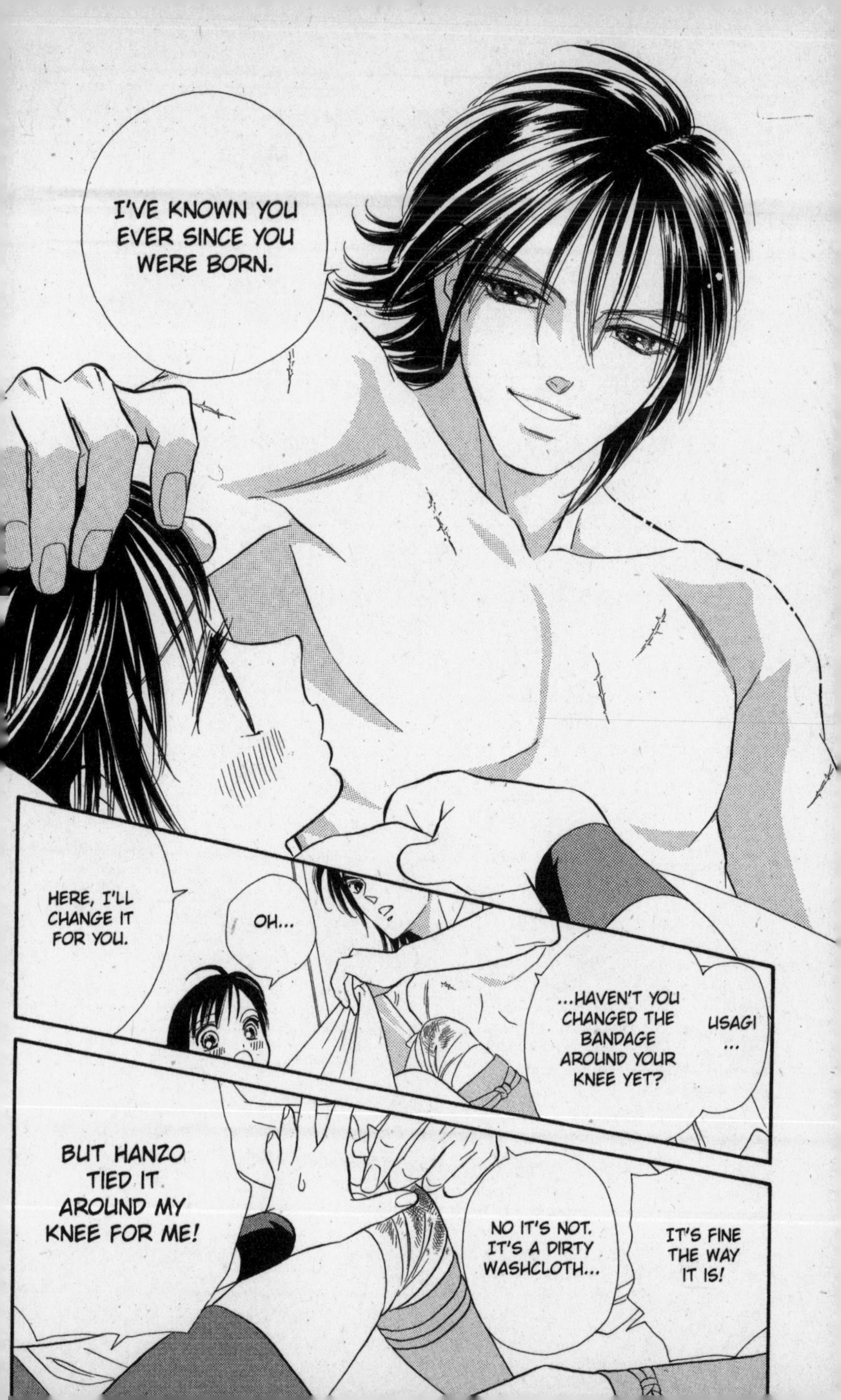
I'VE KNOWN YOU EVER SINCE YOU WERE BORN.
USAGI...
...HAVEN'T YOU CHANGED THE BANDAGE AROUND YOUR KNEE YET?
OH...
HERE, I'LL CHANGE IT FOR YOU.
IT'S FINE THE WAY IT IS!
NO IT'S NOT. IT'S A DIRTY WASHCLOTH...
BUT HANZO TIED IT AROUND MY KNEE FOR ME!

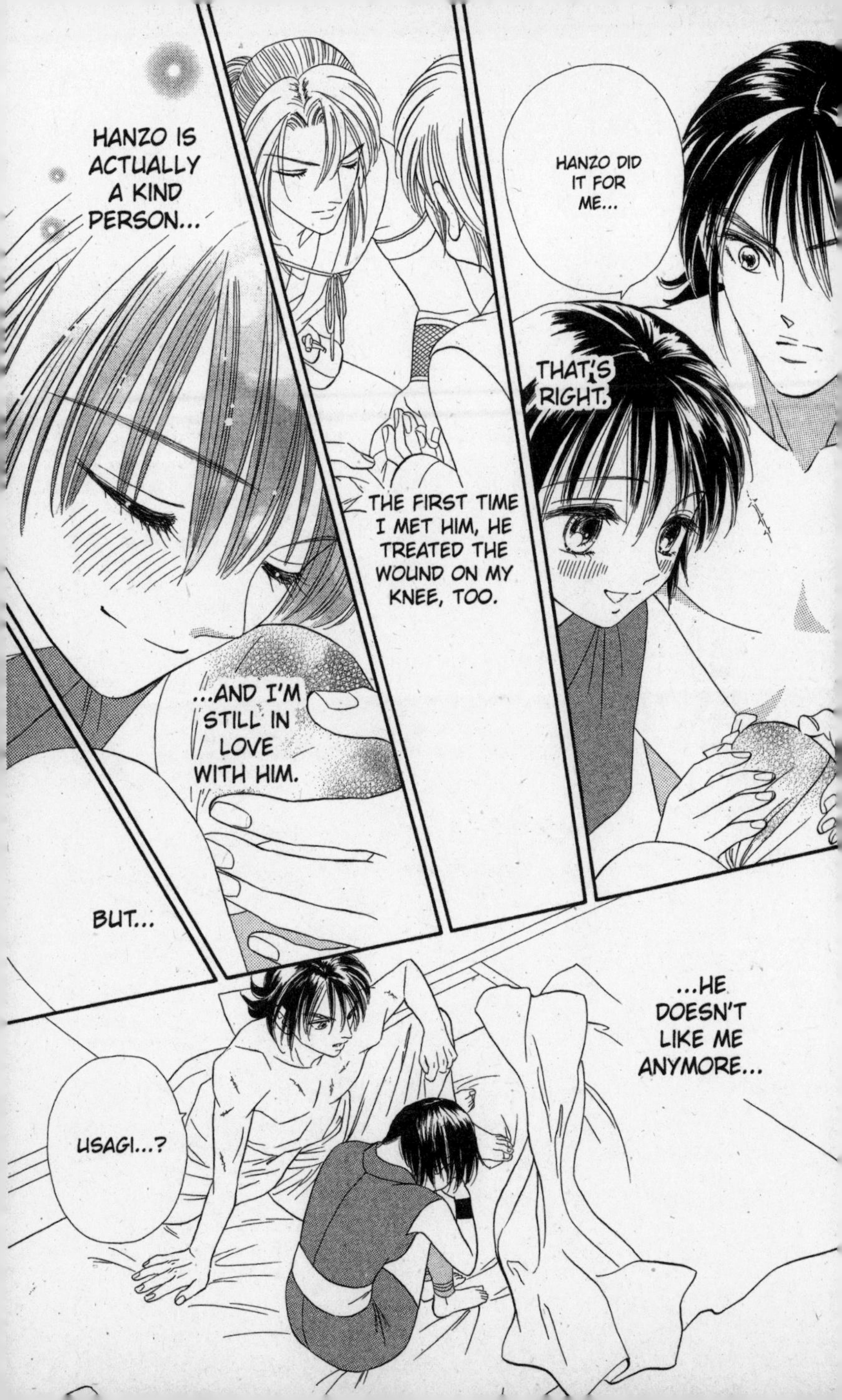
HANZO DID IT FOR ME...
THAT'S RIGHT.
THE FIRST TIME I MET HIM, HE TREATED THE WOUND ON MY KNEE, TOO.
HANZO IS ACTUALLY A KIND PERSON...
...AND I'M STILL IN LOVE WITH HIM.
BUT...
...HE DOESN'T LIKE ME ANYMORE...
USAGI...?

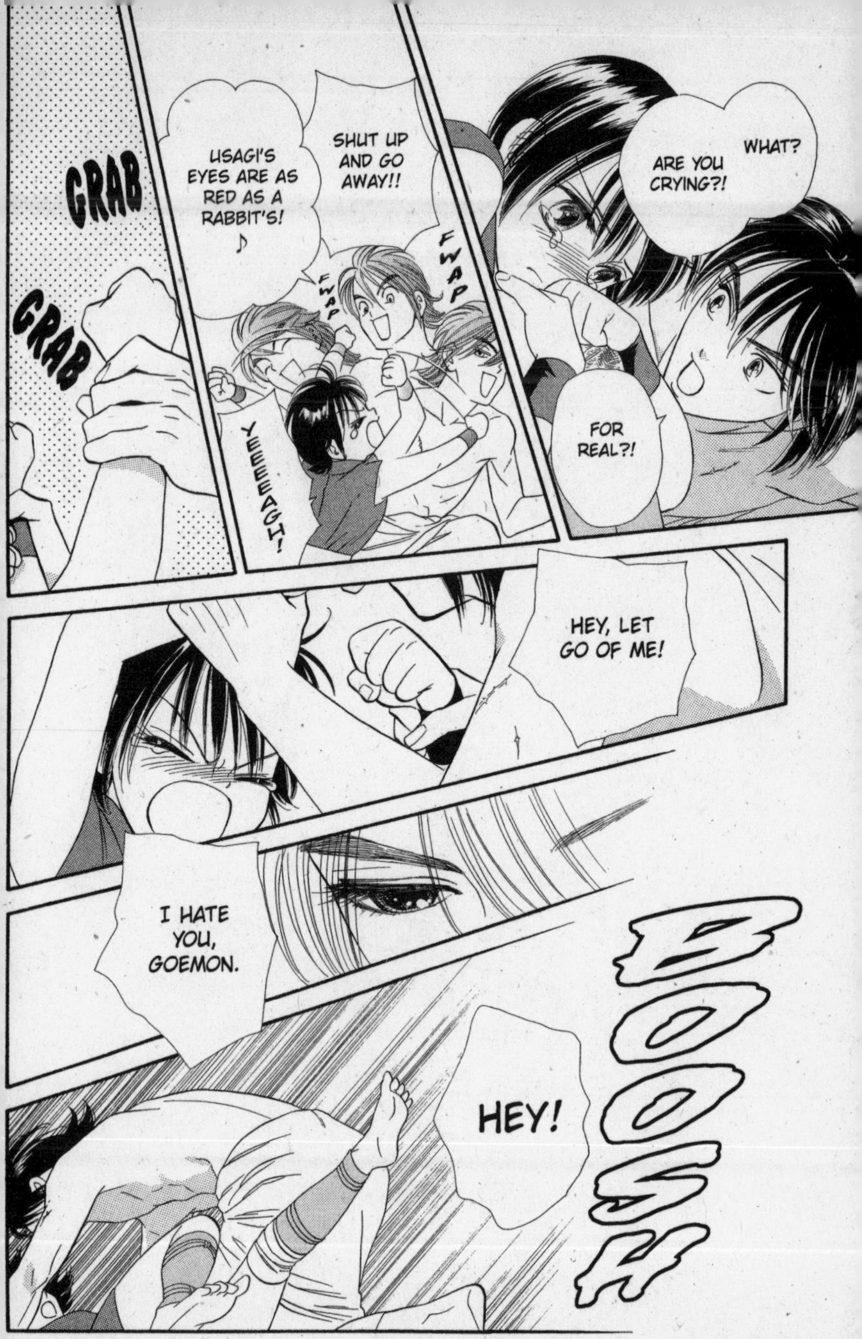
WHAT?
ARE YOU CRYING?!
FOR REAL?!
USAGI'S EYES ARE AS RED AS A RABBIT'S! ♪
SHUT UP AND GO AWAY!!
FWAP
FWAP
YEEEEAGH!
GRAB
GRAB
HEY, LET GO OF ME!
I HATE YOU, GOEMON.
WHOOSH
HEY!

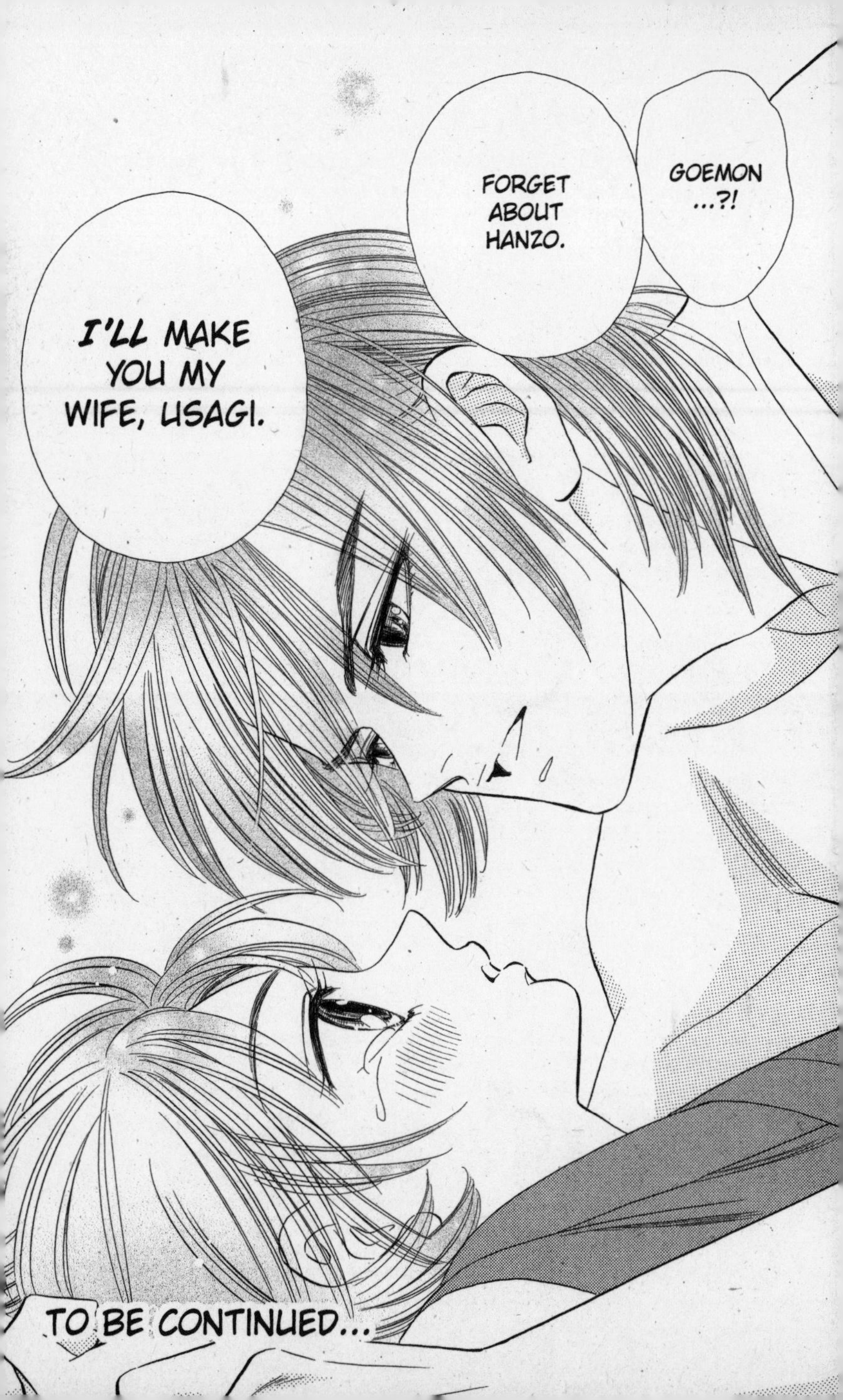
GOEMON ...?!
FORGET ABOUT HANZO.
I'LL MAKE YOU MY WIFE, USAGI.
TO BE CONTINUED...

> *The ways of the ninja are mysterious indeed, so here is a glossary of terms to help you navigate the intricacies of their world.*

Page 8, panel 3: Ninjutsu
The mystical art of the ninja.

Page 17, panel 6: Kurokage
Literally means "Black Shadow," a suitable name for a ninja dog.

Page 22, panel 8: Ninja sword
Called *shinobi-gatana*, which literally means ninja sword, to differentiate it from a samurai sword.

Page 40, panel 7: Water Spider
Water spiders, or *mizu-gumo*, are similar in concept to snow shoes, and allow ninja to walk on water. They are named after the insect with a similar ability.

Page 49, panel 1: High-ranking ninja
There are three ninja ranks. The highest rank is jonin, the middle rank is chunin, and the lowest rank is genin.

Page 49, panel 1: Kunouchi
A term often used for female ninja. The word is spelled くノ一, and when combined, the letters form the kanji for woman, 女.

Page 63, Kankodori
The phrase "the kankodori sings" means a business is not doing well, since the song of the cuckoo is lonely and desolate, just like a store without customers. The word *kankodori* is usually only used in this phrase. The more common name for cuckoo in Japanese is *kakko*.

Page 4, panel 1: Tensho Era
The Tensho Era was from 1573 to 1591. In Japan, every time a new emperor is enthroned, a new era begins in his honor. The current era is Heisei.

Page 4, panel 1: Iga
Iga is a region in Mie prefecture on the main island of Honshu, and also the name of the famous ninja clan that originated there. Another area famous for its ninja is Koga, in the Shiga prefecture on Honshu. Many books claim that these two ninja clans were mortal enemies, but in reality inter-ninja relations were not as bad as stories paint them.

Page 5, panel 3: Slow Kame
Kame can mean turtle in Japanese, although this slow ninja's name is spelled in hiragana, and therefore doesn't have an explicit meaning.

Page 8, panel 3: Asuka Era
This era was named after the capital city of the time and spanned 592-710 CE. This was the time when the Imperial Dynasty was just establishing its sovereignty.

Page 8, panel 3: En-no-Gyojya
Also known as En-no-Ozumu. This semi-mythological sorcerer from the late 7th century is said to have founded Shugendo.

Page 8, panel 3: Shugendo
Literally means "the way of training and testing." It is an ancient ascetic practice to develop spiritual powers by gaining a deeper understanding of Humanity and Nature. It was born from a mixture of indigenous Japanese shamanism, Kannabe Shinko, Buddhism, Taoism, and Confucianism.

Page 143: **Ebisu**
The Seven Gods of Fortune (Shichifukujin) are a group of deities who bring people luck. Daikokuten is the god of wealth and prosperity, Benzaiten is the goddess of fine arts and music, and Bishamonten is the god of war. These three gods all originated in India. Hotei is the god of contentment and happiness, Fukurokuju is the god of wisdom and longevity, and Jurojin is the god of longevity. These three gods all originated in China. Ebisu is the god of fortune and commerce, and originated in Japan.

Page 144, panel 2: **Azuchi**
On Lake Biwa in Shiga Prefecture, where Nobunaga built his castle and the town that were the center of his operations.

Page 148, panel 3: **Tokugawa Ieyasu**
He lived from 1543 to 1616, and became the first Shogun of the Tokugawa Shogunate, and the first person to use Edo (Tokyo) as his capital. Born into a minor noble family, he allied himself with Oda Nobunaga in the 1560s, and continued an uneasy association with Nobunaga's successor Toyotomi Hideyoshi. After Hideyoshi's death, he betrayed Hideyoshi's son (to whom he served as regent) in order to become the first Tokugawa Shogun.

Page 169: **Tonikaku**
This means "after all" or "at any rate" in Japanese, and the characters were chosen for their phonetic sound and not their underlying meaning. It is spelled 兎に角. 兎 is pronounced "to" and means "rabbit," に is the letter "ni," and 角 is pronounced "kaku" (or "tsuno") and means "edge" (or "horn").

Page 169: **Natsume Soseki**
He was one of the most famous literary figures in Japan, and lived from 1867 to 1969. He was on the one thousand yen bill until very recently, when Noguchi Hideo took his place.

Page 192, **Usagi's red eyes**
Goemon is teasing Usagi because her name means "rabbit." Rabbits have red eyes, and Usagi's eyes are red from crying.

Page 95, panel 1: **Oda Nobunaga**
Nobunaga lived from 1534 to 1582, and came close to unifying Japan. He is probably one of the most famous Japanese warlords. He was the first warlord to successfully incorporate the gun in battle, and is notorious for his ruthlessness. He completely razed Mt. Hiei, a major Japanese Buddhist site of the time, and spared no lives in the battle. He was assassinated at the age of 48 by two of his generals.

Page 110, panel 5: **Unagi**
Unagi means "eel" in Japanese. *Usagi* means "rabbit."

Page 117: **Burdock**
Burdock root is called *gobo* in Japanese, and is used extensively in cooking. It is sold as an herbal supplement in the Western market, and is said to have antibacterial and antifungal properties, and to purify blood, clear up skin, lower blood sugar, and even reduce tumors.

Page 121, panel 6: **Okazaki**
Okazaki is in Aichi Prefecture on the main island of Honshu, about 22 miles from Nagoya.

Page 128, panel 4: **Princess**
Sara is not a princess in the European sense of the word. The Japanese word *hime* means a young woman of noble birth.

Page 129, panel 3: **Kami no Hanzou**
The term *kami no* means "the Upper," and can refer to social status. However, since Hanzou is a member of a branch family, it is very unlikely that his status is higher than that of the head of the entire clan, Hanzo. The term *kami no* can also refer to geographic location in relation to an important city center, such as the capital. Hanzou is from Okazaki, which is closer to Edo than Hanzo's home in Segachi.

Page 137, panel 2: **Shimo no Hanzo**
Shimo no means "the Lower," and in this case refers to Hanzo's geographic location rather than social status.

This is the first historical comedy I have ever drawn. Until now, I used to enjoy drawing the pictures, but for this manga, I have been able to really enjoy creating the storyline, too. I drew this manga in a relaxed and comfortable mood, so I hope you will enjoy this in a fun and enjoyable spirit.

–Rinko Ueda

Rinko Ueda is from Nara prefecture. She enjoys listening to the radio, drama CDs, and Rakugo comedy performances. Her works include *Ryo*, a series based on the legend of Gyojo Bridge, *Home*, a story about love crossing national boundaries, and *Tail of the Moon (Tsuki no Shippo)*, a romantic ninja comedy.

TAIL OF THE MOON

Vol. 1

The Shojo Beat Manga Edition

STORY & ART BY
RINKO UEDA

Translation & Adaptation/Tetsuichiro Miyaki
Touch-up Art & Lettering/Kelle Han
Design/Izumi Hirayama
Editor/Pancha Diaz

Managing Editor/Megan Bates
Editorial Director/Elizabeth Kawasaki
VP & Editor in Chief/ Yumi Hoashi
Sr. Director of Acquisitions/Rika Inouye
Sr. VP of Marketing/Liza Coppola
Exec. VP of Sales & Marketing/John Easum
Publisher/Hyoe Narita

Printed in Canada

Published by VIZ Media, LLC
P.O. Box 77064
San Francisco, CA 94107

Shojo Beat Manga Edition
10 9 8 7 6 5 4 3 2 1
First printing, October 2006

store.viz.com

PARENTAL ADVISORY
TAIL OF THE MOON is rated T+ for Older Teen and is recommended for ages 16 and up. This volume contains brief nudity and ninja violence.

Don't Miss an Issue!

Shojo Beat
MANGA from the HEART

THE REAL DRAMA BEGINS IN...

Six of the hottest Shojo manga from Japan—
Nana, Baby & Me, Crimson Hero, Vampire Knight, Kaze Hikaru, and **Absolute Boyfriend** (by superstar creator Yuu Watase!!)**!**

Plus the latest on what's happening in Japanese fashion, music, and art! Save 51% OFF the cover price PLUS enjoy all the benefits of the Sub Club with your paid subscription for only $34.99.

Find the Beat online!
Check us out at

www.shojobeat.com!

Shojo Beat

MANGA FROM THE HEART

COMPLETE OUR SURVEY AND LET US KNOW WHAT YOU THINK!

☐ Yes, I am interested in receiving information and advertising about VIZ Media, Shojo Beat, and any related products, services, news, events, contests, promotions and special offers.

☐ Yes, I am interested in receiving advertising and promotional materials (NOT FOR RESALE) related to VIZ Media, Shojo Beat and/or their business partners.

Name: _____

Address: _____

City: _____ **State:** _____ **Zip:** _____

E-mail: _____

☐ Male ☒ Female   **Date of Birth** (mm/dd/yyyy): 04/09/1994 (Must be 13 and over.)

❶ Do you purchase *Shojo Beat* magazine?

☐ Yes   ☒ No (if no, skip the next two questions)

If **YES**, do you subscribe?

☐ Yes   ☐ No

If you do **NOT** subscribe, why? (please check one)

☐ I prefer to buy each issue at the store.   ☐ I prefer to buy the manga volumes instead.

☐ I share a copy with my friends/family.   ☐ It's too expensive.

☐ My parents/guardian won't let me.   ☒ Other _____

❷ Which particular Shojo Beat Manga did you purchase? (please check one)

☐ Aishiteruze Baby ★★   ☐ Beauty Is the Beast   ☐ Full Moon
☐ Fushigi Yûgi: Genbu Kaiden ☐ Kamikaze Girls   ☐ MeruPuri
☐ Ouran High School Host Club ☐ Socrates In Love   ☐ Tokyo Boys & Girls
☐ Ultra Maniac   ☐ Other _____

Will/did you purchase subsequent volumes?

☐ Yes   ☐ No   ☐ Not Applicable

❸ How did you learn about this title? (check all that apply)

☐ Advertisement   ☐ Article   ☐ Favorite creator/artist
☐ Favorite title   ☐ Gift   ☐ Recommendation
☐ Read a preview online and wanted to read the rest of the story
☐ Read introduction in *Shojo Beat* magazine   ☐ Special offer
☐ Website   ☐ Other _____

4 **Will/did you purchase Shojo Beat Manga volumes of titles serialized in *Shojo Beat* magazine?**

- [x] Yes
- [ ] No

If **YES**, which one(s) will/did you purchase? (check all that apply)

- [ ] Absolute Boyfriend
- [ ] Baby & Me
- [ ] Crimson Hero
- [ ] Kaze Hikaru
- [ ] Nana
- [x] Vampire Knight

If **YES**, what are your reasons for purchasing? (please pick up to 3)

- [ ] Favorite title
- [ ] I want to read the full volume(s) all at once
- [ ] There are extras that aren't in the magazine
- [ ] The quality of printing is better than the magazine
- [ ] Favorite creator/artist
- [x] I want to read it over and over again
- [ ] Recommendation
- [ ] Other ______

If **NO**, why would you not purchase it? (check all that apply)

- [ ] I'm happy just reading it in the magazine
- [ ] All the manga pages are in black and white
- [ ] There are too many to collect for each title
- [ ] Other ______
- [ ] It's not worth buying the graphic novel
- [ ] There are other graphic novels that I prefer
- [ ] It's too small

5 **Of the titles NOT serialized in the magazine, which ones have you purchased? (check all that apply)**

- [ ] Aishiteruze Baby ★★
- [ ] Beauty Is the Beast
- [x] Full Moon
- [ ] Fushigi Yûgi: Genbu Kaiden
- [ ] Godchild
- [ ] Kamikaze Girls
- [ ] MeruPuri
- [ ] Ouran High School Host Club
- [ ] Socrates In Love
- [ ] Tokyo Boys & Girls
- [ ] Ultra Maniac
- [x] Other ______

If you did purchase any of the above, what were your reasons for purchase?

- [ ] Advertisement
- [ ] Article
- [ ] Favorite creator/artist
- [x] Favorite title
- [ ] Gift
- [ ] Recommendation
- [ ] Read a preview online and wanted to read the rest of the story
- [ ] Read introduction in *Shojo Beat* magazine
- [ ] Special offer
- [ ] Website
- [ ] Other ______

Will you purchase subsequent volumes, if available?

- [x] Yes
- [ ] No

6 **Optional: What race/ethnicity do you consider yourself? (please check one)**

- [ ] Asian/Pacific Islander
- [ ] Black/African American
- [ ] Hispanic/Latino
- [ ] Native American/Alaskan Native
- [x] White/Caucasian
- [ ] Other
- [ ] I'd rather not say

THANK YOU! Please send the completed form to:

Shojo Survey
42 Catharine St.
Poughkeepsie, NY 12601

All information provided will be used for internal purposes only. We promise not to sell or otherwise divulge your information.